INSPIRE / PLAN / DISCOVER / EXPERIENCE

CARIBBEAN

Shadows of palm trees on the sands of Punta Cana Beach, Dominican Republic

DK EYEWITNESS

CARIBBEAN

CONTENTS

Vibrant yellow facade of a building in Willemsted, Curaçao

DISCOVER 6

EXPERIENCE 62

NEED TO KNOW 462

DISCOVER

Sunset over English Harbour in Antigua

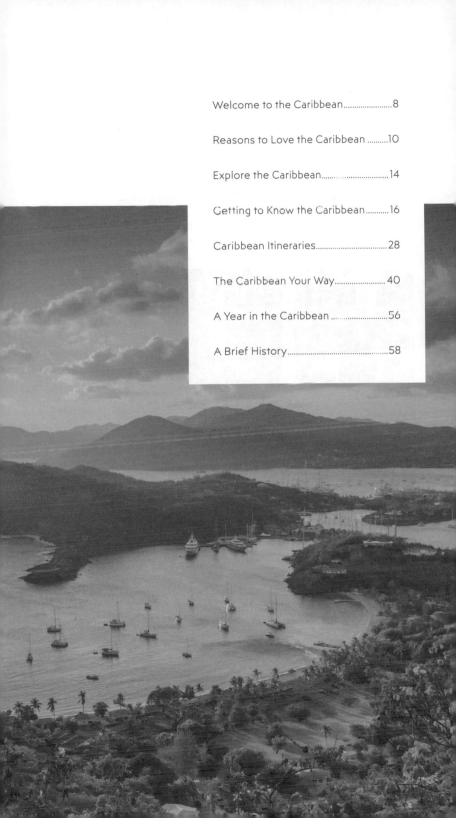

WELCOME TO
THE CARIBBEAN

Sensational beaches lapped by warm, crystal-clear seas. Gorgeous island landscapes concealing incredible natural wonders. Spectacular snorkeling, diving, sailing, and hiking. Colorful carnivals, intoxicating rhythms, and an enticing palette of vivacious cultures. The Caribbean is a rich mosaic. Whatever your dream trip includes, this DK Eyewitness Travel Guide is the perfect companion.

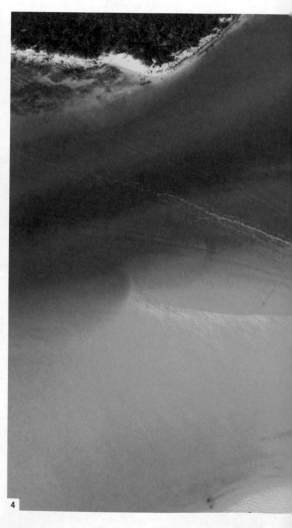

1 Cuban musicians in Havana

2 Santo Domingo Cathedral in the Dominican Republic

3 Petionville district in Port-au-Prince, Haiti

4 The Turks and Caicos

Stretching from the pink sand beaches of The Bahamas to the wind-whipped shores of Aruba, the Caribbean region spans a vast realm of isle-studded aquamarine seas. The islands are immensely varied in size, physical landscapes, and culture. Cuba, the largest island, is a time-warp of old American cars and charming colonial cities, while the Grenadines are a sailor's playground. In between are low-lying beach-wrapped jewels dominated by lush rainforest, desert, and stunning volcanic peaks. Spanish-speaking Puerto Rico exudes modernity, while Guadeloupe is characterized by sleepy villages and a lifestyle that echoes the past.

The cities, too, will not disappoint. Vibrant Havana glories in magnificent museums and yesteryear architecture, and surges with *son* music and sensual salsa. Tattooed with gritty street art, Haiti's Port-au-Prince is an exhilarating blend of color and chaos. Santo Domingo's colonial cathedrals, castles, and cobbled plazas echo to the footsteps of Columbus, while voguish restaurants speak to the city's mouthwatering foodie scene.

The Caribbean can easily overwhelm with the sheer number and diversity of islands, but this guidebook breaks the region down into easily navigable chapters full of expert knowledge and insider tips. Plus, we've created detailed maps and itineraries to help you plan the perfect trip. Whether on a single-island visit, or a multi-island adventure, this Eyewitness Guide will ensure you experience the best the region has to offer. Enjoy the book, and enjoy the Caribbean.

REASONS TO LOVE
THE CARIBBEAN

Abounding in sensational beaches and bathtub-warm waters and infused with vibrant music and passion – there are a thousand reasons to love this diverse region. Here we pick some of our favorites.

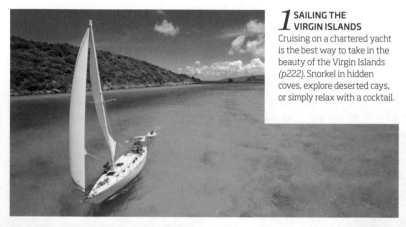

1 SAILING THE VIRGIN ISLANDS

Cruising on a chartered yacht is the best way to take in the beauty of the Virgin Islands *(p222)*. Snorkel in hidden coves, explore deserted cays, or simply relax with a cocktail.

CARNIVAL IN TRINIDAD 2

A hedonistic blowout billed as the biggest street party in the world *(p424)*, this wild and wonderful fantasy-fest proves that Trinidadians know how to party like no other.

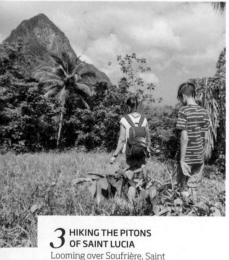

3 HIKING THE PITONS OF SAINT LUCIA

Looming over Soufrière, Saint Lucia's twin volcanic Pitons *(p366)* are majestic from any angle. The unforgettable view from atop Gros Piton is more than worth the demanding hike to the summit.

RHYTHMIC REGGAE 4

Whether you're dancing barefoot in the sand or feeling the vibrations at Sumfest, reggae and the Caribbean are as intertwined as a bass line and drum beat, especially in its home turf – Jamaica *(p136)*.

HISTORIC HAVANA 5

From architecture spanning colonial cathedrals and mobster-era hotels, to classic American cars rumbling down time-worn streets, Havana is a one-of-a-kind city *(p68)*.

SUNDOWNER RUM COCKTAILS 6

Sipping cocktails at sunset is one of the most enjoyable ways to savor the Caribbean. Kick back with a classic mojito in Cuba *(p64)*, or a "Painkiller" in the Virgin Islands *(p222)*.

THE BAHAMAS' PINK SANDS 7

You're spoiled for choice when it comes to superb beaches, but the famous blush-pink sands of Eleuthera and the Exumas *(p131)* in The Bahamas are as lovely as any.

DIVING THE CARIBBEAN SEAS 8

The crystal Caribbean waters teem with kaleidoscopic corals and tropical fish. Don scuba gear to explore wrecks, such as HMS *Endymion*, off Turks and Caicos *(p108)*.

9 WHALE-WATCHING

Watching humpback whales breach in Samana Bay *(p176)* off Dominica *(p352)* or Guadeloupe *(p324)* is one of the most thrilling wildlife encounters in the region.

10 CULTURAL DIVERSITY

The Caribbean is a vibrant tapestry of ethnicities, languages, and customs. Despite its small size, Dominica *(p352)* is especially diverse, while Trinidad *(p424)* is a globe-spanning potpourri.

PUERTO RICO'S BIOLUMINESCENT BAY 11

Swimming in a phosphorescent bay at La Parguera *(p211)* or Vieques' Mosquito Bay *(p215)* in Puerto Rico is a magical, otherworldly experience as luminous dinoflagellates light up around you.

LUXURIOUS RETREATS 12

From Strawberry Hill *(p145)*, in Jamaica's Blue Mountains, to Anguilla's sumptuous beachfront Cap Juluca, the Caribbean is sprinkled with luxury boutique hotels exuding divine comforts and romance.

U.S.A.

Atlantic
Ocean

THE BAHAMAS
p120

TURKS
AND CAICOS
p108

CUBA
p64

CAYMAN
ISLANDS
p96

HAITI
p186

JAMAICA
p136

EXPLORE
THE CARIBBEAN

This guide divides the Caribbean into 24 color-coded
sightseeing areas, as shown on this map. Find out
more about each area on the following pages.

COLOMBIA

CENTRAL AMERICA AND THE CARIBBEAN

U.S.A.

Atlantic Ocean

MEXICO

THE CARIBBEAN

BELIZE

GUATEMALA   HONDURAS   *Caribbean Sea*

EL SALVADOR   NICARAGUA

COSTA RICA   PANAMA

VENEZUELA

COLOMBIA

Pacific Ocean

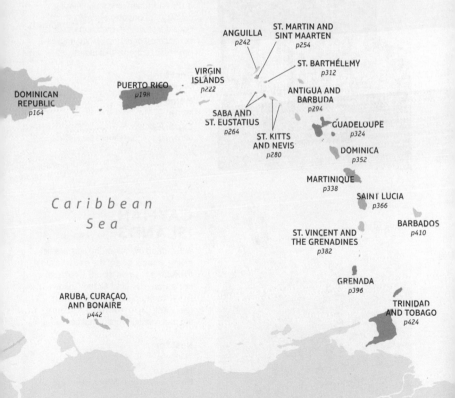

Caribbean Sea

VENEZUELA

0 kilometers   250

0 miles   250

N

GETTING TO KNOW
THE CARIBBEAN

As a vacation destination, the Caribbean conjures up images of white-sand beaches shaded by palms and lapped by crystal seas. But the islands offer so much more, from hikes in rainforests and sailing and diving adventures, to colonial-era sights, creole flavours, and home-grown musical rhythms.

PAGE 64

CUBA

With its time-stood-still Spanish colonial cities and towns, vintage American Cadillacs, absorbing revolutionary history, ubiquitous live music, and the world's best cigars, Cuba is the Caribbean's most stimulating country. Cubans are very welcoming. Consider staying in their homes (casas particulares) or eating in their houses in private restaurants (paladares).

Best for
Live music

Home to
Havana, Trinidad, Valle de Viñales

Experience
Dance and opera in Havana's Gran Teatro

PAGE 96

CAYMAN ISLANDS

With abundant marine life and excellent diving schools, one of the main reasons to visit the Cayman Islands is to explore underwater. On land, Grand Cayman has a cosmopolitan, Floridian resort feel. Little Cayman and Cayman Brac are much smaller, unspoiled getaways.

Best for
Diving

Home to
Bloody Bay Wall and USS Kittiwake dive sites, Seven Mile Beach

Experience
The underwater world in an Atlantis submarine

TURKS AND CAICOS

PAGE 108

The islands of the Turks and Caicos are a beach-lover's nirvana. Many of the strands are truly exceptional, with powder-soft, blindingly white sand bordered by a turquoise ocean. Providenciales is where most visitors stay, by famous Grace Bay beach. On other sleepier islands, you may have miles of sands virtually to yourself. Farther attractions include fantastic diving, whale-watching, and bird spotting, along with soaking up the atmosphere in quaint and historic Grand Turk.

Best for
Beaches and diving

Home to
Providenciales, Grace Bay, Grand Turk

Experience
Observing flocks of flamingos and other birdlife on North, Middle, and South Caicos

PAGE 120

THE BAHAMAS

The islands of The Bahamas offer the full range of vacation experiences. New Providence, home to the capital Nassau, and Paradise Island have high-rise hotels, shopping malls, and casinos. In marked contrast are the Out Islands, characterized by deserted, unforgettable, and sometimes pink-tinged beaches and peaceful little communities. Within the Out Islands there is enormous variety, from chic and quaint Harbour Island to rugged, nature-oriented Andros. Throughout the archipelago, fishing and diving are major draws.

Best for
Beaches and island hopping

Home to
Exuma Cays Land and Sea Park, Lucayan National Park

Experience
Sport fishing in the Gulf Stream's waters off Bimini

$\rightarrow$

PAGE 136

JAMAICA

For many visitors, Jamaica is all about beaches and all-inclusive hotels – the concept was invented here – but it offers so much more. From hip beach bars and Bob Marley tours to beautiful mountain scenery, waterfalls to climb and rivers to raft along, rainforests to zip line over, and plantation houses to visit. Outside of the resorts, in some areas – notably parts of Kingston and Montego Bay – safety can be an issue so it is best to stick to escorted tours.

Best for
Lively nightlife and music scene

Home to
Bob Marley Museum, Blue Mountain Park, Cockpit Country

Experience
A serene trip on a bamboo raft down the Rio Grande or the Martha Brae rivers

PAGE 164

DOMINICAN REPUBLIC

The Dominican Republic offers relaxing stay-put breaks in the numerous large and luxurious hotels that line the beaches at Punta Cana. But the country offers very different faces. From the bohemian watersports mecca of Cabarete and the mountainous center, where activities such as whitewater rafting are popular, to the atmospheric cobbled streets and handsome mansions of Zona Colonial in Santo Domingo.

Best for
Beaches and Spanish colonial architecture

Home to
Santo Domingo, Catedral Primada de América

Experience
A round of golf at the country's many beautifully designed courses

HAITI

PAGE 186

Haiti may be economically impoverished, but culturally it is incredibly rich. Traveling around here is more demanding than anywhere else in the Caribbean, but the rewards are massive – from mysterious vodou ceremonies to heady markets in cast-iron halls, gingerbread mansions, vivid Haitian art, and *taptap* buses decorated like circus caravans. Topping the list of memorable sights has to be La Citadelle, a colossal mountaintop fortress that is a fitting monument against a return to slavery.

Best for
Culture and adventure

Home to
Port-au-Prince, Parc National Historique: Citadelle Laferrière & Palais Sans Souci

Experience
A vodou ceremony, its rituals and trance-induced dances

PUERTO RICO

PAGE 198

Though Puerto Rico has an American infrastructure, the vibe is Hispanic/Caribbean, with Spanish the first language, and rum-based cocktails the order of the day. San Juan offers a wonderful old town to explore, and nightlife as lively as you can cope with. Rent a car and tour beyond the capital, allowing time to relax on beaches, surf in Rincón, hike in El Yunque tropical rainforest, and take in sights such as the impressive Camuy Caves.

Best for
Nightlife, food, and colonial fortresses

Home to
Old San Juan, San Juan National Historic Site, Ponce

Experience
Kayaking after dark on Vieques' bioluminescent Mosquito Bay

→

PAGE 222

VIRGIN ISLANDS

The U.S. Virgin Islands are very different from each other. St. Thomas is a much-visited cruise-ship stop-over, half of St. John is an extremely scenic national park, while the islands' Danish heritage is clearly visible on sleepy St. Croix. The British Virgin Islands are quieter and more exclusive, and above all, a yachter's playground. Days afloat generally involve an isolated beach for a snorkel and picnic lunch, then rum punches at sunset at one of the many beach bars.

Best for
Sailing vacations for all levels of ability

Home to
St. John, St. Croix, Tortola

Experience
Snorkeling in The Baths on Virgin Gorda, where volcanic boulders form natural pools

PAGE 242

ANGUILLA

This little island makes a fair claim to having the Caribbean's finest beaches. There are over 30 of them, many with white sand so talcum-powder soft you sink in up to your ankles. With no mass-market tourism, beaches are generally uncrowded or empty. Other draws are luxury hotels, modernist villas, and gourmet restaurants. While Anguilla attracts its fair share of celebrities, the atmosphere is low-key and laid-back.

Best for
Beaches and fine dining restaurants

Home to
Shoal Bay East, Heritage Collection Museum

Experience
Snorkeling off the beaches and uninhabited offshore cays

ST. MARTIN/SINT MAARTEN

PAGE 252

The two sides of St. Martin/Sint Maarten feel very different from each other. The Dutch half is more developed and busier, particularly in the peak-season when passengers disembark from cruise ships at Philipsburg to visit the duty-free shops and casinos. The French half is more chic, and known for its gourmet restaurants and unspoiled beaches. Blink and you can miss crossing the border between the two sides.

Best for
Beaches, watersports, and restaurants

Home to
Philipsburg, Baie Orientale, Grand Case

Experience
The Flying Dutchman, the world's steepest zip line at Rainforest Adventures, Sint Maarten

PAGE 264

SABA AND ST. EUSTATIUS

Part of the Dutch Caribbean, tiny and little-known Saba (pronounced saybah) and St. Eustatius (often called Statia) are off-the-map, escapist territories. Don't come looking for conventional, relax-on-the-beach Caribbean vacations. Instead, you should visit for brilliant hiking up and around the islands' forested and volcanic peaks, for the profusion of superb, little-explored dive sites, for fascinating histories, and complete and utter tranquility. Accommodation takes the forms of small hotels, inns, and lodges.

Best for
Hiking and diving

Home to
Mount Scenery, The Quill, Saba National Marine Park

Experience
Hiking into The Quill, the rainforest-filled crater of a dormant volcano

$\rightarrow$

PAGE 280

ST. KITTS AND NEVIS

With fascinating colonial-era sights and dramatic, rainforested peaks to climb, St. Kitts and Nevis offer lots to explore as well as inviting beaches. With cruise ships visiting regularly and several large resort hotels, St. Kitts is the busier of the two islands, and generally more developed for tourism. Little Nevis is an immensely beautiful, sleepy backwater with a clutch of atmospheric plantation inns, which you should visit for a meal or two even if you're not staying.

Best for
Colonial heritage and slow-paced island lifestyle

Home to
Brimstone Hill Fortress, Charlestown, Nevis Plantation Inns

Experience
Relaxing in luxury in splendidly restored plantation inns

PAGE 294

ANTIGUA, BARBUDA, AND MONTSERRAT

Antigua is a beach destination par excellence. Many strands have blinding white sand, and there is supposedly one for every day of the year. The island is also a major center for yachting events. Antigua is light on sights, the exception being Nelson's Dockyard, a working Georgian naval harbor. The much quieter sister island of Barbuda has arguably even better beaches and is a bird-watcher's paradise, while the chief reason to visit Montserrat is to see its magnificent volcano.

Best for
Beaches and watersports

Home to
English Harbour and Nelson's Dockyard, Codrington Lagoon

Experience
The Sunday Barbecue party at Shirley Heights Lookout, with live bands and magical sunsets

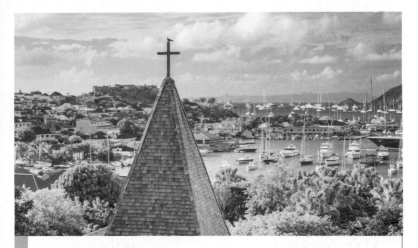

ST. BARTHELEMY

PAGE 312

This ritzy little French outpost is a tropical version of the Côte d'Azur, but with better beaches. St. Barths is as sophisticated – and expensive – as the Caribbean gets. Luxury, small-scale hotels, a plethora of lavish villas up in the hills, and massive yachts in Gustavia port (where the super rich stay) set the scene, as do gourmet restaurants with delicacies imported from the motherland in Europe, and see-and-be-seen beach bars and clubs.

Best for
Dining and beaches

Home to
Gustavia

Experience
Shopping – or at least browsing – in the many designer boutiques in Gustavia

GUADELOUPE

PAGE 324

Part of the French West Indies, Guadeloupe has a stronger Afro-Caribbean feel than France's other territories in the region. The two very different halves of the "mainland" offer a bit of everything, from white-sand beaches, busy resorts, and the powerful Memorial ACTe museum on slavery on Grande-Terre, to rainforests, plunging waterfalls, and a towering, climbable volcano on Basse-Terre. Make day or overnight trips to the offshore islands, the prettiest of which is Terre-de-Haut

Best for
Hiking and island-hopping

Home to
Parc National de la Guadeloupe, Terre-de-Haut

Experience
Trekking up to the summit of steaming volcano La Soufrière

$\rightarrow$

PAGE 338

MARTINIQUE

Martinique is a sophisticated island with a Gallic cachet and Creole spirit, fused together in great French Creole food, plenty of rum, and the distinctive French Antillean rhythms of *zouk* and *beguine*. The fashionable shops on the streets of the capital, Fort-de-France, wouldn't look out of place in Paris. You can expect white-sand beaches in the south, and hiking and sightseeing in the rainforested and mountainous north, including the town of Saint-Pierre, rebuilt after the devastating 1902 earthquake.

Best for
Restaurants and visiting rum distilleries

Home to
Saint-Pierre, Fort-de-France, Route de la Trace

Experience
Diving around the wrecks of sunken ships off Saint-Pierre

PAGE 352

DOMINICA

With a towering, mountainous interior covered in dense rainforest, high-drop waterfalls, thermal springs, and a boiling lake, Dominica is the Jurassic Park of the Caribbean. Hike along trails, bathe under the waterfalls, tube down rivers, snorkel over geothermal springs, and go whale-watching. Stay in delightful, nature-oriented guest-houses; hummingbirds may join you over breakfast. While large cruise ships include Dominica on their itineraries, it is easy to escape from their crowds.

Best for
Hikes and waterfalls

Home to
Morne Trois Pitons National Park, Kalinago Territory

Experience
The eerie volcanic landscape of the Valley of Desolation and the Boiling Lake

PAGE 366

SAINT LUCIA

With its Pitons, a pair of pointy green volcanic cones rising skywards out of the ocean, and mountains blanketed in rainforest, Saint Lucia is one of the most dramatic-looking Caribbean islands. If you're feeling active, you can trek, ride zip lines or an aerial trolley through the jungle, and climb a Piton. Alternatively, if you're seeking romance and relaxation, Saint Lucia is the Caribbean's honeymoon capital. Some hotels offer secluded cottages with private plunge pools and bathrooms with outdoor showers.

Best for
Romantic hotels, dramatic scenery

Home to
The Pitons, Sulphur Springs Park, Marigot Bay, Pigeon Island National Landmark

Experience
A catamaran cruise along the spectacular west coast

PAGE 382

ST. VINCENT AND THE GRENADINES

St. Vincent and the Grenadines all offer very different experiences. You can loll around on exclusive private islands occupied by a single hotel such as Petit St. Vincent and Palm Island, or kick back on glamorous Mustique, famously loved by British royals and celebrities. Bequia, by contrast, is a wonderfully welcoming and sociable place, with enticing bars and restaurants dotted along pretty Admiralty Bay. Mountainous and lush St. Vincent will appeal to those seeking active adventures.

Best for
Escapism, off-the-beaten-path vacations

Home to
Tobago Cays, La Soufrière volcano, Bequia

Experience
Island-hopping under sail around the Grenadines archipelago

$\rightarrow$

PAGE 396

GRENADA

Grenada is a delightfully easy-going and pretty island. It is blessed with some gorgeous soft-sand beaches, particularly in the southwest corner where tourism is concentrated. Even here development is low-rise and fairly unobtrusive. St. George's, the historic capital, is one of the Caribbean's most picturesque ports, while the mountainous and forested interior, where you might spot a monkey or two, is a big draw for hikers. Sightseeing is low-key, revolving around stops at atmospheric chocolate, nutmeg, and rum factories.

Best for
Beaches and lush scenery

Home to
St. George's, Grand Anse Beach, Grand Étang Forest Reserve

Experience
Snorkeling over or diving around the unique Underwater Sculpture Park

PAGE 410

BARBADOS

Barbados is indisputably glamorous, particularly on the Platinum Coast where ritzy hotels, villas, and restaurants back on to a string of beaches. But that is only one face of the island. Head to the interior's rolling cane fields to discover elegant plantation houses and lush tropical gardens. Shoot the breeze with friendly Bajans over a drink or two in one of the many rum shops dotted all over the island.

Best for
British colonial history and gourmet dining

Home to
St. Nicholas Abbey, Garrison Historic Area, Bathsheba

Experience
Oistins Fish Fry, a lively weekly street party with great food, dancing, and music

PAGE 424

TRINIDAD AND TOBAGO

Trinidad is suited to independent, adventurous-minded visitors. Its capital, Port of Spain, holds the Caribbean's most colorful and wildest carnival, and there is world-class bird-watching, especially in the rainforest of the Northern Range. Much smaller Tobago has lovely beaches and fishing villages, and is perfect for a relaxed beach vacation. It's also great for nature lovers, boasting the Western hemisphere's oldest protected forest, a large avian population, and excellent diving.

Best for
Bird-watching and seeing turtles hatch

Home to
Port of Spain, Asa Wright Nature Centre, Tobago Forest Reserve

Experience
Red-billed tropicbirds and boobies soaring at the seabird sanctuary in Little Tobago

PAGE 442

ARUBA, CURAÇAO, AND BONAIRE

These three islands form part of the Dutch Caribbean. Curaçao's cosmopolitan capital, Willemstad, has a historic downtown and a harbor surrounded by pastel-colored gabled buildings – think Amsterdam meets Latin America. Aruba, the smallest but most developed island, offers upscale resort hotels, casinos, excellent beaches, and first-rate windsurfing and kite-surfing. Quiet Bonaire has a coastline entirely protected by a marine park, and is known for its superb diving.

Best for
Beaches and diving

Home to
Willemstad, Eagle Beach, Arikok National Park, Washington Slagbaai National Park

Experience
Fantastic diving directly off the shores of Bonaire in its National Marine Park

←

1 The Baroque facade
of Havana's cathedral

2 Hotel Habana Libre mural

3 A classic mojito

4 A picturesque street
in La Habana Vieja

2 DAYS
in Havana

Day 1

Morning The best place to begin your exploration of Havana is at its foundation site – El Templete – which sits in La Habana Vieja's cobbled Plaza de Armas *(p69)*. Explore the Museo de la Ciudad and Castillo de la Real Fuerza before strolling to Plaza de la Catedral *(p76)*, with its remarkable Baroque cathedral. Pause for a delicious cappuccino at Dulcería Bianchini before continuing down Calle Mercaderes to Plaza Vieja *(p68)* which bustles with local life.

Afternoon Have lunch at La Factoria de Plaza Vieja *(San Ignacio & Muralla; 7866 4453)*, which serves hearty Cuban dishes – best enjoyed alfresco with a refreshing beer. After visiting Plaza Vieja's Cámara Oscura and Museo de Naipes, make your way along Calle Brasil to Plaza del Cristo. Here you'll find the astonishing Capitolio *(p72)*; venture inside and tread the sumptuous marble floors. Don't forget to admire the facade of the Baroque Gran Teatro de La Habana Alicia Alonso as you enter Parque Central *(p70)*.

Evening For the ultimate sunset venue, choose to sip cocktails at the Gran Hotel Manzana Kempinski before taking a ride along the Malecón *(p71)* in a classic convertible car. Ask your driver to take you to La Guarida *(418 Concordia; 7866 9047)*, a real jaw-dropper of a dinner venue. Feast on fine Cuban fusion fare, then head up the decorative spiral staircase to the open-air rooftop bar for a nightcap.

Day 2

Morning Begin your day at Parque Central and walk down the Paseo de Martí. At Calle Trocadero, divert east past the Hotel Sevilla to see the astounding contemporary art collection in the Museo Nacional de Bellas Artes *(p70)*. Your cultural experience continues at the adjacent Museo de la Revolución *(p74)*, where you will learn all about the events of the Cuban revolution. Next, take a leisurely stroll along the Malecón and up La Rampa to admire Amelia Peláez's mural on the facade of the Hotel Habana Libre.

Afternoon The hotel's Café Habana Libre *(Calle M; 7834 6100)* is the perfect place for lunch, topped off by an ice cream at the Coppelia nearby. Next, hop in a taxi to the Necrópolis de Colón *(Calle Zapata esq Calle 12; 7830 4517)* and explore the marble mausoleums of the vast cemetery. Look out for the worshipers praying at La Milagrosa – the "miraculous" tomb that inspired a huge spiritual cult.

Evening For an atmospheric dinner, reserve a table at Café Laurent *(257 Calle M; 7831 2090)* and order the delicious garlic shrimp, followed by the slow-roasted lamb with garlic, mint, and cream reduction. Finally, amble two blocks northeast to the iconic Hotel Nacional *(p71)* to savor some flavorsome *añejo* rum on the garden patio overlooking the Malecón. End the day with a show at the hotel's sensational Cabaret Parisién.

7 DAYS
in Jamaica

Day 1

Morning Begin in Montego Bay. A leisurely stroll along Gloucester Avenue leads past shimmering beaches to the bustling, historic downtown. Wander the Gully fruit and veg market, then along Fort Street to Sam Sharpe Square (p150).

Afternoon Pop inside The Cage before spending an hour exploring the National Museum West, in the Montego Bay Cultural Center (p150). Eat lunch at nearby Ol' Joe Cultural Center and return along Gloucester Avenue, stopping at St. James Craft Market and Doctors Cave Beach.

Evening Dine at Usain Bolt's Tracks & Records Restaurant, and close the evening with cocktails at its Late Lounge.

Day 2

Morning After a leisurely breakfast, take a drive south to Anchovy to Rocklands Bird Sanctuary (p150), then head west along the dramatic shoreline via Lucea to Negril (p148).

Afternoon Lunch at Just Natural and spend the afternoon relaxing on the beach, breaking for snorkeling or an exhilarating banana-tube ride.

Evening End the day with cocktails at Rick's Café (p149) and dinner at the nearby Rockhouse Restaurant.

Day 3

Morning Explore the wetlands of the Great Morass & Royal Palm Preserve (p148) before driving east to Black River (p152). Spot crocodiles on a riverboat safari into the Great Morass (p148).

Afternoon Continue east to reach Treasure Beach (p152). Take a boat to Floyd's Pelican Bar for sunset cocktails.

Evening Idle away the evening with dinner and entertainment at Jakes (p153).

Day 4

Morning Head back to Black River (p152), then turn inland for the parish of St.

1. National Museum West
2. Rick's Cafe at sunset
3. Boats moored at Port Antonio
4. Crocodile basking on the Black River
5. Statue of Noël Coward by Angela Conner on his estate

Elizabeth, stopping at YS Falls (p153) to splash in natural pools and cascades.

Afternoon Pass through Bamboo Avenue on your way to Mandeville (p154) and lunch at OMG Restaurant. Savor the stunning mountain drive as you descend to the southern plains and head east to the capital, Kingston (p140).

Evening Enjoy fusion fare and live music at Red Bones Blues Café (1 Argyle Rd).

Day 5

Morning Spend the morning exploring Kingston. Start at Devon House (p140), then head up Hope Road to the Bob Marley Museum (p142).

Afternoon Take the scenic route up and over the Blue Mountains, enjoying lunch and views at Strawberry Hill (p145).

Evening Call at Old Tavern Estate for an introduction to Blue Mountain Coffee. Take care on the switchback descent to Port Antonio (p154), and enjoy a gourmet meal and stay at Hotel Mockingbird Hill.

Day 6

Morning Take an exhilarating bamboo-raft ride on the Rio Grande before continuing the scenic drive along the north coast. Stop at Noël Coward's former home, Firefly (p158).

Afternoon Lunch beside the sea at Tropical Hut, in Orocabessa, then continue west to Ocho Rios (p158).

Evening Try out your best dance moves at Reggae Inferno (7 James Ave).

Day 7

Morning Start your day with a clamber up Dunn's River Falls (p158), then immerse yourself in the tropical Fantasia of Cranbrook Flower Forest (p160).

Afternoon Lunch at Sharkie's in Runaway Bay (A1 Main Street, Salem).

Evening Continue along the north coast road, stopping at Greenwood Great House (p151) for a sense of plantation history before arriving in Montego Bay.

→

1 Nassau Straw Market

2 Lunch at The Landing on Harbour Island

3 Pig on the beach at Big Major Cay

4 Paddleboarding at sunset in the Exumas

10 DAYS

in The Bahamas and Turks and Caicos

Day 1

Begin in Nassau, the capital of The Bahamas, with a walk around the historic downtown. Start in Parliament Square *(p128)*, admiring the Georgian colonial architecture before walking west to the Nassau Straw Market. Next delve into the Pirates of Nassau Museum, which will enthrall you for hours. Head to Arawak Cay and lunch like a local on conch, before roaming Fort Charlotte. Head back east via off-the-beaten-track Delancy, West Hill, Duke, and Shirley Streets and turn right onto Elisabeth Avenue. Climb the Queen's Staircase to arrive at Fort Fincastle. Dine at Graycliff *(graycliff.com)* and linger for cocktails.

Day 2

This morning, enjoy a Bahamas Fast Ferry ride to Harbour Island, Fleuthera *(p131)*. Rent a bicycle or golf cart to explore Dunmore Town, with its quaint New England architecture. Have lunch at The Landing, then laze away a few hours sunning, swimming, and snorkeling on the famous Pink Sands Beach. In the evening, share a romantic candlelit dinner at the Blue Bar Restaurant, Pink Sands Resort *(pinksandsresort.com)*.

Day 3

Take a water taxi to Spanish Wells on St. George's Cay, just 164 ft (500 m) off the northern tip of Eleuthera. Having arranged a rental car or an excursion in advance, explore the island, with stops at Glass Window Bridge, Preacher's Cave, and Hatchet's Bay Caves. Head back o Harbour Island late afternoon for snorkeling or a spa treatment before dinner at Tippy's *(Banks Rd)*.

Day 4

Transfer to Spanish Wells for the fast ferry ride back to Nassau for a midday flight to George Town *(p131)*, Great Exuma. After lunch at the Peace & Plenty, spend an afternoon fishing, sea kayaking, or scuba diving. Head to the Fish Fry for a memorable dinner of fresh seafood.

Day 5

Take a full day excursion to Exuma Cays Land and Sea Park *(p124)*. Highlights might include snorkeling in Thunderball Grotto; swimming with pigs at Big Major Cay; and marveling at the starfish at Starfish Reserve. Join the locals for dinner at Eddie's Edgewater *(Queen's Highway)*.

→

Day 6

Fly to Miami for a connecting flight to Providenciales *(p114)*, in the Turks and Caicos. In the afternoon, spend a few hours lazing and swimming on the beautiful Grace Bay Beach *(p114)*. After relaxing and soaking up some rays, the country's hallmark beach offers all the watersports you could wish for. Catch the breeze on a Hobie Cat, take a kitesurfing lesson, or maybe gain an exhilarating frigate-bird's view with a parasail ride. Later, walk the beach end-to-end before a relaxing massage or other treatment at your hotel spa. Join the happy-hour crowd at Somewhere *(www.somewherecafeand lounge.com)* to watch the sun go down, then head to Coco Bistro *(cocobistro.tc)* for a romantic alfresco dinner beneath the palms.

Day 7

This morning, explore the island on a guided ATV adventure with Fun Ride Tours *(funridetourstci.com)*, including Discovery Bay Mangroves, Chalk Sound National Park, and Caicos Conch Farm. Enjoy a fresh seafood lunch and a hearty rum at the renowned Da Conch Shack *(daconchshack.com)* atop the sands before an afternoon kayaking or paddleboarding in Mangrove Cay. The wetlands and meandering tidal creeks at the northeast end of Providenciales provide a fabulous introduction to the islands' marine life. Later in the afternoon, dedicate an hour or so for some retail therapy in Ocean Club Plaza or Saltmill Plaza, each with their many art galleries. End the day with dinner at the Crackpot Kitchen *(crackpotkitchen.com)*, and cocktails at the appropriately-named Infiniti Bar at the Grace Bay Club. It is the longest bar in the Caribbean, stretching 90 feet from Grace bay Club to the shore *(www. gracebayresorts.com)*.

Day 8

Fly to Grand Turk (a mere 30-minute journey) in time for lunch at Jack's Shack *(www.jacksshack.tc)*, a delightfully rustic and popular beach bar where you can relax on the sands between bouts of beach volleyball. To explore Cockburn Town *(p117)* this afternoon, hop aboard a Segway with Oasis Divers for a fun guided

1 Da Conch Shack,
Providenciales

2 Conch fritters

3 Grace Bay Beach

4 Hotel Atlantis, Nassau

5 Cabbage Beach watersports

tour that takes in all the main sites of interest including the old-Bermudian style houses and museum. If you prefer, the company can also take you on an excursion to Gibb's Cay to laze on the beach, snorkel the coral reef, and perhaps swim with wild stingrays that can be found here. Have dinner alfresco at the Secret Garden Restaurant at the charming 1850s-era Salt Raker Inn *(www.saltrakerinn.com)*, popular with locals.

Day 9

Start with a short boat ride (or fly with Caicos Express) to Salt Cay *(p116)*. In winter, go whale-watching with Green Flash Whale Tours or Salt Cay Divers. One of the companies' knowledgeable whale experts will add enrichment to your thrilling all-morning excursion. At other times of year, enjoy snorkeling amid a kaleidoscope of colorful corals and fish at Bluff Reef, while divers are spoiled for choice with superb sites, including the 18th-century warship, HMS *Endymion*. After lunch at Porter's Island Thyme, explore Salt Cay's Salinas (good for birding) before returning to Grand Turk.

Spend the rest of the afternoon relaxing before dinner on the veranda at the beachfront Guanahani Restaurant & Bar *(Bohio Dive Resort Waterfront, Pillory Beach, Cockburn Town TKCA 1ZZ)*. On Saturdays there is a live band.

Day 10

Catch an early morning flight to Nassau and head to the plush Hotel Atlantis, Paradise Island *(p129)*, for lunch at Sip Sip beach bar-restaurant. Follow with an afternoon of non-stop fun at Atlantis' Aquaventure Water Park, with its sensational high-speed slides, themed river roller coaster rides, and vast pools (non-guests can purchase a day-pass). After all this adrenalin-charged fun, detox by relaxing on the white sands of Cabbage Beach, or on one of Atlantis' own four beaches. This evening, enjoy a final dinner at Café Matisse in downtown Nassau, then let your hair down at Hammerheads Bar & Grill; or linger at Atlantis for a gourmet Japanese meal at Nobu (which has a special sake cellar), a flutter in the casino, and dancing at Aura nightclub.

←

1 Boats and yachts moored in Cruz Bay, St. John

2 The atmospheric Foxy's Bar in Great Harbour Bay

3 Snorkeling off Virgin Gorda

4 Colorful shops in Road Town, Tortola

2 WEEKS
sailing the Leewards

Day 1

Meet your charter yacht on St. Thomas *(p228)*, a busy cruise-ship destination. Here you can explore Fort Christian and downtown Charlotte Amalie before hoisting sail for the short run to uninhabited Great St. James for some fine snorkeling in Christmas Cove.

Day 2

The Virgins are the most sheltered of the Leeward Islands – perfect for getting a feel for the wind and your vessel as you run east for beautiful St. John *(p230)*. Two-thirds of the island is protected as pristine national park. Step ashore at Cruz Bay to enjoy hiking on the Salt Pond Trail or the Annaberg Plantation Path *(p232)*. Less active travelers can rent a scooter to circumnavigate this hilly isle, or sail to one of the coves tucked along the north shore. End your day with dinner at The Terrace Restaurant in Cruz Bay *(p230)*.

Day 3

Set sail for the British Virgin Islands. Make White Bay, on Jost Van Dyke island, your first stop for lunch and revelry at the Soggy Dollar Bar – a favorite of yachters from around the globe. And you can't say you've visited the Virgin Islands without dropping anchor in Great Harbour Bay for a "Painkiller" at Foxy's Bar *(p239)*.

Day 4

This morning make the short run to Cane Garden Bay and the most tantalizing beach on Tortola island. Head downwind to Smuggler's Cove, stopping to snorkel, before sailing east along Tortola's southern coast to Road Town *(p236)*, abuzz with activity. Head inland to enjoy the serenity of hiking in Sage Mountain National Park *(p237)*. Dine ashore at Pusser's, on the waterfront in Road Town.

Day 5

Head south to uninhabited Norman Island to snorkel in The Caves – three sea caves at the base of cliffs. Now turn east for RMS Rhone Marine Park *(p239)*. You can snorkel above the wreck; or pre-arrange a scuba dive of the steam ship. End your afternoon in the Spanish Town on Virgin Gorda *(p238)*, and dine with your toes in the sand at Coco Maya.

→

Day 6

This morning venture the short distance to The Baths (p238) to spend a couple of hours snorkeling amid natural seawater pools and fantastical granite boulders. Then sail up Virgin Gorda Sound for lunch at the Bitter End Yacht Club. Spend the afternoon threading through the Prickly Pear cays then head north for Anegada, a huge coral with blinding white beaches. Anchor off Pomato Point and enjoy a delicious seafood dinner.

Day 7

A 93 mile (150 km) gap of open ocean separates the easternmost Virgin Islands from Anguilla, so you'll spend most of the day at the helm. An early morning start should put you in sheltered Road Bay, Anguilla (p242), before sundown. For dinner, head ashore to Blanchards Beach Shack, a taxi ride away at Mead's Bay.

Day 8

You'll want a rest day ashore after yesterday's crossing. Explore laid-back Anguilla by car, scooter, or local taxi. Don't miss Wallblake House, Cheddie's Carving Studio, and the Heritage Collection Museum (p247). Ride over to CuisinArt Golf Resort & Spa for lunch and a round of golf or spa treatments. In the evening, enjoy a memorable dinner at Veya Restaurant (North Hill Village 2640).

Day 9

This morning head south on a 3-hour sail to Marigot on St. Martin (p258), with time for shopping in the Creole market and lunch at Mario's Bistro sidewalk cafe. In the early afternoon, head along the northern shore to Île Tintamarre (p260) for fabulous snorkeling in St. Martin Marine Reserve. Sail south for Philipsburg (p256), arriving in time for some duty-free shopping in the capital of the Dutch side of this dual-nationality island. Dine at Chesterfield's before trying your hand at one of Philipsburg's casinos.

Day 10

Sail down to alluringly green and mountainous St. Barthelemy (p312), the chic celebrity isle. First, sail your yacht up

1 A cove in Anguilla

2 Spices for sale at Marigot Market

3 Brimstone Hill Fortress

4 Colorful juice bar in Oranjestad

5 Sentry box at Fort Christiansted

to the snug and protected wharf in Gustavia (p318), with its fine restaurants, French boutiques, and chic bars. Lunch at La Crêperie before sailing the 3 miles (5 km) to Anse de Colombier, at the northern tip of the island. While here, snorkel and take a short hike ashore for sweeping views. In late afternoon, return to Gustavia for shopping, plus a divine dinner then cocktails at Bonito (p319).

Day 11

Set sail at dawn for the 60 mile (97km) southwest passage to St. Kitts (p280). Arriving in early afternoon, lunch at El Fredo's (p291), then walk to Basseterre (p286). There will be time to rent a Moke (a beach buggy) to explore the rest of the island: don't miss Romney Manor Plantation (p286), the Arawak Carvings near Old Road (p287), and Brimstone Hill Fortress (p284). Dine at Serendipity (p290).

Day 12

Head north this morning for the volcanic and mountainous tiny isle of St. Eustatius (p264), just 8 miles (14 km) northwest of

St. Kitts. Expect a spectacular reach in the easterly trades. Anchor in Oranje Bay and go ashore in Oranjestad (p276) for lunch and well-earned cocktails at The Old Gin House. Hike The Quill (p272) in the afternoon – a great appetite-builder for a West Indian dinner at the oceanfront Golden Era Hotel.

Day 13

Your journey 120 miles (195 km) north-west to St Croix (p234) will take all day, so set out at dawn to arrive at the island by early evening. Anchor off Christiansted (p234) and have a well-earned meal at The Buccaneer Hotel, set in a former sugar mill.

Day 14

Spend the morning roaming Chistiansted (p234), with its well-preserved 18th-century buildings within easy walking distance of the waterfront, including Fort Christiansvaern and the old Danish Customs House. After an early lunch, set sail to St. Thomas to end your sailing adventure.

Beaches to Bask On

With so many mesmerizing beaches, you'll struggle to leave your sun lounger. Grace Bay (p114), with its seemingly endless stretches of pearl-white sand, has earned a global reputation for being one of the best beaches in the world. Meanwhile, the blush pink sands of Eleuthera (p131), which is made up of tiny pieces of coral, cleverly stay cool enough for you to luxuriate on.

Couple strolling along the pristine sands at Grace Bay ↑

CARIBBEAN FOR
BREATHTAKING BEACHES

Every Caribbean island is fringed with sensational beaches, where black volcanic sands and dazzling white shores dissolve into dreamy warm seas. From intimate hidden coves to mile-long swathes of sand, there's something for every mood and taste.

TOP 5 CITY BEACH ESCAPES

Playas del Este, Havana
A sunny spot at which to relax and play (p68).

Condado Beach, San Juan
Pristine sands (p205).

Cabbage Beach, Nassau
Brilliant for a range of watersports (p35).

Hellshire Beach, Kingston
The place to party (p155).

Boca Chica, Santo Domingo
Great for snorkeling and diving (p175).

Sensational Sunsets

Those photos of spectacular Caribbean sunsets are real. Head to Havana's Malecón (p71) to snap the 1950s skyline against a flame-red sky. In Jamaica, Negril's West End (p148) is hard to top for sundowner cocktails.

→

The unbelievably gorgeous sunset over Malecón

Party It Up

The Caribbean's beach party scene is as cool as an iced Goombay Smash. Packed with fun bars, there is no better place to salsa with the locals than on the sands of Sosúa *(p177)* in the Dominican Republic. If you're looking for a more festive atmosphere, head to Jost Van Dyke in the Virgin Islands *(p222)* to set your pulse racing with limbo, or join the spring-breakers on Jamaica's Negril *(p148)* to listen and to move to the best live reggae.

↓ Drinking at one of the popular beach bars at Sosúa

↑ The intimate Little Bay Beach in Anguilla

Secluded Beaches

It's easy to discover unsullied sands without the crowds. The uninhabited, blink-and-you-miss-it Prickly Pear Cays, near Anguilla, hits the sweet spot with sugar-like sands and a relaxed beach bar. Anguilla's Little Bay Beach is bookended by cliffs, and worth seeking out for utter seclusion. At Vieques' serenely idyllic Sun Bay, it's just you and wild horses cantering along the sands.

If There's a Will There's a Wave

The Caribbean overflows with watersports, whether you prefer calm or crazy. Kitexcite *(kitexcite.com)* will teach you to scud above the waves at the wind-whipped Cabarete *(p177)*, or you can kayak through placid lagoons at Trinidad's Nariva Swamp *(p432)*.

→

Kite surfing at the Dominican's dreamy Cabarete beach

Spectacular Karst Formations

Disgorged from the sea in great tectonic upheavals, the non-volcanic islands of the Caribbean are a dreamland of dramatic karst (limestone) features. Hotel Los Jazmines' *mirador* (lookout) offers panoramic vistas of Cuba's incredible Valle de Viñales *(p82)*. For an underground adventure, explore the Cuevas de las Maravillas (Caves of Wonders) in the Dominican Republic and gaze at the hundreds of pictographs. Alternatively, marvel at the fantastical dripstone formations in Haiti's lesser known La Grotte Marie Jeanne *(Port-à-Piment)*.

THE CARIBBEAN FOR
NATURAL WONDERS

From magnificent coral reefs to lush rainforests and soaring volcanic peaks, the Caribbean islands are a kaleidoscope of sublime natural seascapes and landscapes. But for all its geographic diversity, the region is bound together by ever-present aquamarine and turquoise seas.

← The Quill volcano rising from the shores of St. Eustatius

Volcanic Grandeur

Bubbling mud pools, steaming vents, and peaks looming sheer from the sea reveal the awesome volcanic origins of many islands. The view of the twin Pitons of Saint Lucia *(p372)* from Anse Chastenet is the most iconic of all Caribbean landscapes. The Volcano Observatory on Montserrat is a great base for exploring the island's "Exclusion Zone". Alternatively, lace up your boots and hike the lush green Crater Trail around The Quill, a stratovolcano on the tiny Dutch island of St. Eustatius *(p272)*.

↑ The unique landscape of Valle de Viñales under the evening sky

CORAL REEFS OF THE CARIBBEAN

The Caribbean's fragile and diverse coral ecosystems are threatened by pollution and global warming; the reefs have diminished by about 80 per-cent in the past four decades. But pockets of healthy coral reefs remain, with abundant marine life – moray eels, sea turtles, octopuses, and an ever-changing ballet of piebald-dappled, striped, polka dot fish. The world's tallest coral column (the "Caribbean Cathedral") probes the waters at Punta Frances, off Cuba's Isla de la Juventud (p84).

Wondrous Waterfalls

Cascading like quicksilver through the lush forests, waterfalls add to the dramatic beauty of mountain terrains. At Cascade aux Écrevisses (p330), on Guadeloupe, slide into the Corossol River like a log down a flume. In Jamaica, link hands in a daisy-chain to clamber prize-winningly pretty Dunn's River Falls (p158). Group adventure tubing down Grenada's Balthazar River is an exhilarating ride.

→ Exploring the rushing water of Dunn's River Falls, a popular spot in Jamaica

Luscious Rainforests

Drenched by the moist trade winds, mountainous regions are enveloped in dense green rainforest. A nirvana to nature lovers, Puerto Rico's El Yunque (p214) is laced with well-maintained trails. In Dominica (p352), experience the verdant splendor on horseback with Rainforest Riding (rainforestriding.com).

← Wandering along a tropical path in El Yunque Rainforest, Puerto Rico

Riding the Waves

Surfing the Caribbean swells offers all the fun and thrills of a rollercoaster. For aficionados, waves that reach 40 feet (12 m) off Rincón *(p210)*, in Puerto Rico, are the ultimate ride. Fun seekers can howl with delight on a "banana-tube" towed by a powerful speedboat off The Bahamas' Paradise Island *(p129)*. Negotiating the rapids on the Río Yaque del Norte on a white-water rafting trip with Rancho Baiguate *(ranchobaiguate.com)* in the Dominican Republic's Jarabacoa *(p179)*, will guarantee plenty of thrills.

↑ Surfing a wave in Puerto Rico's Rincón

THE CARIBBEAN FOR
WATERSPORTS

The Caribbean's scintillating blue waters offer an entire realm of fantastic aquatic adventures. Almost every isle has sensational snorkeling and diving, but the trade winds fuel wind-reliant sports, and you'll also find an abundance of other power-craft options.

Wreck-Diving

Sunken ships hold a special allure for divers, not least because they attract a wealth of marine life. Often, cannons and other artifacts can still be seen, while World War II ships are especially fascinating to explore. Wrecks are scattered all along the Caribbean chain. Bucket-list dives include *Hilma Hooker*, a drug-smuggling vessel condemned to the deep off Bonaire *(p455)*; and HMS *Endymion*, a 44-gun man of war sunk by a storm in 1790 off Turks & Caicos *(p108)*. It is also worth exploring the overloaded freighter *Superior Producer* that sank in 1977, off Curaçoa's southwest coast. At night, an artificial reef is lit by the glow of cup corals.

Diver exploring the *Hilma Hooker* wreck, at 98 ft (30 m) below the surface off Bonaire

Snorkeling and Diving Coral Reefs
Don a breathing tube, face mask, and fins and snorkel like a fish on the water surface. SNUBA (SNorkel + scUBA) tethers compressed air canisters to floating rafts, connecting swimmers to air tubes without heavy restrictive gear. On Aruba, you can explore a German World War II freighter and Lockheed Lodestar plane while SNUBA-diving with Antilla Dives. Beginners should head to Champagne Reef in Soufrière, Dominica *(p359)* to explore the kaleidoscopic sealife teeming just below the surface.

←

Woman snorkeling in the shallow waters around Virgin Gorda, Virgin Islands

> PICTURE PERFECT
> **Shark Shots**
>
> Diving with sharks is not for the faint-hearted, but it is a specialty at Cuba's Jardines de la Reina. Armed with a water-proof camera, capturing a shot of a shark's toothy grin is guaranteed to impress.

Catching the Breeze
The Caribbean is caressed by near-constant trade winds, powering a panoply of breeze-dependent sports. Enjoy a day-sailing excursion from the Grenadines to the tiny Tobago Cays *(p386)*. On Aruba, learn to perform exhilarating aerial kite-surf acrobatics from the experts. Or simply have fun with an easy-to-maneuver Hobie Cat, offered at resort beaches the length of the island chain.

↑ Kite-surfing in Aruba and sailing in Tobago Cays *(inset)*

Awesome Ziplines

Zip lining is an easy, initially intimidating, adventure to get the adrenalin pumping. Fly like Superman at La Bestia, in Puerto Rico; drop 500 ft (150 m) over the ocean on the Dragon's Breath zip line in Haiti; and marvel at Saint Lucia's beauty with Treetop Canopy Adventures. For an unbeatable thrill, give Rainforest Adventures' The Flying Dutchman a try – the world's steepest zip line, at Sint Maarten.

→

Zip lining over lush Labadee in Haiti on the Dragon's Breath

THE CARIBBEAN FOR
OUTDOOR ADVENTURE

The Caribbean isn't just about kicking back in a hammock on a beach. Whether you're seeking to bicycle, parasail, or ride high on a rainforest zipline, the islands offer endless possibilities for outdoor adventure.

Spoke-tacular Cycling

You'll sweat for your reward, but the islands seem even more beautiful from the seat of a bicycle. The Dominican Republic's rugged terrain is perfect for energetic cyclists; Iguana Mama (iguanamama. com) in Cabarete (p177) has trips for beginners through to hardcore cycling junkies. On bike-friendly Tobago, end your ride along forest trails with a cool dip in the sea or at a waterfall; contact Mountain Biking Tobago (mountain bikingtobago.com) for an unforgettable experience.

←

Cycling down the Ciboa Valley in the Dominican Republic

Take a Hike

As geology differs throughout the Caribbean chain, the choice of terrain varies from flat and barren to mountainous and forested. The mountainous isles are laced with excellent trails. Some of the finest trekking is on Saba *(p264)*, with its steep hills, deep vales, and short yet magnificent trails that crisscross the isle. For a full-on adventure, lace up your boots for the overnight trek up the Dominican Republic's Pico Duarte, the Caribbean's highest mountain. The Reef Bay Trail in St. John, Virgin Isands, is also worth a trek, running downhill and past a pool inscribed with petroglyphs.

←

Trekking through lush rainforest in Saba

TOP 5 **TREKS IN THE CARIBBEAN**

Shirley Heights, Antigua
Make this short hike for sunset and the party that follows

Guanapo Gorge, Trinidad
This breathtaking gorge has fascinating geological features.

Mount Jamanota, Aruba
The steep but short trek up the mountain in the Arikok National Park offers fantastic views from the summit.

Seven Sisters Falls, Grenada
A two-hour trek in the Grand Étang Forest Reserve that passes seven lovely waterfalls.

Crispeen Track, Saba
Be transported from Windwardside to The Bottom, with fine views.

Saddling Up

Whether you're seeking a sunset canter along a beach or a lengthier excursion, opportunities for horseback riding abound. In Jamaica, enjoy an exhilarating swim with your horse in the ocean at the renowned Half Moon Equestrian Center *(horsebackridingjamaica.com)*. A riding excursion in the lush and verdant Valle de Viñales *(p82)* is to explore Cuba *a lo cubano* (like a Cuban).

↑ A group riding in Cuba's Valle de Viñales

Seas the Day

The Caribbean's soft sands and warm turquoise waters make the perfect playground for kids of all ages. Children's packages at all-inclusive resorts include building sandcastles and treasure hunts. And family-friendly beaches such as Punta Cana *(p174)*, in Dominican Republic, offer snorkeling, volleyball, plus giant dominoes and other games.

A child enjoying the warm crystal waters of the Caribbean

THE CARIBBEAN FOR
FAMILIES

With its abundance of beaches, nature reserves, and cultural and historical venues, the Caribbean is a fun-filled wonderland for kids. Many islands have family-focused resorts. Plus, the islanders adore children, and interacting with island children will add to your own youngster's delight.

Rainy Day Activities

Thunderstorms don't have to put a stop to the enjoyment of a Caribbean vacation, with scores of museums and educational venues to keep youngsters entertained. Havana's Planetario *(Mercaderes No 311)* features high-tech interactive exhibits on the universe. Or why not take the kids SNUBA diving among the coral reefs off Sint Maarten *(p252)*.

 INSIDER TIP
Family Resorts

Most all-inclusive beach resorts have kids' clubs with special programs for little ones, older children, and teens. Choose a family-focused resort for a fulfilling vacation.

SNUBA diving among coral reefs ↑

Pirate Ships

Youngsters have plenty of opportunity to release their inner Jack Sparrow in settings recalling the heyday of pirates and Buccaneers. Experience a thrilling light-and-sound show pirate raid at Pirates of Nassau in The Bahamas. Party aboard a vessel with Aruba's Jolly Pirates. Or make merry during Pirates Week in the Cayman Islands *(pirates weekfestival.com).*

→

People taking part in a Snorkeling cruise with Aruba's Jolly Pirates

Adventure Parks

Adventure parks offer heaps of fun when kids tire of the beach or when the sun doesn't shine. Splash to your hearts content at Martinique's Aqualand, with its wave pool, water slaloms, and pirate galleon. Saint Lucia's inflatable Splash Island Water Park *(saintluciawaterpark. com)* has lots of obstacle-course style features to keep kids amused.

←

A giant inflatable float at Saint Lucia's Splash Island Water Park

Bringing History to Life

Scores of museums and historic buildings including Pre-Columbian petroglyphs, slave-era plantations, and colonial castles allow children to explore the Caribbean's diverse history. Witness the living indigenous heritage at Kalinago Barana Aute village, on Dominica; visit Citadelle Laferrière *(p195),* in Haiti; and savor a ride on the St. Kitts Scenic Railway Tour *(p280).*

→

Enthralled visitors on the St. Kitts Scenic Railway Tour

Sensational Seafood

The ocean delivers a wealth of great seafood, from conch (The Bahamas' national dish and a Caribbean specialty) and ubiquitous lobster to marlin (a favorite in Cuba), grouper, and even flying fish - a staple of Barbados. Spend an enjoyable day catching your own meal with local fishermen and revel in the sense of heaving earned your reward.

→

Preparing conch on the beach in The Bahamas

THE CARIBBEAN FOR
FOODIES

The gastronomic scene is a vibrant mosaic, with specialties differing from one isle to the next. Indigenous influences meld with those of Africa, Asia, and Europe - plus local exotic fruits and an abundance of seafood - to produce an endlessly creative fusion that is uniquely Caribbean.

Bustling Markets

Teeming with plump, ripe tropical vegetables and fruits, street markets are a riot of color and scents, and a delicious assault on the senses. Fragrant aromas of nutmeg, vanilla, and ginger waft through the air of St. George's Spice Market *(p400)* on Grenada - the "isle of spice." And fisher sell their catch straight from their boats at Montagu Beach Fish Market, in Nassau *(p128)*.

→

St. George's Spice market in Grenada

Heavenly Rum

Locally-produced rum is the spirit of choice in the Caribbean, and the source of dozens of creative (and creatively named) cocktails. Some, such as mojitos and daiquiris, are world-renowned. Others are specific to individual islands, and even to single bars. Visit a distillery such as Barbancourt on Haiti *(p191)*, or those in Guadeloupe *(p332)*, to learn how rum is made and taste the results.

← Daiquiri at El Floridita in Havana, Cuba's famous bar

CLASSIC COCKTAILS

The Painkiller
A Virgin Island blend of rum plus orange juice, pineapple juice, and coconut milk.

Piña Colada
A Caribbean classic combining coconut milk, pineapple juice, and rum.

Frozen rum runners
Slushy blend of rum, fruit liqueurs, orange juice, and grenadine.

Bahama Mama
Rum, coffee liqueur, grenadine, and juices, served over crushed ice.

The Bushwacker
An alcoholic creamy chocolate smoothie containing dark rum.

Caribbean Classics

From conch chowder to curried goat, many dishes are as quintessentially Caribbean as the crystal seas. Start your day with ackee and saltfish, a national dish in Jamaica. Lunch on jerk chicken, or pepperpot stew, both found throughout the region. Dine on *lechón asado* (roast suckling pig), a popular dish on the Spanish-speaking islands.

↑ Pan of spicy jerk chicken, a Caribbean specialty

Listening to Calypso

Calypso, or "steel pan," is the very drumbeat, if not the heartbeat, of Trinidad and Tobago, where the unmistakable tropical sound of tin-drum bands, known as "pannists," resonates through the islands. Faster, syncopated *soca* (which incorporates elements of funk, soul, and zouk) is the quintessential sound of carnival.

→

Playing the tin drums, the sound of calypso

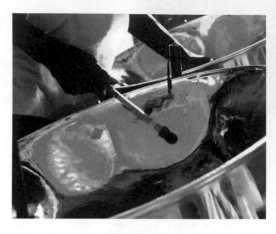

THE CARIBBEAN FOR
RHYTHMS

The melting pot of island cultures has made the Caribbean a major breeding ground for musical genres, and the love of music and dance is difficult to exaggerate. Music festivals and carnivals are a key aspect of the Caribbean heritage, drawing travelers the world over for calypso, reggae, and salsa.

Carnivals

Islands around the Caribbean explode in a riot of color, music, motion, and fanciful costume for carnivals. The biggest of all is in Trinidad, but The Bahamas has its own variant called Junkanoo, Barbados has Crop Over, and Haiti hosts Defile Kanaval (*p56*). The Caribbean concept of Carnival came about during the slave era. Colonial masters allowed their slaves to vent off steam in once-a-year parties. Their irreverent parodies of their masters' pre-Lenten masquerade balls evolved into carnivals – the elaborate spectacles celebrated today in most of the Caribbean.

Learning to Salsa

Visiting Cuba or Puerto Rico without dancing salsa is like visiting France without tasting the wine. To learn the moves and give your hips some attitude, sign up for a dance class and perfect your skills before painting Havana red, hitting the nightclubs of San Juan in Puerto Rico, or sampling the sizzling bars of Santo Domingo in the Dominican Republic.

→

Informal salsa dancing in a Havana Square, Cuba

Dancing to Bachata and Merengue

These twin and twangy musical genres are the music of choice in the Dominican Republic, and like all Caribbean musical genres they have their own dances forms. The two-step beat of fast and lively *merengue* is ideal for dancing with a partner, while mournful *bachata* typically offers slow, plaintive odes to lost loves, although in recent years it has become more upbeat and sometimes incorporates electronic sounds.

↑ Couple dancing to the brisk beats of merengue

Relaxing to Reggae

Born in Jamaica, and forever associated with the spiritually inspired songs of Bob Marley, the island's famous former resident, this is the defining music of the Caribbean. In its island birthplace, you are never far from its infectious syncopated, toe-tapping beat pulsing from buses, beaches, and bars.

←

Woman in elaborate feathered carnival costume in Trinidad and Tobago

→

Flag waving at the Rebel Salute music festival in Jamaica

Superb Soccer

Soccer is a universal favorite here, with impromptu games played on the sands and any available patch of grass. You'll be encouraged to join in, but if you'd rather watch a game, check out Jamaica's national team, the Reggae Boyz, at Kingston's Independence Park.

Soccer on the beach is a commmon sight in the Caribbean

THE CARIBBEAN FOR
SPORTS FANS

The Caribbean's diverse heritage is reflected in the wide variety of sports played here, from cricket to baseball. While the popularity of each game varies between islands, you can expect a lively local spirit wherever you go, whether you're looking to cheer on the sidelines or get stuck in yourself.

Top Golf

Year-round sunshine, fabulous seascapes, and challenging celebrity-designed courses – it's no wonder golfers are drawn to the Caribbean. Tryall Club in Jamaica offers a demanding championship layout with breathtaking views, while Sandy Lane in Barbados has three courses, each with tropical landscaping and perfectly accentuated by natural seascapes.

→

Ready to putt on a perfectly-landscaped, palm-fringed golf course

Crazy About Cricket

The popularity of cricket extends from tiny St. Kitts to powerhouse nations Jamaica and Trinidad. Watch a lively game at Barbados's Kensington Oval, or join a local game, played with makeshift bats and wickets, on one of the Caribbean's beaches.

→

The West Indies playing at Kensington Oval

Brilliant Baseball

U.S. Marines introduced the game to the Spanish-speaking islands in the 19th century, and today, Cuba and the Dominican Republic vie with each other to be the best in the world. Havana's Estadio Latinoamericano is a great place to savor the fervor, but nothing beats the ambience at Santo Domingo's Estadio Quisqueya.

←

Roel Santos of the Cuban National team playing at the Estadio Latinoamericano

 TOP 5 CARIBBEAN SPORT STARS

Usain Bolt
The world's fastest man, the Jamaican competed in three Olympics.

Ana Fidelia Quirot
Cuban runner and a two-time World Champion.

Chris Gayle
This Jamaican cricketer captained the West Indies from 2007–2010.

Shelly-Ann Fraser-Pryce
Sprinter and the first Caribbean woman to win Olympic 100 m gold.

Sammy Sosa
Dominican baseball player who hit more than 600 home runs.

Amazing Athletics

Caribbean nations have produced world-class athletes, and a visit to their training stadiums is an unforgettable experience. Kingston's National Stadium may be the top track, but the blue and yellow track at UWI Cave Hill Campus is equally inspiring, based on the flag of its home, Barbados.

↑ Usain Bolt in his famous pose

A YEAR IN
THE CARIBBEAN

JANUARY

Naniki Music Festival (*mid-Jan*). Three days spanning jazz, R&B, reggae, and more, in the hills of Surinam, Barbados.

△ **Havana International Jazz Festival** (*mid-Jan*). Jazz aficionados flock for nine days of performances by music legends.

FEBRUARY

△ **Trinidad Carnival** (*last week*). Fanciful costumes highlight this week of sensual festivities known as the biggest street party on earth. Port of Spain, Trinidad.

MAY

△ **Dia de los Trabajadores** (*1 May*). Half-a-million people flood through Plaza de la Revolución for Workers' Day. Havana, Cuba.

Saint Lucia Jazz & Arts Festival (*first half of May*). The Caribbean's premier jazz festival draws top international artists for two weeks of performances (*p371*). Saint Lucia.

JUNE

△ **Pineapple Festival** (*early Jun*). All things pineapple, from cooking contests to plaiting the pineapple pole, provide a good excuse to party. Gregory Town, Eleuthera, The Bahamas.

OCTOBER

△ **World Creole Music Festival** (*last week*). World-class Caribbean and international performers celebrate their music over three days and nights. Dominica.

Dominican Republic Jazz Festival (*last weekend*). Jazz legends such as Chuck Mangione and David Sánchez are regulars at this jazzfest. Dominican Republic.

SEPTEMBER

△ **Caribbean Sea Jazz Festival** (*mid-Sep*). Oranjestad pulsates to cool funk, soul, and jazz by maestros from George Benson to Chaka Khan. Aruba.

APRIL

△ **Antigua Sailing Week** (*last week*). Serious sailors compete in this prestigious week-long event known for equally serious partying.

Rara Festival (*Easter week*). Voudou-infused carnival parades highlighted by trumpet-like bamboo instruments and flamboyantly painted celebrants. Jacmel, Haiti.

MARCH

St. Thomas International Regatta (*late-Mar*). Three days of world-class competition and shoreside excitement. St. Thomas, Virgin Islands.

△ **Festival Casals** (*mid-Mar*). Classical music festival in honor of founder and classical musician Pablo Casals. San Juan, Puerto Rico.

AUGUST

Carriacou Regatta (*first week*). Four days of sailing competitions and live entertainment. Grenada.

△ **Crop-Over Festival** (*June-Aug*). A six-week revelry, marking the end of sugar cane harvest, ending in carnival. Georgetown, Barbados.

JULY

△ **Reggae Sumfest** (*mid-Jul*). A six-night line-up of iconic reggae performers starts and ends with a beach party like no other. Montego Bay, Jamaica.

DECEMBER

Junkanoo (*last week*). The Bahamas' most cacophonous street extravaganza includes a carnival parade led by flamboyantly adorned dance troupes. Nassau, The Bahamas.

△ **Parrandas de Remedios** (*last week*). Spectacular home-made fireworks highlight this bombastic carnival pitting two sides of town against one another. Remedios, Cuba.

NOVEMBER

△ **Pirates Week** (*first two weeks*). Light-hearted revelry as locals and visitors make like Jack Sparrow with mock invasions, costume contests, and fireworks. Cayman Islands.

A BRIEF
HISTORY

First inhabited by American Indian tribes, the islands were later conquered by the Spanish, English, French, and Dutch. Once slaves were introduced, the decimated civilizations blended with the Africans and Europeans.

First Inhabitants and the Conquistadores

The Caribbean began to be inhabited around 5000 BC when the Arawak communities migrated from South America. Columbus arrived in 1492, establishing La Isabela on Hispaniola and mapping the islands from Trinidad to Cuba. His arrival spelled doom – in his wake came gold-hungry Spanish conquistadores who settled the major islands, enslaving the natives to mine. Within decades, indigenous peoples were almost wiped out by overwork, massacre, and disease, and as such the Spanish began importing African slaves to supply the need for labor.

1 Columbus landing on the island of Hispaniola

2 1594 map of the Caribbean

3 Depiction of slaves cutting the sugar cane

4 The Millyard in Antigua, 1823

Timeline of events

5000 BC
The Arawak begin moving north from Orinoco Basin, South America

AD 1200
Caribs, also known as the Kalinago, migrate to the Lesser Antilles from South America

1300
The Arawak were driven out a century before Columbus arrived

1492
Christopher Columbus "discovers" the Caribbean by landing on what is now The Bahamas

1503
The first African slaves are transported to Hispaniola

Sugar and Slavery

The phenomenal growth of the sugar industry in the 17th century was made possible by African slave labor. Men, women, and children were captured and packed aboard ships to the New World where most were auctioned to European plantation owners. Britain shipped more than three million Africans to the Caribbean between 1662 and 1807, by which time slaves outnumbered the white population by ten to one. They toiled in the fields with little respite from flogging or worse. Slave masters suppressed rebellions with force, but by the end of the 18th century, uprisings had grown in size and frequency. A rebellion in 1804 in Saint-Domingue led to the creation of the world's first black republic, Haiti. Meanwhile slavery was coming under fire from humanitarians. The rising costs of producing sugar heightened criticism of the "plantocracy". Slavery was abolished in the British colonies in 1833-34, the French in 1848, the Dutch in 1863, in Puerto Rico in 1873, and in Cuba in 1886.

THE AGE OF PIRATES

The wealth of the Caribbean lured pirates in the 16th century, who preyed upon and looted ships sailing from the Caribbean to Europe. They blazed a terror trail, operating out of ports including Port Royal in Jamaica and Tortuga in Haiti. Attacks increased until 1697, when the Treaty of Ryswyck was signed.

1624
The British establish their first Caribbean colony on St. Kitts

1634
The Dutch colonize the southwest Caribbean islands

1635
Guadeloupe and Martinique are colonized by France

1804
Haiti is the first Caribbean nation to gain independence from European powers

1824
Denmark grants emancipation to slaves. Other nations follow

Creole Culture and Island Independence

Each island evolved its own Creole culture which crystallized, into nationalist independence movements. After Haiti and the Dominican Republic gained independence in 1804 and 1844 respectively, the United States declared war on Spain in 1898. This Spanish–American War ended with Spain's defeat. Cuba and Puerto Rico were ceded to the U.S. In 1903, the U.S. granted freedom to Cuba, which experienced a boom-and-bust economy ending in 1959, when Fidel Castro toppled General Batista and the island became a communist nation. Meanwhile, the Danes sold their Virgin Islands to the U.S. back in 1917, and in 1958, an attempt to forge the British-ruled islands into an independent Federation of the West Indies foundered. Jamaica and Trinidad and Tobago were the first British colonies to gain independence in 1962 and others followed. Today Aruba, Curaçao, Bonaire, St. Eustatius, Saba, and Sint Maarten are dependents of the Netherlands; Guadeloupe and Martinique of France; and Anguilla, Montserrat, Cayman Islands, British Virgin Islands, and Turks and Caicos are British Overseas Territories.

↑ Alexander Bustamante and Lyndon Johnson on Jamaican Independence Day in 1962

Timeline of events

1898
U.S. intervenes in Cuba's independence war and seizes Puerto Rico

1902
Mont Pelée erupts on Martinique, destroying St. Pierre

1959
Fidel Castro seizes power in Cuba and begins a Communist revolution

1961
U.S. imposes trade embargo on Cuba

1983
U.S. Marines invade Grenada after Prime Minister is assassinated

The Caribbean Today

The Caribbean is a region of diverse cultures and an eclectic mix of the old and the new. Today, thanks to the gorgeous beaches, sunny climate, and laidback lifestyle, the economic basis for most islands is tourism. Many large resorts were built in the 1950s, and tourism increased dramatically when flights opened up a decade later. The number of visitors rose from 1.3 million in 1959 to four million in 1965, and has continued to increase ever since.

The trend in modern times in the Caribbean is political stability and economic development, and the Caribbean people have succeeded in maintaining democratic forms of government. In a historic meeting in 2015, U.S. President Barack Obama met Raúl Castro to re-establish and normalize relations between Cuba and the U.S. and currently, most trade embargos and travel restrictions have been eased.

In recent years, a series of natural disasters have blighted the region. A powerful earthquake struck Haiti in 2010 and in 2017, hurricanes Harvey, Irma, and Maria wreaked devastation.

1 Creole women ↑
2 Spanish-American war, San Juan, Cuba, 1898
3 Soufriére Hills Volcano on Montserrat
4 Barack Obama and Raúl Castro in 2015

Did You Know

More than 30 million people visit the Caribbean yearly despite some major hurricanes since 2015.

1995
The Soufrière Hills volcano on Montserrat erupts, destroying the capital Plymouth

2010
An earthquake hits Haiti, killing 230,000 people

2012
Partial relaxation of the U.S. trade embargo on Cuba

2017
Harvey, Irma, and Maria hurricanes cause 3,300 deaths

EXPERIENCE

Cobbled street leading to the Trinidad Bell Tower in Cuba

A vintage car parked on the colorful backstreets of Cuba

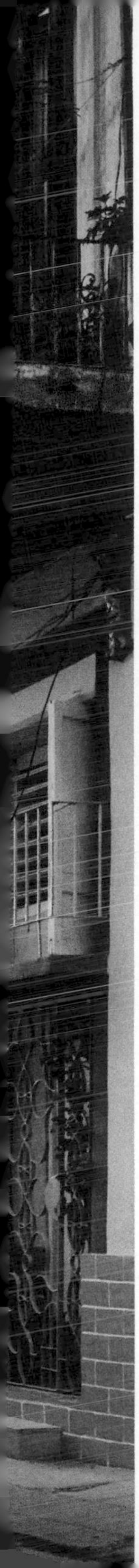

CUBA

The largest island in the Caribbean offers a unique and complex blend of spirited Caribbean culture infused with communism. Its heritage is steeped in struggle. Monuments to the wars of independence with the colonial power Spain, in the late 1800s, and to the revolution in 1959 that swept away the corrupt U.S.-backed regime of Fulgencio Batista, are found in every city. Though long-time president Fidel Castro passed away in 2016, his larger-than-life presence is still everywhere, along with that of the other leading revolutionary hero Che Guevara, in billboards and media exhortations.

The recent thawing of relations with the United States, and consequent easing of travel and trade restrictions, have helped Cuba's beleaguered economy. However, day-to-day life is still a struggle for most Cubans. In the countryside, ox-drawn carts are still a common means of transportation. Nonetheless, despite material hardships, Cuba is an incredibly uplifting place. On the sometimes crumbling, sometimes splendidly restored, streets of colorful, centuries-old towns and cities, the sounds of son, salsa, and rumba fill the air, and *casas de la trova* (open-house clubs) keep traditional forms of music alive. This is the case across the island, in the culturally rich capital of Havana, where nearly a fifth of the island's population of 11 million live, in time-warped little Trinidad in the south, and in sultry Santiago de Cuba in the east.

CUBA

CAPE
Coral

Naples

U.S.A.

Pompano
Beach

Fort Lauderda

Miami

Homestead

Key Largo

Florida
Keys

Key West

HAVANA

MATANZAS

VARADERO

Archipiélago de Sabana

LAS
TERRAZAS

Mariel

José Martí
International
Airport

Juan Gualberto
Gómez Airport

CAYO LEVISA

Candelaria

Batabanó

Güines

Jovellanos

Sagua
la Grande

Remedios

VALLE DE VIÑALES

Golfo de
Batabanó

Jagüey Grande

Colón

SANTA CLARA

Mantua

PINAR
DEL RÍO

PENÍNSULA
DE ZAPATA

Playa
Larga

Isabel Rubio

VUELTA
ABAJO

CIENFUEGOS

SIERRA
ESCAMBRA

Jaime González Airport

Nueva Gerona

Rafael Cabrera
Airport

TOPES DE COLLANTES

MARÍA
LA GORDA

La Victoria

Santa Fe

Vilo Acuña
Airport

TRINIDAD

PLAYA
ANCÓN

VALLE
DE LOS
INGENIC

ISLA DE LA
JUVENTUD

CAYO
LARGO

Caribbean
Sea

CAYMAN
ISLANDS

0 kilometers   100

N

0 miles   100

CUBA

Must Sees

1. Havana
2. Trinidad
3. Valle de Viñales

Experience More

4. Cayo Largo
5. Isla de la Juventud
6. Las Terrazas
7. Pinar del Río
8. Matanzas
9. Cayo Levisa
10. Varadero
11. Península de Zapata
12. María la Gorda
13. Vuelto Abajo
14. Cienfuegos
15. Santa Clara
16. Cayos de Villa Clara
17. Valle de los Ingenios
18. Topes de Collantes
19. Guardalavaca
20. Playa Ancón
21. Holguín
22. Jardines del Rey
23. Camagüey
24. Sierra Escambray
25. Santiago de Cuba
26. Guantanamo
27. Baracoa
28. Gran Parque Nacional Sierra Maestra
29. Bayamo

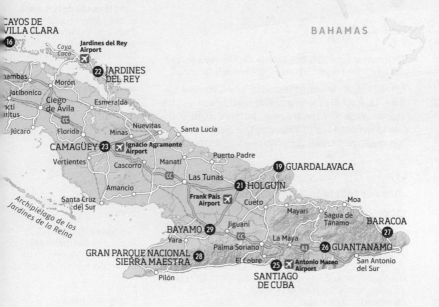

↑ A vintage car cruising down Havana's colorful main street

HAVANA

🏠 N coast of Cuba ✈🚌🚕 🛈 Calle 28 (between 3ra and 5ta Avenida), Playa; (7) 204 0624; www.winfotur.cu

One of the world's great historical cities, Havana is a lively capital full of architectural jewels in various styles. Habana Vieja (Old Havana) was declared a UNESCO World Heritage Site in 1982, and this historic heart has regained its splendor after ongoing restoration.

Plaza de la Catedral

🏠 Calles San Ignacio & Empedrado

This intimate square was once a terminus for the Zanja Real, the royal aqueduct constructed to supply water to ships in the adjoining harbor. The plaza is dominated by the Baroque profile of the Catedral de San Cristóbal, completed in 1777.

In the 18th century, Spanish nobles built their palaces around the square. Most noteworthy is the Casa del Conde de Bayona, today housing the **Museo de Arte Colonial**, full of period furnishings. Women dressed in colonial costume stroll the plaza and pose for photos. Just off the northwest corner, is La Bodeguita del Medio bar-restaurant, where some claim that Ernest Hemingway was once a regular visitor.

Museo de Arte Colonial

♿🏠 Calle San Ignacio 61 📞 (7) 862 6440 🕐 9am–5pm daily

Calle Mercaderes

🏠 Linking Plaza de Armas to Plaza Vieja

This cobblestoned street is lined with restored colonial structures and features a mix of museums, boutiques, and restaurants. Not to be missed is the **Maqueta de la Habana**, an open gallery housing a 1:500 scale model of Habana Vieja. The 17th-century Casa de la Obra Pía is a fine example of colonial architecture.

Maqueta de la Habana

♿ 🏠 Calle Mercaderes 114 📞 (7) 866 4425 🕐 9am–6pm daily

③

Plaza Vieja

🏠 Calles Mercaderes & Brasil

"Old Square" began as Plaza Nueva (New Square) in 1587 and served as Havana's main market place and bullfight

---

 GREAT VIEW
Screen Shots

For a sweeping view of La Habana Vieja, ascend to the rooftop of Edificio Gómez Villa on Plaza Vieja. Here, a Cámara Oscura (a revolving peep-hole camera) projects a real-time panorama onto a screen.

arena. Buildings from four centuries surround the plaza, which has been fully restored. Casa del Conde de Jaruco, built between 1733 and 1737, features colonial details, including *mediopuntos* (half-moon stained-glass windows). The Palacio Cueto is an astonishing Art Nouveau building, currently undergoing a lengthy conversion into a hotel.

④
Calle Obispo

Habana Vieja's liveliest street is the pedestrianized Calle Obispo, which has bustled with activity since colonial days. At its west end, El Floridita is where Ernest Hemingway famously downed daiquiris; today his bronze likeness rests an elbow at the bar. His room (No. 511) at Hotel Ambos Mundos is preserved as a

museum. Another interesting site is Farmacia Taquechel, an old pharmacy with apothecary jars lining the shelves.

Plaza de San Francisco

⌂ Calle Oficios

This airy square once opened onto the colonial waterfront. At its heart, the marble Fuente de los Leones is modeled on a fountain in the Alhambra. The restored Neo-Classical Lonja del Comercio, the former commerce exchange, is topped by a bronze statue of Mercury. Dominating the square, the Basílica Menor de San Francisco de Asís dates back to the 1580s, though it was rebuilt in 1730. In 1762, the British seized Havana and began worshiping in the church, which today is home to a museum of religious art.

EAT

Mama Inés
Fidel's former private chef conjures up superb fusion dishes within a colonial mansion.

⌂ Calle de la Obra Pía, 60
☏ (7) 862 2669 🕘 Sun

$$$

El del Frente
Enjoy tapas and mojitos here, either on the roof terrace or amid the 1950s-inspired interior at this *paladar*.

⌂ Calle O'Reilly, 303
☏ (7) 863 0206

$$$

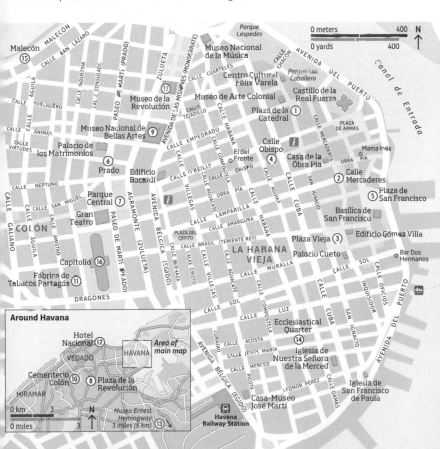

⑥ Prado

🅐 Between Parque Central and Malecón

Officially named Paseo de Martí, this tree-shaded boulevard was redesigned in 1927 by French architect Forestier, and features a raised walkway adorned with bronze lions, wrought-iron lampposts, and marble benches. The many Neo-Moorish buildings include the Hotel Sevilla, from 1908. Nearby, Havana's main wedding venue, the beautiful Neo-Baroque Palacio de los Matrimonios, has an ornately stuccoed interior.

---

⑦
Parque Central

🅐 Paseo de Martí at Calle Neptuno

This spacious park serves as the major gateway between Habana Vieja and the modern districts to the west. Designed in 1877, it has a statue of José Martí in its center. Gracious structures surround the park, including the Hotel Inglaterra and Hotel Plaza, notable for their elegant 19th-century facades. Most striking is the Gran Teatro de la Habana, a Baroque confection adorned with statues.

←

A statue of José Martí, Cuba's foremost national hero, which stands in Parque Central

↑ Image of Guevara on the Plaza de la Revolución

⑧ Plaza de la Revolución

🅐 Paseo between Ave. Carlos M. de Céspedes & Ave. Rancho Boyeros

This monumental plaza has been Cuba's political and administrative center since it was laid out in the 1950s as Plaza Cívica. The facade of the Ministerio del Interior is adorned with a seven-story steel sculpture of Che Guevara. Dominating the plaza, the Memorial José Martí features a marble statue of the national hero, with the Museo de José Martí behind it.

---

⑨
Museo Nacional de Bellas Artes

🅐 Palacio de Bellas Artes: Trocadero e/ Zulueta y Monserrate; Centro Asturiano: San Rafael y Zulueta ⏰ 9am–5pm Tue–Sat, 10am–2pm Sun 🚫 Public hols 🌐 bellasartes.co.cu

Havana's National Fine Arts Museum displays a rich trove across two buildings. The Palacio de Bellas Artes is given over to Cuban art, with sections devoted to colonial and 20th-century works. The Centro Asturiano houses international works, including those of European masters, plus a collection of Egyptian, Greek, and Roman antiquities.

---

⑩
Cementerio Colón

🅐 Zapata y Calle 12 📞 (7) 832 1050 ⏰ 8am–5pm daily

Havana's vast cemetery covers 0.2 sq miles (0.5 sq km) and was arranged in a strict grid in the 1870s. It has been named

---

DRINK

Bar Dos Hermanos
A favored watering hole of Ernest Hemingway, the cocktails here are as good as they were in the writer's day.

🅐 Avenida del Puerto, 305 📞 (7) 861 3514

Dulcería Bianchini II
This tiny, Swiss-run café serves up excellent cappuccinos and other coffees, alongside mouthwatering cakes.

🅐 Callejón del Chorro 📞 (7) 862 8477

a National Historic Monument for its spectacular mausoleums in eclectic styles, from Neo-Classical to avant-garde. At its core is the Capilla Central, a chapel with lavish frescoes.

Fábrica de Tabacos Partagás

🏠 Calle San Carlos 816
📞 (7) 878 5166 🕒 9am-1pm daily

The original cigar factory, which used to be located behind the Capitolio, was founded in 1845 by Jaime Partagás Ravelo, a Catalan businessman. At this location visitors can still take tours of the factory and observe the cigar-making process. Tickets can be bought from a tourist hotel desk.

⑫ 🍴

Hotel Nacional

🏠 Calles O & 21 🌐 hotel nacionaldecuba.com

Overlooking the Malecón, this gem of an Art Deco building opened in 1930. It features a lavish Moorish interior, while cannons stud the lawns.

Considered Havana's finest hotel, its illustrious guest list includes Churchill, Sinatra, Ava Gardner, and Hemingway.

⑬

Museo Ernest Hemingway

🏠 Calle Vigía y Steinhart, San Francisco de Paula
📞 (7) 891 0809 🕒 10am-4pm Mon-Sat, 9am-1pm Sun

Ernest Hemingway's former home, Finca Vigía, is maintained as the author left it, with his possessions in situ. Visitors are not allowed to enter but can look through the open windows and door.

⑭ 🈯

Ecclesiastical Quarter

🏠 S of Plaza Vieja

In colonial days, southern Habana Vieja was a major ecclesiastical center and has many convents and churches. The 17th-century Convento de Santa Clara is an outstanding example of colonial architecture. The Iglesia de Nuestra Señora de la Merced, with a lavish interior and frescoed

 INSIDER TIP
Ferry Tale

Hop on the *lancha* (ferry) that runs between the Emboque de Luz terminus and Regla for superb vistas of the Havana waterfront. It costs a mere 20 centavos (you will need *peso cubano*).

dome ceiling, is popular with both Catholic and Santería (Afro-Cuban) worshipers.

Casa-Museo José Martí is the birthplace of José Martí, and now houses a museum with some of his written works on display.

⑮

Malecón

🏠 Between Prado and Río Almenderes

This seafront boulevard, lined with fanciful buildings, is Havana's main thoroughfare. Highlights include the Monumento al Maine, a memorial to sailors killed when the U.S.S *Maine* exploded in the Havana harbor on February 15, 1898.

↑ Locals relaxing in front of the Malecón's ubiquitous pastel buildings

(16) 🎨 🎭 🛍️

CAPITOLIO

🏛️ Paseo de Martí (Prado), esq San José
📞 (7) 801 1535 ⏰ 10am–3pm Tue & Thu–Sat,
10am–noon Wed & Sun

A symbol of the city, the Capitol (Capitolio) combines the elegance of Neo-Classicism with Art Deco elements. After an extensive renovation, in 2018 it returned to its original role as the seat of Cuba's government.

Standing in an area once occupied by a botanical garden and later by the capital's first railway station, the Capitol is a loose imitation of that in Washington, D.C., but is even taller – the dome was the highest point in the city until the 1950s. During Machado's rule, the building witnessed many major historic events and, after the revolution it became the headquarters of the Ministry of Science, Technology, and the Environment.

↑ The iconic dome dominating the Capitolio's exterior

Did You Know?

The Salón de los Pasos Perdidos (Hall of Lost Steps) takes its name from its unusual acoustics.

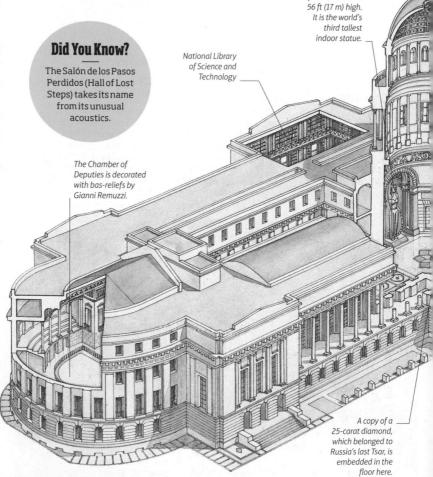

The Statue of the Republic *stands at 56 ft (17 m) high. It is the world's third tallest indoor statue.*

National Library of Science and Technology

The Chamber of Deputies is decorated with bas-reliefs by Gianni Remuzzi.

A copy of a 25-carat diamond, which belonged to Russia's last Tsar, is embedded in the floor here.

EXPERIENCE Cuba

Timeline

1929
△ Gerardo Machado inaugurated the grand building.

1933
△ The police fired on a crowd gathered here during an anti-Machado demonstration.

1959
△ After the revolution, the government leaves the building.

2018
△ The National Assembly moves back to the building.

← The striking dome and sumptuous rooms that make up the Capitolio

The dome is almost 300 ft (92 m) high.

Salón de los Pasos Perdidos

Parliament sits here

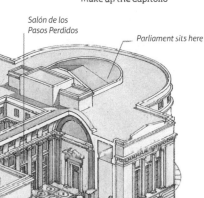

PITOLIO

The bronze doors are ornamented with 30 bas-relief panels by Cuban painter Enrique García Cabrera.

Angelo Zanelli's 20-ft- (7-m-) high bronze sculptures represent work and virtue and each weigh 15 tons.

↑ The *Statue of the Republic*, covered in 22-carat gold leaf

↑ Salón de los Pasos Perdidos, with its vibrant marble floor

MUSEO DE LA REVOLUCIÓN

🏠 Calle Refugio, 1, e/ Avenida de las Misiones y Zulueta 📞 (7) 801 5491 🕐 9:30am–5pm daily (last entry 4:15pm)

This building was once the presidential palace of the overthrown dictator Fulgencio Batista; now, fittingly, it houses the Museum of the Revolution.

Designed by the Cuban architect Rodolfo Maruri and the Belgian architect Paul Belau, the presidential palace was inaugurated in 1920 by Mario García Menocal, and it remained the residence for all subsequent presidents until 1965. The building has Neo-Classical elements, and was decorated by Tiffany & Co. of New York. It contains works by the leading Cuban decorators of the early 1900s and by sculptors such as Juan José Sicre, Esteban Betancourt, and Fernando Boada. In contrast, the museum features documents, photographs, and memorabilia presenting an overview of the Cubans' struggle for independence from the colonial period onward, focusing in particular on the 1959 revolution – from the guerrilla war to the "Special Period" in the 1990s.

→ The former presidential palace's grand exterior and luxurious rooms

GRANMA MEMORIAL

The large glass-and-cement pavilion behind the museum contains the yacht *Granma* (named after its first owner's grandmother). In 1956, this boat brought Fidel Castro and some of his comrades from Mexico to Cuba to begin the struggle against Batista. The yacht is now immortalized in the museum to remind visitors of Castro's bravery and willpower.

The third story contains photos and memorabilia from colonial times to 1959.

The side wing of the palace was home to Batista's office.

↑ A dome topping the Museo de la Revolución's exterior

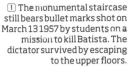

1. The monumental staircase still bears bullet marks shot on March 13 1957 by students on a mission to kill Batista. The dictator survived by escaping to the upper floors.

2. Lined with vast mirrors *(espejos),* the Salón de los Espejos has frescoes by Cuban painters Armando Menocal and Antonio Rodríguez Morey.

3. The collection features many revolutionary paintings.

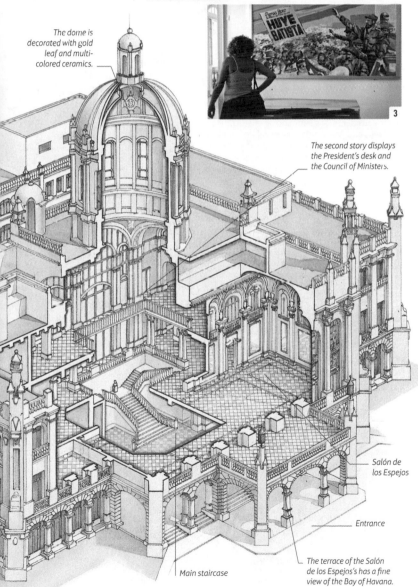

The dome is decorated with gold leaf and multi-colored ceramics.

The second story displays the President's desk and the Council of Ministers.

Salón de los Espejos

Entrance

The terrace of the Salón de los Espejos's has a fine view of the Bay of Havana.

Main staircase

PLAZA DE LA CATEDRAL

Distance 1,968 ft (600 m) **Time** 15 minutes
Nearest bus route P5

Dominated by the elegant profile of its church, Plaza de la Catedral is one of the symbols of La Habana Vieja. A 16th-century plaque in the square marks the spot where the Zanja Real, the city's first aqueduct (and the first Spanish aqueduct in the New World) was located. Reaching the square in 1592, it began at the Almendares river, 7 miles (11 km) away, and was built to provide water to ships docking in the harbor, as well as to local residents. The surrounding aristocratic buildings and present-day cathedral were built in the 18th century. An amble around Plaza de la Catedral is an essential activity for anyone visiting the historic center. Women in colonial costume stroll under the arcades and read fortunes, and there are several bar-restaurants where you can relax in the shade and listen to music.

The modern entrance of the 18th-century **Seminario de San Carlos y San Ambrosio** echoes the Baroque decorative motifs of the cathedral.

Former entrance to the seminary

CALLE SAN IGNACIO

Centro Wifredo Lam, housed in an 18th-century palazzo, promotes contemporary art with exhibitions and lectures.

START

Casa de la Condesa de la Reunión, a 19th-century building surrounding a splendid courtyard, is the headquarters of the Alejo Carpentier Foundation.

CALLE EMPEDRADO

La Bodeguita del Medio is legendary thanks to Ernest Hemingway, who came here to drink mojitos.

The **Taller Experimental de Gráfica** holds theoretical and practical courses in graphic art for locals and visitors, and houses a Gallery of Engravings.

← Ordering a mojito in the iconic La Bodeguita del Medio

↑ The atmospheric surroundings of the Plaza de la Catedral at twilight

Locator Map
For more detail see p69

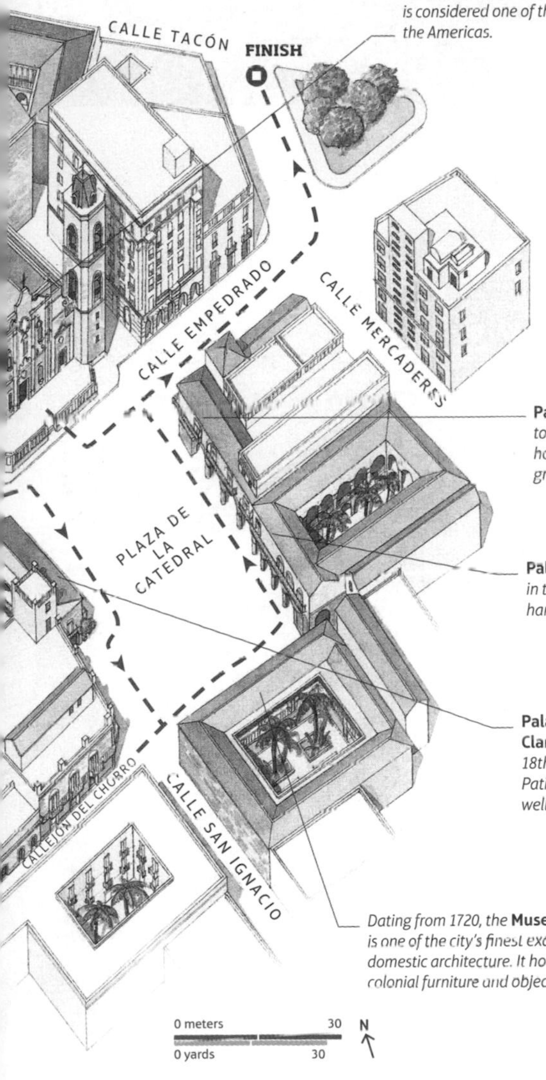

CALLE TACÓN

FINISH

The Baroque façade of **Catedral de San Cristóbal***, declared a national monument, is considered one of the most beautiful in the Americas.*

Did You Know?

Palacio del Marqués de Arcos was once the main post office; the mailbox is still visible on its wall.

CALLE EMPEDRADO

CALLE MERCADERES

PLAZA DE LA CATEDRAL

CALLEJÓN DEL CHORRO

CALLE SAN IGNACIO

Palacio del Conde Lombillo *is home to the Historiador de La Habana, which hosts temporary exhibitions of photographs, paintings, and lithographs.*

Palacio del Marqués de Arcos*, built in the 1700s, houses an art gallery where handicrafts and prints are on sale.*

Palacio de los Marqueses de Aguas Claras *was built in the second half of the 18th century. It is now a bar-restaurant, El Patio, with tables in the inner courtyard as well as in the picturesque square.*

Dating from 1720, the **Museo de Arte Colonial** *is one of the city's finest examples of early colonial domestic architecture. It houses an exhibition of colonial furniture and objects.*

0 meters 30
0 yards 30

N ↑

The colorful center of Trinidad, surrounded by verdant mountains ↑

②

TRINIDAD

 Sancti Spíritus 🚍 Calle Piro Guinart 224, e/ Maceo y Izquierdo, (41) 994 448 🚌 Ave Simón Bolívar 422, (41) 993 348 🛈 Cubatur, Calle Antonio Maceo esq Francisco Javier Zerquera, (41) 996 314; Infotur, Calle Gustavo Izquierdo, (41) 998 258

Trinidad was founded by Diego Velázquez in 1514, but its perfectly preserved cobblestone streets and pastel-colored houses are more a reflection of the landscape of the city in colonial times. From the 17th to 19th centuries, Trinidad was a major player in the sugar trade, and the buildings around the Plaza Mayor bear witness to the wealth of the landowners of the time.

①
Iglesia Parroquial de la Santísima Trinidad

🏠 Plaza Mayor ⏱ 10:30am–1pm Mon–Sat, 11:30am–1pm Sun

Completed in 1892, this austere church, with a Neo-Classical facade, has an elegant four-aisle interior. The church's real attraction, however, is an 18th-century wooden statue made in Spain, the *Señor de la Vera Cruz* (Lord of the True Cross), which is associated with a curious story. The sculpture, made for one of the churches in Vera Cruz, Mexico, left the port of Barcelona in 1731, but three times in succession the ship was driven by strong winds to the port of Casilda, 4 miles (6 km) from the city of Trinidad. While preparing to make a fourth attempt to reach Mexico, the ship's captain decided to leave behind part of the cargo, which included the huge chest containing the statue of Christ. The locals regarded the arrival of the sacred image as a sign from Heaven, and from that time on the *Señor de la Vera Cruz* became an object of fervent worship in Cuba.

← Plaza de los Tres Cruces 545 yds (500 m)

← Cabildo de los Congos Reales de San Antonio 545 yds (500 m)

Taberna La Canchánchera, a typical casa de infusiones housed in an 18th-century building, is known for its namesake cocktail. Live music is also played here.

SHOP

Casa-Estudio Lázaro Niebla

A highly respected contemporary artist, Niebla creates stunning wooden portraits of senior Trinidadians. These tributes are carved on colonial doors and window panels throughout the city.

🏠 **Calle Real del Jigüey 452** 🌐 **lazaroniebla.com**

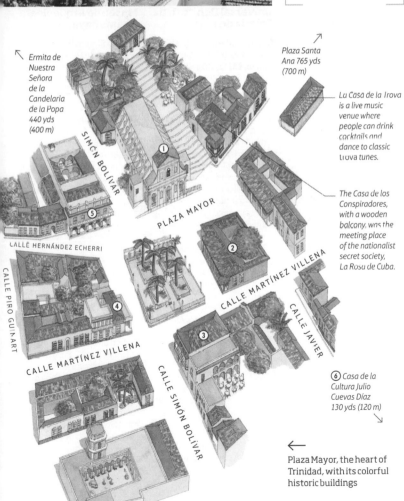

← Ermita de Nuestra Señora de la Candelaria de la Popa 440 yds (400 m)

↗ Plaza Santa Ana 765 yds (700 m)

La Casa de la Trova is a live music venue where people can drink cocktails and dance to classic trova tunes.

The Casa de los Conspiradores, with a wooden balcony, was the meeting place of the nationalist secret society, La Rosa de Cuba.

SIMÓN BOLÍVAR

PLAZA MAYOR

CALLE HERNÁNDEZ ECHERRI

CALLE PIRO GUINART

CALLE MARTÍNEZ VILLENA

CALLE MARTÍNEZ VILLENA

CALLE JAVIER

CALLE SIMÓN BOLÍVAR

⑥ Casa de la Cultura Julio Cuevas Díaz 130 yds (120 m) ↘

← Plaza Mayor, the heart of Trinidad, with its colorful historic buildings

THE ARCHITECTURE OF TRINIDAD

The historic center of Trinidad has an extraordinarily dense concentration of Spanish colonial houses, many still inhabited by the descendants of old local families. The oldest single-story buildings have two corridors and a porch parallel to the street, with a courtyard at the back. In the late 1700s another corridor was introduced to the layout. In the 19th century, the houses formed a square around an open central courtyard. In general, the entrance consists of a large living room that gives way to a dining room, either through an archway or a *mampara* – a half-height double door.

Museo de Arquitectura Colonial

🏛 Calle Ripalda 83, e/ Hernández Echerri y Martínez Villena, Plaza Mayor ☎ (41) 993 208 ⏰ 9am–5pm Sat–Tue

The front of the 18th-century mansion, which is now home to the Museum of Colonial Architecture, features a lovely portico with slim columns, a wrought-iron balustrade, and wooden beams. Originally, the building consisted of two separate houses, both of which belonged to sugar magnate Saturnino Sánchez Iznaga. The houses were joined during the 19th century.

The museum, the only one of its kind in Cuba, covers Trinidad's architecture and illustrates the building techniques used during the colonial period. There is a collection of various locks, latches, doors, hinges, windows, and grilles, as well as parts of walls and tiles.

In one of the bathrooms facing the inner courtyard is a fine example of a 19th-century shower, with a complicated network of pipes supplying hot and cold water.

Universal Benito Ortiz Galería de Arte

🏛 Calle Rubén Martínez Villena y Bolívar, Plaza Mayor ☎ (41) 994 432 ⏰ 9am–5pm Mon–Sat

This beautiful mansion with a long wooden balcony is evocative of the city's golden age. It was built in 1809 for Ortiz de Zúñiga, a former slave trader who later became the mayor of Trinidad. The house currently serves as an art gallery.

The first floor has paintings on display (and for sale) by contemporary Cuban artists, including Antonio Herr, Juan Oliva, Benito Ortiz, Antonio Zerquera, and David Gutiérrez. After admiring the artworks on display, head out onto the wooden balcony for a fine view over the entire Plaza Mayor.

← Porcelain exhibit in the Museo de Arquitectura Colonial

Museo de Arqueología Guamuhaya

🏛 Calle Simón Bolívar 457, e/ Fernando Hernández Echerri y Rubén Martínez Villena, Plaza Mayor ☎ (41) 993 420 ⏰ 9am–5pm Tue–Sun

The building that is now the home of the Archaeological Museum was constructed in the 18th century and was purchased in the 1800s by the wealthy Don Antonio Padrón, who added a portico with brick columns and Ionic capitals.

The Guamuhaya (the indigenous peoples' name for the Sierra Escambray area) collection includes Pre-Columbian archaeological finds as well as objects associated with the Spanish conquest of the island and Cuba's history of slavery. The museum also houses a fascinating collection of stuffed animals, including the *manjuari*, an ancient species of fish that still lives in the Parque Nacional Ciénaga de Zapata swamp.

In the museum's courtyard, there is a bronze bust commemorating the German geographer and naturalist Alexander von Humboldt, who stayed here as Padrón's guest in 1801, during his travels in the New World.

Did You Know?

Legend claims that Mariano Borrell, Palacio Brunet's first owner, made a pact with the devil.

Palacio Brunet (Museo Romántico)

Calle Hernández Echerri 52, esq Simón Bolívar, Plaza Mayor (41) 994 363
For restoration

Built in 1812 as the residence of the wealthy Borrell family, Palacio Brunet now contains the Museo Romántico. Most of the objects on display here belonged to Mariano Borrell, the family's founder. They were inherited by Borrell's daughter, Josefa Angela, the wife of Count Nicolás de la Cruz y Brunet (hence the name Palacio Brunet), in 1830.

The museum's 14 rooms all face the courtyard gallery with its elegant balustrade.

The spacious living room has a Carrara marble floor and a coffered ceiling, furnished with Sèvres vases and Bohemian crystalware. There are also English-made spittoons, which reveal that the 19th-century aristocratic landowners were partial to smoking cigars.

Other rooms of interest are the countess's bedroom, with a bronze baldachin over the bed, and the kitchen, which is still decorated with its original painted earthenware tiles.

Casa de la Cultura Julio Cuevas Díaz

Calle Zerquera 406 (41) 994 308 9:45am-noon & 3-7pm Mon-Fri, 9:45am-noon Sat

During the day, the vestibule of this building is used as exhibition space by local artists (some of whom also have their studios here). In the evening, performances – theater, dance, concerts, and shows for children – are held in the rear courtyard.

EAT

Vista Gourmet

A hilltop restaurant, with a rooftop terrace, Vista Gourmet serves up a great lunchtime buffet.

Callejón de Galdós (41) 996 700

$$$

Sol Ananda

Try the curried shrimp at this quaint antique-filled eatery.

Calle Real 45 y Simón Bolívar (41) 998 281

$$$

Restaurante Plaza Mayor

Although popular with tour groups, this state-run restaurant is worth a visit for the all-you-can-eat buffet.

Calle Zerquera y Villeña (41) 996 470

$$$

← The bright exterior of the Palacio Brunet (Museo Romántico)

EXPERIENCE Cuba

VALLE DE VIÑALES

🏠 Viñales (Pinar del Río) 🚌 Salvador Cisneros 63, (48) 793 112; connections with Havana, Cienfuegos, Pinar del Río, Trinidad, Varadero 🛈 Cubanacán Viajes, Salvador Cisneros 63c, Plaza Viñales, (48) 796 393; Infotur, Salvador Cisneros 63c, (48) 796 263

A unique landscape awaits visitors to the Viñales Valley. With caves, murals, and hot springs, there is plenty to experience in the valley, besides the bizarre *mogotes*.

Resembling sugar loaves, *mogotes* are gigantic karst formations, characteristic of the valley. They are like stone sentinels keeping watch over the corn and tobacco fields, the red earth with majestic royal palm trees, and the farmhouses with roofs of palm leaves. According to legend, centuries ago a group of Spanish sailors who were approaching the coast thought the profile of the *mogotes* they glimpsed in the fog looked like a church organ. Hence the name Sierra de los Órganos, given to the network of hills in this area.

The *mogotes* are all that remains of what was once a limestone plateau. Over a period lasting millions of years, underground aquifers eroded the softer limestone, giving rise to large caverns whose ceilings later collapsed, forming the hollow *mogotes*, with their vast internal caverns. Take a tour of the caves via the Centro de Visitantes *(tel: 48 796 144)*.

Riding a horse *(inset)* through the lush, *mogote*-punctuated Valle de Viñales ↑

Did You Know?

Painter González used cracks in the rock to create special effects of light and color in his mural.

① Between 1959 and 1962, Cuban artist Leovigildo González, a pupil of the Mexican artist Diego Rivera, painted the history of evolution – from ammonites to *Homo sapiens* – on the face of a *mogote*.

② The Iglesia del Sagrado Corazón de Jesús is a pretty church, with a distinctive blue door, in the town of Viñales.

③ The Gran Caverna de Santo Tomás is the largest network of caves in Latin America, with 29 miles (46 km) of galleries and up to eight levels of communicating grottoes.

PICTURE PERFECT
Mogotes

For the best panoramic vistas of the iconic *mogotes*, head to the *mirador* (lookout) beside the Hotel Los Jazmines. Sunrise and sunset are particularly rewarding times to snap that striking shot.

EXPERIENCE MORE

4

Cayo Largo

📍 112 miles (180 km) S of Havana ✈🚢

This 15-mile- (25-km-) long slender, low-lying wisp of an island is a wonderful holiday destination for those who love sun, sea, and sand. Sailing, watersports, and horse-riding are all offered by all-inclusive resorts served by charter flights and overnight excursions from Havana. Cayo Largo is semi-arid and lined along its southern shore by sand as white and fine as powdered sugar dissolving into shallow turquoise seas, perfect for snorkeling and wading. The most impressive beach is Playa Sirena, at the west end of the cay, while the few hotels on the island are concentrated along Playa Lindamar.

There are no inhabitants other than Cuban workers who live in Combinado. Here you'll find the marina and tourist office, as well as the Granja de las Tortuga (Turtle Sanctuary), where eggs laid in the sands by green and leatherback turtles are hatched for release. Scuba-diving and fly-fishing excursions are offered, as well as a sail to nearby Cayo Iguana, named for the endemic iguanas that live here.

The interior and exterior *(inset)* of Presidio Modelo on Isla de la Juventud

5

Isla de la Juventud

📍 94 miles (150 km) S of Havana ✈🚢 ℹ Ecotur; (46) 327 101

The "Isle of Youth" has few major tourist draws, and hence offers a genuine Cuban experience. Nueva Gerona is the main town with colonial homes. The isle's highlight is **Presidio Modelo**, a former prison, now a museum, where Fidel Castro and his men were jailed after they attacked the Moncada Barracks in 1953. They were liberated in a 1955 amnesty.

On the southwest shore, Hotel El Colony at Siguanea Bay is a base for diving to coral formations and shipwrecks. To the south, **Parque Natural Punta Francés** offers good viewing, with a crocodile farm and pre-Columbian petroglyphs at Cuevas de Punta del Este.

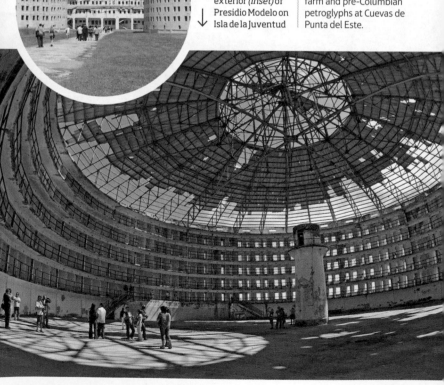

Presidio Modelo
⊛ ⊛ 🚗 3 miles (5 km) E of Nueva Gerona 📞 (46) 32 6369 🕐 9am–4pm Tue–Sat, 9am–1pm Sun

Parque Natural Punta Francés
⊛ 🚗 25 miles (40 km) S of Nueva Gerona 📞 (46) 32 7101 ℹ️ Ecotur, Calles 39 Nueva Gerona

---

Las Terrazas

🚗 Artemisa 🚌 From Havana to Viñales 🌐 lasterrazas.cu

This peaceful and unique rural community, amid the refreshingly cool pine forests of the Sierra del Rosario, was created in 1971 around a lake as part of a reforestation project. One of Cuba's premier eco-tourism sites, it has scenic trails, coffee plantations, and artists' studios. Almost as soon as it was created, the eco-village was colonized by artists who were drawn to the community by its ethos and natural beauty, and there are plenty of artists' studios to explore. Well worth a visit is Casa-Estudio Lester Campa and Casa-Estudio Henry Aloma, where the island's two most prominent artists can be seen at work. Nearby, the Casa-Museo Polo Montañez honors one of Cuba's former preeminent folk-singers; his music is usually playing, tempting visiting Cubans to dance. The Hotel Moka eco-resort nestles above the peaceful village, which is named for the terraces that cover the hillside in coffee and pines. You can sample specialty coffees at Café de María, while a short zipline ride across the lake adds an extra buzz.

A short distance from the village lies the well preserved Cafetal Buenavista – an old coffee plantation, where you can explore the old *barracones* (slave barracks) and huge

stone-wheel *tajona* (mill) used for husking coffee beans. This is the perfect spot for lunch since its restaurant overlooks the plant-punctuated hillside.

Las Terrazas is characterized by its natural beauty. The village is surrounded by scenic trails, where brightly colored birds – including the exquisite tocororo, Cuba's national bird sing from the trees.

The Sendero Las Delicias is a 2-mile (3-km) hike that runs from Cafetal Buenavista to a mountaintop *mirador* (lookout). Nearby, the Río San Juan tumbles over rocky tiers and jade-colored pools to form the Baños del Río San Juan.

Did You Know?
Cubans were not permitted to own cell phones until 2008, when the government ban was lifted.

CUBAN TOBACCO

The tobacco plant *(Nicotiana tabacum)* grows from small, round, golden seeds. Cuban tobacco seeds are in demand throughout the world, because their quality is considered to be so good. The plant reaches its full height in the three or four months from November to February. Like cigar-making, tobacco-growing is the result of age-old expertise handed down from generation to generation. Tobacco plants are quite delicate, and need skilful handling. There are two types: *Corojo*, grown in greenhouses, which has the prettiest leaves and is used as wrapper leaves for the cigars, and *Criollo*, which grows outdoors and provides the other leaves.

Pinar del Río

🚗 109 miles (175 km) SW of Havana 🚌🚍 ℹ️ Infotur, Hotel Vueltabajo, Calle Martí 103; (48) 759 381

Founded in 1669, the orderly capital of Cuba's westernmost province can seem remote and old-fashioned. It has long been a center for the cultivation and industrial processing of tobacco, and is best utilized as a base for exploring the surrounding countryside. Pinar del Río is at its best in the carnival month of July and during November, when stages are set up across the city and colorfully dressed performers on stilts loom over the streets.

The most striking aspect of the historic center of this small, orderly town is the abundance of columns: Ionic or Corinthian, simple or decorated. The most important buildings lie on the arcaded main street, Calle Martí (also known as Calle Real).

8

Matanzas

65 miles (104 km) E of Havana Havanatur, Calle Jovellanos, e/ Medio y Río; (45) 253 856

The capital of the eponymous province, Matanzas fans around a large bay. It grew wealthy in the 17th century from the trade of sugar and slaves, and later developed a rich cultural life, earning the nickname "the Athens of Cuba." The main square, Parque de la Libertad, is pinned by a statue of José Martí and surrounded by attractive buildings, including the 17th-century Catedral de San Carlos. West of the park is the Museo Provincial, which occupies the 1938 Palacio del Junco. It houses an impressive collection of antiques and artifacts from the colonial period.

The restored Teatro Sauto is the city's architectural pride and joy. Designed by Italian architect Daniele Dell'Aglio, it is a solidly built Neo-Classical structure with several Greek-inspired statues made of Carrara marble. Inside, the auditorium is clad in salubrious wood-paneling. Don't skip the Castillo de San Severino, which dates from 1745 and guards the western entrance to the bay. It now hosts a museum on slavery and the Afro-Cuban Santería religion.

9

Cayo Levisa

155 miles (250 km) W of Havana Havanatur, Calle Osmani Arenado, esq Martí; (48) 778 494

This small island, with its white-sand beaches, an offshore coral reef, and mangroves, is the most prepared for tourists in the Los Colorados archipelago, and the only one with diving facilities. Despite this, it is still unspoiled and is home to several species of bird; the surrounding waters, too, have an abundance of fish.

10

Varadero

90 miles (145 km) E of Havana Infotur, Calle 13 y Ave 1; (45) 662 966

Cuba's top resort, which occupies the Península de Hicacos, is connected to the mainland by a drawbridge, a sign of its 19th-century exclusivity. Once a private playground for Cuba's elite, the area opened up to everyone after Castro took power in 1959, and today, Varadero is popular with visitors who are drawn to the clear blue water. The many all-inclusive hotels here all offer watersports, with scuba diving being the main draw.

STAY

Cubanacán Cayon Levisa

This state-run beach-front hotel offers three types of accommodation. Don't miss out on the hotel's extensive watersports program.

Cayo Levisa
cubanacan.cu

$$$

11

Península de Zapata

125 miles (202 km) SE of Havana Cubanacán, Jagüey Grande; (45) 913 224

As well as being the site of the infamous Bay of Pigs

invasion, this vast peninsula is synonymous with unspoiled nature and luxuriant tropical vegetation. The peninsula is protected in the Gran Parque Natural Montemar, and crocodiles and flamingos are among the wildlife that can be seen here. **Boca de Guamá**, the main tourist center of the area, has a crocodile farm. Playa Larga is one of the better beaches along this part of Caribbean coastline, with the coral reef found here offering magnificent dive sites.

North of the Boca de Guamá is Playa Girón, a beach that became famous as the site of the ill-fated, American-backed landing in 1961. Don't miss the small **Museo Playa Girón**, which covers the anti-Castro invasion using photos, documents, weapons, a tank, and the wreckage of airplanes that took part in the last battle, as well as films taken during the invasion.

Boca de Guamá
🍷🍴🛏 ⌂ Carretera Playa Larga Km16 ☎(45) 91 5551 🕐 7am–7pm daily

Museo Playa Girón
🎨🛏 ⌂ Playa Girón ☎(45) 984122 🕐 9am–5pm daily

↑ A diver exploring spectacular coral formations off the coast of Mariá la Gorda

María la Gorda
⌂ 193 miles (310 km) SW of Havana 🛈 Hotel María la Gorda Diving Center; (48) 778 131, 778 077

The best-known bathing spot on the southwestern coast owes its name to a sad legend. A few centuries ago, an overweight girl *(gorda)* named María was abducted by pirates on the Venezuelan coast, transported to Cuba, and abandoned here. To survive, she was forced to trade with buccaneers who passed by, and this section of shoreline still bears her moniker – María the Fat.

The extraordinarily beautiful coral reefs are richly populated by marine life including sea turtles, reef sharks, and a number of rare species of marine creature. This makes these 5 miles (8 km) of coastline a real tropical aquarium. The reefs are also incredibly easy to reach, lying just a short distance from the shore; you don't even need to enter the water to spot vibrant fish swimming around the coral.

←
Bleached driftwood jutting from the sands of a Cayo Levisa beach

Vuelta Abajo
⌂ Pinar del Río

The area between Pinar del Río, San Juan y Martínez, and San Luis produces very high-quality tobacco. The ideal growing conditions are primarily the result of the protection afforded by the Sierra del Rosario mountain range, and the fact that the area's red soil is well drained and rich in nitrogen. Former landowners who left Cuba in 1959 have tried in vain to reproduce the unique environment elsewhere.

At the prestigious Hoyo de Monterrey plantations, plants are protected from the sun by cotton cloth to maintain the softness of the tobacco leaves. There are also windowless curing houses where the leaves are left to dry on long poles.

📷 PICTURE PERFECT
Roll up

The tobacco plantations of Viñales and Vuelto Abajo offer superb photo opportunities. Iconic sights include ox-drawn ploughs framed by royal palms, or *guajiros* (farm workers) tending the fields of tobacco plants.

Antiguo Ayuntamiento, a grand building on Parque José Martí, Cienfuegos ↑

EAT

Kike-Kcho
Found on the tip of the Varadero peninsula, this gourmet restaurant serves sumptuous seafood dishes.

🏠 Marina Gaviota, Varadero 📞 (45) 66 4115

$$$

Salsa Suárez
A classy *paladar* (family-run restaurant) that combines stylish decor with excellent fusion cuisine.

🏠 Calle 31, 103, Varadero 🕐 Tue 🌐 salsasuarez varadero.com

$$$

Finca del Mar
One of the best *paladares* outside Havana, this bay-front alfresco joint offers a tempting international menu.

🏠 Calle 35 between 18 & 20, Cienfuegos 📞 (43) 52 6598

$$$

🔴14 Cienfuegos

🏠 150 miles (242 km) E of Havana 🚉🚌 ℹ️ Ave 56 No 3117 e/ Calles 31 y 33; (43) 514 653

This maritime city has a well-preserved historic core and one of the most captivating bays in the Caribbean Sea – hence the city's nickname, the "Pearl of the South." The central point of Cienfuegos is the Parque José Martí. The vast square was declared a national monument due to its historic importance and notable surrounding buildings; the Neo-Classical Teatro Tomás Terry and the Catedral de la Purísima Concepción, dating from 1870, are unmissable. Nearby, the Cementerio La Reina's Neo-Classical marble tombs are fascinating. The Punta Gorda district is tipped by the **Palacio de Valle**, a 1917 Mughal-inspired mansion that now houses a restaurant.

Palacio de Valle
🏠 Calle 37 y 2 📞 (43) 55 1003 🕐 9:30am–11pm daily

🔴15 Santa Clara

🏠 170 miles (274 km) E of Havana 🚌 ℹ️ Infotur, Calle Cuba 68 e/ Eduardo Machado y Maestra Nicolosa; (42) 227 557

Founded in 1689 when a group from Remedios moved away from the coast to escape pirate raids, Santa Clara became famous in 1958 when it was the setting of the battle, led by Che Guevara, which marked the end of Batista's dictatorship. Cuban sculptor José Delarra commemorated

→ Monumento Ernesto Che Guevara, a huge bronze statue in Santa Clara

this victory at the **Monumento Tren Blindado**, a re-creation of a troop train derailed by Che Guevara's guerrillas, which is worth a visit. At the **Monumento Ernesto Che Guevara**, a statue of the "heroic guerrilla" stands atop an inscribed plinth. Below it is the Museo de Che, with displays of his life.

The main square, Parque Leoncio Vidal, is home to some fine colonial buildings, including the impressive Museo de Artes Decorativas.

Monumento Tren Blindado

 🚩 Carretera Camujuani ☎ (42) 20 2758 🕐 8:30am–5pm Tue–Sat, 9am–1pm Sun

Monumento Ernesto Che Guevara

🚩 Ave de los Desfiles ☎ (42) 20 5878 🕐 Museo de Che: 8:30am–5pm Tue–Sun

---

16

Cayos de Villa Clara

🚩 220 miles (354 km) E of Havana

These beach-fringed isles off the coast of Villa Clara province are accessed by a long *pedraplen* (causeway). A dozen deluxe hotels have been built, and more are planned. Fishing and scuba diving are prime draws, while the mangroves lining the inner shore are perfect for bird-watching.

17

Valle de los Ingenios

 6 miles (10 km) E of Trinidad 📧 ℹ (41) 993 348

This broad fertile valley is named for the numerous *ingenios* (sugar mills) built

here in the late 18th century. The valley is rich in history with ruins providing evidence of the time when the sugar industry was at its peak, and it provides an insight into the social structure of the plantations. Take in great views of the valley at **El Mirador**, a hilltop lookout east of Trinidad.

El Mirador

☺ 🚩 3 miles (5 km) E of Trinidad 🕐 8am–5pm daily

18

Topes de Collantes

🚩 14 miles (22 km) NW of Trinidad ℹ Gaviota Topes de Collantes; (41) 54 0231

The pristine alpine forests of the Sierra Escambray can best be experienced at the Topes de Collantes mountain retreat, 2,625 ft (800 m) above sea level. The Kurhotel Escambray solarium here is used as a recuperative clinic. Hikes lead to Salto de Caburní and its 250-ft (75-m) waterfall, and to

---

BAY OF PIGS INVASION

The narrow Bahía de Cochinos (Bay of Pigs) was the setting for the landing of 1,400 C.I.A-trained anti-Castro Cuban exiles in April 1961. Fidel Castro took charge of the defense. After three days of fighting, the U.S. withdrew its air support and the abandoned invaders were defeated. After 20 months, the captured exiles were exchanged for medicine.

the Hacienda Codina coffee estate, with an orchid garden and medicinal mud pools. The appealing **Museo de Arte Cubano Contemporáneo** displays modern works by famous artists.

Museo de Arte Cubano Contemporáneo

⊛ 🚩 Topes de Collantes 🕐 8am–8pm daily

→

The tumbling waterfalls in the Topes de Collantes reserve

 19

Guardalavaca

 450 miles (724 km) E from Havana

Converted in the mid-1980s into a holiday resort, the beaches of Guardalavaca are among Cuba's most popular vacation destinations. Although the resort is within easy reach of Holguín, 58 km (35 miles) to the southwest, the location still feels remote.

The crescent-shaped main beach has crystal-clear waters, fine sand, and there is a coral reef quite close to the shore.

The name "Guardalavaca" (watch the cow) derives from the Spanish word for the cattle egret, a bird that is common throughout Cuba, and especially in this area.

West of the beach is Bahía de Naranjo, a natural coastal park with karst hills covered with thick vegetation. There

---

 GREAT VIEW
Loma de la Cruz

There are marvelous far-reaching vistas from the top of the Loma de la Cruz (Hill of the Cross) in Holguín. Although the 458 steps to the summit were only added in 1927, this hill was used to plan the original grid layout of the town.

---

are three small islands out in the bay; from Cayo Naranjo, boat tours, diving, and fishing trips can be organized.

 20

Playa Ancón

450 miles (10 km) S of Trinidad

Lining the tendril-thin Ancón peninsula, this stunning white beach is lapped by turquoise waters. Gorgeous coral reefs tempt divers, most notably at Cayo Blanco, a 20-minute boat ride away. La Boca, a village at the neck of the peninsula, is popular with Cubans.

 21

Holguín

450 460 miles (740 km) SE of Havana Infotur, Calle Libertad, esq Martí; (24) 425 013

Called the city of parks due to its many leafy squares, Holguín is a colonial town situated between two hills. It is famed for the active part it played in the wars of

---

independence under the leadership of Calixto García, the famous general who liberated the city from the Spanish in 1972.

To the plaza's north, the **Museo Provincial de Holguín** features five rooms illustrating the cultural development of the town. Catedral de San Isidro, completed in 1720 and consecrated as a cathedral in 1979, stands over Parque Peralta, and Plaza San José is home to a fine church and colonial houses.

Museo Provincial de Holguín

 Calle Frexes 198 (24) 46 3395 8am-4:30pm Tue-Sat, 8am-noon Sun Jan 1, May 1, Jul 26, Oct 10, Dec 25

22

Jardines del Rey

Ciego de Ávila (Camagüey)

In the Atlantic Ocean, the Sabana and Camagüey archipelagos, known collectively as "Jardines del Rey," include about 400 small islands, most uninhabited. They were

> **In the Atlantic Ocean, the Sabana and Camagüey archipelagos, known collectively as "Jardines del Rey," include about 400 small islands, most uninhabited.**

A white-sand, palm-lined beach in the archipelago of Jardines del Rey

"discovered" in 1514 by Diego Velázquez, who was so struck by them that he dedicated them to the king (*rey*), Carlos V. They became a hiding place for pirates and, after the abolition of slavery, a landing point for slave traders.

A causeway, built in 1988 as a link to mainland Cuba, makes it easy for visitors to reach the coral reef and the beach resorts, which are currently concentrated on Cayo Coco and Cayo Guillermo.

 23

Camagüey

📍**165 miles (265 km) E of Trinidad** ✖🚉🚌 ℹ️**Infotur, Calle Ignacio Agramonte 426; (32) 256 794**

This city, declared a UNESCO World Heritage Site in 2008, lies in the middle of a vast area of pastureland. It is nicknamed "the Legendary"

for its traditions of heroism and patriotism, as well as for its Neo-Classical architecture. The irregular, intricate street network that distinguishes Camagüey from other Cuban cities resulted from the need to protect itself from raids.

The former Plaza de Armas is dominated by an equestrian statue of Agramonte, a local independence hero. Buildings of interest on the square include the city's cathedral, the Catedral de Nuestra Señora de la Candelaria, built in 1735.

The cobbled Plaza San Juan de Díos is ringed by examples of vernacular architecture, plus the Iglesia de San Juan de Díos. Life-size figures of real-life residents adorn the Plaza del Carmen. The triangular Plaza de los Trabajadores draws visitors to the Casa Natal

de Ignacio Agramonte (birth-place of Agramonte) and the Baroque Iglesia de la Merced, which contains a Holy Sepul-chre. The Ballet de Camagüey, one of the best regarded dance companies in Latin America, performs at the **Teatro Principal**, which is built in Neo-Classical style.

Teatro Principal
♿ 📍**Calle Padre Valencia 64** 📞**(32) 293 048** 🕐**9am–5pm daily (ballet shows usually from 8pm Fri–Sun)**

24

Sierra Escambray

📍**22 miles (35 km) NW of Trinidad**

This rugged mountain chain – Cuba's second largest – spans Cienfuegos, Santa Clara, and Sancti Spíritus provinces. Smothered in emerald rain-forest, it was the perfect base for Che Guevara's Rebel Army in the late 1950s and, later, for counter-revolutionaries financed by the C.I.A. Today, eco-minded travelers thrill to the birdsong and crash of waterfalls accessed by hiking trails.

On the northwest side, El Nicho is one of the most spectacular waterfalls in Cuba, tumbling 66 ft (20 m) into jade pools. Framed by rainforest, it is reached by following the easy Sendero El Reino de las Aguas hike from the entrance.

Studding the northeastern foothills is Lago Hanabanilla, a man-made *embalse* (reservoir). Hotel Hanabanilla is a popular base for watersports, bird-watching, and guided hikes to El Nicho. Or for a truly unique experience you can journey to El Nicho in an ex-Soviet army truck on a day-long trip from Trinidad.

 Life-size bronze figures by Cuban artist Martha Jiménez in Camagüey's Plaza del Carmen

25

Santiago de Cuba

535 miles (862 km) SE from Havana
Infotur & Cubatur, Ave Garzón e/ 3ra y 4ta; (22) 652 560

This is perhaps the most African, the most musical, and the most passionate city in Cuba. Santiago de Cuba is a lively, exciting place where festivities are celebrated with fervor, never more so than during July's carnival.

Founded in 1515 by Diego Velázquez, the bustling Parque Céspedes lies at the city's heart, surrounded by fine buildings: the Ayuntamiento (town hall); the Neo-Classical Catedral de la Asunción; and the Casa de Diego Velázquez, the original governor's 1522 mansion, now the **Museo de Ambiente Histórico Cubano**.

Not to be missed along Calle Heredia are the Casa de la Trova, the Museo del Carnaval, and the **Museo Emilio Bacardí Moreau**, with eclectic displays ranging from an Egyptian mummy to modern art.

Sprawling around the city's historic core, Santiago's 20th-century districts are full of sites honoring the city's title of "Cradle of the Revolution". The Museo Histórico 26 de Julio, where Fidel Castro launched the revolution in 1953, is near the huge statue of independence hero Antonio Maceo that looms over Plaza de la Revolución. The Avenida Juan Gilberto Gómez connects the plaza to Cementerio de Santa Ifigenia, a monumental cemetery, home to José Martí's tomb.

Museo de Ambiente Histórico Cubano

 Calle Felix Peña 602
(22) 65 2652 9am–5pm daily

Museo Emilio Bacardí Moreau

 Calle Pío Rosado (22) 62 8402 9am–4:30pm Mon–Sat (to 6:30pm Sat); 9am–2:30pm Sun

---

26

Guantanamo

Infotur, Calle Galixto García el Crombet y Emilio Giró; (21) 351 993

If not for the U.S. naval base and the famous song *Guantanamera*, this town would likely only be known to Cubans and music experts. It was founded in 1796 to take in the French fleeing from Haiti.

GREAT VIEW
Mirador La Gobernadora

The U.S. Naval Base, in a Cuban defense zone, is virtually impossible to see, but atop a hill 16 miles (25 km) to the east, the Mirador La Gobernadora restaurant has a viewing tower and provides binoculars.

The town has a few sights of note. Principal Parque Martí is dominated by the Parroquial de Santa Catalina de Riccis, dating from 1863. On Calle Pedro A Pérez is the Palacio de Salcines, designed by José Leticio Salcines in 1919, and which now houses the Museo de Artes Decorativas.

27

Baracoa

98 miles (157 km) E from Santiago de Cuba
Infotur, Calle Maceo 129-A; (21) 641 781

Cuba's first settlement was founded in 1511 and is unusual for its rickety, centuries-old

→ The flat peak of El Yunque, a mountain to the west of Baracoa

wooden homes. It is set on a broad bay framed by lush mountains. The Catedral de Nuestra Señora de la Asunción, on Parque Independencia, exhibits a cross said to have been left by Christopher Columbus in 1492.

Nearby, is the flat-topped El Yunque (the Anvil) mountain, which lures birders and hikers with stunning views. Its lush rainforests are part of a UNESCO Biosphere Reserve protected within Parque Nacional Alejandro Humboldt.

Gran Parque Nacional Sierra Maestra

🏠 Granma, Santiago de Cuba
ℹ️ Ecotur, Hotel Sierra Maestra, Bayamo; (23) 487 006 ext 639

This national park spans the provinces of Santiago de Cuba and Granma. The major peaks of the island are found here, including Pico Turquino, Cuba's highest, at 6,390 ft (1,974 m), as well as sites made famous by the guerrilla war waged by Castro and the rebel forces.

Before you set off, note that much of this area is a military zone therefore lone hiking is not permitted on many of the trails. Ecotur (who have an office in Bayamo) offer regular organized tours into the park. The main starting point for exploring the Sierra Maestra mountain range is Villa Santo Domingo. From here, there is a challenging 3-mile (5-km) journey – on foot or in a good off-road vehicle – to the Alto del Naranjo viewpoint. One of the highlights of the area is Comandancia de la Plata, Castro's headquarters in the 1950s. Here there is a museum, a small camp hospital, and the site from which Che Guevara made his radio broadcasts. Comandancia de la Plata is accessible only via a 90-minute walk. The area was made into a national park in 1980.

The mountain range is great hiking territory, and also attracts rock climbers, but be prepared for spartan facilities.

The coast at the southern edge of the Sierra Maestra is spectacular. The road runs close above the waters of the Caribbean Sea and offers excellent views; take care if driving after dark, however, as the road is in need of repair in some places.

←
The ornate exterior of Santiago de Cuba's Catedral de la Asunción

---

Bayamo

🏠 423 miles (680 km) SE from Havana ✈️🚗🚌
ℹ️ Infotur, Plaza del Himno; (23) 423 468

Founded in 1513, Cuba's second-oldest city was devastated by fire in 1876, during the Ten Years' War. Parque Céspedes, the main square, is overlooked by interesting buildings, including Casa Natal de Carlos Manuel de Céspedes, birthplace of the man behind Cuba's quest for independence, and the lovely church, Iglesia Parroquial Mayor de San Salvador.

DRINK

La Ruina
A popular *bodega*-style beer hall, housed in an old colonial building.

🏠 Calle Galixto García y Gulo, Guantánamo
📞 (21) 929 565

Casa de la Trova
This traditional *trova* pays tribute to local singer and composer Pablo Milanes.

🏠 Calle Martí y Maceo, Bayamo 📞 (23) 425 673

PRACTICAL
INFORMATION

Here you will find all the essential advice and information you will need before and during your stay in Cuba.

AT A GLANCE

CURRENCY
Peso convertible (CUC/$) and peso (CUP)

TIME ZONE
Eastern Standard Time, 5 hours behind GMT. Daylight saving is in effect from March through October

LANGUAGE
Spanish

ELECTRICITY SUPPLY
Power sockets are type F and L, fitting two- and three-pronged plugs. Standard voltage is 220–230v

EMERGENCY NUMBERS

ASISTUR	AMBULANCE
7866 8527	**104**

FIRE SERVICE	POLICE
105	**106**

TAP WATER
Water purity is unreliable so, to be safe, drink bottled water

When to Go

The best period to visit is from December through April, when the weather is pleasant and settled. July and August have torrid rainfall and September to November are prime hurricane months. Rain can occur year-round, but is concentrated from June to November, when hotel and car rental rates drop.

Many key festivals are held in Havana from November to December, including the Festival Internacional del Nuevo Cine Latinoamericano and the Jazz Festival.

Getting There

Charter and regular scheduled flights arrive from Europe, Canada, and Central and South America. Cuba has ten international airports, but most visitors land at either Havana's José Martí International Airport (HAV) or the Juan Gualberto Gómez Airport at Varadero (VRA). Virgin Atlantic has three flights a week from Gatwick to Havana. Cubana flies from Europe. Air Canada serves Cuba from gateways in Canada. Avianca, AeroMexico, and Copa fly from Central America. There are special flights from the US for eligible licensed travelers.

Since late 2015, ferries have also begun to service Cuba from Florida.

Personal Security

Cuba, as a rule, is incredibly safe. However, petty theft does occur, so be careful when carrying cameras and other valuables loose on your shoulder. It is best to keep all of your valuables in sight at all times or locked away in a hotel safe.

Be wary of pickpockets on public transportation and in crowded city centers. If you have anything stolen, report the crime within 24 hours to the nearest police station and take your passport with you. If you need to make an insurance claim, get a copy of the crime report *(denuncia)*. Contact your embassy if your passport is stolen, or in the event of a serious crime or accident.

Health

Emergency medical care for visitors is given at International Clinics and at local hospitals. You will need to show your medical insurance documents. You may be charged a fee for any treatment that you receive, but you may be able to claim the money back later. As such, it is important to arrange medical insurance.

Passports and Visas

Visitors must have a valid passport, onward ticket, proof of travel insurance, and a tourist visa (tarjeta de turista), issued by your airline upon airport check-in. Visas are valid for 30 days (Canadians receive 90 days), and can be extended. US citizens cannot visit Cuba simply for the purpose of tourism. In order to visit Cuba, a license is required from the US Department of the Treasury. The reason for travel must fall under a choice of 12 categories, including family visits, education, and journalism.

LGBT+ Safety

Cuba has liberalized significantly in recent years. The LGBT+ community no longer faces persecution by police, and the government now actively promotes tolerance of same-sex relationships and transgender persons. Informal gay bars and clubs exist in most cities. Countryside populations are generally more conservative, but social acceptance is such that public displays of same-sex affection will result in bemusement, not hostility.

Money

Cuba's currency is the peso, but all tourist transactions are in convertible pesos (designated as CUC$), which can be exchanged for foreign currency at Cadeca exchange bureaux (a surcharge applies for converting US dollars), often located near shops. Euros can be used in Cayo Coco, Varadero, and Cayo Largo. Credit cards are accepted for many tourist transactions. All beach resorts and major cities have state-owned banks serving foreigners but opening times can vary so check before you make a special trip.

Cell Phones and Wi-Fi

Wi-Fi is widely available in most hotels and parks, as well as a few cafes and restaurants. All users must purchase a scratch card issued by **Etecsa**, the state telecommunications company. The card includes a username and password for a specific number of hours' use. A few hotels offer free Wi-Fi, while others charge their own rates.

Visitors bringing cell phones should check with their service providers to determine if they will work in Cuba and if they will be subject to roaming charges. A SIM card can be purchased from **Cubacel** offices for local calls and messages within Cuba. Note that an activation fee also applies.

Etecsa
W etecsa.cu
Cubacel
W etecsa.cu/telefonia_movil

Visitor Information

Official Cubatur offices in the United Kingdom and Canada provide brochures. Infotur has offices in major cities. A huge amount of information about Cuba is available online. All websites originating in Cuba are state-run and care should be taken if making bookings online.

WEBSITES AND APPS

MinTur
Check out Cuba's national tourist board website at www.cubatravel.cu
OnCuba
This is an engaging monthly online magazine, with a weekly calendar, found at www.oncuba.com
Cubanacan
With offices in most towns, this agency runs tours and offers accomodation advice, at www.cubanacan.cu
Ecotur
Book a tour with this eco-tourism agency through www.ecoturcuba.tur.cu

CAYMAN ISLANDS

This trio of low-lying islands – Grand Cayman,
Cayman Brac, and Little Cayman – are the coral-
encrusted summits of the Cayman Ridge submarine
mountain range. The surrounding waters have
a justified reputation for providing some of the
best scuba diving, not only in the Caribbean, but
anywhere in the world. Grand Cayman is the
largest and most developed island, and includes
the capital George Town (where more than half
the population lives) and Seven Mile Beach, which
is actually 5.5-miles- (8.8-km-) long. A short flight
northeast from Grand Cayman takes visitors to
Cayman Brac, a rugged natural paradise, and
Little Cayman, the smallest and least populated
of the islands whose 200 residents are
outnumbered by iguanas ten to one.

Columbus sighted the Cayman Islands in 1503
and called them Las Tortugas due to the many sea
turtles he spotted. However, they soon became
known as the Caimanas due to the crocodile-like
caimans found there. In 1670, the islands fell under
British control. The earliest settlers are believed to
have been deserters from Oliver Cromwell's army
in Jamaica, who survived on farming, and trading
turtle meat with passing ships. Nowadays, the
Cayman Islands are prosperous: as well as being
a popular tourism destination, they are a major
offshore financial center, and for that reason have
the highest wealth per capita in the Caribbean.
The islands are a British Overseas Territory, but
in terms of their culture and lifestyle they feel
undeniably American.

CAYMAN ISLANDS

Experience

Grand Cayman

HELL **2**
West Bay
Head of Barkers
Seven Mile Beach
Welch Point
WEST BAY RD
ESTE RLE?T/BBETTS HIGHWAY
GEORGE TOWN **1**
Owen Roberts International Airport
South Sound

Little Cayman

Spot Bay
Bloody Bay Point
Edward Bodden Airfield
West End Point
South Town

Cayman Brac

Cotton Tree Bay
West End
Charles Kirkconnell International Airport
West End Point

CAYMAN ISLANDS

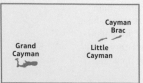

Cayman Brac
Grand Cayman
Little Cayman

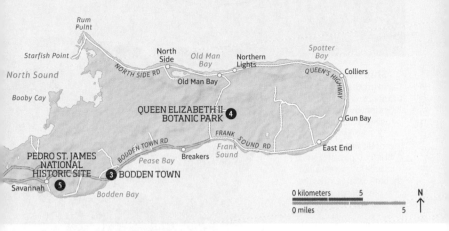

Rum Point
Starfish Point
North Sound
Booby Cay
North Side
NORTH SIDE RD
Old Man Bay
Old Man Bay
Northern Lights
Spotter Bay
QUEEN'S HIGHWAY
Colliers
Gun Bay
East End

QUEEN ELIZABETH II BOTANIC PARK **4**

PEDRO ST. JAMES NATIONAL HISTORIC SITE

BODDEN TOWN RD
Pease Bay
Breakers
FRANK SOUND RD
Frank Sound
FRANK SOUND

Savannah **5**
3 BODDEN TOWN
Bodden Bay

0 kilometers 5
0 miles 5
N

Crawl Bay
Grape Tree Bay
The Bluff
Point of Sand
acksons Point
LITTLE CAYMAN **6**
GUY BANKS RD
Charles Bight
Moody Bay
Tarpon Lake
South Hole Sound
Booby Pond
Owen Island
Blossom Village

0 kilometers 3
0 miles 3
N

North East Bay
Spot Bay
North East Point
Creek
Peter's Cave
Tibbetts Turn
NORTH EAST BAY RD
Great Cave
SOUTH SIDE RD EAST
Pollard Bay
Half Way Ground Cave/Skull Cave
CAYMAN BRAC **7**
Cat Head Bay
Stake Bay
SOUTH SIDE RD
Tom Jennett's Bay
Bat Cave
Sea Feather Bay
South East Bay

0 kilometers 3
0 miles 3
N

Shipwreck Spots

Cayman ocean waters are a tantalizing graveyard of ships, from the Doc Poulson tugboat to the must-see U.S.S. *Kittiwake* just off Seven Mile Beach. Cayman Brac's 50-plus dive sites include four wrecks, but the one to start with is the Russian frigate *M.V. Captain Keith Tibbetts*.

→

The U.S.S. *Kittiwake*, one of the most famous dive wrecks in the Caribbean

THE CAYMAN ISLANDS FOR
DIVERS AND SNORKELERS

With some of the coolest coral in the Caribbean, wicked wrecks, and devilishly deep drop-offs, the Cayman Islands rank among the world's top destinations for diving and snorkeling. More than 350 dive sites offer the delight of getting up close and personal with beautiful marine life.

→

Diver exploring one of the dramatic walls off the Cayman Islands

Pristine Walls

All three isles have walls plummeting into the inky abyss, but Little Cayman's breathtaking Bloody Bay Wall, a short swim from shore, is famed for its dramatic drop-offs, swim-throughs, and rare platinum-yellow tube sponges. The sheer vertical wall begins at 18 ft (5 m) and plunges to more than 6,500 ft (2,000 m). The renowned huge Babylon, along the Grand Cayman's North Wall, also promises beautiful scenery. Look out for parrotfish swimming beside black coral.

Art Installations

For a truly unique gallery viewing, look no farther than the Cayman's underwater worlds. A magical scene comes alive at Sunset Reef, off Grand Cayman, where you can find a 9-ft (3-m) bronze mermaid sculpture. Cayman Brac, meanwhile, features *Oceanic Voyages*, which displays two life-size installations of dolphins and stingrays.

→

The bronze beauty that inhabits the Sunset Reef waters

TOP 5 MARINE CREATURES TO SPOT

Moray Eels
Large, muscular eels that live in crevices in coral reefs and wait to seize passing prey.

Hawksbill Turtles
The smallest of the world's six marine turtle species, this reef-dweller has a patterned shell.

Nurse Sharks
These docile and peaceful bottom-feeders can be seen almost motionless on the shallow seabed.

Parrotfish
The Caribbean has 23 species of these rainbow-hued fish, which nibble at coral to extract algae.

Banded Coral Shrimp
Exquisite, tiny, red-and-white-banded creatures, these flamboyant crustaceans are nocturnal reef dwellers.

Vibrant Reefs

Thankfully, much of Cayman's coral has recovered since a period of devastating decline at the end of the 20th century, and there are plenty of exquisite and healthy reefs in the area which will entice and amaze. Those to the west of Grand Cayman are especially rich, as are the abundant reefs of Little Cayman's Jackson's Bight, where you can marvel at an ever-changing kaleidoscope of marine life.

←

A hawksbill sea turtle and colorful fish swimming around tropical coral reef

EXPERIENCE

①

George Town

📍 West coast of Grand Cayman ✈ ℹ 1320 West Bay Road; 345 949 8522

With a steady stream of cruise ships docking at the port, George Town, the capital of the Cayman Islands, is a busy place all year round. It takes about an hour to casually stroll the streets lined with restaurants and duty-free shops – the city's major attractions. The **Cayman Islands National Museum**, located in one of the few surviving 19th-century structures, has exhibits that document the islands' past.

The Cayman's thriving art community displays local works alongside noted foreign artists at the **National Gallery of the Cayman Islands**. Housed in a striking Modernist industrial space, it exhibits the permanent collection upstairs and temporary collections below. Its Art Café is a lovely space overlooking a sculpture garden. The museum also arranges tours to local studios.

Auto enthusiasts can admire a superb collection of 55 classic and antique cars, plus 18 motorcycles, at the **Cayman Motor Museum**. Don't miss Ugandan dictator Idi Amin's black Mercedes 560 SEC, and the 1930 Rolls-Royce Phantom II that featured alongside actor Omar Sharif in *The Yellow Rolls-Royce*.

Curling north along the west shore like a shepherd's crook, Seven Mile Beach tantalizes with soft white sands that dissolve into calm waters, the color of blue gem stones. One of the most beautiful beaches in the Caribbean, its entire length is lined with luxury homes and hotels, plus bars, restaurants, beach services, and patches of seagrape trees for shade. Seven Mile Beach is divided by name into several beaches. Midway, the wide swath at Governor's Beach, just north of the Governor's Residence, has a healthy shallow reef about 98 ft (30 m) offshore. The best snorkeling is at Cemetery Beach, toward the north end.

BLUE IGUANAS

The Queen Elizabeth II Botanic Park is home to the Blue Iguana Habitat, the center for the National Trust's Blue Iguana Recovery Program. Just two decades ago, the endemic Grand Cayman blue iguana was facing extinction. With a repopulation goal of 1,000, the Habitat is the captive breeding ground for these critically endangered reptiles. The blue iguana grows up to 5 ft (1.5 m) long and can live up to 69 years. While the coloration of male iguanas can vary from dark grey to turquoise blue, females are olive green to pale blue. The National Trust runs safaris (Mon–Sat) with a 1.5-hour guided tour that takes visitors behind the scenes of the breeding facility.

← A cruise ship marine shuttle sailing into the popular port of George Town

HIDDEN GEM
Starfish Point

Perfect for families, this popular beach at the tip of Water Cay Road peninsula is named for the large number of starfish found in its crystal-clear shallows. Visitors can look at, but must not touch, the starfish.

Cayman Islands National Museum

▽◎▽◎◎ ☐ 3 Harbour Dr
🕑 9am–5pm Mon–Fri, 10am–2pm Sat ⓦ museum.ky

National Gallery of the Cayman Islands

◎ ☐ Esterley Tibbetts Hwy
🕑 10am–5pm Mon–Sat
ⓦ nationalgallery.org.ky

Cayman Motor Museum

▽ ☐ 864 NW Point Rd
🕑 Nov–May: 9am–1pm Tue–Sat ⓦ caymanmotormuseum.com

2

Hell

☐ 7 miles (11 km) N of George Town ⓘ Post Office; 345 949 6999

In the village of the same name in West Bay, Hell is a small site featuring 1.5-million-year-old jagged shards of jet-black ironshore (limestone coral and dolomite). Theories abound about how the place got its name. It is popularly believed that the name originated after a local official exclaimed, "This is what hell must look like." The name stuck and the site is now a great tourist attraction, with a hell-themed post office where visitors can send postcards from Hell.

3

Bodden Town

☐ 6 miles (10 km) E of George Town

The atmospheric former capital of the Cayman Islands recalls a more peaceful era, before modernity and mass tourism arrived. Time-worn gingerbread cottages, the ruins of a fort, and the Mission House – a classic early 19th-century Caymanian mansion – make strolling the streets a delight. The Mission House is today run as a museum by the National Trust, with period furnishings and exhibits on the yesteryear lifestyle. Behind the Webster Memorial United Church is the underground Pirates' Cave and, adjoining it, an old cemetery where a dozen or so unmarked graves are said to be those of pirates.

---

4 ▽▽▽▽

Queen Elizabeth II Botanic Park

☐ 15 miles (24 km) E of George Town ⓣ 🕑 9am–5:30pm daily 🕑 Good Friday, Dec 25 ⓦ botanic-park.ky

This park showcases more than half of the plant species native to the Cayman Islands, as well as birds and wildlife, including the rare blue iguanas and 56 species of butterfly. Visitors can walk through the lovely Floral Color Garden, which features hundreds of species of tropical and subtropical plants. Located nearby is the Heritage Garden with its traditional ornamental and medicinal plants, which Caymanians used for various ailments. The garden also has a pretty traditional Cayman house dating back to 1900.

A path near the entrance, named Woodland Trail, gives people the opportunity to view the sprawling natural landscape. Visitors get a chance to see the blue iguana roaming freely in this stretch.

EAT

Cracked Conch

This thatched, open-air joint serves divine fusion seafood dishes. There's deck dining atop a limestone plateau, with the jade Caribbean stretching out in front.

☐ 857 NW Point Rd, West Bay 🕑 Sep ⓦ crackedconch.com.ky

⑤⑤⑤

↑ Palm trees overlooking a lake in the Queen Elizabeth II Botanic Park

↑ The three-story Pedro St. James National Historic Site, the oldest building on the Cayman Islands

⑤ Pedro St. James National Historic Site

🏠 Pedro Castle Rd, Savannah 🚌 ⏰ 8:30am-5pm daily 🚫 Good Friday, Dec 25 🌐 pedrostjames.ky

Located high above Pedro Bluff, Pedro St. James is the oldest building on the Cayman Islands. William Eden, a wealthy Englishman, used Jamaican slave labor to construct this three-story stone building in 1780. In 1831, the first Cayman government was formed within it. The building later suffered damage from hurricanes, fire, and even lightning, but in 1992 the government decided to restore it. Guides are dressed in period costumes, and a tour of the house reveals antique furniture with mahogany floors and staircases, timber beams, and gabled framework. The visitors' center features an excellent 3D multi-sensory theater, where viewers can experience 200 years of Cayman history in just 20 minutes. There are breathtaking views from the house, and the site is a popular location for concerts, weddings, and parties. A memorial commemorates the 2004 Hurricane Ivan.

⑥ Little Cayman

🏠 89 miles (143 km) NE of Grand Cayman 🚤

A mere 10-sq-mile (25-sq-km) island, Little Cayman is the smallest of the three Cayman islands and is inhabited by fewer than 200 residents. Nature rules this laid-back, one-road island, with iguanas and birds outnumbering humans. The island is a popular day trip destination from Grand Cayman for travelers who mainly come here for solitude or diving. Bloody Bay Wall in Bloody Bay Marine Park (p100) offers one of the Caribbean's finest drop-offs.

Blossom Village is the only town on the island. Close by is the Booby Pond Nature Reserve, a nesting ground for 20,000 red-footed boobies, as well as the magnificent frigatebirds and waterbirds. The **National Trust House** at Blossom Village offers viewing platforms with telescopes to observe the birdlife. Just across the reserve is **Little Cayman Museum**, which features displays on the island's history. Point of Sand, at the eastern tip, has a pretty little beach. Offshore lies Owen Island, a tiny white beach cay, ideal for picnics and kayaking.

National Trust House

🕐 🏠 Guy Banks Rd, Blossom Village 📞 345 623 1107 ⏰ 9am-5pm Mon-Fri

Little Cayman Museum

🏠 Blossom Village ⏰ 1:30-4pm Mon-Sat 🌐 littlecayman museum.org

⑦ Cayman Brac

🏠 90 miles (144 km) NE of Grand Cayman 🚤 ℹ West End Community Park; www. itsyourstoexplore.com

Brac, the Gaelic word for "bluff," is a suitable name for this Cayman isle that has the most dramatic topography of the group, dominated by a limestone cliff reaching up to 146 ft (44 m) on its eastern tip. The island has several caves

Did You Know?

The islands were named the "Caimanes" after the Kalina word for the crocodiles once found here.

and many trails to explore. A 3-hour hike from Spot Bay leads to an old lighthouse from where there are splendid views of the ocean. Halfway down the trail is Little Cayman Brac Outlook (a large rock), where bird enthusiasts can see nesting brown boobies.

Another interesting hike is south off Bight Road. This is the National Trust Parrot Reserve and Nature Trail, which protects the endemic Cayman Brac parrot, along with other birds, plants, and native trees. On South Side Road visitors can see Rebecca's Cave, a historic site where islanders took shelter during Cuba's worst ever hurricane in 1932. It contains the grave of Rebecca Bodden, a baby girl who died in the cave during the storm. Just beside the cave the challenging Salt Water Pond trail begins, which takes hikers

from the south to north coast. At its end is Salt Water Pond, a sanctuary for a tern colony. Hikers can also visit the beautiful **Cayman Brac Heritage House** on North East Bay Road, where local artisans display their work. Be on the lookout for jewelery made of caymanite, a local stone used by the island's artisans that makes for the perfect Cayman Rab souvenir. Nearby is the island's first museum, **Cayman Brac Museum**, opened in 1983. It has exhibits on ship-building and displays on the islanders' lifestyles during the 1930s.

Cayman Brac Heritage House
Ⓐ Ⓐ ⬛ 218 NE Bay Rd ☎ 345 948 0563 🕒 8:30am–noon & 1–5pm Mon–Wed, 8:30am–1pm Fri

Cayman Brac Museum
Ⓐ Ⓐ ⬛ 279 Stake Bay Rd ☎ 345 948 2222 🕒 9am–noon & 1–4pm Mon–Fri; 9am–noon Sat

TOP 3 CAYMAN ISLANDS BOAT TRIPS

Bioluminescent Tour
ⓦ caymankayaks.com
Marvel as tiny dino-flagellates emit lingering bursts of bright spectral blue light as you explore Bioluminescent Bay by kayak or electric boat.

Sunset Cruise
ⓦ fivestarcharters cayman.com
Celebrate sundown in style with hors d'oeuvres and champagne on ice aboard a luxurious private yacht.

Atlantis Submarine
ⓦ caymanislands submarines.com
Marvel at the incredible underwater world aboard this 48-passenger submersible with huge windows for fab views, plus spotlights for really cool night entertainment.

The ruggedly beautiful Cayman Brac, home to a number of nesting brown boobies *(inset)*

PRACTICAL
INFORMATION

Here you will find all the essential advice and information you will need before and during your stay in the Cayman Islands.

AT A GLANCE

CURRENCY
CI dollar (CI$)

TIME ZONE
Eastern Standard Time (EST), 5 hours behind Greenwich Mean Time (GMT). The islands do not observe daylight savings

LANGUAGE
English

ELECTRICITY SUPPLY
The electrical system delivers 110 volts at 60 cycles. US-style plugs are used. European appliances will require adaptors and transformers

EMERGENCY NUMBERS
AMBULANCE, POLICE, FIRE SERVICE

911

TAP WATER
Tap water is safe to drink

When To Go

December to April is when most people visit the Cayman Islands. The year-round temperature ranges between 70° F and 90° F (21° C and 32° C). The dry season lasts from November to April, while the rainy season runs mid-May through October. August to October are prime hurricane months. The islands' unique Hurricane Guarantee covers any cancellations made prior to arrival and offers compensation if vacation time is cut short because of inclement weather.

Getting There

All international flights arrive at Grand Cayman's Owen Roberts International Airport. Scheduled flights to Grand Cayman are available on Air Canada, American Airlines, British Airways, Delta, JetBlue, United Airlines, US Airways, and WestJet. Cayman Airways is the national flag carrier, offering flights from the US. A host of charters also provide non-stop flights from US cities. Inter-island daily service from Grand Cayman to the sister islands is provided by Cayman Airways and its affiliate Cayman Airways Express. Charter flights can be booked with Island Air. There is no ferry service.

Personal Security

The Caymans are one of the Caribbean's safest destinations, with a low crime rate. However, petty theft and pickpocketing does occur, and it is advisable to keep valuables in the hotel safe. The islands are hassle-free, with no street or beach vendors.

Health

The government's Cayman Islands Hospital and the private Chrissie Tomlinson Memorial Hospital have modern facilities and are well equipped to deal with emergencies. The state-run Faith Hospital is in Cayman Brac, while Little Cayman has the Little Cayman Clinic. Medical insurance is mandatory and should be taken out before your trip.

Passports and Visas

A valid passport is required, along with a return ticket. UK, Canadian and US nationals do not need a visa to enter the Caymans, but many other countries, including several Caribbean states, do. The Immigration Department website has details of countries requiring and those exempted from visas. A departure tax is included in the airline ticket.

LGBT+ Safety

Same-sex relations were legalized in 2001 in the Cayman Islands under Britain's directives, and same-sex marriage was legalized in March 2019. However, local conservative politicians and religious figures have been consistently homophobic, and in 1998, the government famously refused permission to berth for a cruise ship carrying gay passengers. There are no gay clubs or beaches, and displays of same-sex affection are severely frowned upon.

Money

The Cayman Islands has its own currency, the CI dollar (CI$), but the US dollar is accepted everywhere and there is a fixed rate of exchange. Major credit cards and traveler's checks are widely accepted. ATM machines are available all over Grand Cayman. There is only one on Cayman Brac and one on Little Cayman. There is one branch of the Cayman National Bank on both Cayman Brac and Little Cayman. The branch on Cayman Brac is open Monday through Friday and that on Little Cayman is open only on Mondays and Thursdays.

Cell Phones and Wi-Fi

The international dialing code is 345, followed by a seven-digit local number. Public phones are available throughout the islands. The two cell phone providers, Digicel and LIME, offer prepaid phone plans. Visitors bringing their own cell phones should check with their service providers to determine if they will work in the Cayman Islands. Wi-Fi, either free or for a small fee, is available at airports, most hotels, cafes, and some restaurants.

Getting Around

Renting a car or taking a guided tour is the best way to explore the islands. Visitors must be at least 21 years to drive and have a Visitor's Permit issued at any car rental firm. Vehicles can be hired from most major car rental companies on Grand Cayman; CB Rent-A-Car at the Cayman Brac airport; and from McLaughlin Car & Moped Rentals is the only car rental firm in Little Cayman, although scooters can also be rented from Scooten! Scooters! Driving is on the left. Main roads are paved and in good condition. Taxis are readily available at all resorts and airports. There is a taxi stand in George Town. Daily public bus service on Grand Cayman generally runs from 6am until midnight depending on the route and the day.

Visitor Information

The **Cayman Islands Department of Tourism** has its head office in Grand Cayman. **District Administration** has information on the sister islands. The **Tourism Attraction Board** and **Sister Islands Tourism Association** also provide useful information.
Cayman Islands Department of Tourism
w caymanislands.ky
District Administration Cayman Brac
w itsyourstoexplore.com
Sister Islands Tourism Association
w sita.ky
Tourism Attraction Board
w tab.ky

A striking pink beachfront house in the Turks and Caicos

TURKS AND CAICOS

The 40 low-lying islands and cays that make up the Turks and Caicos are part of the Bahama Archipelago and lie in the Atlantic Ocean, not the Caribbean Sea. Only eight islands are inhabited. The capital and center of government is Cockburn Town on Grand Turk, the easternmost isle, though the most populated and developed island is the westernmost, Providenciales. "Provo" is also the most visited, in no small part due to the allure of Grace Bay, often rated as one of the world's best beaches. Flat as pancakes, the islands sit atop an underwater plateau with walls that plunge to the bottom of deep ocean trenches.

The islands' history is closely associated with salt, the "white gold" extracted from *salinas* – natural saltwater ponds and lagoons. Commercial salt raking was begun by visiting Bermudans in the late 1600s and continued for nearly 300 years. It was big business on Salt Cay and Grand Turk, where *salinas* and canals can still be seen. Most of today's "Belonger" population are descended from Africans brought to work at the salt pans, and later on the cotton plantations set up by defeated Loyalists after the American War of Independence. Nowadays, traditional livelihoods continue such as boatbuilding and fishing for conch – an integral element in local cuisine and culture. However, the islands are dependent for their prosperity on tourism and, as a zero-tax jurisdiction, offshore finance. Although Turks and Caicos is a British Overseas Territory, the islands' communities are a blend of African, Caribbean, and American cultures.

Three Mary Cays
Sanctuary

Whitby
Beach

Cottage
Pond

North Caicos
Airport

Parrot Cay

Kew

Flamingo
Pond

East Bay Islands
National Park

Pine Cay

Bottle Creek

Mudjin
Harbor

Northwest
Point

Wheeland
Beach

Little Water Cay

NORTH
CAICOS

Conch Bar

Blue Hills

4

Middle Caicos
Airport

Pigeon Pond

GRACE BAY

Caicos
Conch Farm

5

PROVIDENCIALES

1

2

Long Bay Beach

**MIDDLE
CAICOS**

Chalk Sound
National Park

Providenciales
International Airport

West Caicos

Yankee
Town

Lake Catherine

3 **WEST CAICOS**

*Caribbean
Sea*

**TURKS AND
CAICOS**

Atlantic Ocean

ambarra Beach
Bambarra

Lorimers Point

Drum Point

East Caicos

Bell Sound Nature Reserve

South Caicos Airport

SOUTH CAICOS 6

Cockburn Harbor

Turks Island Passage

GRAND TURK 8

Flamingo Beach

Pillory Beach Cockburn Town

JAGS McCartney International Airport

White Sand Beach

East Cay

SALT CAY 7

Cotton Cuy

Balfour Town

Big Ambergris Cay

Little Ambergris Cay

0 kilometers   15

0 miles   15

N

→
Caribbean flamingos flying over the North Caicos Islands

TURKS AND CAICOS FOR
WILDLIFE ENCOUNTERS

While sensational sands and turquoise seas are the top draw for visitors to Turks and Caicos, its wetlands, dry forests, and marine ecosystems abound with wildlife. From bottlenose dolphins and humpback whales to the Bahama woodstar hummingbird, these isles have plenty to entice ecotourists.

Discover the Depths

The lush waters surrounding the Turks and Caicos teem with marine life, including spectacular reefs. At Elephant Ear Canyon, brown eagle rays swarm alongside moray eels, stingrays, and a spectrum of panchromatic reef fish and corals. Sharks are common throughout these waters but Shark Hotel, off Northwest Point in Providenciales, is usually thronged with reef, lemon, and hammerhead sharks.

→
A grouper fish blending in with vibrant coral

Birds of a Feather

Around 230 bird species reside in the Turks and Caicos, including several endemics. On Providenciales, Northwest Point National Park and Frenchman's Creek Nature Reserves provide the best chance to spot osprey and White-tailed tropicbirds. Less-visited North, Middle, and South Caicos are the best sites for keen twitchers – flamingos, mangrove cuckoos, and reddish egrets are key draws to the Ramsar Nature Reserve.

← A brown pelican on the beach

TOP 3 BIRDS IN THE TURKS AND CAICOS

Bahama Woodstar
The only resident hummingbird in the region has a glittering purple gorget.

White-tailed Tropicbird
With its spectacular long trailing tail, this snow-white tropical marine species swoops over the ocean.

Greater Caribbean Flamingo
This gregarious wading bird gets its pink color from algae that it sieves using its bill upside down underwater.

INSIDER TIP
Watch in Winter

Whale-watching excursions operate from Grand Turk from January to April. Reputable companies include Oasis Divers (oasisdivers.com) and Salt Cay Divers (saltcaydivers.com).

→ Graceful humpback whales swimming in shallow waters

Whale-Watching

Winter months offer the promise of eye-to-eye encounters with humpback whales as they migrate from the Northern Atlantic to the warm waters off the Turks and Caicos. The best place to spot them is Island Passage, between Grand Turk and Salt Cays. Humpbacks and pilot whales can often be seen from dive boats operating from Providenciales.

EXPERIENCE

① Providenciales

🏝 **Second-westernmost isle of Turks and Caicos** ✈🚢
ℹ Stubbs Diamond Plaza;
649 946 4970

This ox-jaw-shaped isle, known locally as Provo, is renowned for the crescent of seemingly never-ending beach at Grace Bay. "Downtown" is the island's business center and has a few shops and offices. **Cheshire Hall Plantation**, one of the few remaining historical sites in the area, features stone ruins of a late 1700s cotton

---

🔍 HIDDEN GEM
Little Water Cay

Make time to visit this tiny island within Princess Alexandra National Park. Rock iguanas waddle down to shore to greet arrivals on the otherwise uninhabited, scrub-covered cay just east of Providenciales.

---

plantation. It's located on a hilltop near Downtown.

The isle tapers east from Northwest Point, which is pinned by a lighthouse and reached by rough sandy trails. Most of the west shore is protected within two nature reserves – North West Point Pond reserve and Pigeon Pond and Frenchman's Creek reserve – sheltering wetlands, mangroves, tidal flats, and offshore reefs. Chalk Sound National Park, along the south shore, has particularly beautiful blue waters. For a fine view, head to South Rock, where rock slabs are carved with mariners' markings from the 18th and 19th centuries.

Boat excursions depart from near the farm for snorkeling and party cruises, to a string of tiny cays off the east coast, including Little Water Cay, which is crawling with iguanas. Pine Cay is a private jewel and setting for The Meridian Club, an all-inclusive resort with sports facilities that range from Hobie Cats to the resort's own yacht. Wrapped in snowy

sands and turquoise waters, Parrot Cay, to the northeast of Providenciales, hosts an eponymous resort with a fine-dining restaurant and deluxe rooms. Its luxurious COMO Shambhala spa, on a 2-mile- (3-km-) long beach, is the perfect place to relax. For a true local flavor of Provo, head to Bight Park on Thursday evenings. More than a dozen food vendors have set up shop here, and live music and entertainment adds to the fun.

Cheshire Hall Plantation
♿🅿🚻🍴 🏛 Leeward Hwy
☎ 649 941 5710 ⏰ 9am–4pm Mon–Fri

---

② Grace Bay

🏝 **N coast of Providenciales**

The stupendously beautiful Grace Bay, curling along the north shore for 3 miles (5 km), is lined with talcum-white sands shelving into

↑ Colorful watercraft dotting the turquoise waters off the island of Providenciales

→ Divers exploring the drop-off within West Caicos Marine National Park

shallows, and some of the best snorkeling spots on the island. This is all protected within the 10-sq-mile (26-sq-km) Princess Alexandra Land and Sea National Park, home to with iguanas, ospreys, and a variety of marine life.

The beach, tufted with wispy grasses peeping up from sand dunes, is lined with upscale hotels and has plenty of watersports, but there are plenty of quiet spots, too.

Among the most deluxe hotel options on Grace Bay, the Andalusian-style Grace Bay Club is acclaimed for its Infiniti restaurant. Sprawling over 479,150 sq ft (44,500 sq m), the all-suite resort offers tennis and watersports, among many other facilities.

West Caicos

 15 miles (24 km) SW of
Providenciales

A tiny island of 11 sq miles (29 sq km), West Caicos is inhabited by iguanas, lizards, and birds. In the 1890s, the island's Yankee Town was a center for salt extraction, and ruins of old buildings and railroads still stand here. Bird-watchers can spot flamingos at the Lake Catherine Nature Reserve, while divers can explore the West Caicos Marine National Park. This reserve has some of the best diving sites in the region, including a submerged plateau wall that plunges into a 7,000 ft (2,133 m) abyss.

 North Caicos

12 miles (19 km) NE of
Providenciales

With its dense and lush vegetation, North Caicos is widely accepted as the most beautiful of all the Turks and Caicos islands. Its verdant plantlife has earned it the nickname "Green Island" among locals. A short distance from Kew village in the north, Wade's Green Plantation recalls the days when sisal and cotton were grown. Ancient cannons still stand sentinel on Fort George Cay nearby. Hotels are concentrated at Whitby Beach, the best of several ultra-white sands, while a boat ride delivers visitors to East Bay Islands National Park, where iguanas and marine turtles can be seen.

Birders flock to Cottage Pond, a sinkhole with jade waters, to see ducks and grebes; and to the appropriately named Flamingo Pond to observe flamingos. Just offshore is Three Mary Cays Sanctuary, which is a habitat for ospreys.

EAT

Bugaloo's Conch Crawl
This beachfront eatery offers fresh local cuisine with a large selection of conch dishes, while live bands tempt patrons to dance on the sands.

Five Cays Rd,
Providenciales
W bugaloostci.com

$$$

Guanahani
Irresistible globe-spanning cuisine, ranging from coconut shrimp to chicken tikka masala. Themed nights include Reggae BBQ.

Bohio Dive Resort,
Grand Turk W bohio
resort.com

$$$

Infiniti
A gourmet alfresco restaurant at the Grace Bay Club, offering fusion seafood and a dramatic "infinity-edge" bar.

1 Grace Bay Circle Rd,
Providenciales Lunch
W gracebayresorts.com

$$$

> The stupendously beautiful Grace Bay, curling along the north shore for 3 miles (5 km), is lined with talcum-white sands shelving into shallows and some of the best snorkeling spots on the island.

↑ Exploring Conch Bar Caves National Park, Middle Caicos, by torchlight

5 Middle Caicos

 15 miles (24 km) E of North Caicos

This sparsely populated isle was once a major center of the Lucayan civilization, remains of which can be seen at the Armstrong Pond Village Historical Site, one of the many pre-Columbian sites in the area. This, and some plantation ruins, are accessible via the well-signed Middle Caicos Reserve and Trail System. Stalactites and stalagmites can be admired in Conch Bar Caves National Park, a haven for bats. The remote Vine Point and Ocean Hole Nature Reserve, on the south coast, is named in part for its massive blue hole, and is popular with divers and birders. Mudjin Harbor Beach, near the main settlement of Conch Bar, is framed by dramatic cliffs cusping sheltered coves. Bambarra Beach offers excellent

Did You Know?

The Turks and Caicos flag once featured an igloo, after the design – meant to show salt mounds – was mistaken.

snorkeling and hosts the annual Valentine's Day Cup, a sailboat race using scale models handcrafted by local artisans.

Located about 2 miles (3 km) east of Middle Caicos is the unpopulated East Caicos. Once a sisal plantation, it is now a habitat for several bird species, including flamingos.

6 South Caicos

 15 miles (24 km) SE of Middle Caicos

This diminutive and arid isle, home to a population of just over 1,500 and almost entirely lacking in resorts, combines superb wall dives and excel-lent bonefishing in the jade-blue Bell Sound Nature Reserve and Admiral Cockburn Nature Reserve. Pink flamingos flock around the briny *salinas* (salt ponds), within sight of the down-at-heels town of Cockburn Harbour, which is the isle's main settlement. The town was severely damaged by Hurricane Irma and Hurricane Maria in 2017, but has since fully recovered. Every May, the streets of Cockburn Harbour burst into life for the Big South Regatta, which includes speedboat races, beauty pageants, float parades, and donkey races.

7 Salt Cay

8 miles (13 km) SW of Grand Turk ✈🚢 🌐 saltcay.org

An arid, arrow-shaped speck of an isle, Salt Cay is named for the salt ponds that became the foundation for the region's salt production industry, which was a successful international enterprise from the mid-17th to the ealy 20th century. Many

→ Colonial houses lining the beachfront of Cockburn Town, Grand Turk

of the warehouses, homes, and other limestone structures built by Bermudan salt traders have been restored, making tiny Balfour Town a delightful capsule of vernacular industrial architecture. Most locals get around by bicycle or golf cart; cars are virtually unknown.

The salt ponds are one of the Caribbean's premier sites for spotting ospreys and wading birds. In winter, humpback whales gather in the waters southeast of Salt Cay and can be seen close to shore.

In 1790 a storm claimed H.M.S. *Endymion*, a British man-o'-war that sank south of Salt Cay. Today, the wreck of the 44-gun frigate is a world-renowned diving site and draws divers keen to explore its remains and the unspoiled habitat that surrounds it.

---

❽ Grand Turk

🏠 120 miles (195 km) E of Providenciales ✈🚢 🛈 Front St; 649 946 2321

The small, semi-arid Grand Turk is an unlikely outpost for Turks and Caicos's capital, Cockburn Town. Strolling the streets of its charming historic center feels like stepping back in time. Bermudan-style limestone-and-clapboard structures line the sand-blown streets. Built of ships' timber, 19th-century Guinep House hosts the **Turks and Caicos National Museum**, which features fine exhibits from the Molasses Reef shipwreck dating from 1513.

The town overlooks coral-tinged Pillory Beach, one of a string of beaches lining the windward shore. Locals believe that Christopher Columbus made his first New World landfall here on October 12, 1492. The offshore reef is protected within Columbus Landfall Marine National Park. The leeward shore is also sprinkled with long, lonesome beaches with soft powdery sands. Two of the most beautiful beaches are Governor's Beach, with its crystal clear water and shallow depths, and White Sands Beach, which is perfect for kiteboarding.

Turks and Caicos National Museum

♿♨ 🏠 Front St ⏰ Times vary, check website 🌐 tcmuseum.org

TOP 5 DIVE SITES IN THE TURKS AND CAICOS

H.M.S. *Endymion*
A spectacular shallow wreck dive south of Salt Cay, the cannons of this British warship are encrusted in coral.

Shark Hotel
Located off northwest Providenciales, this is a good spot to swim with Caribbean reef sharks.

Black Forest
Named for its black coral, this site off Grand Turk has rare Grasyby grouper.

Elephant Ear Canyon
A West Caicos site with huge elephant ear sponges, stingrays, and plentiful black coral.

Thunderdome
This artificial reef on the northwest coast of Providenciales is enthralling at night.

PRACTICAL
INFORMATION

Here you will find all the essential advice and information you will need before and during your stay in the Turks and Caicos.

CURRENCY
US Dollar (US$)

TIME ZONE
Eastern Standard Time (EST), 5 hours behind Greenwich Mean Time (GMT). Daylight Savings is in effect the first Sunday of March through the first Sunday of November

LANGUAGE
English

ELECTRICITY SUPPLY
Turks and Caicos operates on 110 volts. Outlets use US two-prong plugs

EMERGENCY NUMBERS

TEL

911

TAP WATER
In most cases it is safe, yet bottled water is the common choice due to the poor taste of piped water

When To Go

These breeze-swept isles are pleasant year-round, although the best weather is from December through April, when there is hardly any rain and the temperatures are near perfect – 73–84°F (between 23–28°C). The midsummer months can be torrid, while the weather can get sticky during the hurricane season (June through November). Cultural events are mostly held during the winter months, but rates tend to be higher then than in summer.

Getting There

Charter and regular scheduled flights arrive at Providenciales International Airport from North America. There are a few direct flights from North America to Grand Turk International Airport. Private charter planes connect all the other islands to Grand Turk and Providenciales. Delta, US Airways, JetBlue, United Airlines, and American Airlines fly to Providenciales from various US gateways. British Airways serves Providenciales via the Bahamas and Antigua. The Bahamas is also served by Bahamasair. Air Canada has direct flights from Montreal, Ottawa, and Toronto to Providenciales. WestJet also offers direct flights from Montreal and Toronto.

Personal Security

Theft and crime affecting tourists is rare in Turks and Caicos, but it is best to keep valuables in a hotel safe, and to avoid wearing expensive jewelry when out and about.

Health

There are public clinics on each island, and a general hospital on Grand Turk, but many may not meet the standards that most people are used to. Private clinics such as Grace Bay Medical Centre and Cockburn Town Medical Centre are usually preferred by tourists. Some all-inclusive resorts have a nurse on staff. Providenciales also has a hyperbaric chamber.

Passports and Visas

Most visitors do not require a visa for a stay of up to 90 days but must have a valid passport and a ticket for onward travel.

LGBT+ Safety

Same-sex sexual activities have been legal in the Turks and Caicos , a British overseas territory, since 2001, through an order of the UK's Privy Council. However, marriage and civil unions of same-sex couples have not been legalized and the culture of the island is not very LGBT+- friendly. There are a number of high-end resorts that are non-judgemental and offer luxurious holidays and privacy to LGBT+ visitors.

Money

The US dollar is the official currency of Turks and Caicos, which also issues its own crown and quarter. Traveler's checks in US dollars are accepted in most hotels, taxi services, and restaurants in Providenciales, and can be cashed at local banks. However, cash and credit cards are preferred on other islands, where banks may be fewer. Most major credit cards are accepted. There is no limit on the amount of money that visitors may bring to the islands.

Mobile Phones and Wi-Fi

The Turks and Caicos has efficient mobile and telephone services operated by Digicel and LIME. To call abroad from the Turks and Caicos, dial 011 and the country code, then the area code and number. To call Turks and Caicos from North America, dial 1, then 649 and the local number; from the UK, dial 00 for international access, then 649 and the local number. Calls within the islands require only the seven-digit number. Visitors bringing their own mobile phones should check with their service providers to determine if they will work in the Turks and Caicos. Most hotels and restaurants offer Wi-Fi. There are also Internet cafés on the islands.

Getting Around

The Turks and Caicos has a total land area of 166 sq miles (430 sq km) scattered across 100,000 sq miles (26,000 sq km) of ocean. The isles are connected by a few ferry services and scheduled, small plane charters. A bridge connects North and Middle Caicos. Providenciales is served by tourist taxis and cars.

Holders of an International Drivers License and citizens of the UK, US, and Canada are permitted to drive on their own license for up to 30 days. Reputable rental companies are AVIS, Hertz, and Grace Bay Car Rentals. Hotels can also arrange for car rentals. Scooters can be rented from companies such as Tony's Car Rental on Grand Turk, which also hires out bicycles. It is advisable to wear helmets. Minivans operate taxi services on all islands and can be used for touring. Rates can be expensive, so be sure to negotiate an agreed fare before setting off. The concierge or front desk staff of most hotels will help visitors call for a taxi from a reputable company.

Visitor Information

The **Turks and Caicos Islands Tourist Board** has offices in the US, Canada, and the UK. Within the Turks and Caicos, it has offices on Grand Turk and on Providenciales (at the airport and at Turtle Cove Marina). Hotel tour desks can also give advice on organized excursions and entertainment. The **Turks and Caicos Hotel and Tourism Association** and **Visit Turks and Caicos Islands** websites provide helpful information and recommendations.

Turks and Caicos Islands Tourist Board
🆆 turksandcaicostourism.com
Turks and Caicos Hotel and Tourism Association
🆆 turksandcaicoshta.com
Visit Turks and Caicos Islands
🆆 visittci.com

THE BAHAMAS

The Bahamas comprises an archipelago of some 700 low-lying islands and cays spread over 100,000 sq miles (259,000 sq km) of the Atlantic Ocean. Most Bahamians live on New Providence, location of the country's capital, Nassau. The Out Islands – the term used to cover all the islands except New Providence and Grand Bahama – are sparsely populated or uninhabited, unspoiled idylls. Columbus made his first landfall in the Americas on the easternmost Bahamian island of San Salvador in 1492. The Spanish soon wiped out the peaceful Lucayans who were already living in The Bahamas, transporting many to work in mines on Hispaniola. European colonization was taken up in earnest by English settlers from Bermuda on Eleuthera in 1647, then New Providence two decades later. These were lawless times, with the looting of cargo ships across the shallow waters around the islands. Blackbeard was one of the many pirates operating at the time.

After the American Revolution (1765–83), many defeated Loyalists arrived in The Bahamas with slaves, and set up cotton plantations. During the American Civil War in the 1860s, The Bahamas was a haven for blockade runners associated with the Confederate states. Later, during Prohibition in the U.S. in the 1920s, rum-running from Bahamian ports to Florida became big business. The Bahamas gained independence from Britain in 1973, and tourism has developed as the mainstay of the country's economy, with most visitors coming from North America.

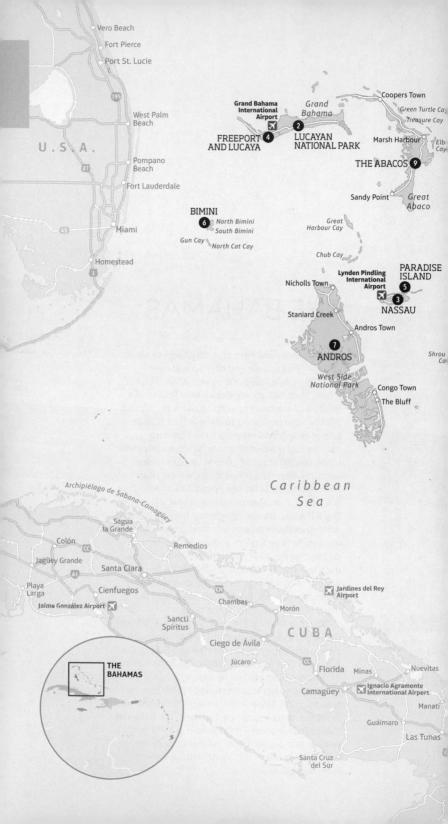

THE BAHAMAS

Must Sees

1 Exuma Cays Land and Sea Park
2 Lucayan National Park

Experience More

3 Nassau
4 Freeport and Lucaya
5 Paradise Island
6 Bimini
7 Andros
8 Long Island
9 The Abacos
10 The Exumas
11 Eleuthera
12 The Inaguas
13 Cat Island
14 San Salvador

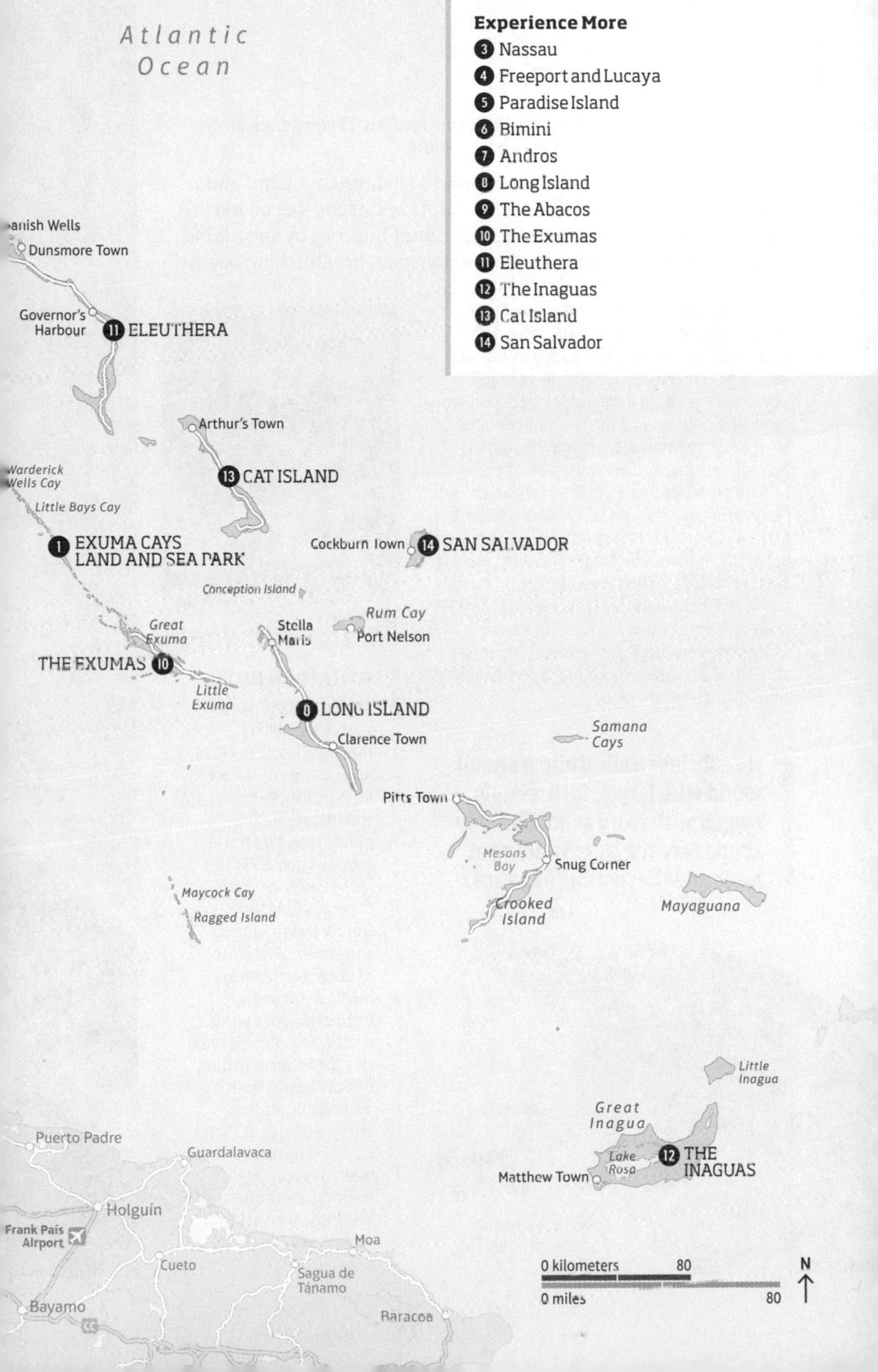

Atlantic Ocean

anish Wells
Dunsmore Town

Governor's Harbour **11** ELEUTHERA

Arthur's Town

Warderick Wells Cay

Little Bays Cay

13 CAT ISLAND

1 EXUMA CAYS LAND AND SEA PARK

Cockburn Town **14** SAN SALVADOR

Conception Island

Rum Cay
Port Nelson

Great Exuma

Stella Maris

THE EXUMAS **10**

Little Exuma

8 LONG ISLAND

Clarence Town

Samana Cays

Pitts Town

Mesons Bay Snug Corner

Maycock Cay

Ragged Island

Crooked Island

Mayaguana

Little Inagua

Great Inagua

Lake Rosa **12** THE INAGUAS

Matthew Town

Puerto Padre

Guardalavaca

Holguín

Frank País Airport

Moa

Cueto

Sagua de Tánamo

Bayamo

Baracoa

0 kilometers   80
0 miles   80

N

❶ 🎨 🍴

EXUMA CAYS LAND AND SEA PARK

📍 76 miles (123 km) SE of Nassau ✈🚢 From Nassau ℹ Warderick Wells Cay; www.bnt.bs/exuma-cays-land-sea-park

The world's first land-and-sea reserve, the Exuma Cays Land and Sea Park protects an archipelago of coral cays strung like pearls in a 22-mile (35-km) line south of Nassau. Island-hopping by speedboat is an exhilarating introduction to The Bahamas' breathtaking beauty.

Spanning 453 sq-km (175 sq miles) of pavonine seas, this remote ecological preserve and wildlife refuge is accessible solely by boat or seaplane. It enshrines a blissfully tranquil world with larger, lush islands ringed with ivory sand. The only sounds are the caterwauling of birds and the rustling of palms. The park is a no-fishing zone, and anchoring amid coral reefs is prohibited. Hence, the reefs teem with marine turtles, moray eels, and polychromatic fish – a nirvana for diving. Ashore, endangered Bahamian iguana, curly-tailed lizards, and the nocturnal hutia scurry around. Shroud Cay and Warderick Wells Cay (which has nature trails and a trail map) are nesting sites for white-tailed tropicbirds, while rocky dundas, off Little Bells Cay, offers superb snorkeling amid dripstone formations.

> **It enshrines a blissfully tranquil world with larger, lush islands ringed with ivory sand. The only sounds are the caterwauling of birds and the rustling of palms.**

BAHAMIAN HUTIA

The only Bahamian native terrestrial mammal is the hutia, an endangered short-limbed, rabbit-sized rodent resembling a guinea pig. The hutia is one of about 20 sub-species of the Capromyidae rodent family that includes the arboreal tree rat of Cuba. Hutias were hunted close to extinction following colonization and it was thought they had died out until the 1960s but a small population survived on East Plana Cay. The hutia has since been reintroduced to Exuma Cays Land and Sea Park in an attempt to diversify its range.

↑ A curly-tailed lizard, one of the inhabitants of the park

Did You Know?

Created in 1958, the
Exuma Cays Land and
Sea Park was the first
national park in
the Bahamas.

↑ Inviting turquoise and
teal waters and sandy,
light-salmon shoals

LUCAYAN NATIONAL PARK

🏠 Grand Bahama Hwy, 14 miles (23 km) E of Lucaya ⛴ From Nassau
🕐 9am–5pm daily 🌐 bnt.bs/lucayan-national-park

Grand Bahama's crown jewel, Lucayan National Park boasts a wealth of gorgeous flora and fauna. A realm of pristine mangrove wetlands, stunning sands, and a limestone plateau riddled with one of the world's longest known underwater cave systems await discovery.

A rejuvenating dip in the freshwater springs of Lucayan National Park is just one reason to visit this fascinating habitat, where all six Bahamian ecological zones are displayed. The main draw is the dwarf palm forest and mangrove forest, including Mangrove Wash, dominated by bromeliads and orchids.

A stunning array of wildlife can be seen in the park's distinct ecosystems, including curly-tailed lizards and raccoons. Small stingrays flap above the mud flats, while tiny fish swim amid the tangled root maze that helps keep out larger predators, and keen-eyed wading birds stake out a meal.

A short staircase spirals down into Ben's Cave, filled with an impossibly turquoise freshwater pool above a denser layer of salt water about 6 feet (2 m) down. Nearby Burial Mound Cave is named for the fossilized human remains of pre-Columbian Lucayan people found buried here. Swimming in the caves is prohibited, but scuba diving is allowed with a permit and a guide arranged through UNEXSO (unexso.com), a company based at the beautiful marina in Lucaya (p128).

Gold Rock Creek flows through the mangrove swamp and sidles between dunes that spill onto Gold Rock Beach, a gorgeous expanse of white sand unspooling along the shore as far as the eye can see, where turtles emerge from the waves by night to lay their eggs in the warm sands.

Did You Know?

The park's caves are home to a blind, transparent crustacean, *Speleonectes lucayensis*.

The sun setting over the white sandy beach and its rich forest ↑

① Ben's Cave is perfect for scuba diving.

② Snaking boardwalks form an easily-walked loop through the various ecosystems.

③ Kayaking is a fun, non-intrusive way to navigate the waterways.

TOP 5 TREES IN THE PARK

Red Mangrove
These broad-leafed, salt-tolerant ever-greens emerge from brackish coastal waters on multiple prop roots.

Swamp Cabbage Palm
Salt and drought hardy, this palm species grows well in swamp.

Poisonwood
Growing abundantly along Bahamian shores, this member of the cashew family produces a toxic resin.

Sea Grape
A native of Caribbean beaches, this broad-leafed, deciduous tree produces bunches of edible "grapes."

Bahamian Pine
Native pines cover half of Grand Bahama and depend on frequent fires to maintain their ecological niche.

EXPERIENCE MORE

EAT

Cafe Matisse

Housed in a centenary mansion with patio dining, this spot serves Italian cuisine plus creative fusion dishes, such as shrimp in red curry sauce. As expected, the walls are hung with Matisse prints.

🅰 Bank Lane, Nassau 🕒 Mon & Sun 🌐 cafe-matisse.com

The Fish Fry

This no-frills beachfront enclave of small stalls and a restaurant is a favorite with locals for its all-things-conch menu, including a delicious ceviche, plus other seafood. Try D'Water Café, which has live music in the evenings.

🅰 Arawak Cay, West Bay St, Nassau 🌐 fishfrynassau.com

---

3 🗺🍴🖥🛍

Nassau

ℹ Festival Place; 242 302 2000

Almost two-thirds of the nation's populace live on New Providence, and Nassau is the Bahamas' bustling capital city. The gritty yang to the calm yin of the Out Islands, Nassau is awash with cruise-ship passengers and a rum-happy party crowd. But it is also blessed with old Georgian buildings, fine beaches, and a fistful of intriguing museums.

Spend a day exploring the historic downtown, beginning at the Welcome Center that adjoins the cruise piers. One block south, Parliament Square is pinned by a statue of Queen Victoria and surrounded by government buildings. The lively Straw Market is interesting, and beyond it is the **Pompey Museum of Slavery & Emancipation**, housed in an 18th-century mansion where slaves were once sold. The enthralling **Pirates of Nassau** is nearby, an interactive museum that transports visitors back to 1716 with light and sound shows and eerily real exhibits. Rising atop Bennet's Hill to the southeast, Fort Fincastle was built in 1793 in the shape of a paddle-wheel steamer; reach it via the Queen's Staircase, hewn by slaves from solid limestone.

Farther west is the more grandiose Fort Charlotte, built in 1788 and commanding fine views over pearly white Cable Beach. Don't miss Clifton Heritage National Park, where trails wind through a variety of ecosystems and past the remains of a pre-Columbian Lucayan village. Visitors can also rent snorkel gear and swim to the Sir Nicholas Nuttall Coral Reef Sculpture Garden, the world's largest underwater gallery of sculptures.

Pompey Museum of Slavery & Emancipation

♿ 🅰 Bay St ☎ 242 356 0495 🕒 9:30am–4:30pm Mon-Sat (till 1pm Thu)

Pirates of Nassau

♿ 🅰 Cnr King & George sts 🕒 8:30am–5:30pm Mon-Sat, 9am–2pm Sun 🌐 piratesofnassau.com

---

4 🗺🍴🖥🛍

Freeport and Lucaya

ℹ Port Lucaya Marketplace; 242 373 8988

Dominating the western end of Grand Bahama – a low-lying isle covered in scrub and

> **The gritty yang to the calm yin of the Out Islands, Nassau is awash with cruise-ship passengers and a rum-happy party crowd.**

casuarinas – the sprawling twin cities of Freeport and Lucaya were laid out in the 1950s as a duty-free destination to lure early pleasure-seekers. The uninspiring grid of soulless buildings and wide streets is somewhat enlivened by the International Bazaar, a duty-free enclave entered by Torii gates and teeming with cruise ship passengers. Inside, the highlight is a visit to the Fragrance of the Bahamas perfume factory, which is located in a pink 18th-century mansion and offers free tours.

A wealth of beaches lines the south shore. Closest to downtown is Xanadu Beach, where eccentric billionaire Howard Hughes holed up for his final years, inside the now-faded Xanadu Resort. Today's beachfront action centers farther east in the Lucaya suburb. Lucaya Beach, the island's most popular sand strip, is served by watersports and the Port Lucaya Marketplace, a marina and tourist complex.

A five-minute drive east of Freeport, the Garden of the

Grove botanical garden offers a lush respite from the sand of the region; trails weave through tamarind groves and past artificial cascades. Beyond, the paved Grand Bahama Highway strings along the southern shore through a virtually uninhabited morass of scrub and marsh.

Paradise Island

🏠 **4 miles (7 km) NE of Nassau**

Linked to Nassau by twin bridges, Paradise Island is the capital's hedonistic little sister, and is synonymous with wild bachelor parties, over-the-top weddings, and unabashed ostentation.

Shaped like an ox-jaw, the entire length of the isle's north shore is lined its with 4 miles (6 km) of white-sand beaches. Excursion boats will run visitors a short distance offshore to Blue Lagoon Island (bahamas bluelagoon.com), a long sliver of land that offers an aquapark and watersports. Paradise Island Golf Course and nearby Versailles Garden – a terraced garden spanning the isle north to south – provide distractions from the beach.

Undoubtedly the island's biggest draw, however, is **Atlantis Paradise Island Bahamas**, an ocean-themed

mega-resort, as fun-filled and extravagant as any product of Las Vegas, Walt Disney World® Resort, or even Hollywood. Opened in 1998, the huge resort includes a massive casino that sits alongside a vast Aquaventure waterpark. The park is home to the largest open-air aquarium in the world and (for confirmed thrill-seekers only) a Mayan Temple's Leap of Faith water-slide that propels riders through a shark-filled lagoon. You can also see the predators close up through an underwater Plexiglass walkway, and the resort offers a variety of marine-based adventures.

Atlantis Paradise Island Bahamas
🏠 1 Casino Dr ⓦ atlantis bahamas.com

TOP 4

SUNDOWNER HOTSPOTS

Pete's Pub & Gallery, Abaco
ⓦ petespub.com
A waterfront pub with metal sculpture foundry and its own signature rum cocktail.

Miss Emily's Blue Bee Bar, Green Turtle Cay
ⓦ missemilysbluebeebar.com
Renowned for its Goombay Smash that is sold by the gallon, this hole-in-the-wall also serves delicious meals.

End of the World Saloon, Bimini
🏠 Queen's Hwy, Alice Town
A tiny, sandy-floored bar, where locals play dominoes and - supposedly - Hemingway once caroused.

Nippers Bar, Abaco
ⓦ nippersbar.com
This colorful beach bar is party central; its Nipper Juice cocktail is particularly potent.

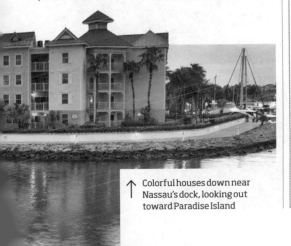

↑ Colorful houses down near Nassau's dock, looking out toward Paradise Island

6 Bimini

i Bimini Craft Center, Alice Town; 242 347 3528

Perched at the edge of the Gulf Stream just 50 miles (80 km) from Florida, tiny Bimini – comprising North Bimini, South Bimini, and a sprinkling of uninhabited cays – is renowned as a former base for Prohibition-era rum-runners. It was also a favored hangout for Ernest Hemingway, who was lured here by the region's first-rate sportfishing.

Today raffish Alice Town, Bimini's sole settlement, has been outclassed by the new Resorts World complex, with its swanky casino overlooking a pristine pearly beach. Divers delight in exploring Bimini Road, where underwater formations resembling giant building blocks inspire fantasies that this could be the fabled Atlantis.

Did You Know?

Alice Town, in Bimini, was briefly the busiest port in the Bahamas due to Prohibition-era rum-running.

HIDDEN GEM
Abaco National Park

Located at the southern end of Great Abaco, this park was created in 1994 to protect the endangered Abaco Parrot. About 1,000 of the birds remain, nesting in limestone cavities at the site.

7 Andros

i Mayou Plaza, Queen's Hwy, Andros Town; 242 368 2286

The largest and wildest of the Bahamian islands, Andros is a flat-as-a-flounder wilderness of pine forests, palm savannas, and sprawling wetlands pitted with "blue holes" – deep, water-filled sinkholes – and freshwater lakes. Half a dozen small settlements speckle the eastern shore, centered on Andros Town. Androsia, a workshop there producing handmade batiks, is worth a visit.

Most vacationers come for sensational bonefishing or to dive blue holes and coral reefs. To the east, the world's third-longest fringing reef plunges to more than 6,600 ft (2,000 m) off the Tongue of the Ocean wall.

Northwest of Andros Town, Blue Holes National Park has many trails along which visitors may spot Bahamian endemic birds.

8 Long Island

i Queen's Hwy, Salt Pond; 242 338 8668

One of the prettiest Out Islands, Long Island is a slender sliver of land and a study in contrasts. Atlantic waves crash against cliffs that tower over its eastern shore, while the calm lee side is scalloped with pink- and white-sand bays. Dean's Blue Hole, near the main settlement of Clarence Town, is the world's second-deepest blue hole and occupies a beach-fringed bay. Hamilton Cave is a draw of a different sort, displaying well-preserved indigenous Lucayan pictographs. In the far north, Stella Maris Resort is famous for its dives with sharks and to the Comberbach wreck.

↑ A snorkeler skirting the S.S. *Sapona* wreck off the coast of Bimini

 Pretty Elbow Reef lighthouse, located on one of the Abacos's "Loyalist Cays"

STAY

⑨ The Abacos

ℹ️ Harbour Place Bldg, Queen Elizabeth Dr, Marsh Harbour; 242 699 0152

Rich in history, the boomerang-shaped Abacos chain comprises Great Abaco and the necklace of Abaco Cays. The cays shelter the calm Sea of Abaco, to the delight of yachters. Although hardly a metropolis, Marsh Harbour is the third-largest town in the Bahamas. Boats depart its marina for the four small "Loyalist Cays", named for the British Loyalists who settled here after the American Revolution of 1776: Green Turtle, Great Guana, Man o' War, and Elbow. With their picture-perfect gingerbread cottages lining narrow lanes overflowing with bougainvillea, the cays are the Abacos's main draw. Elbow Cay is the most significant, centered on pretty Hope Town. Its harbor is pinned by the candy-striped Elbow Reef Lighthouse, the most iconic of Bahamian lighthouses; climb the 101 steps for a bird's-eye view over Hope Town.

On Green Turtle Cay, the Albert Lowe Museum displays model ships and historic artifacts in the former home of British Prime Minister Neville Chamberlain. Nearby, the Loyalist Sculpture Garden is laid out in the form of the Union Jack, and displays busts of prominent Loyalists.

---

⑩ The Exumas

ℹ️ Turnquest Star Plaza, George Town, Great Exuma; 242 336 2430

Claiming 365 reef-fringed cays and isles scattered like pearls across the jade waters of the central Bahamas, the Exumas are haloed by footprint-free beaches and are renowned for luxurious resorts and excellent diving. Great Exuma and Little Exuma – with resort hotels, Loyalist ruins, and the Family Island Regatta in April – are the populous pendants at the southern end of the Exuma Cays. A significant swatch of this chain of gorgeous, mostly uninhabited cays is protected within Exuma Cays Land & Sea Park, which teems with marine life and is perfect for kayaking and snorkeling.

---

⑪ Eleuthera

ℹ️ Queen's Hwy, Governors Harbour; 242 332 2142

A tendril-thin bow lined for much of its length by blush-pink sands, Eleuthera has long been a favorite of high-class socialites. Virtually the entire population lives in the small lobstering community of Spanish Wells at Eleuthera's northern tip; or in irresistibly quaint Dunsmore Town on Harbour Island. Visitors to the latter are delighted by its pretty 18th-century clapboard cottages and appropriately named Pink Sands Beach. Chic boutique hotels line sands the color of rosé, made even more striking by electric-blue waters lapping at their edge. At Glass Window Bridge, just south of Harbour Island, the Prussian-blue Atlantic is separated from the turquoise Bight of Eleuthera by a mere 30-ft (10-m) span.

A bright flock of flamingos wading through a river in Great Inagua National Park

 The Inaguas

ℹ Gregory St, Matthew Town; 242 339 1271

A far cry from the upscale resorts, watersports, and luxurious treatments found elsewhere in the Caribbean, the Inaguas are all about eco-tourism. They are the southern-most isles in the Bahamian chain: offbeat, semi-arid, salt-encrusted Great Inagua and uninhabited Little Inagua.

> **More than 80,000 flamingos tip-toe the saltwater lagoons of Great Inagua National Park, which covers almost half the island.**

More than 80,000 flamingos tip-toe the saltwater lagoons of Great Inagua National Park, which covers almost half the island. And some 140 other native and migratory bird species can be seen here, including the endangered Bahama Parrot. Other wildlife also abounds; the endemic Inagua slider turtle clings to life in rare freshwater pools, while green and hawksbill turtles haul ashore to nest on Inagua beaches. Anglers can cast for hard-fighting bonefish, arranged through Great Inagua Outback Lodge. Sun-beaten Matthew Town, the Inaguas' only community, thrives on salt production, and the vast site of the **Morton Salt Factory** can be toured.

Morton Salt Factory
Ⓢ ⬚ Matthew Town
📞 242 339 1300

 Cat Island

ℹ Queen's Hwy, Salt Pond; 242 338 8668

Cat Island is little troubled by tourists, despite its 8-mile (13-km) Pink Sand Beach to rival that of Eleuthera (p131), and a lifestyle steeped in traditional Afro-Bahamian culture. The narrow, hook-shaped isle is freckled with small limestone homes, built around the ruins of former Loyalist cotton plantations. Retired islanders play rake 'n' scrape music beneath trees festooned with bottles to ward off evil spirits – an *obeah* (spiritualist) belief. Trails wind through rolling hills that rise to Mount Alvernia, the highest point in the country; studded by a Medieval-style mini-

 PICTURE PERFECT
Flamboyance of Flamingos

Flamingos are shy birds and may fly away if you get too close, so to capture a sharp photograph you will need a telephoto lens. The stunning color of the flamingos is best shot in the morning or evening light.

⑭ San Salvador

🛈 Queen's Hwy, Cockburn Town; 242 331 1928

The outermost Bahamian island is small, but plays an outsized role in history. Five monuments commemorate Christopher Columbus's landfall in the Americas here on October 12, 1492 – these include a large stone cross at Long Bay, where the explorer is thought to have first stepped ashore. He named this isle "The Holy Savior," and it is ringed its entire length by beaches and coral reefs. There are more than 50 diving sites in the area, including the S.S. *Frascate* wreck, which sank here in 1902.

The island interior is a morass of briny lakes that comprise Great Lake Preserve, established to protect the endangered San Salvador rock iguana. A perimeter road leads past several ghost settlements, Loyalist plantation ruins, and the Dixon House Lighthouse.

monastery. Sleepy Arthur's Town, in the north, was the childhood home of Sidney Poitier, who became the first Caribbean actor to win an Academy Award in 1964.

COLUMBUS
1492.

→ A striking statue of Christopher Columbus in San Salvador

AMERICAS "DISCOVERED"

Everyone except residents of Turks and Caicos agrees that Christopher Columbus first touched land in the Americas in The Bahamas, visiting several islands. But exactly where he first stepped ashore is unknown. Many ancient scholars argued that a direct route west from Europe to Asia was possible. Genoese explorer Columbus was the first to seek a sailing route to the Indies. He set sail in August 1492 and in October, stumbled upon the unknown Americas, believing he had reached the Indies (hence the Caribbean islands are today called the West Indies). He made three other Americas voyages, in 1493, 1498 and 1502, but never returned to Bahamian waters.

↑ Depiction of Columbus landing on San Salvador in The Bahamas

PRACTICAL
INFORMATION

Here you will find all the essential advice and information you will need before and during your stay in The Bahamas.

CURRENCY
Bahamian Dollar
(BSD)

TIME ZONE
EST GMT - 5. The
Bahamas observes
Daylight saving time
April through October

LANGUAGE
English

ELECTRICITY SUPPLY
Outlets are 60 cycles/
120 volts, which is
compatible with
American devices.
British and European
appliances require a
two-pin flat adapter

EMERGENCY NUMBERS

**EMERGENCY
(APPLIES TO ALL SERVICES)**

911 or 919

TAP WATER
It is generally safe in
major urban centers,
but it's best to stick to
bottled water farther
afield

When To Go

The best time for visiting is December through April, the dry season. Temperatures are ideal, although hotel prices are higher. Hotels and car rental companies often offer discounts during hurricane season, June through November, when temperatures are higher and rains more frequent. Cultural events occur throughout the year.

Getting There

Although Nassau's Lynden Pindling International Airport (NAS) is the main airport, a few international flights arrive and depart from regional airports at Paradise Island, Freeport, George Town, and Marsh Harbour. The main US hubs are Miami, Fort Lauderdale and Orlando, but direct flights also depart Chicago, New York and other cities. American Airlines, Delta, Bahamasair, JetBlue, Southwest Airlines and United Airlines offer frequent service. Air Canada and Westjet provide direct service from Canada. British Airways flies non-stop between London and Nassau.

Personal Security

Violent street crime is mostly relegated to low-income zones away from touristy areas. But opportunistic crimes such as bag snatching are common. Be very careful with your belongings, and beware of pickpocketing, especially in crowded areas such as markets and casinos. Be alert to your surroundings, and use your common sense. Report any theft to the police, and get a copy of the report, if you wish to make an insurance claim. Contact your embassy or consulate if your passport is stolen, or in the event of a serious crime or accident.

Health

Sunburn is the most common ailment. Use sunscreen and shade hat, avoid midday sun where possible, and drink plenty of water. Sunstroke and heatstroke require prompt

medical attention. Minor stomach upsets, caused by unfamiliar food or poor hygiene, are not uncommon. Rest and rehydration are the main treatments; for stomach issues, seek advice from a pharmacy or clinic if there is no improvement after a couple of days. Mosquitoes are a nuisance around dawn and dusk. Cover up and use repellent, and avoid the beach at these hours.

Passports and Visas

Visitors to The Bahamas are not required to carry ID at all times, but it is a good idea to keep at least a photocopy of the information pages of your passport on your person.

LGBT+ Safety

Homosexuality is not illegal in The Bahamas. However, there are no laws against discrimination or harassment of LGBT+ people and many Bahamians are very conservative towards gay and lesbian issues. Public displays of affection by same-sex couples are generally frowned upon, and occasional acts of violence against LGBT+ people have occurred.

Money

The Bahamas' currency is the Bahamian Dollar (BSD), equivalent in value to the US dollar, which is also accepted everywhere. Euros and pounds Sterling can be exchanged at banks, including RBC Caribbean, and at foreign-exchange booths. Most shops and tourist outlets accept major credit cards, except on more remote Out Islands. Most banks in Nassau and Freeport have ATMs, but there are very few on the Out Islands, where you should plan to operate on a cash-only basis.

Cell Phones and Wi-Fi

The international dialing code for The Bahamas is 242. Most foreign cellphones service plans won't work in The Bahamas but it may be worth checking with your service provider before you go. Unlocked cell phones can be used with Bahamian SIM cards, and locked phones can only be used with expensive roaming. Almost all hotels have Wi-Fi, as do many restaurants.

In both regards, service on the Out Islands is generally poor.

Getting Around

Nassau's historic core is easily negotiated on foot, while taxis are ideal for getting around the greater metropolis, and cars can be rented for exploring further afield. Bahamasair flies between all the islands, although getting between adjacent Out Islands may involve flying via Nassau. Flamingo Air, Pineapple Air, and Western Air also have Out Island service. Some remote islands are served only once or twice a week, but private charter planes can be hired. Bahamas Ferries offers high-speed ferry service from Nassau to six Out Islands. Adventurous travelers might consider inexpensive and slower mail-boats, which depart Nassau on overnight passage to the Out Islands. The Abacos Cays are connected by water taxis, but getting around most Out Islands can be a challenge. Infrequent communal minibuses operate on most islands, where taxis and car rental options are limited and expensive.

Visitor Information

The Bahamas' Ministry of Tourism has offices in New York, Plantation (FL), Houston, and Atlanta, plus Toronto and UK. The two local offices are in Rawson Square, Nassau, and in International Bazaar, Freeport.

WEBSITES AND APPS

bahamas.com
The official government tourism website provides excellent information for accommodations, dining, exploring, and transportation.

nassauparadiseisland.com
Excellent in-depth information on Nassau and Paradise Island.

Bahamas Ridei
The Bahamas' answer to UBER lets you get a ride in minutes with the tap of a button.

JAMAICA

The Caribbean's third-largest island –146 miles
(234 km) long and up to 50 miles (80 km) wide –
encompasses white-sand beaches, tumbling
cascades, and the misty Blue Mountain range.
Its reggae and dancehall music and spicy jerk
cuisine have helped make the country famous,
as has a certain Jamaican called Usain Bolt, the
fastest man in the world.

Jamaica's natural abundance was the major
draw for the island's various colonizers. First to
settle were Amerindians from South America,
who farmed and fished here until the arrival of
Christopher Columbus in 1494. He claimed the
island on behalf of Spain, initiating the
establishment of the slave-driven plantation
economy which the English developed when
they captured Jamaica in 1655. Freed slaves –
the Maroons – were a thorn in the side of the
plantocracy, who used guerrilla tactics to win
armed campaigns against English forces. Slavery
was finally abolished in 1834, and Jamaica
gained independence from Britain in 1962.

The once all-important sugar and banana
industries continue, but are now eclipsed in
economic importance by tourism. To the west lie
the dazzling beaches and limestone cliffs of the
laid-back resort of Negril. Montego Bay and Ocho
Rios, ports of call for cruise ships, are the big
resorts in the north, while Port Antonio over in
the east has a slow-paced, old-world charm. For a
taste of the "real Jamaica," head down to Kingston,
the capital, an intense, edgy but rewarding city,
overlooked by the coffee-growing Blue Mountains.

Caribbean
Sea

ROSE HALL
Sangster
International Airport ✈ **11** GREENWOOD **11**
11 ○ Falmouth
RUNAWAY AND
DISCOVERY BAYS
Lucea A1 Duncans **26**
MONTEGO BAY **8** **28**
MAYFIELD ROCKLANDS Good GREEN
9 BIRD SANCTUARY ○ Hope Clark's GROTTO
FALLS Anchovy Town CAVES
Negril
Aerodrome **6** ANIMAL Kensington Windsor ○ Alexandria
10 FARM B5 B3
Long GREAT MORASS **7** ROARING RIVER
Bay AND ROYAL PALM **3** Albert Dry Harbor
RESERVE Town Mountains
5
4 Sheffield Petersfield Seaford Town COCKPIT
NEGRIL COUNTRY
7 Savanna- B6 Christiana Frankfield
BLUE HOLE la-Mar YS Falls Maggoty
MINERAL A2 Appleton Estate
SPRING Bluefields ST. ELIZABETH **14** Shooter's Hill
Whitehouse Middle Lacovia **15** MANDEVILLE
Quarters Santa A2
BLACK RIVER **13** Cruz
Malvern Downs Toll Gate
TREASURE BEACH **12** Santa Cruz
Mountains
Calabash Bay
Great Bay Alligator
Pond

JAMAICA

Must Sees

1 Kingston
2 Blue and John Crow Mountains National Park
3 Cockpit Country

Experience More

4 Negril
5 Great Morass and Royal Palm Reserve
6 Mayfield Falls
7 Blue Hole Mineral Spring and Roaring River
8 Montego Bay
9 Rocklands Bird Sanctuary
10 Animal Farm
11 Rose Hall and Greenwood
12 Treasure Beach
13 Black River
14 St. Elizabeth

15 Mandeville
16 Port Antonio
17 Hellshire
18 Port Royal
19 Long Bay
20 Winnifred Beach
21 Frenchman's Cove and the Blue Lagoon
22 Reach Falls
23 Firefly
24 Dunn's River Falls
25 Ocho Rios
26 Runaway and Discovery Bays
27 Cranbrook Flower Forest
28 Green Grotto Caves
29 Bob Marley Centre and Mausoleum
30 Oracabessa

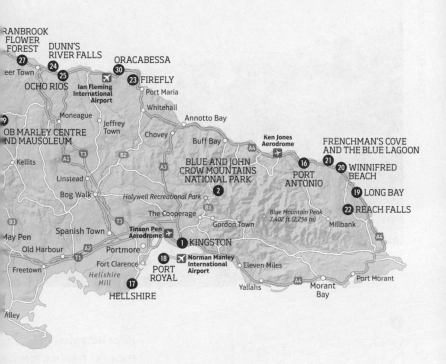

CRANBROOK
FLOWER
FOREST
27
eer Town

DUNN'S
RIVER FALLS
24
25
OCHO RIOS

ORACABESSA
30
23 FIREFLY
Ian Fleming
International
Airport
Port Maria

Whitehall

9

OB MARLEY CENTRE
ND MAUSOLEUM

Moneague

Jeffrey
Town

Chovey

Annotto Bay

Kellits

A1
T3

B2

Linstead

Bog Walk

Holywell Recreational Park

Buff Bay

A4

Ken Jones
Aerodrome

FRENCHMAN'S COVE
AND THE BLUE LAGOON
21
16
20 WINNIFRED
BEACH

BLUE AND JOHN
CROW MOUNTAINS
NATIONAL PARK
2

PORT
ANTONIO

19 LONG BAY

The Cooperage

B1

Blue Mountain Peak
7,402 ft (2,256 m)

22 REACH FALLS

Millbank

Gordon Town

B3

Spanish Town

T3

Tinson Pen
Aerodrome

A4

May Pen

A2

Old Harbour

T1

Portmore

1 KINGSTON

Freetown

Fort Clarence

18

Hellshire
Hill

Fort
Royal

PORT
ROYAL

Norman Manley
International
Airport

Eleven Miles

Port Morant

Yallahs

A4

Morant
Bay

17

Alley

HELLSHIRE

Caribbean
Sea

JAMAICA

The city hills of
Kingston, spilling down
to the large harbor

1

KINGSTON

⌂ 119 miles (190 km) SE of Montego Bay ✈ ℹ Jamaica
Tourist Board, 64 Knutsford Boulevard; 876 929 9200

Spreading inland from a natural harbor and cradled
by the peaks of the Blue Mountain range, Kingston is
Jamaica's cultural and commercial center. The city is
loosely divided into two halves: New Kingston holds the
manicured Emancipation Park, while Downtown is home
to banks, offices, and most of the city's historic buildings.

1

Devon House

⌂ 26 Hope Rd ⏰ 9:30am–
5pm Mon–Sat, 2–6pm Sun
& public hols 🌐 devon
houseja.com

Shady gardens surround the
splendid Devon House, built in
the late 19th century by the
nation's first black millionaire,

George Stiebel. Today a
national monument, the
museum – a blend of
Georgian and Caribbean
architecture – is furnished as
if he had never left. The larger
complex and gardens, with
their lush green lawns, are
populated with restaurants,
boutiques, and a spa, is a
popular place to head for a
snack or to relax outside.

2

Hope Botanical

⌂ Hope Rd ☎ 876 970 3505
⏰ 6am–6pm daily

At the northern end of Hope
Road are the Hope Botanical
Gardens. Colloquially known as
"Hope Gardens", these are set
in a former sugar estate and
filled with rare trees, plants,
and animals. The many rare
species include Jamaica's
national tree, the blue
mahoe (*Hibiscus elatus*).

On the waterfront,
behind the lawns
and swaying palms
of Ocean Boulevard,
the National Gallery
houses the best collec-
tion of homegrown
art in the country.

Gallery houses the best collection of homegrown art in the country. The superb repertoire ranges from pre-Columbian days to the present. Its varied events program often includes film screenings and musical performances alongside the exhibits.

Institute of Jamaica

🏛 10–16 East St 🕐 9am–4pm Mon–Thu, 9am–3pm Fri
🌐 instituteofjamaica.org.jm

This multi-faceted gem spans three buildings and several museums relating to Jamaica's heritage. The principal venue is the National Museum, which is home to over 17,000 exhibits, while the Natural History Museum also fascinates with its bug- and beast-themed displays. The Jamaica Music Museum documents the rise of the island's indigenous genres.

Parade

🏛 William Grant Park, junction of King & Queen sts

The pulsing heart of Downtown is centered on leafy William Grant Park, pinned by a statue of Queen Victoria. The park is surrounded by colonial-era buildings, including Bramwell Booth Memorial Hall and Ward Theater on the north side.

National Gallery

🏛 12 Ocean Blvd 🕐 10am–4:30pm Tue–Thu, 10am–4pm Fri, 10am–3pm Sat
🌐 nationalgalleryof jamaica.wordpress.com

On the waterfront, behind the lawns and swaying palms of Ocean Boulevard, the National

STAY

Terra Nova Hotel
This luxurious retreat, a former Great House, offers stylish period furnishings and a popular bar. The dining is superb.

🏛 17 Waterloo Rd
🌐 terranovajamaica.com

$$$

The Courtleigh
An old-school charmer that fuses traditional and contemporary styling. Don't miss the weekly poolside BBQ with live music.

🏛 85 Knutsford Blvd
🌐 courtleigh.com

$$$

⑥ 🗡 Ⓜ 🖥 🎒

BOB MARLEY MUSEUM

🏠 56 Hope Rd ⏰ 9:30am–4pm Mon-Sat
🌐 bobmarleymuseum.com

The former home and studio of the Reggae superstar after he moved "uptown" from Trench Town, the museum celebrates the life of the legendary musician and Jamaica's most famous son.

You'll learn all there is to know about Marley on an hour-long tour of the colonial-era wooden home where he lived and worked between 1975 and his death in 1981. The main room is festooned with awards that include Jamaica's Order of Merit, plus gold and platinum discs. The adjoining room is papered with press clippings, plus posters and a life-size 3D hologram from his 1978 One Love Peace Concert. Upstairs exhibits include a replica of Marley's Wail' N Soul 'M, the original rocksteady record label's recording studio created in 1966. Disc labels festoon the soundproof booth with original mixing board and three-legged stool.

Marley's bedroom is kept in its original state, with his favorite guitar (painted with birds and flowers) propped against the bed, and a poster of Rastafari icon Haile Selassie above. The former recording studio in the backyard is now a theater and exhibition space, showing a film on Marley's life.

↑ Statue of Bob Marley, sculpted by Pierre Rouzier

→ Lion Order mural by Like Minded Productions

BOB MARLEY

Born on February 6, 1945, Bob (Robert Nesta) Marley remains the biggest reggae star in the world. Having grown up in the country, Marley moved to Kingston with his mother after his father died of a heart attack. They lived in the government "Yard" where he met Peter Tosh and Bunny Livingstone, with whom he formed the Wailers. Chris Blackwell of Island Records introduced them to the world. Their first album was an instant success, and more followed. But Livingstone and Tosh became disillusioned with Blackwell and with Marley's dominance in the band and left to pursue solo careers. In 1980, Marley was diagnosed with cancer and died on May 11, 1981, in Miami.

↑ The wooden exterior of Marley's former home and now museum

↑ Former US President Barack Obama surveying the exhibits with a museum guide

Did You Know?

Assassins tried to kill Marley after he agreed to perform at a peace concert organied by Michael Manley.

143

2 ⊗ ▭

BLUE AND JOHN CROW MOUNTAINS NATIONAL PARK

ℹ 25 Eastwood Park Road, Kingston; www.blueandjohncrowmountains.org

Passing tiny mountain towns, whispering eucalyptus trees shrouded in mist, and famed coffee plantations, the 28-mile (45-km) stretch of the Blue Mountains makes for the most scenic drive on the island.

At the Holywell Recreational Park, you will find the main visitors' center for the Blue and John Crow Mountains National Park, a World Heritage Site, with cabins to stay in. With its highest peak reaching 7,402 ft (2,256 m), the Blue Mountain range is Jamaica's largest. Its lower canopy of soapwood, dogwood, and Caribbean cedar is interspersed with coffee plantations, and its upper slopes care overed with stunted montane rainforest.

From Papine and Kingston, there are two main driving routes. The road divides at The Cooperage, with one fork heading toward Holywell Recreational Park, taking in coffee plantations and a glitzy hotel en route, and the other toward Gordon Town and Mavis Bank, where jeeps can be rented to reach the start of the hiking trail to Blue Mountain Peak. A full day is necessary to see both the Holywell and Mavis Bank sides of the mountains. Be sure to drive slowly, and avoid the hills if it is raining, since landslides are fairly common.

BLUE MOUNTAIN COFFEE

Widely acknowledged as one of the best in the world, Blue Mountain coffee is grown at 2,000–5,000 ft (609–1,524 m). The climate and rich soil produce the distinctive beans, which are hand-picked, washed, then rested before being hulled, sorted into grades, roasted, and packed.

↑ The impressive Blue Mountains rising behind lush forest

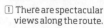

① There are spectacular views along the route.

② Strawberry Hill Hotel in Irish Town, where Bob Marley convalesced after being shot in 1976.

③ Old Tavern Coffee, the only estate in the mountains to process its own single-estate coffee.

145

COCKPIT COUNTRY

⌂ 36 miles (58 km) SE of Montego Bay 🚌 Infrequent minibuses run to Windsor
🌐 Southern Trelawny Environmental Agency; www.stea.net

A vast wilderness covering some 500 sq miles (1,294 sq km), the largely uninhabited Cockpit Country is one of Jamaica's most ecologically important areas. Home to innumerable rare plants and animals, it is characterized by the bizarre karst topography of conical hills separated by deep sinkholes in the limestone.

Cockpit Country served as an important place of protection for runaway slaves in the 17th century, who fought British authorities in its hills up until 1739. The best place to appreciate the Cockpit's serene remoteness is Windsor, a tiny hamlet on the northern fringes of the area and gateway to the nearby Windsor Caves, a bat colony carpeted with pungent guano. There are also some great trekking trails into the Cockpit's fringes. A good base for exploring is Good Hope, an 18th-century house with spectacular views over Cockpit Country. The house was bought by John Tharp, the largest land- and slave-owner in Jamaica, in 1767, with money he had made from plantations and the slave trade. Visits are arranged via Chukka Adventures *(chukka.com)*.

> The best place to appreciate the Cockpit's serene remoteness is Windsor, a tiny hamlet on the northern fringes of the area.

TOP 4 TREKS IN COCKPIT COUNTRY

Windsor Loop
A great introduction to Cockpit Country, this short trail can be trekked in 2–3 hours.

Burnt Hill Nature Trail
A steeply undulating east-west (or vice versa) trek between Clark's Town and Albert West.

Bunker Hill to Clear River
A relaxed trek to Dromilly Cave, Dromilly Great House ruins, and Clear River ends with a picnic and a refreshing dip in a natural pool.

Windsor to Troy
This guided but arduous, 10 mile (16 km), day-long trek spans Cockpit Country north to south.

Did You Know?

Cockpit Country has the deepest of Jamaica's sinkholes – deep pits with sheer edges.

← The gardens surrounding the Good Hope Estate and the outlying landscape *(inset)*

🔍 HIDDEN GEM
Good Hope Gallery

Acclaimed ceramic artist David Pinto invites visitors to his rustic studio *(jamaicapottery. com)* at Good Hope. You may even feel inspired to take one of his classes.

↑ The verdant hills that make up the landscape of the atmospheric Cockpit Country

EXPERIENCE MORE

4

Negril

 52 miles (83 km) SW of Montego Bay ☀🚌 ⓘ Negril Chamber of Commerce, Vendors Plaza, West End Rd; www.negril.com

Perhaps the most popular of Jamaica's three main resort areas, Negril is split between its 7 miles (12 km) of picture-perfect white sand and the limestone cliffs that make up the island's extreme western tip. Both cliffs and beach are lined with hotels, restaurants, and the ever-busy bars that have helped to give the area its reputation for nightlife; visitors can dance in the sand to live reggae most nights of the week.

With its clear warm waters, sheltered by a reef and almost mirror calm, the beach is one of the Caribbean's best. However, the beauty of the place also means crowds of people, including vendors selling everything from hair braids to glass-bottom boat rides. For a quieter environment, it is best to head east along the sand toward Long Bay beach park, where the buildings thin out and the

hustle and bustles diminishes accordingly.

Ranged along pockmarked cliffs that sheer off into deep, crystal-clear waters studded with lovely reefs, the West End, south of downtown Negril, is a world away from the beach. It is quieter, though still home to some seriously upscale hotels, as well as more budget options. The swimming is fantastic, and many venues have stairs down the cliffs and ladders to get in and out – but it can be tricky when the water is choppy.

The West End also provides the perfect spot to watch the sun set, with bars offering live music, happy hour, and cliff-diving displays.

5

Great Morass and Royal Palm Reserve

🏠 Sheffield Rd, 2 miles (5 km) E of Negril 📞 876 364 7407 🚌 🕐 Times vary, call ahead

Running inland from Norman Manley Boulevard and

> ### HEDONISTIC NEGRIL
>
> First "discovered" in the 1970s, hippies descended on Negril to laze on the beaches in a ganja-wreathed haze. Many are still drawn here by Negril's reputation, which has been built around intemperance. Drugs (especially marijuana and magic mushrooms) remain part of the fabric, but these days the area's most bacchanalian aspect is its nightlife.

covering some 9 sq miles (24 sq km), the Great Morass is Jamaica's second-largest wetland. It can be accessed by bus or route taxi from Negril to Savanna-la-Mar, but it is a long walk away from the nearest stop. It is best to take a chartered taxi.

The Great Morass is a peaty, reed-covered expanse that provides a habitat to a number of rare animals and plants,

including the many trees around which the Royal Palm Reserve has been created. With wooden boardwalks that lead right out onto the morass, the air alive with the chirping of crickets, cicadas, frogs, and with every inch of surface covered in thick greenery, it is a great place for a walk. Also a good spot for bird-watching, the reserve has a couple of observation towers and more than 50 species of bird to look out for. Visitors can try their luck at fishing as well.

↑ A cascading waterfall near the intriguing dive site of Blue Hole Mineral Spring

Mayfield Falls

🏠 Glenbrook 🌐 original mayfieldfalls.com

Inland from the northwest coast, in the heart of the Dolphin Head Mountains, lies Mayfield Falls, where 21 cascades tumble along a river shaded by arching bamboo thickets. Change into swimwear, rent water shoes, and hire a guide at the base to wade upstream, scramble up the rushing cascades, and plunge into jade-colored pools. At the end of the tour, visitors are led back through pastures lined with fruit trees for lunch at a picturesque restaurant. The falls can be hard to find, but all the local taxi drivers know the way there, and tour companies offer excursions from Negril and Montego Bay.

Blue Hole Mineral Spring and Roaring River

🏠 6 miles (10 km) SE of Negril

The hinterland east of Negril is pocked with refreshing

← A lively beach bar in Negril, filling with partygoers just as the sun begins to set

"blue holes" and mineral springs. The most impressive is Blue Hole Mineral Spring, a turquoise pool encased within an exquisite karst grotto in the hills above Little Bay. Daredevils take the plunge from a cavernous opening in the ground, but a metal ladder is a safer option for entering the 35-ft (10-m) deep pool. Inside, it feels a little like being inside a giant lava lamp. There is also a hotel at the site, with a spectacular rooftop bar; the perfect spot for a post-swim drink. There is also plenty of entertainment for those not keen to enter the pool, since the staff and local divers often perform acrobatic jumps into the pool.

From the dusty market town and parish capital of Savanna-la-Mar, signposts lead visitors northeast to Roaring River Park, just outside the small community of Petersfield. Set in a former plantation, the park has a series of deep limestone caverns to explore.

However, the real draw is a nearby deep blue spring-water pool, overhung with greenery that makes it a magical place for a swim. It is best to take a guided tour to the site from Negril, since unofficial guides have been known to conduct tours in an unsafe manner.

DRINK

Collette's Bar
This colorful, no-frills downtown shack serves up ice-cold Red Stripe and good vibes, which draw locals and tourists alike.

🏠 Fire Station Rd, Negril
📞 876 429 3636

Rick's Café
The perfect place for kicking back and watching local cliff divers as Marley melodies fill the air. Afternoon pool parties (Thu & Sat) get particularly packed.

🏠 West End Rd, Negril
🌐 rickscafejamaica.com

Floyd's Pelican Bar
A 15-minute boat ride from shore, this quirky, Robinson Crusoe-esque thatched bar is perched atop a sandbar reef and makes the perfect day-trip destination.

🏠 12 miles (20 km) NW of Treasure Beach
📞 876 354 4218

↑ A relaxing beach bar at the edge of Doctor's Cave Beach, near Montego Bay

⑧ Montego Bay

 NW Coast 🚗🏖️🍴
ℹ️ Montego Bay Convention Centre; www.montego-bay-jamaica.com

Enclosed by a cradle of hills with stunning views of the western coastline, Montego Bay's lovely beaches are the main reason for its enduring popularity. A favorite stopover for cruise ships, and the destination for most international flights to Jamaica, it is a busy place, with most activity concentrated along the length of Gloucester Avenue, christened the Hip Strip for promotion purposes. The first point of interest along the Strip is **Walter Fletcher Beach** (formerly known as Aquasol). It is popular with locals and has a kids' play area, water-sports facilities, and tennis courts.

Past the tacky facades of the Margaritaville bar is the entrance to the famed white sand and crystal-clear water of Doctor's Cave Beach and Cornwall Beach.

Downtown Montego Bay provides a refreshing antidote to the glitz of Gloucester Avenue, with a couple of sights to look out for. Across the road at the end of the Strip is Fort Street, which threads past the chaotic Gully fruit and vegetable market to Sam Sharpe Square, named after one of Jamaica's national heroes *(see box)*. In the northwest corner, next to the cut-stone Cage built by the British as a lockup for runaway slaves, is a sculpture of Sam Sharpe preaching to his followers. Just around the corner, the **Montego Bay Cultural Centre** houses the National Museum West, which explores the nation's history, with an emphasis on Montego Bay. For an insight into the Rasta philosophy and lifestyle, check in at **Rastari Indigenous Village**, a living cultural center on the outskirts of town. Here rastafarians share their core values, and lead tours of the village and surrounding area.

Walter Fletcher Beach

♿🚹🍴 Gloucester Ave
📞 876 979 9447 Wed–Sun; hours vary

Montego Bay Cultural Centre

♿🍴🎫 Sam Sharpe Square 📞 876 971 3920
9am–5pm Tue–Sun

Rastari Indigenous Village

Fairfield Rd, 3 miles (5 km) E of downtown By appt 🌐 rastavillage.com

⑨ ♿🚫 Rocklands Bird Sanctuary

Rocklands Rd, Anchovy
📞 876 952 2009 🚌
10am–5pm daily

Just past the Lethe turnoff at Anchovy, Rocklands Bird Sanctuary offers bird-lovers one of Jamaica's most unforgettable experiences. The former home of the celebrated ornithologist Lisa Salmon (d. 2000), it is a favored spot for a multitude of birds that come here to feed each day. Buses from Montego Bay to Savanna-la-Mar run past

SAM SHARPE

The Christmas Rebellion of 1831 was perhaps the most significant slave uprising in Jamaica's history. The slave trade had been outlawed in 1807, but thousands of Africans were still working in the sugar estates, unaware of the legislation. Sam Sharpe, a house slave who had taught himself to read due to his position as deacon, learned of abolitionist activities in Britain, and preached that freedom was close. The news spread quickly, and by December 27, non-violent protests had developed into full rebellion. The British response was brutal, but the uprising was the first step to complete abolition in 1838.

the approach road, but it is a steep and difficult walk up to the sanctuary, so it is advisable to charter a taxi all the way from Montego Bay.

On arrival, visitors are given a feeder of sugar-water to entice the diners – mostly different kinds of humming-bird – to perch on people's hands to drink the water, the whirr of their wings vibrating musically in the air. Other species of bird can also be spotted here, including the greater Antillean bullfinch and the gorgeous black-throated blue warbler. A nature walk through thick vegetation is also included in the entry fee.

Animal Farm

📍 10 miles (16 km) SW of Montego Bay 📞 876 899 0040 🕐 10am-5pm daily

Located in the Montpelier Hills, Animal Farm & Nature Reserve is an eco-friendly farm. Spread over

6 acres (2.5 ha), the farm is primarily dedicated to aviculture – the breeding and rearing of birds – and has over 70 varieties of exotic bird, including the "Rasta Fowl", named after their distinctive plumage resembling Rastafarian dreadlocks. Animals on the farm include pigs, turtles, rabbits, sheep, guinea pigs, and a donkey.

The farm organizes bird-watching tours, which are led by skilled guides. Visitors can even hand-feed the birds in a large walk-in aviary. Hiking tours around the surrounding valley and bamboo rafting trips along the Great River are also offered.

The expansive grounds have a lovely herb garden, as well as a friendly petting zoo and a playground for children.

Rose Hall and Greenwood

🕐 9am-6pm daily
ℹ️ Rose Hall: 10 miles (16 km) E of Montego Bay, 876 953 2323, www.rosehall.com; Greenwood: 12 miles (19 km) E of Montego Bay, 435 Belgrade Ave; 876 953 1077, www.greenwoodgreathouse.com

East of Montego Bay, the era of plantation slavery comes to

the fore in the form of two palatial great houses that have been opened up as tourist attractions. Rose Hall and Greenwood are signposted from the main coastal high-way, and buses along that road pass the entrances to both.

Closest to Montego Bay is Rose Hall Great House, the 18th-century former home of the "White Witch" Annie Palmer. She came to Rose Hall as the wife of its owner, John Rose Palmer, and soon unleashed a reign of terror. Her wicked deeds are detailed by the tour guides. The supposedly haunted house has been slickly renovated in period style, with lavish furnishings and antiques. The tours start from the gift shop which has displays of old photographs.

Far more atmospheric, Greenwood Great House is also a more handsome structure, commanding amazing coastal views and filled with original fittings and curiosities. The house once belonged to relatives of the renowned British poet Elizabeth Barrett Browning. In addition to an extensive collection of Jamaican antiques, it houses a large and rare collection of musical instruments, as well as a library.

↓ The handsome facade of Rose Hall Great House, built in 1770

→
Swimmers enjoying the natural pools and swinging vines at YS Falls

HIDDEN GEM
Alligator Pond

Far from the madding tourist crowd, this south coast fishing hamlet is lined with colorful *pirogues* (traditional boats) and fishers selling their catch. On weekends, it gets lively with Kingstonians.

12
Treasure Beach

56 miles (90 km) S of Montego Bay 🚍🛈

In direct contrast to the glitz and concrete of the north coast, the string of peaceful fishing villages that make up the relaxed and laid-back Treasure Beach offer a more authentic island experience than the resorts. Tourism has developed sustainably here, with the community getting tangible benefits from the industry, both by being directly involved – most of the hotels and restaurants are owned by locals – and by way of initiatives such as the BREDS

foundation. A non-profit organization funded largely by visitor donations, BREDS has created an emergency medical response unit for the community and purchased an ambulance, as well as equipping schools with computers, and fishermen with radios, and much more.

Located between the sea and the arid flatlands that spread out below the Santa Cruz Mountains, Calabash Bay is the heart of the community. To the north, Frenchman's Bay offers great opportunities for swimming and bodysurfing, and the scenic beach is ideal for sunbathing, too. South of Calabash and Frenchman's bays is Great Bay, with another fine beach and a thriving fishing industry. Though the sand here is brown rather than white, the waters are clear and extremely clean, and the odd wave makes a refreshing change to the millpond-like northern shore.

It is easy to while away an entire vacation dividing time between the beaches, but it is well worth arranging a boat trip along the coast to the unique Floyd's Pelican Bar *(p149)*. Built on stilts stuck into a sandspit offshore of Parottee Point near Black River, this ramshackle thatch-roofed bar is a one-of-a-kind experience. Guests can paddle around the shallows, snorkel in the surrounding waters, or just sit in the bar and have a meal or a beer, enjoying the sunset, which is especially atmospheric here.

13
Black River

46 miles (73 km) S of Montego Bay 🚍🛈

Black River, the weather-beaten capital of St. Elizabeth, may be the largest town in the parish but that is not saying much, given the region's bucolic feel. It is certainly not a tourist hot spot, though there are a few interesting buildings along the waterfront. Most notable among these is the elaborate Invercauld House, built in 1894 when Black River was one of the island's main ports.

The main reason people come here, though, is to take a boat safari up the Black River

↑ Diners lingering at a charming open-air restaurant in Treasure Beach

Great Morass, a wetland populated by Jamaican crocodiles. Boats leave from the depot at the main town bridge, and meander upstream, passing thick clumps of twisted mangrove that provide a habitat for many bird and marine species. The crocodiles are used to visitors, and many of them have been named by the boat captains. **Black River Safari** offers crocodile viewing trips from Black River.

Black River Safari
 ⌂ 1 Crane Rd ☎ 876 965 2513 ⏰ 9am–4pm Mon–Sat

⑭
St. Elizabeth
⌂ 60 miles (100 km) S of Montego Bay

Characterized by bauxite-rich red earth and rolling cattle pastures, St. Elizabeth is one of Jamaica's most beautiful parishes, with a few places worth visiting by way of a driving tour from Treasure Beach.

Heading north from Black River, the quaint little village of Middle Quarters reveals itself through a crowd of women selling bags of the spicy pepper shrimp that the area is known for. Just past here, the signposted road to the left leads toward YS, a huge

cattle and horse farm that is also home to the lovely **YS Falls**, surrounded by lush pastures and jungle-covered hills. Reached via a short tractor-trailer ride, the falls are an absolute delight. Several end in deep pools that are great for swimming, but some are too rocky. There is a spring-water swimming pool near the snack shop, which is ideal for kids. When water levels allow, tubing along the river is a lot of fun, and there are three zip lines that allow visitors to whoosh overhead.

Beyond YS, the road gets even narrower. Past the tiny community of Maggotty, is the **Appleton Estate**, which is surrounded by endless fields of sugar cane. Appleton is the oldest producer of rum in Jamaica; the estate dates back to 1655 although distilling began only in 1749. The tour inside the factory complex takes guests through the whole production process, from the selection of the sugar cane to the bottling of the rum, and ends with a chance to sample some of its excellent brands.

YS Falls
⊛⊛🍴🛈 ⌂ 3 miles (5 km) N of Middle Quarters
⏰ 9:30am–3:30pm Tue–Sun
🌐 ysfalls.com

Appleton Estate
⊛⊛😋🛈 ⌂ 8 miles (13 km) NE of Middle Quarters
⏰ 9am–4pm Mon–Sat
🌐 appletonestate.com

EAT

Pork Pit
This open-air restaurant is renowned for its finger-lickin' jerk pork, chicken, and fish, served with all the trimmings.

⌂ 27 Gloucester Ave, Montego Bay
☎ 876 940 3008

 ⑤⑤⑤

Niah's Patties
The go-to spot for delicious Jamaican patties. An array of fillings are on offer, from spiced potato to lobster.

⌂ West End Rd, Negril
☎ 876 399 6823

 ⑤⑤⑤

Jakes Country Cuisine
There is vibrant decor, a fun ambience, and stellar Jamaican classics and fusion fare at this hip hotel restaurant.

⌂ Jakes Hotel, Treasure Beach 🌐 jakeshotel.com

 ⑤⑤⑤

EXPERIENCE Jamaica

15

Mandeville

🏔 65 miles (104 km) SE of Montego Bay 🚌

The capital of Manchester, Mandeville is one of Jamaica's most beautiful spots, set among hills some 2,000 ft (600 m) above sea level. It was established by the Duke of Manchester – once governor of Jamaica – and named for his son, the Viscount of Mandeville, in 1816. The town showcases Jamaican architecture – a classic Georgian style using local materials. The Mandeville Court House, built in 1817, has a portico supported by Doric columns; also noteworthy are the Manchester Parish Church, the Mandeville Jail and Workhouse, and the Mandeville Hotel.

16

Port Antonio

🏔 61 miles (98 km) NE of Kingston 🚌🚇

A quiet little town that grew around its deep twin harbors,

Port Antonio owes its origins as a tourist spot to actor Errol Flynn (1909–59). Having run aground here aboard his private yacht, Flynn took a liking to the Portland area, and ended up buying Navy Island just off-shore, and a hotel that used to stand on the Titchfield Peninsula – the western tip of Port Antonio's East harbor. By the 1950s, he was well known for inviting a string of celebrities, including Bette Davis and Ginger Rogers, to Jamaica to stay and go rafting on the Rio Grande – an excursion that can still be undertaken today.

Although little remains to be seen of the Flynn legacy today, the area does retain a sense of faded glamor, especially in the palatial resorts east of town. Port Antonio still has a certain shabby charm, with a few colonial-era buildings that feature typical overhanging verandas along its main street. There is a bustling fruit and vegetable market and the Port Antonio Court House, housed in a grand old Georgian building.

TOP 3 RIVER TRIPS IN JAMAICA

Martha Brae Rafting
An expert captain poles you down the jade Martha Brae river (*jamaicarafting.com*).

White River Tubing
This high-adrenaline tubing trip includes seven mini rapids (*chukka.com*).

Rio Grande Rafting
Begin at Berridale for a lazy and romantic three-hour raft ride, which ends at Rafters Rest (*876 993 5778*).

Facing Navy Island is the Port Antonio Marina, now known as the Errol Flynn Marina. The marina offers world-class facilities, including waterfront paths for promenading, a designated helicopter landing area, manicured lawns, a slip of white-sand beach, and an upscale restaurant.

Unfortunately, Navy Island is officially closed to visitors, though local fishermen still take people to its lovely secluded beaches for a swim and to snorkel.

⓱
Hellshire

📍 10 miles (16 km) SW of
New Kingston 🚌

On the other side of the harbor
from Kingston, and accessible
via the toll highway to the
huge dormitory suburb of
Portmore, the Hellshire Hills
are an arid, cactus-strewn
expanse jutting down into
the Caribbean Sea. The main
reason people visit is for a
swim at **Fort Clarence Beach**
– a stretch of white sand that
is popular with Kingstonians –
or to have a plate of fried fish
at the neighboring village of
Hellshire, known island-wide
for its outstandingly good
seafood. Here, ramshackle
restaurants sell fried fish with
a vinegary pepper sauce and
bammy or cornbread fritters.
It is a thoroughly Jamaican
scene at weekends, when huge
speakers blast out reggae and
local families hit the beach.

Past Hellshire, the **Two
Sisters Caves** are a series of
deep caverns in the limestone
made accessible by wooden
walkways and stairs. Guides

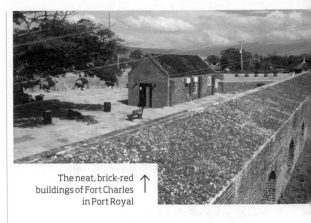

↑ The neat, brick-red
buildings of Fort Charles
in Port Royal

explain the caves' history and
point out an pre-Colombian
petroglyph on one of the
cave walls.

Fort Clarence Beach
🏄 🍴 🚻 📍 Main Rd, Hellshire
📞 876 364 3628 🕙 10am-6pm
Mon-Fri, 9am-6pm Sat & Sun

Two Sisters Caves
🏄 📍 Main Rd, Hellshire
📞 876 656 8031 🕙 Group
tours only, call ahead

⓲
Port Royal

📍 5 miles (8 km) SW of New
Kingston 🚌

Port Royal is a series of small
cays that joined together to
form a breakwater between
Kingston's harbor and the
open ocean. This atmospheric
fishing village, with a colorful
past of piracy and naval might,
was scarred by a catastrophic
natural disaster. A thriving
town under the English, it
suffered a massive earthquake
in 1692 that destroyed most
of the place and killed thousands of people, effectively
ending its importance.

Port Royal still holds several
of the original English-built
fortifications, the largest of
which is **Fort Charles**, the first
of five bastions built here from
bricks that had served as
ballast on English ships. The

Maritime Museum in the courtyard has a small but intriguing
collection of artifacts from the
ruins of the original town.
Back toward the main square,
you can visit St. Peter's Church
and the tomb of Lewis Galdy,
who was swallowed by the
earth during the earthquake,
and miraculously regurgitated
seconds later. Alternatively,
take a boat to Lime Cay, a tiny
island with white sands and
clear waters.

Fort Charles
🏛 🕙 📞 876 967 8438
🕙 9am-5pm daily 🚫 Good
Friday & Dec 25

> **PIRATES OF
> PORT ROYAL**
>
> When the English took
> Jamaica from Spain in
> 1655, Nelson himself
> employed pirates to
> help defend the island.
> The pirates - referred to
> as privateers - began
> eagerly plundering
> treasure-laden Spanish
> ships sailing to their
> New World colonies.
> These profitable days
> ended when England
> signed a peace treaty
> with Spain in 1670.
> Attempts were made
> to persuade privateers
> into a life of peace, and
> those who refused were
> hunted and often killed.

↑ A rafter poling his way
along the Rio Grande in
Port Antonio

Locals selling paintings and other colorful souvenirs at Long Bay

small reef, ideal for snorkeling; equipment can be rented at the beach.

This lovely place is as popular with locals as it is with visitors. However, the regulars are in an ongoing dispute with the government, whose redevelopment plans could irrevocably alter the character of Winnifred Beach.

Long Bay

🏠 12 miles (19 km) E of Port Antonio 🚌

The wide beach of Long Bay, a glorious stretch of yellow sand and crashing waves, has only a few hotels and restaurants overlooking the water. Tourism has developed over the years with young Europeans coming here to relax and go surfing. Currents can be dangerous, so take local guidance before swimming. It is usually safe though, and the waves make an invigorating change to most of Jamaica's beaches. This windswept shore has also become popular in recent years for kiteboarding, thanks to its consistent swells and dependable trade wind. Visitors can negotiate sea trips with the local fishermen who draw their small craft up onto the sands.

PICTURE PERFECT
Turtle Bay

With its crashing waves, crystal tidepools, and sea stacks rising from the ocean like church spires, this rocky shore is a landscape photographer's dream. The east-facing beach is perfect at sunrise.

Winnifred Beach

🏠 5 miles (8 km) E of Port Antonio at Fairy Hill

Laid-back Winnifred Beach is a rarity in Jamaica. This spectacular white-sand cove has still not fallen victim to development and thus retains its pristine quality.

People can walk down to the beach from the main road, just opposite the Jamaica Crest Resort. The only buildings breaking the view are the odd shacks selling food and drink alongside the basic changing facilities. There is a

Frenchman's Cove and the Blue Lagoon

🏠 5 miles (8 km) E of Port Antonio 🌐 frenchmanscove.com

The coastline east of Port Antonio (p154) is one of the most beautiful in the country. Watered by frequent rain showers that bounce off the Blue Mountains, the jungle-like tangle of ferns, flowers, and palms cascade down the inland side of the coast road. The turquoise waters offshore are spectacular, with the odd palm-covered island just adding to the perfection. Local hoteliers have long tried to capitalize on the Portland area's natural attractions by developing it as a tourist resort. However, the lack of

> **The location was also made famous by the 1980 movie _The Blue Lagoon_, starring Brooke Shields and Christopher Atkins.**

decent roads means it is still relatively unspoiled, with just a handful of hotels and a sprinkling of guesthouses.

Just a short distance from Port Antonio, a weather-beaten sign marks the entrance to Frenchman's Cove, perhaps the most beautiful of Jamaica's beaches. It is a perfect horseshoe of sand enclosed by jungle-clad hills and with a cool, sandy floored river running into the bay beneath Frenchman's Cove Resort.

A short way farther east along the main road, signposts indicate the turnoff for the Blue Lagoon. At this almost circular pool of unknown depth, chilly springwater mixes with the warm seawater to amazing effect, making the pretty lagoon an unforgettable place to swim and snorkel. The location was also made famous by the 1980 movie _The Blue Lagoon_, starring Brooke Shields and Christopher Atkins. Visitors are

advised to be wary of the local "guides" who may ask for unnecessary entrance fees. One way to visit is on a bamboo raft trip from Frenchman's Cove.

Reach Falls

🏠 6 miles (9 km) SW of Long Bay 🚌 📞 876 993 6606
🕗 8:30am–4:30pm Wed-Sun

Beyond Long Bay, the coast road sweeps spectacularly below cliffs and around the calm reaches of Manchioneal Bay before turning inland again. A road to the right winds upward through the rainforest to the beautiful Reach Falls that cascade from Drivers River. The green pools at the bottom of the fall are at least 4-ft (1.2-m) deep, with crystal-clear water and pebbled floor.

The surrounding area has been developed by the government and now has changing facilities, a visitors' center, and food outlets – although the falls have lost a little of their unspoiled quality as a result. Still, the deep main pool is beautiful and visitors can follow the river upstream to seek out underground caves and swimming spots.

↑ Swimmers enjoying the startlingly blue waters of Frenchman's Cove

EXPERIENCE Jamaica

㉓

Firefly

📍 43 miles (70 km) NW of Kingston 🚌 🕐 9am–5pm Mon-Thu & Sat 🌐 firefly-jamaica.com

Sitting pretty above the village of Port Maria, Firefly was the Jamaican home of the well-known English playwright, actor, and songwriter Noël Coward (1899–1973) and his partner, Graham Payn (1918–2005), who both lived here until Coward's death. The 1950s house – which Coward bought for $150 as a retreat from his first Jamaican home Blue Harbour, which had become overrun with house-guests – has been left as it was. Photographs on the walls show the famous visitors to his residence, from Sophia Loren and Audrey Hepburn to Queen Elizabeth II. Perhaps best known for such quintes-sentially English ditties as "Mad Dogs and Englishmen," Coward also wrote many plays, some of them in this house. However, a key reason that visitors from across the world still flock to the site is the fabulous view that Firefly affords of the coastline below, with verdant Cabarita Island in the foreground.

←
A bronze sculpture of Noël Coward by Angela Conner, which sits at the playwright's Firefly residence

㉔

Dunn's River Falls

📍 2 miles (3 km) W of Ocho Rios 🕐 8:30am–4pm daily 🌐 dunnsriverfallsja.com

Jamaica's most well-known natural feature and definitely one of its top tourist attrac-tions, Dunn's River Falls is as iconic as rum, Rastas, and reefers. This magnificent cascade comprises dozens of cataracts tumbling through a tree-shaded vale to the sea. The wedding-cake tiers are formed by travertine (calcium carbonate) deposited as the water flows from one turquoise pool to another. The setting is made more attractive by a natural frame of ferns, ginger lilies, and bamboos, and by light filtering through the forest canopy.

Linking hands to clamber up the falls in a daisy-chain led by experienced guides is exhilarating despite the hordes of other visitors, especially on cruise ship days. Water shoes are mandatory, and are avail-able for rent at the entrance.

While the surrounding land has undergone extensive development, the falls them-selves remain spectacular, as does the white-sand beach at their base. There is also a lively reef offshore and it is possible to rent snorkel gear.

A short distance east, opposite Reynold's Pier, a road leads uphill to **Mystic Mountain**. This environ-mentally-friendly adventure theme park is a must for thrill-seekers, with its zipline, rain-forest chairlift through lush greenery, and bobsled ride.

Mystic Mountain
🎢 🍴 🛍 🕐 9am–5pm daily 🌐 rainforestadventure.com

↑
Visitors tackling the thrilling uphill climb at Dunn's River Falls

㉕

Ocho Rios

📍 54 miles (86 km) NW of Kingston ✈ 🚌 ⛴ ℹ TPDCO Information Office, Ocean Village Plaza, Main St; www.ochorios.com

Very much on the beaten path, Ocho Rios (or Ochi as it is often known) has grown up around the tourist industry, and these days its principal sources of income are the massive cruise ships that overshadow the harbor most days of the week. Built around a wide bay with a sweeping arc of hotel-lined beach, Ocho Rios is well-equipped to meet the limited time constraints of cruise passengers, with several attractions that can easily be seen in half a day. Buses and minibuses arrive and depart at the terminal on Main Street, and route taxis cover all the main local roads.

The port town's chief attraction is Island Village, at the far west end of Main Street. This entertainment complex – a slick collection of shops, restaurants, and bars with a private beach (open to

patrons) – also has its own cinema. Another highlight here is **Margaritaville**, a Caribbean-themed restaurant and bar that provides family-friendly fun during the day; there is a rooftop hot tub, a two-story waterslide, and a freshwater pool with a swim-up bar. After dark, Margaritaville transforms into a nightclub with a sophisticated Afro-Cuban vibe.

Ocho Rios Bay Beach, also known as Turtle Beach, is worth a visit to laze on the pristine, regularly raked white sands. It also offers changing facilities, lifeguards, and watersports on-site. Other than the beach, the area's main attractions overlook the town at Murphy Hill, where the restful **Shaw Park Botanical Gardens** sit some 550 ft (167 m) above sea level. The gardens have beautiful views of the town, and are home to rare plants and trees, as well as a pretty waterfall. The gardens are tiered, which allows a variety of plants that thrive at different altitudes to grow here.

Just down the road is **Konoko Falls and Park** (for-merly named Coyaba River Garden), which offers equally striking views. It is more compact than the Shaw Park Botanical Gardens, with paths threading past pools and streams. The park also has a small zoo, mostly given over to aviaries that house a variety of birds endemic to Jamaica, and a museum that is dedicated to local history. Out in the garden, there is a waterfall in which visitors can take a quick, refreshing splash.

Margaritaville
◉◉ ⌂Island Village ⓦmargaritavillecaribbean.com

Ocho Rios Bay Beach
◉◉◉ ⌂Main St ☎876 656 8031 ◷8:30am–4pm daily

Shaw Park Botanical Gardens
◉◉ ⌂Shaw Park Rd ☎876 974 2723 ◷8am–4pm daily

Konoko Falls and Park
◉◉◉ ⌂Shaw Park Rd ◷8am–4:30pm daily ⓦkonokofalls.com

EAT

Evita's
Located in an utterly charming 1860s manse high above Ochi, Evita's serves up fine Italian and Caribbean fusion fare, paired with unbeatable views. It's been a local favorite for over 30 years, and first-time visitors will quickly see why.

⌂Eden Bower Rd, Ocho Rios ⓦevitas jamaica.com

___

Miss T's Kitchen
Head here for a celebration of authentic Jamaican culture and cooking, run by self-taught chef Miss T. Expect such classics as oxtail stew, rundown, and curried goat, dished up in an outrageously colorful restaurant with a lush garden.

⌂65 Main St, Ocho Rios ⓦmisstskitchen.com

$$$

___

Mille Fleurs
Reservations are a must at this *prix fixe* Caribbean fusion delight, which offers alfresco candlelit dining in the hills high above Port Antonio. The food is local and achingly fresh – with vegetables sourced where possible from the hotel's own garden – and the terrace views are breathtaking.

⌂Hotel Mockingbird Hill, Port Antonio ⓦhotelmockingbird hill.com

26

Runaway and Discovery Bays

📍 25 miles (40 km) W of Ocho Rios 🚌

Unlike Ocho Rios (p158) or Montego Bay (p150), the neighboring towns of Runaway Bay and Discovery Bay are made up of a string of huge all-inclusive resorts that line the coast, interspersed with a few roadside restaurants and a couple of good beaches.

Runaway Bay has the Cardiff Hall Public Beach, a handsome strip of white sand that is popular with the locals. There is no entry fee, and no facilities to speak of except for a small bar and a snack shop. Located on Discovery Bay is the **Puerto Seco Beach**, which has a strip of pristine white sand and all expected facilities, as well as a waterpark.

Puerto Seco Beach

 📍 Main Rd, Discovery Bay 🕒 9am–5pm daily

27

Cranbrook Flower Forest

📍 18 miles (29 km) W of Ocho Rios 📞 876 770 8071 🚌 🕒 9am–5pm daily

The perfect antidote to busy Ocho Rios, the Cranbrook Flower Forest offers 0.2 sq miles (0.5 sq km) of beautifully landscaped gardens and a thriving forest, all threaded with paths. Shaded by palms and planted with all kinds of beautiful tropical blooms, from heliconias, philodendrons, birds of paradise, hibiscus, and begonias to an amazing display of orchids, the flower gardens are exquisite.

The other highlight is the River Head Adventure Tour, which begins at the entrance lawns. It is a delightful walk through the unspoiled tropical forest along the bank of the Little River. The trail leads up to where the river rises from a spring to form a 20-ft- (6-m-) wide intensely blue natural pool.

Elsewhere on-site, visitors can fish for tilapia; picnic on the lawns surrounding the central building (a restored sugar mill); go bird-watching; or take part in an adrenaline-filled canopy tour.

The lush grounds make this a popular place for weddings and it is possible to rent just the location or have Cranbrook make all the arrangements. There is also a small gift and snack shop near the entrance.

28

Green Grotto Caves

 22 miles (35 km) W of Ocho Rios   9am–4pm daily W greengrotto cavesja.com

On the main road between the Runaway and Discovery Bays, Green Grotto Caves is an extensive network of limestone caverns with a subterranean lake and plenty of impressive stalactites and stalagmites. Guided tours take visitors through the history of the caves, which were used by indigenous peoples as a place of worship, and later as a hideout by Spanish troops, pirates, and slaves.

29

Bob Marley Centre & Mausoleum

25 miles (40 km) SW of Ocho Rios 876 843 0498 9am–4pm daily

High in the St. Ann hills amid a gorgeous landscape of rich red earth and grassy cattle pastures, the Bob Marley Centre & Mausoleum is located in the hamlet of Nine Mile, where Marley was born in February 1945. He spent his early childhood here before moving to Kingston at the age of 13. Encircled by a high fence and with Rasta red, gold, and green flags flapping in the wind, the compound is centered around the tiny wooden shack where the Marleys lived when Bob was aged between 6 and 13 years.

The mausoleum itself is a simple whitewashed building that holds Marley's marble tomb. Incense burns and the stained-glass windows filter colors on to the stone, creating

A green mineral spring, winding through Cranbrook Flower Forest

↑ Reggae musicians entertaining visitors at the Bob Marley Centre & Mausoleum

a moving atmosphere. Also located on the property is a restaurant as well as a gift shop which sells CDs and various Marley memorabilia. There is also a Rastafarian-colored "meditation stone" where Marley used to rest his head while contemplating.

Chukka Adventures takes visitors to the mausoleum either in a jeep or on an old-time country bus. Each year on February 6, the anniversary of Marley's birth, the village comes alive with a massive concert as part of a week-long tribute to Jamaica's best-known musician, who remains the biggest reggae star in the world.

30

Oracabessa

60 miles (95 km) NW of Kingston W oracabessa. com

A nondescript little place, Oracabessa was the center of banana export until the 1900s. Today, however, the town's main claim to fame is that it drew the attention of author Ian Fleming, who built a house and wrote most of his James Bond novels here. It may seem like an unlikely setting for a fictional world of

Did You Know?

Ian Fleming used Jamaica as the setting for two of his 007 novels – *Doctor No* and *The Man with the Golden Gun.*

spies, villains, and fantastical gadgets, but Fleming fell in love with Jamaica during a visit in 1943. Following in the footsteps of his friend, Noël Coward, who built two houses just down the coast *(p158)*, Fleming created Goldeneye as a retreat from the bleak English winter.

Today, the house is part of the exclusive Goldeneye Hotel *(p157)* and is closed to non-guests. However, the 007 connection remains with the **James Bond Beach**, just down the coast from Goldeneye. It was opened in the mid-1990s by Jamaican-born impresario Chris Blackwell, who produced most of Bob Marley's albums and owns 0.1 sq miles (0.3 sq km) of Oracabessa beachfront. There are bathrooms, changing rooms, and watersports on site.

James Bond Beach
Old Wharf Rd
9am–6pm Tue–Sun

PRACTICAL
INFORMATION

Here you will find all the essential advice and information you will need before and during your stay in Jamaica.

AT A GLANCE

CURRENCY
Jamaican dollar
(J$)

TIME ZONE
Eastern Standard Time, 5 hours behind GMT. It does not observe daylight savings

LANGUAGE
English, but everyone also speaks the patois version, heavily accented and sprinkled with local slang

ELECTRICITY SUPPLY
The electric current is 110 volt but some hotels may have 220 volt, 60 cycles. Plug sockets usually take two flat prongs

EMERGENCY NUMBERS

AMBULANCE & FIRE SERVICE	POLICE
110	**119**

TAP WATER
Water purity is unreliable so, to be safe, drink bottled water

When To Go

Jamaica, like much of the Caribbean, is at its best from mid-December through mid-April, when there is less rainfall and the heat is tempered by cooling trade winds. June through November is hurricane season, with the threat reaching its peak in September. The summer months, particularly July and August, can get uncomfortably hot. Rates tend to be cheaper at these times.

Getting There

Jamaica is well served by direct charter and scheduled flights from Europe, the US and Canada, which land at Donald Sangster International Airport in Montego Bay, or Norman Manley International Airport in Kingston. Caribbean Airlines and Fly Jamaica fly from several US and Canadian cities to Kingston and Montego Bay, and American Airlines, Delta, JetBlue, Spirit Airlines and United Airlines also offer direct services from the US. There are direct flights from Toronto and other Canadian cities with WestJet, Caribbean Airlines, Sunwing, and Air Canada. From the UK, British Airways and Caribbean Airlines fly to both Kingston and Montego Bay, as do several charter operators.

Personal Security

The island is not altogether crime-free and there are incidents of drug-related violence especially in Kingston. It is best to avoid the town during any tension. Keep to the main streets and avoid lonely areas. Do not walk alone late at night in the cities or along beaches. Women travelers can expect to receive very graphic and forward comments; these tend to be directed at all women in Jamaica.

Health

Jamaica is generally safe health-wise. Visitors may bring their own prescription medicines. No vaccinations are required to enter the island unless visitors have been to an affected area.

Passports and Visas

Citizens of the European Union, the US, Canada, Australia, New Zealand, Japan, Israel, South Africa, South Korea, and Mexico have no visa requirements for a stay of less than three or six months depending on the country of origin. All visitors need a valid passport and an onward ticket. Citizens of other countries may require a visa, which can often be obtained on arrival in Jamaica with production of a valid onward ticket.

LGBT+ Safety

Jamaica , generally considered the most violently homophobic nation in the Caribbean, has become slightly more liberal towards the LGBT+ community in recent years. However, sexual relations between males (but not women) remains illegal, and violent acts against LGBT+ individuals are frequent in Jamaica's stereotypical macho culture, where dancehall lyrics are often explicitly homophobic. Displays of affection between same-sex couples should be avoided.

Money

The local currency is the Jamaican dollar (J$), with notes available in the denomination of J$1,000, J$500, J$100, and J$50. Bureaux de change are widespread in the resorts, generally offering better rates than the banks. There are ATMs at all banks and also scattered around the big resorts; in the latter, some dispense US dollars rather than local currency.

Cell Phones and Wi-Fi

Visitors bringing their own cell phones should check with their service providers to determine if they will work in Jamaica. Most international cell phones will work, but you may incur hefty roaming charges with your carrier. Local pay-as-you-go SIM cards are widely available from supermarkets and convenience shops, either from Digicel or FLOW, the two main cell-phone operators in the country.

Most hotels have Internet service; many have Wi-Fi. Internet access tends to be restricted in rural areas.

Getting Around

The best option for getting around the island is to hire a car or a local driver. If you're thinking of hiring a car, there are outlets in all the resorts. AVIS and Island Car Rental are the major players. In terms of public transportation, with the exception of Kingston, where city buses are government-run and quite efficient, all buses (usually minibuses) are owned and run by private individuals and tend to be chaotic with no set schedules. Routes are painted on the front or the side of the bus. Knutsford Express offers a regular bus service from Kingston to Montego Bay, Negril, and Ocho Rios. Route taxis running set routes are great for short trips. Taxis are freely available in all the resorts; the national association of drivers is JUTA.

Jamaica's tour companies range from one-man shows to huge outfits with fleets of buses that ferry visitors between the island's most popular attractions. There are plenty of outfits in the middle of these two extremes. Some of the renowned ones are **Barrett Adventures**, **Caribic Vacations**, **Sun Venture Tours Jamaica**, and **Treasure Tours**.

Barrett Adventures
w barrettadventures.com
Caribic Vacations
w caribicvacations.com
Sun Venture Tours Jamaica
w sunventuretours.com
Treasure Tours
w treasuretoursjamaica.com

Visitor Information

The **Jamaica Tourist Board** has offices in Montego Bay and Kingston, as well as booths at cruise ship ports and at the airports. Their website also provides detailed information.
Jamaica Tourist Board
w visitjamaica.com

DOMINICAN REPUBLIC

Occupying the eastern two-thirds of the island of Hispaniola, the Dominican Republic is the Caribbean's second-biggest country. The capital, Santo Domingo, is a large, modern metropolis where almost a third of the country's 10 million inhabitants reside, with the oldest colonial city in the Americas at its core.

The country's history pre-dates Columbian times, when the Taíno people adorned caverns with art that is still visible today. In 1492, Columbus landed on Hispaniola and Europe's first permanent colonial settlement was established at La Isabela a year later, marking the start of Spanish rule. Subsequent centuries saw the arrival of slavery; uprisings; battles between the Spanish, French, British, and also with neighboring Haiti. The country established its independence in 1844, but underwent U.S. occupation from 1916 to 1924, then decades of authoritarian rule under Rafael Trujillo. The republic now has a democratic government.

The culture of the Dominican Republic reflects its ethnically diverse population. Spanish is the official language. Dominicans swing to the fast-paced *merengue* and sensual *bachata*, and although it is a Catholic nation, many people worship Taíno/African spirits. Add to the mix the national passion of baseball, introduced here in the late 19th century by Cuban immigrants.

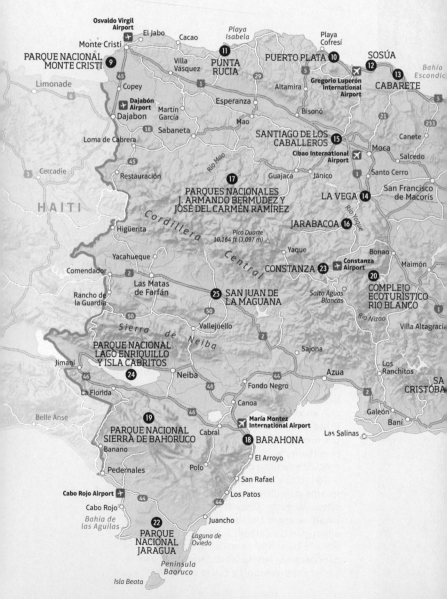

DOMINICAN REPUBLIC

Must Sees
1. Santo Domingo

Experience More
2. La Romana
3. Parque Nacional los Haitises
4. Parque Nacional Cotubanamá and Isla Saona
5. Punta Cana and East Coast
6. Playa Bayahibe
7. Boca Chica
8. Peninsula de Samaná
9. Parque Nacional Monte Cristi
10. Puerto Plata
11. Punta Rucia
12. Sosúa
13. Cabarete
14. La Vega
15. Santiago de los Caballeros
16. Jarabacoa
17. Parques Nacionales J. Armando Bermudez y Jose del Carmen Ramirez
18. Barahona
19. Parque Nacional Sierra de Bahoruco
20. Complejo Ecoturistico Rio Blanco
21. San Cristóbal
22. Parque Nacional Jaragua
23. Constanza
24. Parque Nacional Lago Enriquillo y Isla Cabritos
25. San Juan de la Maguana

↑ Visitors admiring the magnificent buildings of Fortaleza Ozama

❶

SANTO DOMINGO

🏠 S coast of Dominican Republic 🚕🚌🚐 ℹ️ Plaza Colón, Calle Isabel la Católica 103; 809 686 3858.

Santo Domingo's main sites are concentrated in the Zona Colonial, the historic heart of the city. This once-walled enclave of cobbled streets and leafy plazas features some of the oldest colonial buildings in the Western Hemisphere. Calle Las Damas echoes to the bootsteps of the first Spanish *conquistadores*, who set sail from here to conquer Latin America. Today, the district bustles with life, while beyond the colonial core a quiltwork of districts radiates inland.

❶

Fortaleza Ozama

🏠 Calle Las Damas 📞 809 686 0222 🕐 9am-5pm Tue-Sun

Overlooking the mouth of the Río Ozama, which bisects the Dominican Republic's capital city, this fortress was begun in 1502 and is the oldest colonial military edifice in the Americas. At its heart, the Torre del Homenaje (Tower of Homage) stands tall over a surrounding green swath. Originally a watch-tower, Fortaleza Ozama later served as a prison. Interior tunnels and dungeons, where many of the prisoners were held, can be explored during a tour of the site. Rusting cannons stand atop the river-front wall and armaments are displayed in the esplanade, pinned by a statue of the renowned Spanish military commander Gonzalo Fernández de Oviedo, who died in 1557.

❷

Parque Colón

🏠 Calle El Conde & Calle Arzobispo Meriño

Named for Christopher Columbus, whose statue dominates the square, this wide, tree-shaded plaza is a center for social life. Looming over the southern half is the grandiose Catedral Primada de América. The park is also surrounded by colonial and 19th-century buildings.

One block south, the **Museo de Larimar** has exhibits on larimar, a semi-precious blue stone that is mined solely in the Dominican Republic. On the plaza's northwest corner, Antiguo Palacio Consistorial, built in Neo-Classical style, is the former town hall.

🔍 HIDDEN GEM
Mercado Modelo

Few venues in Santo Domingo offer such an off-beat experience as this town's main market. Forsake the tourist souvenirs section and seek out *botánicas* (herbalist stores) in the northwest corner.

Nearby, Plazoleta Padre Billini is named after a 19th-century priest who founded a hospital for the poor. It is the setting for the Museo de la Familia Dominicana del Siglo XIX, which is furnished to replicate a typical middle-class 19th-century home. Visitors can also stop by at many souvenir and cigar shops, located north of the park.

Museo de Larimar
Calle Isabella Católica 54 809 689 6605 9am-6pm Mon-Sat, 9am-3pm Sun

---

3

Plaza España

Calle Isabel La Católica & Calle La Atarazana

This broad, virtually treeless plaza is the setting for two pre-eminent museums. The **Museo de las Casas Reales**, in the Renaissance-style former chamber of the Royal Court, showcases colonial artifacts, from antique weaponry and suits of armor to exhibits on Columbus's voyages. A massive Reloj del Sol (sundial) stands outside the entrance.

Once the home of Christopher Columbus's son Diego, a two-story Mudéjar-style building that dates from 1517 has been magnificently restored to house the **Museo Alcázar de Colón**. It re-creates the Columbus household with many original pieces, such as silverware and mahogany furniture, that once belonged to the family. At night, the plaza comes alive as its many bars and restaurants fill up.

Located two blocks west, the ruins of the 16th-century Monasterio de San Francisco form a backdrop for occasional concerts. Nearby, the **Museo Mundo de Ambar** displays splendid examples of the semi-precious gem, amber.

Museo de las Casas Reales
Calle Las Damas cnr Calle Mercedes 809 682 4202 9am-5pm Tue-Sun

Museo Alcázar de Colón
Plaza de España 809 682 4750 9am-5pm Tue-Sat, 9am-4pm Sun

Museo Mundo de Ambar
Calle Arzobispo Meriño 452 9am-6pm Mon-Sat, 9am-1pm Sun amberworldmuseum.com

STAY

Boutique Hotel Palacio
Located in the colonial district, this 18th-century venue offers modern conveniences.
Calle Duarte 106
hotel-palacio.com
$$$

Casas del XVI
Blissful comforts await in these elegantly furnished townhouses.
Calle Padre Billini 252
casasdelxvi.net
$$$

Hostal Nicolas de Ovando
An atmospheric hotel, built around the 16th-century home of a *conquistador*.
Calle Las Damas
hodelpanicolasdeovando.com
$$$

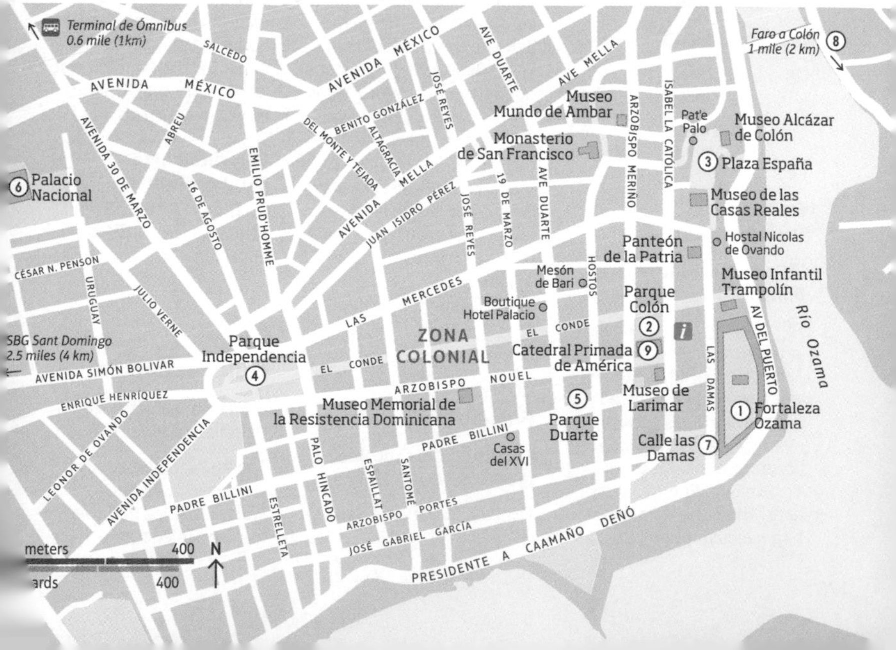

EAT

Pat'e Palo

This lively, open-air brasserie serves creative and delicious fare, with dishes including risotto in squid ink and tuna carpaccio.

🏠 Calle Atarazanas 25
🌐 patepalo.com

$$$

Mesón de Bari

Loved by neighborhood bohemians and festooned with local artworks, this colorful joint is renowned for its *cangrejo guisado* (crab stew).

🏠 Calle Hostos 302
📞 (809) 689 5546

$$$

SBG Sant Domingo

Chic and airy, SBG (formerly Sophia's) draws sophisticates for eclectic international dishes that span churrasco to sushi.

🏠 Calle Paseo de los Locutores
🌐 sbggroup.com.do

$$$

↑ The colorful facade of Galería de Arte Cándido Bidó, near the Palacio Nacional

---

Parque Independencia

🏠 Calle Palo Hincado & Av. Bolívar

This bustling plaza is located at the western end of the Zona Colonial. It has beautiful landscaped lawns, dotted with fountains, and is a popular meeting place. One of the plaza's entrances is via the 17th-century Puerta del Conde gate, where the Dominican flag was first raised in 1844.

The Republic's three principal heroes – Juan Pablo Duarte, Francisco del Rosario Sánchez, and Ramón Matías Mella – rest within the Altar de la Patria, a marble mausoleum where an eternal flame burns in their honor. The tomb is guarded by a soldier in uniform.

Parque Duarte

🏠 Calle Padre Billini & Calle Hostos

The most intimate of Santo Domingo's colonial plazas, this small square is a gathering spot for locals to gossip beneath the statue of Juan Pablo Duarte. On the eastern side, Iglesia y Convento de los Padres Dominicos is famous for its stone zodiac wheel in the chapel.

To the northwest of Parque Duarte, the Museo Memorial de la Resistencia Dominicana both honors the resistance to Tujillo's tyranny and raises awareness of human rights.

Palacio Nacional

🏠 Calle Dr. Delgado Báez
📞 809 695 8000 ⏰ By appt

The Palacio Nacional was completed in 1947 as a palace for dictator-president Rafael Trujillo. The Neo-Classical structure, made of pink roseate Samaná marble and featuring a domed roof, was designed by renowned Italian architect Guido D'Alessandro. Prior permission is required to view the exquisite interior, and a formal dress code is enforced (shorts, sandals, and tennis shoes are not allowed). The Salón de las Cariátides, with its walls lined with 44 elegant caryatids (draped female figures), is a highlight.

A short stroll southwest of the Palacio Nacional brings visitors to **Galería de Arte Cándido Bidó**. This 1950s mansion is the former studio-home of the republic's most famous artist, Cándido Bidó, who died in 2011. His colorful artworks are on display.

Galería de Arte Cándido Bidó

⊗ 🏠 Calle Dr. Báez 5
📞 809 685 5310 ⏰ 9am–6pm Mon-Fri

Calle Las Damas

🏠 Between Fortaleza Ozama and Plaza España

The first cobbled colonial street laid out in the New World is named for Doña María de Toledo (wife of Diego

> **Calle Las Damas is lined with beautifully restored historic buildings, including the Panteón de la Patria, completed in 1743 as a Neo-Classical Jesuit church.**

Columbus) and other ladies of the nobility. Calle Las Damas is lined with beautifully restored historic buildings, including the **Panteón de la Patria**, completed in 1743 as a Neo-Classical Jesuit church. Having once been used as a theater, today it is a somber mausoleum for national heroes, and is guarded by a uniformed soldier.

Kids will enjoy the **Museo Infantil Trampolín**, a funfilled educational forum covering earth sciences to social affairs.

Panteón de la Patria

🏛 Calle Las Damas & Plazoleta de María Toledo 📞 809 689 6010 🕐 9am-5pm Tue-Sun

Museo Infantil Trampolín

🎨🎨 🏛 Calle Las Damas 🕐 9am-5pm Tue-Fri, 10am-6pm Sat & Sun 🌐 trampolin.org.do

---

⑧

Faro a Colón

🏛 Av. Estados Unidos, Parque Mirador del Este 📞 809 591 1492 🕐 9am-5:30pm Tue-Sun

This massive monument in honor of Christopher Columbus was initiated in 1929 and completed only in 1992, when it was dedicated for the quincentennial celebration of the explorer's arrival. The "Columbus Lighthouse" was designed in the shape of a cross by neophyte British architect Joseph Lea Gleave. Soaring ten stories high over Parque Mirador del Este, the 680-ft- (207-m-) long concrete structure is stepped in tiered

layers. Hollow within, it houses a Gothic marble sepulcher by Spanish sculptor Pere Carbonell i Huguet. This contains a bronze urn, filled, supposedly, with Columbus's ashes, which were transferred from the Catedral Primada de América. On special occasions, high-power beams are turned on to cast a cross-shaped light in the sky.

Stretching out near the Río Ozama, woody and pretty Parque Mirador del Este is the city's chief recreational area, with various sports arenas and centers. At its far eastern end, Cueva Los Tres Ojos (Three Eyes Cave) is named for three water-filled limestone sinkholes, a popular visiting spot for families on weekends.

The **Acuario Nacional** (National Aquarium) overlooks the Atlantic Ocean and has displays of marine life such as sharks, rays, and eels. Opposite the aquarium stands the Agua Splash, a fun waterpark for families with plenty of pools and slides.

Acuario Nacional

🎨 🏛 Av. España 75 📞 809 766 1709 🕐 9:30am-5:30pm Tue-Sun

↑ The towering Faro a Colón, often referred to as the "Columbus Lighthouse"

CATEDRAL PRIMADA DE AMÉRICA

🏛 Parque Colón, Calle Arzobispo Nouel & Arzobispo Meriño 🕐 9am-4pm daily

Considered the oldest cathedral in the Americas, the Catedral Primada de América has a fascinating history within its well-preserved walls. Once housing the remains of Christopher Columbus, the gold-tinted building is also an intriging mix of architectural movements through the ages.

Diego Columbus laid the foundation stone of this cathedral in 1514. The original architect, Alonso de Rodríguez, was inspired by the design of the cathedral in Seville, Spain. Revised by Luis de Moya and Rodrigo de Liendo, the building was finally completed in 1541, but was added to throughout the 18th century. In 1920, Pope Benedict XV elevated it to the status of Basílica menor de la Virgen de la Anunciación. The building also contains a treasury, which has an interesting collection of furnishings and jewelry. Take care to dress appropriately when visiting the cathedral.

←

Supported by 14 columns, the ceiling soars above a floor of checkered marble

The north facade of the Catedral Primada de América lit up at night ↑

EXPERIENCE Dominican Republic

↓ The ornate altarpiece at the Catedral Primada de América

↑ Altos de Chavón, a replica of a 16th-century town, near La Romana

EXPERIENCE MORE

② La Romana

🏛 80 miles (129 km) E of Santo Domingo 🚗🚉 Av Libertad 7; 809 550 6922

This coastal port town is the republic's principal center for sugar production. Although modern, it retains many colonial structures centered on Parque Central, which is studded with wrought-iron sculptures in the shade of Iglesia Santa Rosa de Lima. El Obelisco, at the juncture of Avenida Libertad at Calle Francisco del Castillo, shows the nation's history. The main draw is Altos de Chavón, a fantastical 1970s re-creation of a Tuscan hill town complete with a "Roman amphitheater" that is used as a music venue by its owners, the nearby Casa de Campo resort. Its St. Stanislaus Church is named after Poland's patron saint, whose ashes were brought here by Pope John Paul II during his visit in 1979. It is one of the most beautiful churches in the Dominican Republic, with a terracotta roof and wide stripes of stone comprising the upper walls. The church also houses the Regional Museum of Archaeology, which displays pre-Columbian Taíno artifacts.

About 5 miles (8 km) to the southwest of La Romana is Isla Catalina, a small island with great beaches. On the main road to San Pedro de Macoris is **Cueva de las Maravillas**, an underground cave-cum-museum with natural dripstone formations and over 500 pictographs.

Cueva de las Maravillas
♿🚫⏱🅿 ⏰9am–5pm Tue–Sun 🌐cuevadelas maravillas.com

↑ Parque Nacional los Haitises, home to over a hundred species of bird *(inset)*

3

Parque Nacional los Haitises

⌂ 47 miles (75 km) NE of Santo Domingo ⏱ 8am–5pm daily

This national park protects a region of rugged limestone terrain studded with *mogotes* (ancient limestone plateaus) and riddled with caverns. The dense forests are home to at least 112 bird species, including swallows that swarm Cueva de las Golondrinas and seabirds nesting on Islade los Pájaros. The easiest access is on guided boat trips arranged by **Paraíso Caño Hondo**, an activity center.

Paraíso Caño Hondo

⌂ 7 miles (11 km) W of Sabana de la Mar ⓦ paraisocano hondo.com

4

Parque Nacional Cotubanamá and Isla Saona

⌂ Guaragua, 3 miles (5 km) S of Bayahibe 📞 829 833 0879

Renamed in 2014 for a Taíno *cacique* (chieftain) who resisted the Spanish, the park formerly known as Parque Nacional del Este protects 307 sq miles (796 sq km) of tropical humid and rare seasonal deciduous forest, plus various marine ecosystems. A rugged limestone plateau, at the Republic's southeast extreme, is pockmarked with *cenotes* (sinkholes) and caverns daubed with precious pre-Columbian pictographs. The forests teem with wildlife: rhinoceros iguanas; the endangered solenodon (resembling a shrew on steroids); the jutía, a rabbit-sized, herbivorous rat; as well as 122 bird species,

including the Hispaniolan parrot, red-footed boobies, and frigatebirds.

The park's main entrance is at Guaraguo. A coastal trail leads to lovely Playa Tortuga and Cueva de Panchito, the entrance of which is guarded by a Taíno figure with raised arms. Ranger-guided hikes lead to Cueva de Jose María, with the best galleries of Taíno pictographs. You can also access the park to the east via Boca de Yuma. Nearby is the fortified Casa Ponce de León, built in 1505.

Boat excursions zip over to picture-perfect Isla Saona, which offers gorgeous beaches, a lake full of flamingos, and Piscina Natural – a turquoise lagoon cusped by a sandbar with sea stars.

5

Punta Cana and East Coast

⌂ 2 miles (3 km) S of Punta Cana airport ⓦ punta cana.com

This coastal zone is the setting for the majority of the

country's all-inclusive resorts. Stunning beaches, from snow white to gold, unspool along some 31 miles (50 km) of picture-perfect coconut palm-lined coast. Resort development concentrates around Punta Cana and Playa Bávaro, but other resort areas by Uvero Alto are evolving to the north, where the virginal Playa Lavacama and Playa Los Muertos are great places to escape the crowds. The Puntacana Resort & Club's Indigenous Eyes Ecological Park & Reserve protects a pocket of endangered flora and fauna, and you can swim in rejuvenating freshwater lagoons by arrangement.

A short distance inland is the regional capital city, Higüey, renowned for its Modernist concrete cathedral, **Basílica de Nuestra Señora de la Altagracia**. This is the nation's largest church, designed in 1950 by French architects André Dunoyer de Segonzac and Pierre Dupré.

Basílica de Nuestra Señora de la Altagracia
 Ave. Juan XXIII & Sánchez ☎ 809 554 2291 ◷ 6am–7pm daily

6
Playa Bayahibe

 89 miles (142 km) SE of Santo Domingo

Considered one of the best places to dive in the country, the Bayahibe area has endless white-sand beaches, notably Playa Dominicus and Playa Bayahibe. The original fishing village is diminishing with the spread of all-inclusive resorts.

7
Boca Chica

 20 miles (32 km) E of Santo Domingo

This compact beach area, a 30-minute drive from the capital, gets packed on weekends and holidays when people spill out of the bars onto the narrow streets. Be aware, though, that Boca Chica is known for its brazen sex tourism industry.

Palm-fringed sands dissolve into peacock-blue shallows, good for snorkeling. Wade out to the Isla La Matica and Isla Los Pinos, where mangroves harbor a wealth of birdlife. Divers can head out to the **Parque Nacional Submarino La Caleta**, where 28 excellent dive sites include the wrecks of the *Hickory*, *El Limón*, and *Captain Alsina*.

Parque Nacional Submarino La Caleta
✪ 5 miles (8 km) W of Boca Chica 🛈 Tropical Sea Divers; www.tropicalseadivers.com

← The Lighthouse Beach Bar at sunset, in Playa Bayahibe

8

Península de Samaná

 110 miles (177 km) NE of Santo Domingo Calle Santa Barbara 4; 809 538 2332

Jutting into the Atlantic Ocean, this slender peninsula is lined by white-sand beaches along its north and east shores. On the southern shore, rivers cascade down from a thickly forested mountain to the Bahía de Samaná, a favored wintering spot for humpback whales.

The regional capital, Santa Bárbara de Samaná, is a good base for exploring. Just north of town is Salto El Limón waterfall, which makes for a great day-trip on horseback. Nearby, at Samana Zipline Tour, visitors can tackle a choice of ziplines and take a safari truck trip.

9

Parque Nacional Monte Cristi

Monte Cristi

Tucked away at the delta of the Río Yaqui del Norte, little-visited Parque Nacional Monte

> **On the southern shore, rivers cascade down from a thickly forested mountain to the Bahía de Samaná, a favored wintering spot for humpback whales.**

Cristi protects a sprawling expanse of cactus-studded semi-desert, lagoon-pocked marshland, and pristine ocean. Its seven ecosystems include almost half of the nation's mangrove forests, which are home to more than 160 bird species.

From the park entrance, a trail leads to the tangerine sands of Playa Detras del Morro, in the shadow of El Morro clifftop. Offshore, a necklace of coral surrounds the Cayos de lso Siete Hermanos, popular with marine turtles for nesting, and with American oystercatchers and boobies. "Pipe Wreck" – an 18th-century merchantman that sank with its load of clay pipes – lies 3 miles (5 km) down off Isla Cabras. Excursions, plus diving, are offered from Marina del Mar, including a chance to spy manatees in the lagoons.

The park spreads north and south of the town of San Fernando de Monte Cristi, surrounded by saltpans from which much of North America's table-salt is derived.

10

Puerto Plata

145 miles (233 km) NW of Santo Domingo Calle José del Carmen Arizo 45; 809 586 5059

Founded in 1502, this port town is replete with historic buildings, notably in the Zona Victoriana with its cluster of 19th-century wooden gingerbread houses. At its heart lies Parque Independencia, which has the Catedral San Felipe Apostól on the south side, and, two blocks east, the popular **Museo del Ambar**, housed in a 1919 mansion. Also worth visiting is the 1577 **Fortaleza San Felipe**, one of the oldest colonial forts of the New World.

Beyond the historic core, the modern city is an ungainly sprawl. Boutique hotels are clustered on Playa Dorada, named for its palm-shaded golden sands, while locals gather at Playa Cofresí, a laid-back beach with few watersports but some restaurants.

↑ Charming Victorian-era gingerbread houses in Puerto Plata

The **Monte Isabel de Torres** lures visitors to its trail-crossed summit. A cable car to the peak, accessed from Avenida Teleférico, provides stupendous views of the city.

Museo del Ambar
 Calle Duarte 61
9am-6pm Mon-Sat
ambermuseum.com

Fortaleza San Felipe
Av Gregorio Luperón
9am-5pm daily

Monte Isabel de Torres
Av Manuel Tavárez Justo **8:30am-5pm daily**
telefericopuertoplata.com

Punta Rucia

20 miles (32 km) W of Puerto Plata

Graced by cottony sands that shelve gently into azure waters, this remote beach is a favorite of day-trippers who arrive on boat excursions from Puerto Plata. Most trips include a visit to Cayo Paraíso, an idyllic cay with crystal waters colored by a kaleidoscopic palette of fish.

A dirt track leads to Refugio de Manatís Estero Hondo, a mangrove-fringed lagoon protecting manatees. Farther east is **Parque Nacional La Isabela**, which preserves the ruins of the New World's first permanent settlement, established by Columbus in 1492.

Parque Nacional La Isabela
El Castillo **9am-5:30pm daily**

Sosúa

110 miles (175 km) NW of Santo Domingo **Calle Duarte 1; 809 571 4808**

This clifftop beach town is laid out on either side of the long Playa Sosúa. The town itself

is divided into two areas: Los Charamicos to the west and El Batey to the east, where German and Austrian Jewish refugees settled during the 1940s. Fine wooden architecture, including the synagogue and adjoining **Museo Judío Sosúa**, can be seen here. A coral reef nearby offers scuba diving, and dive operators offer trips to the wreck of the *Zingura*, scuttled in 1993.

Museo Judío Sosúa
Calle Dr Alejo Martínez **809 571 2633** **Timings vary, call ahead**

Cabarete

119 miles (190 km) NW of Santo Domingo **Calle Principal; 809 571 0962**

With a vibrant nightlife, Cabarete is both the Republic's party beach resort and its watersports capital. The wind-whipped beaches are among the best in the Caribbean for kiteboarding and wind-surfing. Small hotels and colorful bar-restaurants edge up to the sands of this beach village.

Just east of Cabarete is an entrance to the **Parque Nacional El Choco**, which has trails, caves, and a lagoon with a waterfall. Another popular excursion from Cabarete is to the **27 Charcos De Demajagua**

Natural Monument to the south. Visitors can hike along a riverbed to a series of cascades and natural waterslides.

Parque Nacional El Choco
Callejón de la Loma **829 779 1975** **9am-4:30pm daily**

27 Charcos De Demajagua Natural Monument
Imbert **8am-3pm daily** **27charcos.com**

TOP 4 RAINY DAY ACTIVITIES

Plaza de la Culture
With museums covering art, history, and geography, you could spend all day at this Santo Domingo gem.

Dive Bayahibe
Escape the rain via full immersion, at the 1724 Guadalupe Underwater Archaeological Preserve.

ChocoMuseo
Sate your sweet tooth at a "Bean to Bar" workshop *(chocomuseo.com)*.

Cueva Fun Fun
Exploration meets adventure in this underground cavern, complete with subterranean grotto pools.

↑ Kiteboarders catching some early evening waves off a beach in Cabarete

14

La Vega

📍 70 miles (113 km) NW of Santo Domingo 🛈 Calle Mella esq Durangé; 809 242 3231

Founded in 1562, La Vega is a sprawling, chaotic city on the banks of Río Camú in the heart of El Cibao Valley. It is renowned for its lively Carnival and for its Catedral de la Concepción de la Vega, a post-Modernist, industrial-style design that visitors either love or hate. The dramatic exterior, with Gothic elements, offers a garish

EAT

Jellyfish
Great ambience and superb seafood cuisine make this on-the-sands restaurant an unforgettable dining experience.

📍 Playa Bávaro, Punta Cana 🌐 jellyfish restaurant.com

$$$

Sam's Bar & Grill
This long-running institution, now located at L'oase Resort, serves up classic dishes alongside movie screenings.

📍 21 Playa Real, Puerto Plata 🌐 samsbardr.com

$$$

Lax
Have dinner with the sand between your toes at this lively beach bar, which serves burgers, tapas, and other finger food-style favorites.

📍 Playa Encuentro, Cabarete 📞 829 745 8811

$$$

counterpoint to the sparse interior with a simple altar. The city's other sights of interest include the Neo-Classical Palacio Municipal and Palacio de Justicia.

Northeast of La Vega lies the Santo Cerro (Holy Hill), where an annual pilgrimage is made every September 24 to Iglesia Las Mercedes. The simple church is considered to be the site of a miracle during the colonial days. Nearby is the original settlement of La Concepción de la Vega, founded in 1494 as a base for gold-mining but destroyed by an earthquake in 1562. The ruins are preserved within **Parque Nacional Arqueológico Histórico La Vega Vieja**.

Parque Nacional Arqueológico Histórico La Vega Vieja
 📍 Carretera Moca, Santo Cerro 🕐 8am–5pm Mon–Sat

15

Santiago de los Caballeros

📍 88 miles (138 km) NW of Santo Domingo 🚆 🛈 Parque Duarte & Calle del Sol; 809 582 5885

Built on the banks of the Río Yaque in the center of El Cibao Valley, the Republic's second-largest city thrums with energy and traffic. The hub of agriculture and commerce outside Santo

Domingo, this wealthy city also boasts fine attractions, including an easily walked colonial core and many monuments that recall its past status as a tobacco boom town. Cigar manufacture remains its most important industry; deft hands can be seen rolling fine cigars at Fábrica de Cigarros La Aurora, part of **Centro León**, a cultural institute with a contemporary art gallery and an anthropology museum.

Any tour should begin at Parque Duarte, surrounded by an eclectic assemblage of colonial structures, including Catedral Santiago Apóstol. Nearby, Fortaleza San Luís has been restored and displays pre-Columbian artifacts.

The soaring Monumento a los Héroes de la Restauración was erected in 1940 by the dictator Rafael Trujillo (1891–1961). The Museo Folklórico Don Tomás Morel offers an introduction to the city's vibrant Carnival culture.

Around 45 miles (72 km) east of Santiago, **Reserva Científica Loma Quita Espuela** has trails into rainforest, where the Hispaniola parrot and other endemic birds can be spotted.

← The towering Monumento a los Héroes de la Restauración in Santiago de los Caballeros

↑ A lone trekker approaching Salto de Jimenoa waterfall, in Jarabacoa

Another interesting place to visit is **Casa Museo Hermanas Mirabal**, in Salcedo, 30 miles (48 km) east of Santiago. It is where the sisters María Teresa, Minerva, and Patria Mirabal, who opposed Trujillo, grew up in a middle-class home, and is now maintained as a shrine.

Centro León

 ◉ 🏛 Av 27 de Febrero 146
🕐 10am–7pm Tue–Sun
🌐 centroleon.org.do

Reserva Científica Loma Quita Espuela

◈ 🐾 ☎ 809 588 4156
🕐 8am–4pm daily

Casa Museo Hermanas Mirabal

◈ 🐾 Carretera Salcedo, Tenares ☎ 809 587 0530
🕐 9am–5pm Tue–Fri, 9am–6pm Sat & Sun

16

Jarabacoa

📍 96 miles (154 km) NW of Santo Domingo 🅸 Calle Independencia; 809 574 6810

Deep in the Cordillera Central, at a height of 1,750 ft (533 m), this agricultural town attracts those escaping the heat of the lowlands for a crisp alpine climate. Parque Mario Nelsón Galán, the small town square, is a good spot to watch life

go by. The town nestles in the valley of the Río Yaque del Norte and is a base for white-water rafting, horseback riding, and for hiking, including to three local waterfalls: Salto de Baiguate, Salto de Jimenoa, and Salto de Jimenoa Alto. Jarabacoa is also the gateway to Pico Duarte, the tallest mountain in the Caribbean.

17

Parques Nacionales J. Armando Bermúdez y José del Carmén Ramírez

📍 16 miles (26 km) NW of Jarabacoa ☎ 809 472 4204

The Cordillera Central forms a rugged backbone here, rising to 10,164 ft (3,097 m) atop Pico Duarte, accessed from the mountain hamlet of La Ciénaga. The hulking mass is a popular, albeit challenging three-day round-trip hike to the summit, where the Dominican flag flutters above a bust of Juan Pablo Duarte (1813–76), father of the nation. This mountain terrain of razorback ridges and plunging gorges is known as the "Dominican Alps," and is enshrined within the Armando Bermúdez and José del Carmén Ramírez National Parks. Rainforest smothers the lower flanks, while trails lead up through the mist-shrouded cloud forest and then pine forest above. Birding is particularly superb here.

FACELESS DOLLS

The towns of El Cibao, and specifically Moca, are known for making ceramic *muñecas sin rostros* (faceless dolls), meant to symbolize the nation's multi-ethnic make-up in which no racial group is favored. The tiny, brightly painted dolls purposefully have no facial features and come in various skin tones. The dolls usually portray country women wearing headscarves or straw hats, and holding flowers or *tinajones* (earthenware jars). They were first created by Dominican artist Liliana Mera Limé in 1981.

↑ A swimmer sampling the crystal waters of a deserted pool in Barahona

20

Complejo Ecoturístico Río Blanco

🏠 11 miles (17 km) SW of Bonao 📞 809 296 8208

Nestled beside the Río Yamu, in the mountains west of Bonao, the Complejo Ecoturístico Río Blanco is a great place to stay for travelers who want varied activities nearby. Organized tour options include horseback rides, guided hikes to local coffee- and cocoa-growing farms, and a visit to a bamboo furniture workshop.

There are nine comfortable cabins, while other options include a large dormitory-style room or a campground.

18

Barahona

🏠 120 miles (193 km) SW of Santo Domingo 🚌🚖
ℹ️ Oficina de Turismo, Av Enriquillo; 809 524 3650

Founded in 1802 by Haitian general Toussaint L'Ouverture, Barahona, at the head of Bahía de Neiba, evolved as a center for sugar production in the 20th century and is today a port city. It is the gateway to a little-visited region of huge natural beauty. Palm-fringed beaches unfurl south along a roller coaster road named Vía Panorámica, a scenic drive framed by the turquoise ocean.

South of the city, Playa San Rafael is a popular beach with its cool pools fed by natural spring waters. And west of Barahona is Polo Magnético, an optical illusion in which the road, sloping in one direction, appears to slope the other way. Also worth visiting is **Reserva Científica Laguna de Cabral**, to the northwest. It has board-walk trails from which to spot waterfowl and wading birds.

Reserva Científica Laguna de Cabral
 🏠 Cabral 🕐 8am–6pm daily

19

Parque Nacional Sierra de Bahoruco

🏠 116 miles (186 km) SW of Santo Domingo 🕐 9am–4:40pm Tue–Sun

One of the least visited in the country due to its remoteness and rugged terrain, this park is a must for bird enthusiasts – it has over 100 species. Its landscape ranges from dry deciduous lowland forests to cloud forests and pines at higher altitudes. White-necked crows and narrow-billed todies can be seen around Laguna La Charca and near the visitors' center at Hoyo Pelempito. The park's rich vegetation includes 180 orchid species.

21

San Cristóbal

🏠 17 miles (27 km) W of Santo Domingo 🚌 ℹ️ Gober-nación, Av Constitución 25, 809 528 0395

Founded in the late 16th century, San Cristóbal is

→ The bustling main square of San Cristóbal

a city steeped in historical significance. The capital of the province of the same name, this sprawling, busy city was originally named Trujillo after the dictator, Rafael Leonidas Trujillo. The name, however, was changed after he was gunned down in 1961. During his dictatorship, he built many monuments in the town to honor himself. One of them is the domed, mustard-colored **Catedral de Nuestra Señora de la Consolación**. This church also had a tomb intended for Trujillo, but he was eventually buried in Paris. The interior is decorated with murals by Spanish artist José Vela Zanetti. His work also adorns Trujillo's hilltop mansion, Castillo del Cerro, which was once embellished with gold leaf and murals. It is now a police academy and is closed to the public. Other noteworthy buildings include Casa de la Cultura, on the south side of Parque Cristóbal Colón, the city's main square. On Parque Duarte is Iglesia Parroquial, a pretty church, built in 1946 to honor Trujillo's hometown.

Located just 2 miles (3 km) northwest of the city is Reserva Antropológica El Pomier, which protects 55 caves adorned with pre-Columbian pictographs. More than 6,500 ancient pictographs and petroglyphs have been identified, most being spiritual symbols and animal figures. Paved paths lead through the major caverns, populated by harmless bats. There is a museum, shop, and café at the reserve.

Catedral de Nuestra Señora de la Consolación

Ⓐ Av Constitución
Ⓒ 8am–5pm daily

Parque Nacional Jaragua

Ⓐ 124 miles (200 km) SW of Santo Domingo Ⓣ
Ⓘ Grupo Jaragua; www.grupojaragua.org.do

The nation's largest national park, Jaragua offers great wildlife viewing, although most of this semi-arid terrain is off-limits. Endangered Ricord's and rhinoceros iguanas inhabit the park, accessed by trails from Fondo Paradí. Flamingos and roseate spoonbills can be seen in Laguna Oviedo, where the visitors' center has a lookout tower. Marine turtles nest at Bahía de las Águilas, accessible by boat or jeep.

> **Colonia Japonesa, a hamlet on the northern outskirts of Constanza, was founded in the 1950s by Japanese farmers lured here by dictator Trujillo.**

Constanza

Ⓐ 16 miles (26 km) NW of Santo Domingo
Ⓘ Constanza National Airport; 809 539 1022

With an exquisite location surrounded by mountains at 4,000 ft (1,219 m), this town is set in a broad valley that is the breadbasket of the nation. A quiltwork of fields produce much of the nation's fruit and a variety of flowers. With crisp mountain air and splendid scenery, Constanza is a good starting point for hikes, though it has been bypassed by tourism. Mountain drives by jeep guarantee great scenery. Colonia Japonesa, a hamlet on the northern outskirts of Constanza, was founded in the 1950s by Japanese farmers lured here by dictator Trujillo. Several structures here are in traditional Japanese style.

A challenging yet beautiful drive south of Constanza leads to Salto Aguas Blancas, a duo of waterfalls cascading into a chilly pool. The highest free waterfall in the Caribbean, it is fringed by pretty ferns and other vegetation that clings to the sheer rock faces of the canyons.

Parque Nacional Lago Enriquillo y Isla Cabritos

 112 miles (180 km) W of Santo Domingo ⏰ 7am–5pm daily ℹ Asociación de Guías Ecoturísticos del Lago Enriquillo; 809 880 0871

Encircled by mountains, super-saline Lago Enriquillo is the largest lake in the Caribbean as well as its lowest point, at 140 ft (43 m) below sea level. The lake is a remnant of the Caribbean Sea left land-locked by ancient tectonic movements. Hundreds of American crocodiles inhabit the lake and are easily seen on Isla Cabritos. Flamingos tiptoe about the waters, which are home to more than 60 other bird species, including roseate spoonbills. Visitors will find plenty of rhinoceros iguanas around the ranger station at La Azufrada, from where boats leave on guided tours.

Nearby Las Caritas, outside the hamlet of Postrer Río, has rocks etched with pre-Columbian petroglyphs showing human faces. At the western end of the lake is Jimaní, a border town abutting Haiti, known for its bustling market and brightly painted Haitian buses called *taptaps*.

San Juan de la Maguana

112 140 miles (225 km) NW of Santo Domingo

Founded in 1503, this city is now the capital of San Juan province. Although most of the early colonial structures were destroyed during the 19th-century Haitian invasions, it still boasts some intriguing sites, centered on Parque Central. Dating from 1958, the domed, eclectic-style Catedral San Juan Bautista features Baroque and Rococo ornamentation and an exterior spiral metal staircase. On the eastern side of town, Parque Duarte is home to the Neo-Classical Palacio Ayuntamiento and Modernist Palacio de Justicia.

Also worth visiting is El Corral de los Indios, a pre-Columbian site located 4 miles (6 km) north of town. It has a wide stone circle used as a *batey* (ball court).

Against the backdrop of the magnificent mountain range of Cordillera Central lies the **Presa de Sabana Yegua**, a popular man-made lake known for its bass and tilapia. However, droughts have reduced the water level to an all-time low.

Presa de Sabana Yegua
🏛 15 miles (24 km) E of San Juan de la Maguana ⏰ Ask at military guardpost for entry

Did You Know?

The Dominican Republic's flag is the only one in the world to include an image of the Bible.

The ornate interior of ↑ Catedral San Juan Bautista in San Juan de la Maguana

LUXURY GOLF COURSES IN THE DOMINICAN REPUBLIC

Considered the Caribbean's undisputed top golf destination, the Dominican Republic is carpeted with dozens of emerald palm-studded fairways laid out by Gary Player, Jack Nicklaus, Nick Faldo, and other celebrity golf-pro designers. A major forte of the island, new world-class courses open every year, many of them ocean-fringed beauties associated with premier resort hotels and constructed by the leading names in golf design.

PUNTA ESPADA

The first of three Jack Nicklaus Signature courses at Cap Cana, this magnificent and intricate course *(puntaespadagolf. com)* opened in 2006 with coast-hugging fairways and ocean views from every hole. The signature 13th hole requires a tee shot over the ocean. GolfWeek magazine ranks it the number one course in the Caribbean.

TEETH OF THE DOG COURSE

Named for the sharp limestone terrain known locally as *diente del perro* (dog's teeth), this spectacular championship course is rated the best in the Caribbean. One of three Pete Dye-designed ocean-front courses at the Casa de Campo resort *(casadecampo.com)*, outside La Romana, it regularly gets updated with tricky bunkers that add to its coral-fanged bite.

CORALES GOLF COURSE

Designed by golf architect Tom Fazio, this beauty at the Puntacana Resort and Club *(puntacana.com/golf)* is a classic oceanfront course, with holes perched atop cliffs. A must-play for any golfer visiting the beautiful Punta Cana, it culminates with a forced carry over the narrow, bluff-edged Bay of Corales to the 18th green.

↑ The scenic Punta Espada course, with palm trees swaying in the breeze

↑ U.S. golfer Max Scodro taking a shot on the Teeth of the Dog Golf Course

↑ Denny McCarthy playing on the Corales Golf Course beside the ocean

PRACTICAL
INFORMATION

Here you will find all the essential advice and information you will need before and during your stay in the Dominican Republic.

AT A GLANCE

CURRENCY
Peso (RD$)

TIME ZONE
Atlantic Standard Time (AST), 4 hours behind GMT and 1 hour ahead of EST

LANGUAGE
Spanish

ELECTRICITY SUPPLY
The Dominican Republic operates on 110 volts, but 220 volts is sometimes found. Outlets use US two-prong or three-prong plugs

EMERGENCY NUMBERS

POLICE, FIRE, AMBULANCE

911

TAP WATER
Tap water is not safe to drink – it is best to stick to bottled water

When To Go

The best time for visiting the Dominican Republic is November through April, the dry season, when temperatures are pleasantly moderate. Summers (June through August) can be exceedingly hot, although often hotels and car rental companies offer discounts. Temperatures can vary with elevation; Cordillera Central is delightfully cool year-round. Cultural events occur throughout the year, but much of the country comes to a halt in March/April for Semana Santa (Holy Week).

Getting There

Although Santo Domingo's Las Américas International Airport (SDQ) is the main airport, most international flights serving beach resorts land at Punta Cana International Airport (PUJ), while other flights also arrive and depart from regional airports such as Aeropuerto Internacional Gregorio Luperón (POP), in Puerto Plata. American Airlines, Delta, JetBlue, Spirit Airlines, United Airlines, and US Airways offer services to the Dominican Republic, as do many charter airlines. Air Canada and WestJet provide direct flights from Toronto and Montreal to Punta Cana. Several European airlines connect through Miami.

Personal Security

A few safety precautions are advisable, as petty theft and crime is endemic in visitor venues and remote and unlit places at night. Leave all valuables in the hotel safe when exploring on foot. Driving on isolated rural roads at night is risky due to poor lighting, so avoid if possible and use extreme caution.

Health

Most destinations in the Dominican Republic are safe, and endemic tropical diseases are limited to dengue, and malaria (a rare occurrence primarily along the Caribbean coast). Additional threats include sunburn, dehydration, and

riptides; check conditions with locals before swimming. Private doctors and clinics are found in every town, and basic government-run *centros de salud* (health centers) serve most communities. Hospiten operates medical clinics and an ambulance service in major resorts.

Passports and Visas

All foreign citizens need a passport plus proof of onward travel to visit the Dominican Republic. A tourist card ($10), valid for 30 days, is issued upon arrival or can be bought online in advance. Extensions for an additional 90 days cost $25 from the **Dirección General de Migración**
w migracion.gob.do

LGBT+ Safety

The Dominican Republic has an active gay scene, and Santo Domingo has several (somewhat discreet) gay bars and nightclubs. However, this predominantly Catholic country is still fairly close-minded about LBGT+ rights and equality. Displays of public affection between same-sex couples of either gender may elicit a negative verbal response, or worse.

Money

The Dominican currency is the peso (RDS), but the US dollar is accepted everywhere. Euros and pounds Sterling can be exchanged at banks, including BanReservas, and foreign-exchange booths. Most shops and tourist outlets accept major credit cards. Traveler's checks in US dollars are accepted in very few places. Most banks have ATMs, but they frequently run out of cash.

Cell Phones and Wi-Fi

Visitors can buy prepaid phones or SIM cards from main service providers such as Claro, Altice and Viva. If you are bringing your own mobile phone, check with your service providers to determine if it will work in the Dominican Republic. Calls from hotels incur a hefty surcharge. The Republic's international dialing codes are 809 and 829. Calls within Santo Domingo require the ten-digit number including the area code, which should be preceded by 1 when dialing beyond Santo Domingo. Most hotels have Internet service; many have Wi-Fi.

Getting Around

Santo Domingo's Zona Colonial is easily negotiated on foot, while taxis are ideal for getting around the great metropolis. Tourist taxis await visitors outside most hotels. Locals rely on *carros públicos* (private unmetered cars) that operate as communal taxis, but are best avoided, as drivers tend to overcharge. *Moto-conchos* (motorcycle taxis) form the main transport for locals outside Santo Domingo and are best avoided as well. The rest of the country is most easily explored on organized excursions or buses, since self-drive can be a daunting experience despite the efficent road network. Air-conditioned buses link most destinations nationwide.

A 50-minute ferry ride links Samana to Sabanade la Mar, while there are air services between Puerto Plata and Punta Cana to Santo Domingo and other citles.

Visitor Information

The Dominican Republic's **Ministry of Tourism** has offices in the US, Canada, and UK, as well as in major tourist centers in the Republic. The key local offices include one on Santo Domingo's Parque Colón, in Bávaro, and Puerto Plata.
Ministry of Tourism
w godominicanrepublic.com

HAITI

Haiti fills the mountainous western third of the island of Hispaniola. During the 1700s, the French turned what was then called Saint-Domingue into its richest overseas possession, its huge workforce of enslaved Africans producing vast quantities of sugar and coffee. In the late 1700s, Toussaint Louverture led a revolution of nearly half a million slaves. After a prolonged armed struggle, Haiti was able to declare its independence in 1804. By doing so it became the world's first black-led republic, and the first state in the Caribbean to throw off the shackles of European colonial rule. In return, it was forced to pay crippling reparations to France, a debt that took over 120 years to settle. The country has also had to deal with dictatorships (notably François "Papa Doc" Duvalier in the 1960s) and natural disasters. In January 2010, an earthquake with a 7.0 magnitude struck close to the capital, Port-au-Prince, killing an estimated 300,000 people. All these factors contribute to Haiti having the unenviable status of being the poorest nation in the western hemisphere.

Haiti's unique cultural elements – its creole language, renowned art, vodou religious practices, and *kompa* music (like a modern *merengue*) – have all developed from, and reflect, its African and French heritage. About 95 percent of its population are of African descent.

HAITI

Experience

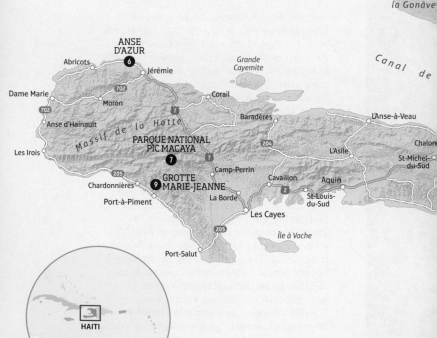

EXPERIENCE

EXPERIENCE Haiti

❶

Port-Au-Prince

📍 8, rue Légitime; 509 3816 0100

Exciting, vibrant, and riotously colorful, the Haitian capital is a surprisingly loveable city, despite its juxtaposition of poverty and luxury, and cluttered streets that are a chaotic cacophony. Although the city is still visibly recovering from the devastating 2010 earthquake, pulsating Port-au-Prince is a testament to the self-reliance, resourcefulness, ingenuity, and indefatigable good humor of its people.

Place du Champs de Mars, the city's main sight in the heart of downtown, is a mosaic of grassy squares and broad boulevards (and site of the demolished Palais Nacional) that are studded with busts of national heroes. Don't miss *Le Negre Marron* by Haitian sculptor Albert Mangonès, a powerful monument that was commissioned by the Duvalier government to commemorate the landmark slave revolt against France. Also in the square is the subterranean **Musée du Pantheón National**, which survived the earthquake virtually unscathed, and chronicles Haitian culture and history, from pre-Columbian Taino to the modern day. Highlights include the rusted anchor from Columbus's *Santa María*, exorbitant crowns of Henri Christophe and Emperor Faustin, and "Papa" Doc's black hat and cane.

Did You Know?

Author Graham Greene was banned from Haiti after his novel *The Comedians* depicted the island in a bad light.

For the fullest assault on the senses, head to Marché de Fer, a remarkable cast-iron, Islamic-style market built in 1889 (and rebuilt since it burned down in the aftermath of the 2010 hurricane). Duck inside the appealing red structure to rummage through the teeming craft market or lose yourself in the food hall.

To the south, admire more avant-garde metal designs at 622 Grand Rue, where several artists' studios conjure found scrap into amazing phallic, political and voodoo figures. The yin to this yang is Maison Dufort on Rue du Travail, a wonderful and lovingly restored gingerbread manse that is open to the public. The building is an excellent example of quintessential Haitian architecture, which is now a rare sight on the island.

Atop a hill 10 miles (16 km) southeast of Port-au-Prince, Fort Jacques was built in 1806 and named for Jean-Jacques Dessaline. High amid cool pine forests, this well-preserved fortress in the shape of an irregular star has fine views over Port-au-Prince.

Musée du Pantheón National

♿ 🏛 Pl. du Champs de Mars 📞 3417 4435

 ←
Gleaming marble interiors of the Musée du Pantheón National in Port-au-Prince

2

Parc Historique de la Canne à Sucre

 48, blvd. 15 Octobre, Chateaublond ⏰ 9am–4pm Mon–Sat, 1–4pm Sun 🌐 parchistorique.ht

On the northeast side of town, Parc Historique de la Canne à Sucre (Historical Park of Sugar Cane) recalls the height of sugar production during the French colonial era (1627–1804) through to its use in more modern times. The museum occupies the former Chateaublond plantation and 19th-century sugar mill, originally owned by French planter Louis de Taveau de Chambrun Chateaublond. Visitors to the site receive a walk-through history lesson on plantation life and the evolution of the sugar industry in Haiti. A waterwheel and various mechanical parts from the early mill are displayed beneath outdoor pavilions, while other exhibits speak to the nightmare of slavery. The Afro-Caribbean Room displays Pre-Columbian artifacts, while other key attractions include a narrow-gauge railway and a Baldwin steam train.

After breathing in the history, enjoy a freshly-squeezed cane juice and meal in the museum's Le Relais restaurant. The park often hosts music concerts and other live events.

↑ Visitors touring the packed cellar of the renowned Barbancourt Rum Distillery

3

Barbancourt Rum Distillery

 16, rue Bonne Foi, Damiens 🌐 barbancourt.net

Tucked amid sugarcane fields on the outskirts of Port-Au-Prince, the Barbancourt Rum Distillery was founded by Frenchman Dupré Barbancourt in 1862, the same year that the United States first recognized Haiti as a country. The self-sufficient factory – one of Haiti's oldest – still uses the famed double-distillation process of Cognac, familiar from Barbancourt's home region of France, but includes pure sugarcane juice instead of the more common molasses for a more flavorful product.

Guided tours (which run on weekdays Nov–Jun, in French) offer visitors an inside perspective on the production of this iconic brand, still distilled in the traditional manner by the socially responsible Societé du Rhum Barbancourt company. The factory hums busily as tractors haul sugarcane to the mill for crushing amid the grinding of steam-powered machinery. You will also learn about fermentation and distilling, then aging in oak barrels stored in brick-and-stone warehouses. The factory produces 11 types of rum using more than 200 tons of cane daily.

As with all good distillery tours, this one ends with a tasting, which is served on the tree-shaded lawn. Visitors are invited to test Barbancourt's 150-year history of excellence by sampling extensively from its line of rums, including its signature 15-year Estate Reserve rum.

> ## VOODOO IN HAITI
>
> Haiti is officially Catholic but Vodou (or voodoo), which originated in Benin and was brought to Haiti by slaves, is the de facto national religion. Adherents worship loa - family spirits that intercede on behalf of Bondye, the Supreme Creator, and which have duality with Catholic saints. This pantheon of anthropomorphic figures all have distinct personalities and characteristics, and are honored through offerings and rituals - including dances in which believers enter into trances - intended to cultivate good relations and beseech favors.

④ Bassin Bleu

Pack your bathing suit for a visit to this series of mystically translucent pools in an extra-ordinarily pretty gorge 7 miles (12 km) west of Jacmel. The "blue pool" is actually a triptych of tiered cascades that tumble into three natural rock bassins: Bassin Clair, Bassin Bleu, and Bassin Palmiste. The refreshing cascades are surrounded by fern-festooned cliffs. According to local lore, mermaids inhabit Bassin Bleu and come out by night.

The journey to the pools or *bassins* begins with a mountain ride on a "donkey" (Haitian slang for a pick-up truck), then a 20-minute hike that includes navigating stepping stones across the Petite Rivière de Jacmel.

Site access is restricted to a limited number of visitors daily, and beach shoes are recommended for traction on the slippery rocks. Rent a local guide who will be able to show you a safe spot atop the falls from which to jump into the middle pool.

⑤ Jacmel

🄰 60 miles (95 km) SW of Port-au-Prince
🄸 Experience Jacmel; 3722 5757

Haiti's fourth-largest city nestles in a large bay on the south coast of the Péninsule de Tiburon. It is an alluring and tranquil hill town, and is one of Haiti's most popular destinations for festivities, culminating in the annual

carnival. The pillars and balconies within its cast-iron buildings were an inspiration for New Orleans, in Louisiana. Although large sections of the historic center were demo-lished by the 2010 earthquake, Jacmel has been slowly rebuild-ing. Its downtown area is enlivened by elegant town houses that evoke its 19th-century wealth as a coffee-exporting hub. Maison Cadet, with its pointy "witch's hat" roof, is a stellar example. Nearby, the impressive Cathédrale de St Phillippe et St Jacques is undergoing repair, as is the cast-iron market that was imported from Belgium in 1895.

Jacmel's arts and crafts scene teems with creative ven-ues and cultural events. Scores of papier-mâché artisans can be seen making their masks for the carnival, and walls are festooned with street art; stroll the new Promenade du Bord de Mer to admire its colorful urban mosaics.

⑥ Anse d'Azur

Haiti has dozens of stunning beaches, but this swatch of creamy-colored sand dissol-ving into a turquoise sea is irresistible. Descending the narrow path that snakes past an old fort, you can make out the dark silhouette of a shipwreck merely 66 ft (20 m) from shore. It is commonly considered to be a sunken German U-boat. However, a 2004 investigation found the

A swimmer floating beneath the waterfall at Bassin Bleu ↑

A broad-billed tody, found in the Parque National La Visite

wreck to be not a submarine, but the late 19th-century gunboat *Reynaud*, which sank after colliding with an English Royal Mail Company steamer. Bring a snorkel and fins to swim out and explore the coral-encrusted remains.

7

Parc National Pic Macaya

 Haut Camp, Camp Perrin; 509 4893 5457

A paradise for eco-tourists, Parc National Pic Macaya is cusped within the Massif de la Hotte, a dragon's-back spine running the length of the Péninsule de Tiburon. This sanctuary protects Haiti's last stand of virgin cloud and dwarf forest, and reaches 7,700 ft (2,347 m) atop Pic Macaya, Haiti's second tallest mountain. A hotspot of biodiversity, with a unique ecology that includes the world's greatest concentration of endemic amphibians and reptiles, the area was declared a Biosphere Reserve in 2016. Visitors must request a permit and rent a guide for hikes.

8

Parc National La Visite

⌖ 14 miles (22 km) S of Port-au-Prince ⓘ Haiti National Trust, 12, Impasse Besse; 509 2949 9000; www.haititrust.org/la-visite

Tiny Parc National La Visite offers a calming, bucolic escape from the city into the cool Montagnes du Cibao mountains. It was established in 1983 to protect a remnant of Hispaniolan pine and montane broadleaf forest on the slopes of Morne du Cibao, Haiti's third highest peak. This fragile pocket of biodiversity is home to 17 frog species, 18 reptile species, and more than 80 bird species, including the endemic Hispaniolan spindalis and broad-billed tody. The standard trek is from Furcy to Seguin, a half-day mostly uphill hike. The snaking trail is rocky in places (and muddy after rains); bring water and raingear. The weather at this altitude is fickle, and temperatures can plunge when clouds form, soaking you in a chill mist. An early start ensures that most of your hike will be in the cool hours. Options for an overnight stay include the simple Auberge La Visite near Seguin, or a more stylish setting at The Lodge at Furcy.

9

Grotte Marie-Jeanne

⌚ 8am–4pm daily

Haiti's best-known (and biggest) cave riddles the hills above Port-à-Piment, near the tip of the Péninsule de Tiburon. Much of this limestone labyrinth – a tri-level system with

36 known chambers – remains unexplored, but you can delve inside three chambers to admire the pre-Columbian pictographs and stupendous dripstone formations, which include overhead "cathedral bells" and flowstones resembling plicated curtains.

Just getting to the caves is an Indiana Jones-style adventure. The narrow trail includes a jungly clamber over roots and gnarly limestone outcrops. English-speaking guides (who will unlock the entrance gates) can be rented in the coastal village of Port-à-Piment; ask for Jean-Baptiste Eliovil, who helped map the caves.

A paradise for eco-tourists, Parc National Pic Macaya is cusped within the Massif de la Hotte, a dragon's-back spine running the length of the Péninsule de Tiburon.

EAT

Papaye

An uber-hip venue that delivers excellent Caribbean-Creole fusion dishes.

⌂ 48 Rue Métellus, Port-Au-Prince 📞 509 4656 2482 🗙 Sun

$$$

Lolo

Enjoy hearty Italian dishes served on a lamplit patio. Seafood fans should try the conch pizza.

⌂ Blvd. Carenage, Cap-Haïtien 📞 509 3778 9635 🗙 Sun

$$$

Lakou Lakay

A friendly lunchtime spot perfect for those visiting the Parc National Historique, with tasty Creole fare.

⌂ Rue du Palais, Milot 📞 509 3614 2485

$$$

⑩

Cap-Haïtien

ℹ 115, Rue 13B, Cap-Haïtien; 2817 3555

This relaxed port city – known as La Cap (or "O-Kap") to locals – is Haïti's top tourist destination. It is a great base both for those keen to explore Palais Sans Souci or La Citadelle, or for those simply looking to laze on nearby beaches, but the former "Paris of the Antilles" also has its own charm. Cap-Haïtien was founded in 1670 as Cap-Française and served as Saint-Domingue's capital until 1770. It prospered as the wealthiest city on the island, garnering many fine buildings with arched doors and filigreed iron balustrades. The city survived the 2010 earthquake relatively unscathed, and enough exquisite (albeit much-faded) architecture remains that you can spend hours exploring streets that resemble a slightly disheveled New Orleans.

Cap-Haïtien's gem is the recently restored Cathédrale Notre-Dame de l'Assomption on Place d'Armes. Monuments of Toussaint Louverture and Jean-Jacques Dessalines stud the square, where the

 ↑ Visitors aboard a speedboat off the coast, north of Cap-Haïtien

liberation of slaves was proclaimed in 1783. The colorful cast-iron Marché de Cluny, built in 1890, is another unmissable highlight.

Cap-Haïtien has an international airport, is linked by highway to Port-au-Prince, and is easily reached from the Dominican Republic by bus.

---

⑪

L'Île-à-Rat

A tiny, idyllic coral cay ringed by a sun-bleached beach and teal waters, L'Île-à-Rat studs the Baie de l'Acul du Nord, about 4 miles (6 km) offshore of the ramshackle fishing village of Labadie. The cay is haloed by a coral reef and calm waters. Snorkelers may spot rusted cannons and other relics amid the coral.

The cay is easily reached by water taxi from Labadie, or Gaia Tours in Cap-Haïtien offer excursions. Fishermen come and go and will cook freshly-caught lobster or grilled fish served on the beach. With luck, you'll have this jewel to yourself, but on some days, groups of cruise ship passengers (to whom it's promoted as Amiga Island) arrive from Royal Caribbean Cruise's nearby resort.

Parc National Historique

📍 11 miles (18 km) SE of Cap-Haïtien ⏰ 7am–4pm daily

Inaugurated in 1978 and recognized as a UNESCO World Heritage Site four years later, the Parc National Historique preserves Haiti's two most impressive historic sites. Both were built by ex-slave and self-proclaimed King of Haiti, Henri Christophe, and rise above the small town of Milot, southeast of Cap-Haïtien.

Deservedly nicknamed the "Versailles of the Caribbean," Sans Souci was the largest of nine palaces built by the autocratic Christophe. He lived here with his wife, Queen Marie-Louise, and – inspired by the baroque taste then fashionable in Europe – held opulent parties and feasts until the collapse of the kingdom in 1820. The palace was wrecked by the 1842 earthquake, and today only

> **Inaugurated in 1978 and recognized as a UNESCO World Heritage Site four years later, the Parc National Historique preserves Haiti's two most impressive historic sites.**

skeletal walls remain amid the immense gardens and waterworks. At the entrance, opposite the ticket office, stands the circular, domed, and well-preserved Immaculée Conception de Milot church.

From here it's a 2-mile (4-km) uphill trek to La Citadelle, a mammoth fortress cemented to the mist-wreathed summit of Pic Laferrière. Christophe was an unpopular monarch and ruled with an iron fist, imposing forced labor on 20,000 newly-freed slaves, who toiled for 15 years on the mighty enterprise (1805–1820). Despite La Citadelle's unpalatable genesis, UNESCO declares that the twin sites of Sans Souci and La Citadelle "serve as universal symbols of liberty, being the first monuments constructed

by black slaves who had gained their freedom."

The walls of La Citadelle soar 130 ft (40 m), making the fortress impregnable against potential attacks. Beyond the drawbridge, the awe-inspiring complex has royal quarters, dungeons, an excellent museum, and several cannon batteries that offer commanding views in every direction. Guides can be rented by the entrance to Sans Souci (try asking for Maurice Etienne). They can offer an informed and entertaining tour, although tales of Christophe ordering soldiers to march into the abyss to test their loyalty are apocryphal.

Spectacular mountain views from La Citadelle *(inset)* in the Parc National Historique ↓

PRACTICAL
INFORMATION

Here you will find all the essential advice and information you will need before and during your stay in Haiti.

AT A GLANCE

CURRENCY
Haitian gourde
(HTG/ GDE)

TIME ZONE
Eastern Standard
Time, GMT- 5.
Daylight saving are
observed April–Oct

LANGUAGE
French

ELECTRICITY SUPPLY
The electrical system
delivers 110 volts at
60 cycles. US-style
plugs are used

EMERGENCY NUMBERS

AMBULANCE	FIRE SERVICE
115	**116**

POLICE
114

TAP WATER
Water purity is
unreliable so, to be
safe, drink bottled
water

When To Go

The best time for visiting Haiti is November through April, the dry season, when temperatures are pleasantly moderate. Summers can be exceedingly hot and rainy (particularly July and August) and hurricanes are a slim possibility. Hotels and car rental companies generally offer discounts at this time of year. Temperatures vary with elevation; the Cordillera Septentrional, Massif du Nord and Chaîne des Matheux are delightfully cool year-round.

Cultural festivals occur throughout the year, but key events such as La Festival de Rhum and Carnival, are held in winter (November and February respectively).

Getting There

Most flights arrive Toussaint Louverture International Airport (PAP), the main airport, in Port-au-Prince, while flights serving beach resorts of the north coast land at Hugo Chávez International Airport (CAP) in Cap Haïtien. American Airlines, Delta, JetBlue, and Spirit Airlines serve Haiti with flights from Atlanta, Fort Lauderdale, Miami, New York and Orlando. Air Canada flies from Montreal. Air France has direct service from Paris, and several carriers connect Haiti with other Caribbean islands, plus Central and South America.

Personal Security

Although warnings of violent crime, including kidnapping, can be overstated, Haiti does have a high crime rate and special vigilance is required. Avoid demonstrations of wealth, such as jewelry and flamboyant watches, and take precautions against pickpockets in crowded places. Violent street protests are frequent, and it's wise to check ahead for any known political activity. Sexual assault is prevalent and female visitors should take extra precautions.

Contact your embassy or consulate if your passport is stolen, or in the event of a serious crime or accident.

Health

Healthcare provision in Haiti is sporadic and often substandard, and good facilities are few and far between. You will be expected to pay for medical treatment on the spot, in cash. Emergency evacuation insurance is recommended. The most common illnesses relate to eating or drinking contaminated food and water so take care about what you eat and drink. Mosquitoes are a nuisance and malaria and zika are prevalent in some areas. Cover up in the evenings and use repellents, and consult your doctor in advance for an appropriate prophylactic. Use sunscreen and shade hat to prevent sunburn, and drink plenty of bottled water to prevent dehydration.

Passport and Visas

Tourists are not legally required to carry ID, though it is a good idea to keep at least a photocopy of the information pages of your passport on your person at all times.

LGBT+ Safety

Although same-sex relations are legal in Haiti, many community leaders and Christian pastors vehemently condemn them. Hence, intimidation of, and violence against, LGBT+ individuals is common. Although many same-sex Haitians hold hands as a sign of platonic affection and friendship, gay and lesbian travelers should refrain from demonstrating physical affection in public.

Money

Haiti's currency is the gourde, written as HTG or GDE, and divided into 100 centimes. Haitians refer to five gourdes as one "dollar" (H$). Confusedly, many shops and outlets quote in US dollars, which are widely accepted. Most banks in Port-au-Prince and Cap-Haïtien have ATMs, but they often run out of cash; elsewhere, ATMs are rare. Most hotels and some shops and tourist outlets accept major credit cards. It's wise to plan to operate on a cash-only basis. US dollars, plus Euros and pounds Sterling can be exchanged at banks and supermarkets, which have foreign-exchange counters.

Cell Phones and Wi-Fi

The international dialing code for Haiti is 509. Connectivity of landlines is patchy at best. The country's two biggest cellular providers, Digicel and Natcom, have roaming service agreements with major U.S. carriers on the GSM network, and service is generally good. Visitors bringing their own cell phones should check with their service providers to determine if they will work; however, it may be cheaper to buy a local SIM card in Haiti. Wi-Fi access is widespread: most hotels have Wi-Fi, and Internet cafes are ubiquitous – as are electricity outages.

Getting Around

Moto-taxis and *publiques* (collective taxis) are ubiquitous in all towns, and radio-taxis operate in Port-au-Prince and Cap Haïtien. Large air-conditioned buses connect major cities and tourist destinations, and a chaotic system of less comfortable minibuses connects everywhere else. Crude *taptaps* (converted pick-up trucks) are often the only transport in rural areas. Major car rental companies have offices at Toussaint Louverture International Airport, but driving has its risks and is suited for skilled, confident, and adventurous drivers only. Sunrise Air and Mission Aviation offer domestic flights from Aérogare Guy Malary airport, in Port-au-Prince.

Visitor Information

Haiti's Ministry of Tourism *(8 rue Légitime, Port-au-Prince)* has no offices outside Haiti, but it has information bureaus at the airports in Port-au-Prince and Cap Haïtien, and an office in Jacmel.

WEBSITES AND APPS

experiencehaiti.org
   The Haiti Tourist Board's official website is a good starting point
travelinghaiti.com
   Plenty of handy information on this commercial resource
gov.uk/foreign-travel-advice/Haiti
   A useful resource of up-to-date information on health and safety issues

PUERTO RICO

With elegant Spanish colonial architecture lining vibrant streets infused with the sounds of heady salsa and bomba music, and the flavours of Spanish–African criollo cuisine, Puerto Rico is a treat for the senses. The island's fascinating history has imbued the Island with a distinct cultural identity. When Columbus arrived in 1493, the island was inhabited by the Taíno. The first settlement was established in 1508 by Juan Ponce de León, who christened it Puerto Rico (Rich Port). In 1521, San Juan was founded and became the capital. African slaves were subsequently brought in to work on sugar cane, coffee, and tobacco estates, and the Dutch, French, and English tried, unsuccessfully, to wrest the island from the Spanish. Following the Spanish–American War in 1898, the island was ceded to the United States, the foundation for its present status as a commonwealth of the U.S. and partially self-governing territory. The tension and complications in this arrangement were put under the spotlight following the destruction inflicted on Puerto Rico by Hurricane Maria in September 2017, and the issue of where aid was due to come from.

In terms of the lie of the land, Puerto Rico is around 100 miles (160 km)long and 35 miles (56 km)wide. There are 300 miles (482 km) of coastline, and a mountainous backbone running across its interior that is traversed by a driveable panoramic route, La Ruta Panorámica. San Juan, the political and cultural capital, is a cosmopolitan city with a beautifully preserved colonial core. Vieques and Culebra – the Spanish Virgin Islands – lie off the northeast shore of the mainland.

PUERTO RICO

Must See

① San Juan

Experience More

② Arecibo Observatory
③ Dorado
④ Parque Las Cavernas del Río Camuy
⑤ Playa Jobos
⑥ Parque Cermonial Indígena Caguana
⑦ Mayagüez
⑧ Boquerón
⑨ Rincón
⑩ San Germán
⑪ Hacienda Buena Vista
⑫ Ponce
⑬ Bosque Estatal de Guánica
⑭ Centro Ceremonial Indígena de Tibes
⑮ El Yunque National Forest
⑯ Playa Piñones
⑰ Luquillo
⑱ Fajardo
⑲ Vieques
⑳ Culebra

Atlantic
Ocean

DORADO
**SAN
JUAN**
**PLAYA
PIÑONES**
① Condado
③
187 ⑯ Loíza Aldea
✈
**Luis Muñoz Marín
International Airport**
LUQUILLO
ayamón
Río Piedras
3 ⑰
Guaynabo
⑳ Río
Grande
⑱ **FAJARDO**
**Benjamín Rivera
Noriega Airport**
167 174
66
Playa Flámenco
✈ ⑳
Naranjito
1
181 Trujillo
Alto
⑮ Ceiba Dewey **CULEDRA**
Comerío Gurabo **EL YUNQUE
NATIONAL FOREST**
✈ **José Aponte de la
Torre Airport**
173 Caguas
Juncos Naguabo
172 ⑳ Río Blanco
Cidra San Lorenzo 53
Cayey ⑰ Las Piedras **Antonio Rivera
Rodríguez Airport** ✈ Isabel Segunda
182 **Humacao** ⑲ **VIEQUES**
*Bosque
Estatal
de Carite* *Esperanza*
179
⑮
Guayama 181
Patillas Yabucoa
53
3 Maunabo
Arroyo
Central
Aguirre

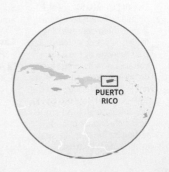

**PUERTO
RICO**

❶

SAN JUAN

 N coast of Puerto Rico ✈🚢🚌 ℹ️ La Casita, 500 Calle Tanca; 800 866 7827

Founded in 1521, San Juan was laid out in a grid on a headland protecting a large bay. Known as San Juan Viejo ("old"), this historic core has been restored, with pastel-painted 17th- and 18th-century buildings lining the cobblestoned streets. Two castles guard the colonial city, a popular port of call for cruise ships. Inland, modern San Juan has an altogether different feel.

①
Plaza del Quinto Centenario

📍 Calle Norzagaray and Calle del Cristo

This triple-tiered plaza, built in 1992 for the 500th anniversary of Columbus's arrival, is pinned by Totem Telúrico, a granite totem representing the island's peoples. The plaza is surrounded by the Ballajá barracks, now housing **Museo de las Américas**, with exhibits on New World culture, and the 16th-century Convento de los Dominicos. Nearby, is Parque de Beneficencia, a peaceful setting for the Neo-Classical Instituto de la Cultural

Puertorriqueña, displaying historical artifacts. Built in 1521, Casa Blanca now serves as a museum depicting early colonial life.

Museo de las Américas

♿ 📍 Calle del Morro 🕐 9am-noon, 1–4pm Tue–Fri; noon-5pm Sat & Sun 🌐 museolas americas.org

Casa Blanca

♿ 🚫 📍 Calle San Sebastián 1 📞 787 725 1454 🕐 8am-4:30pm Wed–Sun

②
Plaza de San José

📍 Calle del Cristo and Calle San Sebastián

This intimate colonial plaza has at its heart a statue of the conquistador Ponce de León (1474–1521), the island's first governor. Along Calle San Sebastián, quaint colonial mansions come alive at night as lively bars and restaurants. Step inside Iglesia San José to view the muraled ceiling, then browse the **Museo de Pablo Casals**, celebrating the life of

→

A bronze statue of Ponce de León, which stands in the Plaza de San José

One of San Juan's narrow cobblestoned streets, lit by lamps as dusk falls

Spanish-born cellist Pablo Casals (1876–1973), who lived his later life in San Juan.

Museo de Pablo Casals

 Calle San Sebastián 101 787 723 9185 9:30am–4:30pm Tue–Sat

---

③

Calle del Cristo

Between Calle Tetuán and Calle Norzagaray

Sloping downhill from Plaza de San José, the Calle del

Did You Know?

San Juan is paved with blue cobblestones brought from Spain; they were cast from furnace slag, hence their color.

Cristo is paved with blue-tiled cobblestones, and lined with two-story town-houses that double as cafés, art galleries, and boutiques. A good time to explore is on the first Tuesday of the month, during Noche de Galerías, when the galleries remain open late. The Neo-Classical Catedral de San Juan Bautista was completed in 1852 atop the site of the city's first cathedral. Admire the trompe-l'oeil ceiling and the marble mausoleum containing the remains of Ponce de León.

---

④

Plaza de Armas

Calle San José and Calle San Francisco

San Juan Viejo's central plaza originated as a 16th-century parade ground and later became the administrative center. Open and airy, it has lost much of its early charm to fast-food outlets, although the 1789 Alcaldía (City Hall) still impresses, as do the Neo-Classical Diputación Provincial Delegation and Intendencia, now State Department offices.

EAT

St. Germaine Bistro & Café

This quirky, French-run venue specializes in crêpes, sandwiches, and signature salads.

Sol St 156 787 725 5830 Mon

$$$

Zest

The neon-lit restaurant of the Water Beach Club Hotel offers tasty Latin fusion cuisine.

Tartak St 2 waterbeachhotel.com

$$$

Marmalade

An über-chic lounge bar and restaurant, with excellent build-your-own tasting menus.

Fortaleza St 317 Sun marmaladepr.com

$$$

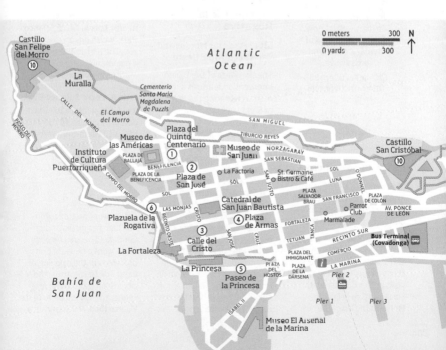

DRINK

Mist Rooftop Bar

This chic, open-air bar atop the San Juan Water Beach Club Hotel is an excellent place to chill. Head here to sip cocktails and mingle with the city's cool cats.

⬜ Playa Isla Verde, Carolina 🌐 waterbeach hotel.com

La Factoria

Combining a laidback, speakeasy-style ambience with killer craft cocktails, it's no wonder this spot draws *la farándula* – the young, bohemian in-crowd. Settle back and enjoy drinks beneath a ceiling strung with twinkling fairy lights.

⬜ San Sebastian St 📞 787 412 4251

Parrot Club

A long-standing local favorite, this colorful bar and dance club is located in the heart of San Juan, and is known for its vibrant mix of live jazz, salsa, and bossa nova.

⬜ Calle Fortaleza 363 🌐 parrotclubpr.com

↑ Locals strolling within the tree-lined area of Paseo de la Princesa

Paseo de la Princesa

⬜ Between Calle La Marina and El Morro headland
ℹ Puerto Rico Tourism Company; 787 721 2400

This waterfront promenade begins at the dock-front and leads west, tracing the course of the towering city walls and ending beneath Fortaleza San Felipe del Morro, at the tip of the headland. The 1.5-mile- (2.4-km-) long walkway of the Princess esplanade is elegantly lined with wrought-iron street lamps. Tree-shaded Plaza del Inmigrante has several fascinating buildings and, soaring over the north side, the Art Deco Banco Popular. Walking west you will pass the former La Princesa prison, now the Puerto Rico Tourism Company's headquarters.

Plazuela de la Rogativa

⬜ Caleta de las Monjas and Calle Recinto del Oeste

The tiny Plaza of the Divine Intervention features a monument celebrating the delivery of San Juan from a British siege in 1797. The Modernist bronze statue shows a bishop leading a torch-lit procession that fooled the invaders into believing that the civilian torch-bearers were a large garrison of Spanish troops.

To the south, the plaza offers fine views of La Fortaleza, the governor's mansion built in 1533, as well as the Puerta de San Juan, at the end of Paseo de la Princesa, which was the main entrance to the walled city in colonial days, and still bears its heavy wooden gates.

Bacardi Rum Distillery

⬜ Carretera 165, Cataño
🕐 9am–4:30pm Tue–Sun
🌐 bacardi.com

Spanning 0.2 sq miles (0.5 sq km) of carefully landscaped grounds, Bacardi, the world's largest rum distillery, produces more than 100,000 gallons (378,540 liters) of rum on a daily basis. Visitors are given a (compulsory) tour that traces the history of the company and of rum manufacture, and are offered a tasting in the bar. Afterward, visit the nearby **Luis A. Ferré Science Park**, which has an excellent zoo. The park is also home to a planetarium and an aerospace museum.

Luis A. Ferré Science Park
🎡🦁 ⬜ Carretera 167, Plaza del Sol Bayamón 📞 787 740 6868 🕐 10am–5pm Wed–Fri, 10am–6pm Sat & Sun

---

Santurce

The heart of metropolitan San Juan lies just inland of Condado. The area recently underwent a rejuvenation process with the opening of Centro de Bellas Artes, the city's main performing arts venue; and **Museo de Arte de Puerto Rico**, which boasts a

superb collection by Puerto Rican artists spanning three centuries. The Plaza del Mercado de Santurce, a traditional market, is housed in a Renaissance-style structure that was erected in 1909. Santurce merges west into Miramar, the most desirable residential address in the city. The nation's premier university, Universidad de Puerto Rico, is located in Hato Rey district, southwest of Santurce, and hosts the Museo de Historia, Antropología y Arte. It displays Puerto Rico's foremost collection of pre-Columbian exhibits. Nearby, **Fundación Luis Muñoz Marín** honors the politician considered the "father" of modern Puerto Rico.

Museo de Arte de Puerto Rico

⊗⊗⊙⊙⊙ 🏛 Av de Diego 299 ⏰10am–5pm Thu–Sat, 10am–8pm Wed, 11am–5pm Sun 🌐mapr.org

Fundación Luis Muñoz Marín

⊗⊗ 🏛Carretera Estatal 877 ⏰10am–2pm Mon–Fri, 10:30am–1pm Sat & Sun 🌐luismunozmarin.org

⑨ Condado

Puerto Rico's first resort, built in the 1950s, Condado became popular with tourists only after the 1980s. Lined with towering high-rise hotels and condominiums, this upscale district occupies a slender isthmus wedged between the Atlantic Ocean and Laguna Condado.

The main thoroughfare, Avenida Ashford, is a favored shopping district among locals and visitors alike. Only 2 miles (3 km) from the avenida, Condado Beach, a talcum-white strand lining the seashore, draws sun-seeking locals on weekends. The place is also well-known for its great nightlife, with plenty of bars and restaurants that come to life after sunset.

Connecting Condado eastward is the trendy neighborhood of Ocean Park, favored by beach-going youth. The coast here is a great place to enjoy parasailing and other watersports. Good beaches extend east from this residential area to the Isla Verde, the stunning setting of some of the city's finest hotels.

> Connecting Condado eastward is the trendy neighborhood of Ocean Park, favored by beach-going youth. The coast here is a great place to enjoy parasailing and other watersports.

Diners within La Perla, one of Condado's lively upscale restaurants

↑ Castillo San Felipe del Morro, viewed from the sea

⑩ 🏃 🎨

SAN JUAN NATIONAL HISTORIC PARK

📍 Avenida Muñoz Rivera and Calle Norzagary, San Juan
🕐 9am-6pm daily 🌐 nps.gov/saju

Encompassing Castillo San Felipe del Morro and Castillo San Cristóbal, plus three-quarters of the remaining colonial-era city wall, this massive military complex is a potent symbol of the once mighty power of Spain.

↑ A scenic watchtower at Castillo San Cristóbal

With tunnels, watchtowers, armories, sentry posts, and museums sufficient to fill an entire day, this UNESCO World Heritage Site is best explored with a guide. The fortresses are separated by the windswept Campo del Morro headland and linked by the perimeter wall.

Commanding the clifftop at San Juan Viejo's eastern entrance, Castillo San Cristóbal was initiated in 1634 and completed in 1783. It was designed by military engineers to prevent a land assault, with successive lines of defense and a moat. The barracks have eight rooms, with one furnished as it was 200 years ago.

Begun in 1539 to guard the harbor entrance, nearby Castillo San Felipe del Morro was completed in 1786. The lighthouse offers fine views of the castle and the El Canuelo fort. A museum displays an interesting collection of swords and military costumes.

→
Devil's
Sentry Box,
in Castillo
San Cristóbal

↑ An entrance way at Fort Castillo San
  Felipe del Morro

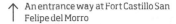

↑ One of the vaulted rooms in the soldiers'
  barracks at Castillo San Cristóbal

PASEO DEL MORRO

This marvelous pedestrian esplanade
snakes along the edge of the harbor
channel at the foot of La Muralla. It
begins at the Puerta de San Juan – the
only remaining gate of six in the soaring
perimeter wall – and runs to the very tip
of El Morro headland. It is punctuated by
fascinating interpretive signs, and by
garitas hovering overhead. There's no
access to Castillo del Morro, but cooled
by balmy sea breezes, the walk is its
own reward (especially at sunset).

EXPERIENCE MORE

②
Arecibo Observatory

⌂ 55 miles (88 km) W of San Juan ⓣ ⓞ 9am–4pm Wed–Sun ⓦ naic.edu

The world's second largest single-dish radio telescope is a bowl suspended between towering *mogotes* in the Gaurionex Mountains (it was nudged out of first place in 2016 by a telescope in China that has a reflector the size of 30 soccer pitches).

The observatory opened in 1963 under the Department of Defense to study the upper atmosphere and outer space using radio frequency transmission. Officially known as the National Astronomy and Ionosphere Center, and operated by the National Science Foundation, it is the headquarters of the Search for Extraterrestrial Intelligence. The observatory's Angel Ramos Foundation Visitor Center has excellent, though dated, informational exhibits.

James Bond fans may also recognize Arecibo as the setting for a dramatic fight scene in the 1995 movie, *Goldeneye*.

③
Dorado

⌂ 15 miles (24 km) W of San Juan ⓣ

Named for the golden sands stretching along the palm-shaded shore, Dorado provides a gateway to the beaches for San Juan families, and deluxe hotels command the best beachside turf. It became a fashionable spot in the 1950s, with the former Dorado Beach Hotel (now a Ritz-Carlton Reserve) attracting celebrities such as the Kennedys. The best public beaches include Cerro Gordo and Playa Sardinera. The town has a main square, Plaza de Recreo, and local history exhibits can be seen at **Museo La Casa del Rey**, built as a parador in 1823, and later used as a Spanish garrison.

West of Dorado, Guajataca Forest Reserve protects a vast tropical forest. Nearby is the Lago Guajataca, which has picnic and fishing facilities.

Museo La Casa del Rey
 ⌂ Calle Méndez Vigo 292 ☎ 787 796 1030 ⓞ 8am–4:30pm Mon–Fri

←

Interior of the Arecibo Observatory's museum, which also offers breathtaking views *(inset)*

4

Parque Las Cavernas del Río Camuy

📍 57 miles (92 km) SW of San Juan 📞 787 898 3136
🕐 🟢 8:30am–5pm Wed–Sun

Puerto Rico's largest cave system is also the world's third largest, with over 220 caverns, though only 16 can be visited on guided tours. These begin with a steep downhill trolley ride to the Cueva Clara de Enpalma, followed by a snaking, hour-long walk through the cool cavern, which soars 170 ft (52 m) high. Key dripstone formations are spotlit. Bats flit overhead and a blind endemic fish species swims in the black underground river. Next up is a ride in the trolley to Tres Pueblos Sinkhole, plunging 400 ft (122 m). The caves closed following damage by Hurricane Maria, but are undergoing restoration and should reopen by 2020.

5

Playa Jobos

📍 82 miles (132 km) W of San Juan

Surfers ride the Atlantic breakers that wash ashore at this long beach which shines like silver lamé. The sands here have been whipped into dunes by the winds. Beach bars, restaurants, and hotels line twin beaches separated by a craggy headland of ironshore (limestone-coral formation). El Pozo de Jacinto (Jacinto's Well), on the western side of the beach, is a small natural blowhole that attracts many visitors.

Punta Borinquen, southwest of Playa Jobos, has some spectacular beaches, including Playa Crash Boat, which offers great diving just offshore, and is popular with surfers. The point previously served as a U.S. Air Force base, and visitors can enjoy a round on the old Base Ramey golf course.

Columbus first set foot on the island near the town of Aguadilla, where the Caribbean's largest aquatic theme park, **Parque Acuático Las Cascadas**, is now located.

Parque Acuático Las Cascadas

📍 2 Puerto Rico, Aguadilla 📞 787 819 1030
🕐 Mar–Sep: 9am–5pm daily

6

Parque Ceremonial Indígena Caguana

📍 65 miles (105 km) W of San Juan 📞 787 894 0370
🕐 🟢 8am–4:30pm daily

Surrounded by lush montane forests, Parque Ceremonial Indígena Caguana provides an excellent overview of ancient Taíno culture. The archaeological site – which was excavated in 1915 – was once used for both ceremonial and recreational purposes. It features 10 ceremonial

→

An ancient petroglyph at the Parque Ceremonial Indígena Caguana

bateyes (ball courts) surrounded by monolithic granite slabs that are etched with petroglyphs of human figures. The most notable among these is the Mujer de Caguana, a fertility figure showing a woman in childbirth. A small museum at the site displays ancient artifacts, and a gift shop sells *zemis* (worshiped figures).

Did You Know?

Puerto Rico was one of Spain's last two colonies in the New World (the other being Cuba).

7

Mayagüez

⌂ **100 miles (150 km) SW of San Juan**

Named for the river upon which it sits, Mayagüez is translated as "Land of the Clear Waters." Though the town was founded in 1760, little sign of its early past remains following a series of devastating fires. Nonetheless, its spacious main square – Plaza Colón – is adorned with fine buildings, most notably the Neo-Classical Town Hall and behind it, the Teatro Yagüez. The latter, declared a National Historic Landmark in 1976, remains a major hub of performing arts, culture, and education in the town. Also of interest are the square's 16 bronze statues, and that of Christopher Columbus. Locals gather here to play dominoes beneath jacaranda trees.

Home to seven colleges and universities, and with a student population of over 13,000, Mayagüez offers a lively nightlife scene and plenty of good eateries to choose from. The town is also a popular departure point for sportfishing.

8

Boquerón

⌂ **15 miles (24 km) S of Mayagüez**

Locals flock to this slightly rough-around-the edges beach town, which has a lovely strand hidden behind old clapboard houses and a string of restaurants and bars. A special treat is to buy freshly caught oysters from street stands. Bosque Estatal de Boquerón, the area's state forest, is a dry tropical and mangrove forest which offers tremendous birding. The beaches that line its shore are also popular, with snorkelers hoping to glimpse some of the local marine life. The nearby **Refugio de Aves de Boquerón** is similarly good for birding, and also has blinds for close-up viewing of various waterfowl and manatees.

South of town lies the Cabo Rojo Peninsula, where a semi-derelict lighthouse pins a dramatic headland that is named for its red-hued rocks. Nearby, simple accommodations at Playa El Combate cater for island families who gather to sunbathe and party on this narrow beach.

An hour's drive east of Boquerón, the south coast community of La Parguera is one of Puerto Rico's liveliest coastal resorts. The mangrove-fringed bay is unfortunately spoiled by the buzz of jet skis and excessive construction, but its a good place to organize a boat trip to Isla Magueyes and Phosphorescent Bay.

Refugio de Aves de Boquerón

⊗ ⌂ Carretera 301 Km 5.1 787 851 4795 ⏰ 8am–4pm Tue-Sun

9

Rincón

⌂ **Carretera 115, 88 miles (140 km) W of San Juan** ✈ **Aguadilla Airport, 5 miles (8 km)** ⓘ

Considered the premier surfing spot in Puerto Rico, this beach resort midway down the west side of the island

↑ The colorful town hall in Plaza Colón, Mayagüez's tree-lined main square

combines rugged beauty with a laid-back social scene and a lively nightlife. A network of roads link several beaches and rustic communities, including Rincón, spread across the pointy Punta Higuero peninsula. Tide-pooling here is fun, while snorkeling is great (in the protection of the scattered reefs), and open waters offer superb diving. Winds whip up waves that can reach as high as 40 ft (12 m), drawing surfing aficionados in search of the ultimate ride. Sunsets in Rincón are a blaze of sensational color, and humpback whales are often sighted from shore as they migrate through the Mona Passage during winter.

Rincón faces the Mona Passage, studded by Isla Mona, a rocky, uninhabited outcrop populated by birds, iguanas, and marine turtles. This wildlife refuge requires a permit from Departamento de Recursos Naturales y Ambientales to visit. Moca, inland of Rincón, produces *mundillo* (lace) and hosts the Mundillo Festival each June. Festivities include lace-weaving demos, along with traditional music, and plenty of food and drink.

10 San Germán

🏠 30 miles (48 km) SE of Mayagüez

This quaint hillside town was founded in 1512 – the second settlement established by the Spanish in Puerto Rico – and is home to the most intact colonial core outside San Juan Viejo. Colorful reminders of the wealth generated by the 19th-century coffee boom adorn its leafy plazas: 249 buildings are listed on the National Register of Historic Places. The Iglesia Porta Coeli, which dates from 1606 and is the second-oldest church in Puerto Rico, exhibits religious statuary and *santos* in the Museo de Arte Religioso. The church stands over the Plaza Santo Domingo, which is noteworthy for the 19th-century gingerbread Casa Morales. A short walk west leads to the Plaza Francisco Mariano Quiñones, graced by the Neo-Classical Iglesia de San Germán de Auxerre, which was rebuilt in 1737 after an earthquake.

> Sunsets in Rincón are a blaze of sensational color, and humpback whales are often sighted from shore as they migrate through the Mona Passage during winter.

11   Hacienda Buena Vista

🏠 7 miles (11 km) N of Ponce ☎ 787 722 5882 ⏰ Tours only, book ahead

Deep in the mountains north of Ponce, this beautiful plantation can be traced to 1833. Although a primary producer of coffee, it also grew rice and maize. Original mill machinery shows how the maize was milled and the still-working water-turbine can be seen alongside other memorabilia, the elegant great house, warehouses, and slave quarters. It is managed by the Conservation Trust of Puerto Rico, which has resurrected the farm as a working coffee estate.

PHOSPHORESCENT BAYS IN PUERTO RICO

One of the coolest and most magical experiences of a Puerto Rico visit is the spectral glow of a bioluminescent lagoon on moonless nights. Puerto Rico has three such other-worldly lagoons, which are lit by microscopic dinoflagellates - single-celled organisms that emit a pulsing electric-blue light when disturbed by passing fish, turtles, or humans. Most impressive is Bioluminescent Bay (also known as Mosquito Bay) on Vieques *(p215)*, where visitors can take a kayak trip, slipping into the water to spark their own halo. The others are Laguna Grande, in Cabezas de San Juan Nature Reserve near Fajardo, and La Parguera Bay, in the southwest.

Ponce

78 miles (125 km) SW of San Juan ✈🚌 **ℹ Plaza las Delicias; 787 841 8044;**

Founded in 1692, Ponce still remains an important port city and abounds in cultural institutions that reflect its historical preeminence as a center for artists and political thinkers. Architecturally distinct from San Juan, its downtown area reminds many visitors of New Orleans, notably so during its renowned Carnival, when dancers parade through the streets in extravagant *vejigante* (horned) masks. The city was a major slave-trading port during the early colonial days and African heritage is firmly rooted in local culture.

The city witnessed a steady decline in the 20th century. Fortunately, the "Ponce en marcha" restoration project was initiated in the mid-1980s, and most of the city's notable historic buildings are once again gleaming.

At the heart of Ponce, the spacious Plaza Las Delicias goes by various other names, including Plaza Central. It actually comprises two squares: Plaza Luis Muñoz Rivera and Plaza Federico Degetau, to the north and south, respectively, of the Catedral Nuestra Señora de la Guadalupe and the famous black-and-red-striped **Parque de Bombas**. This whimsical fire station has an antique fire truck and vintage cars on display. The twin squares have several statues, and the Lion's Fountain, which looks splendid when floodlit at night. The buildings around the square are a medley of architectural styles spanning three centuries and ranging from Spanish colonial to Neo-Classical and Art Deco. The most commanding building is the Neo-Classical Teatro La Perla, which has served as a performing arts center since 1941. The surrounding streets are graced by pretty homes fronted by wrought-iron grills. Adjoining the theater, the **Museo de la Historia de Ponce** is the nation's foremost history museum. One block east, Casa Serrallés is an exem-

💬 INSIDER TIP
Whale Watch

Every winter, humpback whales migrate to the Mona Passage to mate and calve in the tropical waters. Rincón lighthouse is a great spot to view them from shore, or get closer with Taino Divers *(tainodivers.com)*.

plar of Art Nouveau styling. Today it houses the **Museo de la Música Puertorriqueña**, which traces the evolution of music on the island.

Toward the north, the city is flanked by Loma Vigía (Watchman's Hill), which is dominated by La Cruceta de Vigía, a huge cement cross. At its base, **Castillo Serrallés**, a Spanish Revival mansion built in 1926 for the rum magnate Don Juan Serrallés, is furnished with a few splendid colonial pieces and also serves as a Museum of Sugar & Rum. The gardens in its complex are exquisite. The **Museo de Arte de Ponce**, a Modernist structure designed by Edward Durell Stone, has works by artists such as Gainsborough, Diego Rivera, and Delacroix, as well as some avant-garde Puerto Rican artists.

Parque de Bombas
Plaza Las Delicias
☏ 787 284 3338 🕘 9am-6pm Wed-Mon

Museo de la Historia de Ponce
♿ **Calle Isabel 53**
☏ 787 844 7071 🕘 9am-4pm Tue-Sun

Museo de la Música Puertorriqueña
Calle Isabel 45 ☏ 787 848 7016 🕘 8:30am-4:30pm Tue-Sun

→
A reconstructed tribal hut within the Centro Ceremonial Indígena de Tibes

Castillo Serrallés
  🅰 Cruzeta El Vigía 17 🕒 9:30am–5:30pm Tue–Sun 🔲 museocastilloserralles.com

Museo de Arte de Ponce
🅰 Av Las Américas 2325 🕒 9am–5pm Thu–Sun 🔲 Pub hols 🔲 museoarte ponce.org

13

Bosque Estatal de Guánica

🅰 3 miles (5 km) E of Guánica 📞 787 821 5706

Protecting a rare stand of seasonally deciduous subtropical dry forest, this United Nations Biosphere Reserve spans the small town of Guánica. It covers 9,900 acres (4,000 ha) of gnarly dwarf tree species – including campeche, gumbo limbo, and ancient guayacán, among others – festooned with mistletoe, bromeliads, and Spanish moss. Additional ecosystems include pockets of semi-desert that are studded with cactuses, agaves, and yuccas, as well as mangroves, coral reefs, and rocky shoreline with white-sand beaches where green and leatherback turtles nest.

The larger eastern section is the easiest part to explore. Carretera 334 climbs to the ranger station, where you can pick up a map and begin most of the reserve's 12 trails. Be sure to wear sturdy footwear, and bring lots of water and a pair of binoculars to spy the many bird species, which include nine of Puerto Rico's 14 endemics.

←
The eye-catching striped facade of the Parque de Bombas in Ponce

14

Centro Ceremonial Indígena de Tibes

🅰 2 miles (3 km) N of Ponce 📞 787 840 2255 🕒 9am–3:30pm Tue–Sun

Discovered after Hurricane Eloise in 1975, Centro Ceremonial Indígena de Tibes is a pre-Columbian site which is still being excavated. Today, it is one of the largest and most important ceremonial sites in Puerto Rico, covering 217,800 sq ft (20,250 sq m), and includes nine *bateyes* (ball courts) plus burial grounds, all hemmed in by boulders etched with petroglyphs. The site displays signs of two cultures: the Igneris, who settled on the island around AD 300, and the Taíno, who overran the Igneris around AD 1000. A small museum displays remarkable exhibits including pottery, axe-heads, and *cemi (p218)* excavated at this site, along with an adult skeleton curled up in a fetal position. A reconstruction of a traditional Taíno village helps educate visitors on the lifestyle of the indigenous people. Visits are by guided tour only and it is advisable to make reservations in advance.

EAT

Blossoms

A long-running local favorite that offers an array of Asian dishes, from Szechuan to sushi.

⬤ El Conquistador Resort, Fajardo
ⓦ elconresort.com

$⑤$$⑤$⑤

Susie's Restaurant

This cozy restaurant features patio dining lit by tiki torches.

⬤ Rte 250, Dewey, Culebra ☏ 787 340 7058
☒ Wed & Thu

$⑤$$⑤$⑤

El Quenepo

An elegant option, known for its fusion menu and craft beers.

⬤ Calle Flamboyan 148, Vieques ☒ Sun & Mon
ⓦ elquenepovieques.com

$⑤$$⑤$⑤

 15

El Yunque National Forest

⬤ 25 miles (40 km) SE of San Juan ◷ 7:30am–6pm daily ⓦ fs.usda.gov/elyunque

The 44 sq mile (114 sq km) El Yunque National Forest – formerly the Caribbean National Forest – is the only tropical rainforest within the U.S. National Forest system. Ranging from an elevation of 30 ft (9 m) at its base to 3,533 ft (1,077 m) at the top of Cerro El Toro, the rain-sodden park (named for a flat-topped mountain, "the anvil") features various ecosystems, including high mountain cloud forest and dwarf forest atop the highest slopes. El Portal Rain Forest Center, the main visitors' center (due to reopen in late 2019 following hurricane damage), offers splendid exhibits on local geology, geography, and ecosystems. The park has a number of hiking trails, from easy to strenuous among plunging waterfalls and steep ravines. This region offers hikers some of the best birding and wildlife viewing on the island.

16

Playa Piñones

⬤ 19 miles (30 km) E of San Juan

This golden beach, located on Carretera 187, is favored by the locals on weekends, when families set up picnics beneath the palms. Weekend traffic jams the roads, so it is better to visit the beach on weekdays. Roadside restaurants sell tempting fried seafoods. Paseo Piñones Recreational Trail runs along the shore, providing a scenic thoroughfare for cyclists, joggers, and strollers.

The beach extends east to Playa Vacia Talega, known for its "cemented" sand dunes. Farther inland is Bosque Estatal Piñones, which protects a prize wetland habitat for waterfowl and wading birds. Occupying the coastal flatlands east of Playa Vacia Talega, the small, relatively impoverished town of Loíza Aldea is a center for African culture. Every year in late July it plays host to the colorful, week-long Fiesta de Santiago Apóstol, Puerto Rico's premier carnival.

Hikers exploring the dramatic scenery of El Yunque National Forest

⑰ Luquillo

🏠 45 miles (72 km) E of San Juan

A string of golden-white beaches decorate the northeast shore between the towns of Río Grande and Luquillo. The sands meld into warm, reef-protected waters of peacock blues and greens, great for snorkeling and tidepooling. Playa Luquillo is lined with a number of upscale resorts. To the west, Playa Río Mar is a relatively uncrowded setting for the vast Wyndham Grand and Rio Mar Country Club. East of Playa Luquillo are the wind-whipped Playa Azul and Playa La Selva, where breakers bring surfers ashore.

⑱ Fajardo

🏠 36 miles (58 km) SE of San Juan 🚆🚌

The sprawling coastal town of Fajardo is a major maritime center for sportfishing and sailing charters, available at Puerto del Rey Marina. Scheduled ferries also depart here for Vieques and Culebra.

The small **Las Cabezas de San Juan Nature Reserve**, immediately north of Fajardo, protects a mangrove forest where manatees swim in freshwater lagoons and dozens of waterfowl can be seen on the boardwalk trail (reservations are required). The El Faro lighthouse, built in 1882, is well preserved. Nearby, Playa Seven Seas offers good snorkeling in reef-protected shallows.

Las Cabezas de San Juan Nature Reserve
☺☺ 🏠 Carretera 987
📞 787 722 5882

⑲ Vieques

🏠 20 miles (32 km) SE of Fajardo 🚆🚌

The largest of the 24 isles of the Spanish Virgin archipelago surrounding Puerto Rico, Vieques takes life at a laidback pace. Most of the inhabitants live in Isabel Segunda, a small town that remains charmingly old-world, with little traffic. During World War II the U.S. Navy used the isle for gunnery practice – a deterrent to development during the next five decades. The bombardment

> **The largest of the 24 isles of the Spanish Virgin archipelago surrounding Puerto Rico, Vieques takes life at a laidback pace.**

ceased in 2003, when the navy pulled out. Today, Vieques is a chic spot for off-the-beaten-path charm and the chance to see deer, manatee, and four species of marine turtles at Vieques National Wildlife Refuge. Hotels are found mostly around Esperanza, a sleepy village overlooking a gorgeous bay. Nearby, Bioluminescent Bay (p211) comes alive at night, when bioluminescent microorganisms glow when disturbed. Manatees also frequent the coastal lagoons. In addition, Vieques is a major nesting site for marine turtles. The **Vieques Art and History Museum**, in Fort Conde Mirasol, has exhibits on island history.

Vieques Art and History Museum
☺☺☺ 🏠 El Fortín Conde de Mirasol, Isabel Segunda
📞 787 741 1717 🕙 9am–4pm Wed–Sun

⑳ Culebra

🏠 27 miles (43 km) E of Fajardo 🚆🚌

Vieques's even sleepier smaller sister is renowned for its scintillating beaches, including undisputably Puerto Rico's finest: Playa Flamenco, a broad curve of pure white sand and gorgeous ocean waters drawing day-trippers from Puerto Rico on weekends. Nearby Playa Carlos Rosario has a coral reef close to shore, perfect for snorkeling, while Playas Resaca, Brava, and Flamenco are protected as marine turtle-nesting sites within Culebra National Wildlife Refuge.

↑ Sun-worshipers relaxing beneath the shade of palm trees on Playa Luquillo

HIKING ADVENTURES IN PUERTO RICO

Puerto Rico is a hiker's nirvana. Active travelers can lace up their boots to explore a kaleidoscope of ecosystems and fabulous landscapes. From the lush El Yunque rainforest to the arid, cactus-stippled Bosque Estatal de Guánica, the isle's 14 forest reserves offer walks, hikes, and treks for every ability.

SHORT AND EASY

Things don't get much easier than at Reserva Las Cabezas de San Juan, at the northeast tip of the island. A trolley ride leads to a half a mile- (1 km-) long board-walk trail where you might spot mana-tees in Laguna Grande. In Bosque Estatal Guajataca, 25 miles (40 km) of trails weave among *mogotes* – isolated, sheer-faced limestone mountains laced with caverns and canyons.

STAIRMASTER WORKOUT

The Caribbean National Forest has 23 well-serviced trails through virginal montane forests. Most are short and make easy loops. To test your stamina, take to the rugged 6 mile- (10 km-) long El Toro Trail, passing through all four tropical forest ecosystems as you summit Mount Toro. Farther west, Reserva Forestal Toro Negro has steep trails through forest shrouded in mist.

FOR WILDLIFE LOVERS

Isla Mona, a 3-hour boat ride from Mayagüez, is called the "Galapagos of the Caribbean." Two hiking trails offer up-close viewing of Mona iguanas, red-footed boobies, and frigatebirds. The easy 1 mile- (2-km-) long Ballena Trail in Bosque Estatal de Guánica showcases a mosaic of habitats where hawks swoop overhead, iguanas scurry, and thimble-size frogs hop about underfoot.

↑ Hiker marveling at La Mina Falls in El Yunque (Caribbean National Forest)

↑ Densely forested path through the jungle at El Yunque

TOP 5 WILDLIFE SPECIES

Look out for these amazing species while hiking through Puerto Rico's ample rainforest.

Coqui

Puerto Rico's adorably tiny mascot, and the world's smallest frog, is named for its surprisingly loud two-note "ko-KEE" chirp. There is a Puerto Rican expression, "Soy de aqui, como el coquí," which translates to "I'm from here, like the coquí."

Puerto Rican Giant Anole

This large, bright-green tree-dwelling lizard extends a red dewlap to attract females and ward off other males. It moves by jumping from branch to branch within the canopy, for which it has evolved long hind limbs.

Puerto Rican Emerald Hummingbird

The diminutive zumbadorcito weighs 3 grams (0.1 ounce) and was worshiped by the Taíno as a "god bird." The male has iridescent green feathers on its body and a black tail, while the female has a white breast and white tail feathers. They are very territorial and often defend their patch with elaborate aerial pursuits.

Mona Iguana

Found only on Isla Mona, this iguana species can reach 3.3 ft (1 m) in length. Despite its dragon-like appearance, it's a harmless vegetarian and spends most of the day basking in the sun or underground, conserving energy.

Puerto Rican Parrot

The island's endemic green parrot is critically endangered; fewer than 50 remain in the wild, and only in the El Yunque National Forest.

1 A tiny coqui – the world's smallest frog

2 The long-limbed giant anole

3 An iridescent male hummingbird

4 The heavily armored Mona iguana

5 A striking green Puerto Rican parrot

A DRIVING TOUR
LA RUTA PANORÁMICA

Length 165 miles (265 km) **Stopping-off points**
Roadside lechonerías at Guavate, for roast pork on the
spit. For lodging, stop at the historic Hacienda Gripiñas

This panoramic route, officially known as Ruta
Panorámica Luis Muñoz Marín, runs along the
island's mountainous backbone from Yabucoa
to Mayagüez. About 40 separate highways
make up the clearly marked, well-paved route.
It passes Cerro de Punta, the island's highest
peak, as well as a variety of montane forests.
The route is best traversed with at least one
overnight stay at a parador.

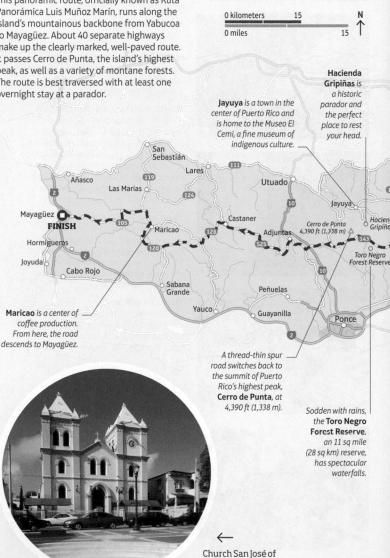

0 kilometers — 15
0 miles — 15
N ↑

Hacienda Gripiñas is a historic parador and the perfect place to rest your head.

Jayuya is a town in the center of Puerto Rico and is home to the Museo El Cemi, a fine museum of indigenous culture.

San Sebastián
Añasco
Las Marias
Lares
111
119
124
Utuado
10
Jayuya
14

Mayagüez
FINISH
Hormigueros
Joyuda
Cabo Rojo
105
Maricao
120
128
Castaner
Adjuntas
525
Cerro de Punta 4,390 ft (1,338 m)
143
Hacienda Gripiñas
Toro Negro Forest Reserve
10
2

Sabana Grande
Yauco
Peñuelas
Guayanilla
Ponce
2

Maricao *is a center of coffee production. From here, the road descends to Mayagüez.*

A thread-thin spur road switches back to the summit of Puerto Rico's highest peak, **Cerro de Punta,** *at 4,390 ft (1,338 m).*

Sodden with rains, the **Toro Negro Forest Reserve***, an 11 sq mile (28 sq km) reserve, has spectacular waterfalls.*

← Church San José of Aibonito in Puerto Rico's highest town

↑ The Museo El Cemi in Jayuya is designed like a giant
cemi – an earthly representation of Taíno divinities

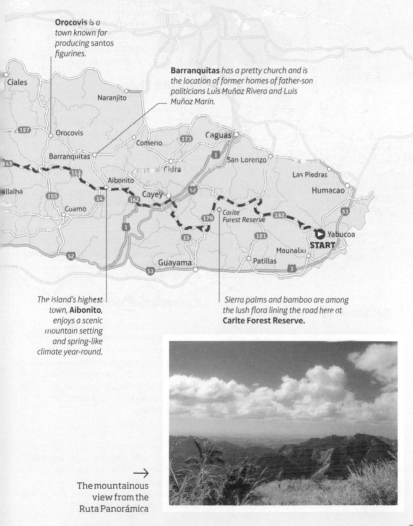

Orocovis *is a
town known for
producing santos
figurines.*

Barranquitas *has a pretty church and is
the location of former homes of father-son
politicians Luis Muñoz Rivera and Luis
Muñoz Marín.*

*The island's highest
town,* **Aibonito**,
*enjoys a scenic
mountain setting
and spring-like
climate year-round.*

*Sierra palms and bamboo are among
the lush flora lining the road here at*
Carite Forest Reserve.

→
The mountainous
view from the
Ruta Panorámica

PRACTICAL
INFORMATION

Here you will find all the essential advice and information you will need before and during your stay in Puerto Rico.

AT A GLANCE

CURRENCY
US Dollar (US$)

TIME ZONE
Eastern Standard Time, 5 hours behind GMT

LANGUAGE
Spanish

ELECTRICITY SUPPLY
Puerto Rico operates on 110 volts. Outlets use US two- or three-prong plugs

EMERGENCY NUMBERS

TEL

911

TAP WATER
Water purity is unreliable so, to be safe, drink bottled water

When To Go

As in most of the Caribbean, the best weather here is from December through April. The other months get more rain and are hotter, although breezes help keep things cool year-round. Parts of the south-west are in a rain shadow and also receive few breezes. Accommodation rates are generally lower during summer months (June through August), but cultural events are spread throughout the year.

Getting There

Most scheduled flights arrive at San Juan's Luis Muñoz Marín International Airport (SJU), with flights from more than 20 US cities. Some flights arrive at regional airports in Ponce, Mayagüez, and San Juan's Isla Grande Airport (SIG). American Airlines, Delta, JetBlue, Spirit Airlines, United Airlines, and US Airways offer services to Puerto Rico, as do Air Canada and numerous charter airlines. Several European airlines such as British Airways connect through Miami, while Iberia has direct flights. The regional partner of American Airlines, Air Flamenco connects the provincial airports within Puerto Rico, including Vieques and Culebra, which can also be reached by ferry from Fajardo.

Personal Security

Violent crime against visitors is rare, but carjackings and opportunistic snatch-and-grab theft are not uncommon in San Juan. Avoid wearing jewelry in public and keep valuables locked in a hotel safe. Puerto Rican drivers have little regard for traffic rules, so drive cautiously. Check with locals about tidal conditions before swimming.

Health

Puerto Rico is safe and there are no endemic tropical diseases. Private medical clinics, such as Clínica Las Américas, are ubiquitous and all major towns have hospitals. Hotels can arrange for a doctor in any emergency.

Passports and Visas

All visitors, except US citizens, must show a passport when visiting Puerto Rico. Visitors from Europe may enter the country for 90 days without a visa, but must register with ESTA online. This can take up to 72 hours for approval and there is a charge. Travel requirements may change – check before travel. All visitors must have a ticket for onward travel.

LGBT+ Safety

Puerto Rico is perhaps the Caribbean's most liberal enclave regarding LGBT+ rights, including legal protections, and the Puerto Rico Tourism Company actively promotes gay and lesbian travel. San Juan's gay scene is well-developed and open, and several key beach destinations and hotels are LGBT+ friendly. However, small towns and rural areas are much more conservative, and here a level of discretion is advised to avoid a negative response.

Money

The US dollar is the official and sole currency of Puerto Rico, although locals still use the term "peso" or "billetes" for the dollar. Traveler's checks in US dollars are accepted in some hotels, restaurants, and stores, although credit cards are always preferable. There are banks with ATMs in almost every town.

Cell Phones and Wi-Fi

Visitors bringing their own cell phones should check with their service providers to determine if they will work in Puerto Rico.

The local carrier is Claro, but major US carriers such as AT&T, Sprint, and T-Mobile are also accessible. Most hotels, restaurants, and cafes offer Wi-Fi, either free or for a fee.

Getting Around

The easiest way of discovering the island is to hire a rental car or to stitch together a series of island excursions. These can be taxi tours, day trips offered by tour companies, plus hiking and caving outings, and even sailing trips. Domestic flights connect San Juan to Vieques and Culebra – the Spanish Virgins – but the most pleasant way to visit these outlying islands is by ferry from Fajardo, which takes about an hour.

Crowded minivans provide public transportation between towns. Driving in Puerto Rico has its own challenges and traffic jams are ubiquitous in urban centers. The island has an extensive road system, but congestion is severe, and a frightening disregard for traffic regulations makes driving in Puerto Rico quite risky. Most major international car rental companies, such as AVIS, Hertz, and Budget, are represented. Renting a scooter is a good option for exploring Vieques and Culebra, but be sure to wear a helmet. Taxis offer efficient service within San Juan. The hotel concierge or front desk can call for a taxi waiting outside most tourist hotels. Locals rely on públicos (private mini-vans) that operate communal taxi services for town-to-town travel. Puerto Rico Tourism Company can provide information on taxi companies.

Visitor Information

The Puerto Rico Tourism Company has offices in the US, Canada, Germany, Spain, and the UK that provide brochures. Within Puerto Rico, it has offices on Paseo de la Princesa and by the cruise port in San Juan. The **Official Tourism website** provides lots of helpful information and inspiration for your trip.

Puerto Rico Tourism Company
 w seepuertorico.com
Official Tourism Website
 w discoverpuertorico.com

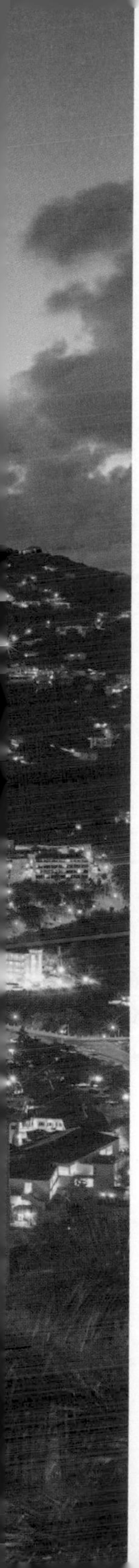

VIRGIN ISLANDS

The Virgin Islands is an archipelago of mostly hilly green isles, many of which are uninhabited, ringed with gorgeous sandy beaches and turquoise waters. Following catastrophic damage inflicted by Hurricane Irma in September 2017, the affected islands are gradually returning to their status as a getaway paradise.

On the western side of the archipelago lie the U.S. Virgin Islands, an unincorporated U.S. territory. The main islands of St Thomas, St. John, and St. Croix were colonized by Denmark from the late 1600s and developed as slave-trading ports and plantations. The Danish legacy is still very much in evidence in the buildings and street names of Charlotte Amalie on St. Thomas, and in Frederiksted and Christiansted on St. Croix. Fearing they might be used by Germany as submarine bases, the United States purchased the islands in 1917 for U.S.$25 million.

The 60 or so islands that make up the British Virgin Islands have been under some form of British jurisdiction for some 350 years, and are an internally self-governing British overseas territory. Tourism, especially sailing, is key, but as a tax haven, financial services are important too. Of the four main islands, Tortola is the largest, liveliest and most developed, while Virgin Gorda is slower paced. Jost Van Dyke island, named after a Dutch pirate, is known for its beach bars, while low-lying, reef-fringed Anegada is a snorkeler's dream. The islands' most famous resident is Richard Branson, who lives on the private Necker Island.

VIRGIN ISLANDS

Experience

0 kilometers 6
0 miles 6

N ↑

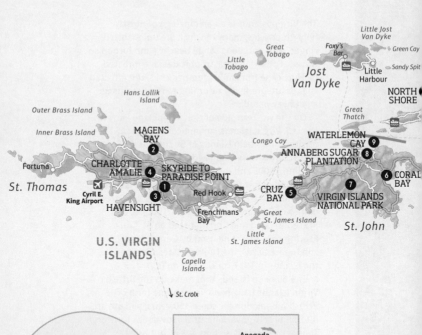

Cow Wreck
Bay
Jack
Bay
Tuble Bay
**Auguste George
Airport**
The Settlement
Anegada
Lower
Bay
White
Bay

BRITISH
VIRGIN ISLANDS

*Virgin
Gorda*

Necker
Island
Prickly Pear
Island
Mosquito
Island
21 GORDA PEAK
NATIONAL PARK

Great
Camanoe
George
Dog
West
Dog
Great
Dog
*Savannah
Bay*

Guana
Island
Scrub
Island
15 MARINA
CAY
20 VIRGIN GORDA

**Terrance B. Lettsome
International Airport**
Spanish Town
✈ **Virgin Gorda Airport**

IR O'NEAL
BOTANIC GARDENS
18
17 ROAD TOWN
Tortola
*Baths
National Park*

19 SAGE MOUNTAIN
NATIONAL PARK

Salt
Island
*Ginger
Island*

22
RMS *RHONE*
MARINE PARK
Cooper
Island

Peter Island

*Norman
Island*

*C a r i b b e a n
S e a*

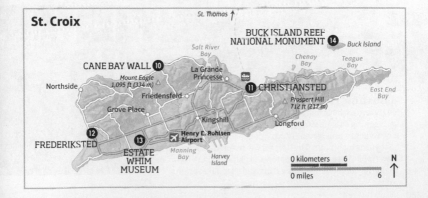

St. Croix

St. Thomas ↑

BUCK ISLAND REEF
NATIONAL MONUMENT **14** *Buck Island*

CANE BAY WALL **10**
Salt River
Bay
La Grande
Princesse
*Chenay
Bay*
*Teague
Bay*

Northside
*Mount Eagle
1,095 ft (334 m)*
Friedensfeld
11 CHRISTIANSTED
*East End
Bay*

Grove Place
Kingshill
△ *Prospect Hill
712 ft (217 m)*
Longford

12
FREDERIKSTED
13
ESTATE
WHIM
MUSEUM
✈ **Henry E. Rohlsen
Airport**
*Manning
Bay*
*Harvey
Island*

0 kilometers   6

0 miles   6

N
↑

◁ Party Spots

The plentiful bars and restaurants at Cane Garden Bay *(p236)* make it a fun party venue, perfect for whiling away the hours and escaping galley duties. Plus, the anchorages are close to shore so you can simply swim or wade up to the beach. For more eclectic bars, sail to the east of the island and Trellis Bay just next to the airport, which offers plenty of moorings and a monthly full moon party on the picturesque beach.

THE VIRGIN ISLANDS FOR
SMOOTH SAILING

With aquamarine waters, sun-soaked harbors, and white-sand beaches, the Virgin Islands are the Caribbean's premier sailing destination. Sail, swim, and snorkel by day, then head to shore in the evening to a beach bar or restaurant for rum cocktails and a fine French-Caribbean dinner.

△ Bustling Marinas

Lively and sociable marinas have facilities to accommodate vacationing charters, long-term residents, and visiting mega-yachts, and generally provide slips or mooring balls and boat yards for repairs. The horseshoe-shaped harbor at Road Town *(p236)* also features customs facilities, while Virgin Gorda Yacht Harbor has numerous eating and shopping options.

◁ Peaceful Escapes

With several anchorages around Jost Van Dyke, sailors can relax at Foxy's Bar *(p239)* in Great Harbor – an idylic spot reached only by boat. Alternatively, sail around to White Bay in the west for a quiet stroll along the long stretch of sheltered sand.

▷ Drink Like a Pirate

Put hair on your chest by knocking back a "painkiller" – a heady concoction of rum, pineapple and orange juice, coconut cream, and nutmeg – at Pusser's Bar in the B.V.I *(pussers.com)*. Set on the tiny speck of Marina Cay in a sheltered, emerald-green lagoon, this spot lures sailors from far and wide since it's easily accessible from the Sir Francis Drake Channel.

◁ Abandon Ship

Head to tiny and uninhabited Salt Island to the south of Tortola for some excellent scuba diving or snorkeling at one of the Caribbean's best wreck sites. The Royal Mail steamer R.M.S. *Rhone* that sank in a hurricane in 1867 is today part of the R.M.S. *Rhone* Marine Park *(p239)*. Snorkel over the top of the wreck while anchored at Lee Bay or take an excursion with a dive operator. Also hike around the island and visit the salt ponds and the cemetery for sailors who went down with the *Rhone*.

▷ Rent a Boat

Tortola in the B.V.I. is the obvious location for renting boats, most of which are moored at Road Town. You can arrive here by ferry from the U.S. Virgin Islands or across the bridge from Terrance B. Lettsome International Airport on Beef Island. Companies also charter "bareboats," where experienced sailors serve as captain, or yachts or catamarans complete with captain and crew. Charters also set sail from St. Thomas and St. John in the U.S. Virgin Islands.

ST. THOMAS

1

Skyride to Paradise Point

Estate Thomas **9am-10pm daily (when cruise ships are in)** **paradisepointvi.com**

Located directly across from the Havensight shopping mall, and popular with cruise ship passengers, this aerial cable car whisks visitors more than 700 ft (213 m) up Flag Hill in just seven minutes. On the spacious observation decks at the top are expansive views of Charlotte Amalie's harbor, the cruise ships in port, planes landing and taking off at Cyril

E. King International Airport, and even glimpses of Puerto Rico in the distance during clear weather. The summit restaurant and bar serves the Bushwacker, a surprisingly potent frozen rum cocktail made with Bailey's Irish Cream. There's also a short nature trail around the hill and a number of shops selling tourist trinkets. For the best ambience, visit around sunset.

2

Magens Bay

Rt 35 **magensbayauthority.com**

Ever popular Magens Bay beach stretches along a U-shaped bay. This beach

↓ Skyride to Paradise Point cable cars *(inset)*, and the spectacular view that awaits travelers at the top

Did You Know?

Columbus named the islands "Las Virgenes" after the famed beauty of St. Ursula and her 11,000 virgin companions.

has a snack bar, snorkel gear and small sailboat rentals, a beachwear shop, showers, and bathrooms. On cruise ship days the beach can get a little crowded. Locals like to party here on weekends and holidays, when music gets very loud and the atmosphere more than lively. For some solitude, it is best to stroll down to either end of the beach.

Inland from the beach is the Magens Bay Arboretum, a splendid botanical garden that is home to both native and imported plants.

Havensight

📍 2 miles (3 km) SE of
Charlotte Amalie 🚌🚕
ℹ️ Dept of Tourism: 340
774 0784

Home to the world's busiest
cruise ship dock, Havensight
bustles with activity. Those
who arrive on a cruise ship
can join their sailing, scuba,
or exploring excursions at the
dock. A short stroll from the
dock is the vast Havensight
shopping area. It stretches
from Havensight Mall to Port
of Sale Mall, and around the
corner past Wendy's fast food
restaurant to Yacht Haven
Grande Mall. Several downtown Charlotte Amalie stores
have branches in the area.
Visitors also buy liquor here,
since it is available at better
prices than anywhere else.

The area is home to many
restaurants, so cruise ship
passengers not eating on
board will not go hungry.

Relaxing in a shaded green
space in downtown
Charlotte Amalie ↑

Charlotte Amalie

 SW coast of St. Thomas
✈️🚌🚕

While there are ample stores
filled with everything from
T-shirts to crafts to luxury
items that beckon, Charlotte
Amalie, long the center of
commerce, offers more than
just shopping opportunities.
The island's history reveals
itself in stores that formerly
served as warehouses or
merchants' homes centuries
ago. A short walk takes visitors
to Fort Christian, a military
construction begun in 1672
by the Danish, who controlled
the island at the time. Today,
it has been converted into a
museum that displays exhibits on the island's history
and culture. Just across the
Veterans Drive from Fort
Christian, the big green building that now serves as home
to the local Legislature was

the site for the transfer of
power from Denmark to the
U.S. of St. Thomas, St. John,
and St. Croix on March 31,
1917. The purchase cost the
U.S. government $25 million.
Every year on the same day,
local residents observe the
transfer anniversary in the
Legislature's garden.

For those inclined to take
advantage of the shopping
opportunities, however,
Charlotte Amalie presents a
paradise of sorts. Vendor's
Plaza offers great bargains,
while various art galleries
are scattered around the
Shopping District.

Two streets inland from the
Shopping District's Main Street,
St. Thomas Synagogue has
served as the spiritual home to
the island's Jewish population
since 1833. Other historic
churches are scattered around
the city as well. The Neo-
Classical white building, from
the Shopping District, is the
seat of the local government's
administrative branch, and
houses the governor's office.

Lunch can be enjoyed at any
of the numerous restaurants
that sit along Main Street, and
on the streets and alleys that
connect Main Street to the
waterfront and the streets
inland. The restaurants range
from simple sandwich eateries
to more formal venues.

→

Relaxing on Cruz Bay beach;
(inset) boats in the bay's
picturesque habor

ST. JOHN

⑤

Cruz Bay

🏠 W coast of St. John 🚌🚢
ℹ Henry Samuel St; 340
776 6450

St. John is the smallest of
the three U.S. Virgin Islands,
but arguably offers the most
spectacular natural beauty.
Most vacationers pass through
Cruz Bay, St. John's main town:

 INSIDER TIP
Old Wife

Try the national dish,
"Old Wife" – boiled whole
fish served with fungi
(pronounced foon-ji).
Fungi is an Antiguan
version of polenta or
grits, made by forming
a cornmeal and okra
paste into balls.

---

ferries from St. Thomas and
the British Virgin Islands pull
into the port; it has the widest
choice of restaurants and
shops; and many watersports
excursions depart from here.
Near the ferry dock, in Cruz
Bay Park, taxi drivers wait to
pick up visitors, and people
relax on the benches
scattered around the park.
Shops and restaurants are
anchored by Wharfside Village
shopping center, sitting beachfront near the ferry dock,
while the Mongoose Junction
shopping center is located
where North Shore Road starts
uphill and out of Cruz Bay.

The town is home to a few
historical sites. The red-roofed
Battery, on the north side of
the harbor, dates back to
1825 and is currently the seat
of the territorial government.
Farther afield, at Tamarind
Court, is the Elaine Ione

Sprauve Library located in a
restored apricot-hued plantation house dating from 1757.

---

⑥

Coral Bay

🏠 6 miles (10 km) E of Cruz
Bay 🚕

About 200 years ago, Coral
Bay was the only large settlement on St. John. Today, it is
home to a handful of shops
and restaurants that lie along
the main road. It is anchored
by the Skinny Legs Bar
and Grill complex and the
Cocoloba shopping center
to the south. The Emmaus
Moravian Church is an important historical site. The parish
dates to 1756, but the church
was rebuilt after it was
severely damaged during
the 1916 hurricane.

Trunk Bay
An ever-popular spot, with crystal water, towering palms, and a snorkeling trail.

Salt Pond Bay
The curve of white sand here offers great swimming and snorkeling, and is the starting point for many hikes.

Cinnamon Bay
A good bet for a day out, with a watersports center that offers kayaks and snorkeling, and the scenic Cinnamon Bay Trail.

Lameshur Bay
This remote and well protected bay has a talcum-soft sandy beach with good snorkeling along the east edge. It's also a great place to spot sea turtles and rays.

Maho Bay
This gorgeous strand is popular with families, thanks to the shallow water and abundance of shady spots. There are also a number of barbecue grills and picnic tables.

⑦ 🏊 🏔

Virgin Islands National Park

🅰 4 miles (6 km) E of Cruz Bay 🕐 🕑 24 hours daily
ℹ Cruz Bay Visitors' Center; www.nps.gov/viis

Covering nearly two-thirds of St. John, the Virgin Islands National Park encompasses 11 sq miles (29 sq km) above ground and 9 sq miles (23 sq km) of marine sanctuary. It was established in 1956, thanks to land donations by American philanthropist Laurance S. Rockefeller. The Visitors' Center in Cruz Bay has exhibits, books for sale, and rangers on duty to answer questions. Brochures about various beach, watersports, and hiking opportunities are also available to pick up from the center. The park also offers guided programs including beach walks and birding trips.

→
Park ranger on a sea kayak at Virgin Islands National Park, St. John

8
Annaberg Sugar Plantation

📍 North Shore Rd, St. John
🕐 8am–5pm daily

Once one of 25 active sugar mills on St. John, Annaberg was a leading producer of sugar, molasses, and rum back in the 19th century. Today, the plantation is the best preserved and most accessible of the old sugar mills, and lies within the Virgin Islands National Park (p231). Visitors can explore the site via a trail that takes in the ruins of the windmill, slave quarters, the rum still, and a dungeon. The latter served as a means of punishment for enslaved laborers. Informative signboards dotted throughout the site explain how sugar was produced; how slaves worked in the fields planting and harvesting sugarcane; while skilled coopers, blacksmiths, and sugar cookers worked in the factory. Ranger-led tours are also available, and can be organized through the National Park visitor center.

> **Once one of 25 active sugar mills on St. John, Annaberg was a leading producer of sugar, molasses, and rum back in the 19th century.**

The plantation's 38-ft- (12-m-) tall windmill is a highlight of the site, and is the largest such windmill in the Virgin Islands. It dates to 1830 and was state-of-the-art machinery for that period, being able to produce 300–500 gallons (1,140–1,900 liters) of juice in an hour.

While the historic ruins are what first attracts vistors to Annaberg, lovely views of Leinster Bay, the Sir Frances Drake Channel, and a few of the British Virgin Islands also make a trip worthwhile.

9
Waterlemon Cay

📍 North Shore Rd, St. John
🕐 8am–5pm daily
🌐 watermelon-cay.com

Waterlemon Cay is nestled just a few meters off shore on the eastern end of Leinster Bay, approximately a 20-minute walk along the main shoreline from the parking lot at Annaberg Sugar Plantation. The word "cay" originally translated as a small islet,and this one has a sandy spit and is surrounded by a fringing reef and grassy sea beds that teem with 40 species of coral and hundreds of tropical fish, as well as green turtles, stingrays, starfish, dolphins, and nurse sharks. It's considered to be one of the best snorkeling spots on St. John.

Water entry is at a pebble beach adjacent to the cay. Once in the water, head for the western edge, which is protected from wind and waves, making for easier and far more pleasant snorkeling than that at the far point or eastern side.

Back on the main shore, the beach trail also leads up to Windy Hill where there are some ruins of an old Danish Guard House, and appealing views back down to the cay and Leinster Bay.

↑ Remains of a windmill at the Annaberg Sugar Plantation

↑ Stunning views from the Salt Pond Trail

HIKING IN ST. JOHN

St. John is the U.S. Virgin Islands' premier hiking destination and will appeal to both the experienced hiker and the casual stroller. The Reef Bay guided hike is the most popular, with trips departing from the Virgin Islands National Park's Cruz Bay Visitors' Center several times a week. The island also has other trails including the walk through the Annaberg Plantation and the Ram's Head Trail along the southern shore. A brochure available at the Visitors' Center covers around 20 hikes, ranging in length and difficulty.

↑ Hikers descending the hill on a ranger-led hike of the Reef Bay Trail

↑ Ancient petroglyphs on the edge of a rockpool at Reef Bay

REEF BAY TRAIL

The 2-mile- (3-km-) long Reef Bay Trail begins on Centerline Road, from where it heads downhill to a sandy beach. On the walk you will pass Reef Bay Great House, now in ruins - a remnant of bygone days when plantations dotted St. John - and ancient petroglyphs, possibly carved by Taínos along the edges of rock pools. The Reef Bay sugar factory ruins and beach mark the end of the Reef Bay Trail. The old mill has been partially restored and the grave of former owner Will Marsh is tucked back in the bushes. A boat picks up hikers for the return trip to Cruz Bay.

SHORTER HIKES

St. John has several fairly easy hiking trails that cut across flat terrain. Many of these are no more than 1 mile (2 km) long.

The Annaberg Plantation path leads visitors through a 0.8 sq mile (2 sq km) sugar plantation. Now in ruins, the plantation's sugar mill, factory, and kitchen date back to the 18th century.

The Ram's Head Trail, beginning at Salt Pond Bay, stretches across a rocky beach with a short climb uphill to an overlook with fantastic views of the Caribbean Sea.

The Salt Pond Trail offers pleasant hiking through arid vegetation to the pretty Salt Pond Bay Beach and takes less than 20 minutes to complete.

ST. CROIX

⑩
Cane Bay Wall

 7 miles (12 km) W of Christiansted ⓣ

Stretching along St. Croix's north side, the famous Cane Bay Wall attracts divers from around the world. Most prefer to go out on a boat with dive operators, but The Wall is also accessible from Cane Bay Beach and other locations along the island's north shore. It sits just 100 ft (30 m) to 200 ft (60 m) offshore. Canyons plummet over 2,000–3,000 ft (610–920 m) down, giving novice and experienced divers

Did You Know?

The U.S. Virgin Islands is the only place in the United States where you drive on the left side of the road.

a view of colorful corals (including the rare black coral), sponges, and fish, as well as the occasional shark.

---

⑪
Christiansted

 N coast of St. Croix 🚐🚌ⓣ
ℹ Government House, King Street; 340 773 1404

Home to Christiansted National Historic Site and its massive waterfront Fort Christiansvaern, this charming town is also the jumping-off point for trips to Buck Island Reef National Monument. Rangers at the fort offer information on the site's highlights. Christiansted was erected in the 18th century and most of the buildings date back to that time. These have been restored, and transformed into stores and restaurants. The Tourism Department office, in the Government House, has maps and brochures about St. Croix. Tours

of this historic structure, built as a home for a Danish merchant in 1747, are available.

Visitors can stroll on the Christiansted Boardwalk that winds along the harbor past Fort Christiansvaern, with benches strategically placed for prime harbor viewing. The town is also home to a handful of small hotels, but note that the closest beach is at the Hotel on the Cay, located in the midst of the Christiansted Harbor.

---

⑫
Frederiksted

🏠 12 miles (19 km) SW of Christiansted 🚌ⓣ

St. Croix's second town is a sleepy place. However, it is the site of the territory's most historic event. On July 3, 1848, about 8,000 slaves marched from nearby Estate LaGrange to Fort Frederik to demand their freedom. Standing in a carriage parked in front of the

← Colorful buildings lining the waterfront in Christiansted

fort, Danish Governor-General Peter von Scholten announced that freedom was theirs. The Danish government called von Scholten home, while the former slaves continued to work the plantations. Frederiksted was later the scene of other labor uprisings by discontented workers.

The town does not have many shops, and only a few restaurants and a small hotel in the downtown area, but when cruise ships sail in, this is where they arrive. A lovely white sandy beach stretches north from Fort Frederik.

13

Estate Whim Museum

🏠 Centerline Rd, Rte 76
📞 340 772 0598 🕐 10am-3pm Wed-Sat (plus cruise ship days) 🚫 Sun

This historical landmark is one of the oldest plantations on St. Croix. Its history dates back to 1743, when it started as a cotton plantation with slaves brought here from West Africa. After cotton, sugarcane

was grown until 1952. The museum includes the restored great house, sugar factory ruins and mills, plots of sugar cane, and gardens.

14

Buck Island Reef National Monument

🏠 1 mile (1.5 km) NE of Christiansted 🚢
🕐 Sunrise-sunset daily
🌐 nps.gov/buis

Day-sail and power boats leave from Christiansted waterfront and Green Cay Marina to this 29-sq-mile (77-sq-km) national park. The rainbow reefs that make up the underwater trail at the eastern side of the monument offer some good snorkeling. After the snorkel stop, most boats anchor off a gorgeous white sandy beach at the western end. Visitors can also hike uphill to the island's highest point, at 328 ft (99 m) above sea level.

EAT

Eat @ Cane Bay
A pleasant, open-air spot that dishes up some of the best food on the island. Try the Crab Cake Benedict for Sunday brunch.

🏠 110c Cane Bay, St. Croix
🚫 Tue & Sun eve
🌐 eatatcanebay.com

$$$

Virgilio's
Top-end Italian cuisine, from great homemade pasta with made-to-order sauces, to delectable tiramisu.

🏠 5150 Dronnigens Gade, St. Thomas 🚫 Sun
🌐 virgiliosvi.com

$$$

→ Snorkelers at the Buck Island Reef Monument, hoping to glimpse the coral beneath the surface *(inset)*

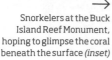

A catamaran afloat in turquoise waters, just off Marina Cay

TORTOLA

 15

Marina Cay

🏠 Off Tortola's NE coast 🚢
📞 284 494 2174

Home to Pusser's Marina Cay Hotel and a popular boating anchorage, Marina Cay makes an interesting day trip from Tortola. American newlyweds Robb and Rodie White set up house on the island in 1937 and lived here for three years. In his 1985 book, *Two on the Isle*, Robb White tells the story of their adventures. What is left of their home serves as part of the hotel, and guests can wander the grounds, take a dip in the ocean from the sandy beach, and enjoy the salty ambience of the bar and restaurant. Activities include snorkeling reefs sitting just off the island's soft white beach. Those with a thirst for greater adventure can try scuba diving from the beach or a boat.

 16

North Shore

Visitors may enjoy spending part of their day in Tortola driving the North Coast Road for some glorious ocean views and a glimpse into the island's local life. The drive can be challenging in spots, with lots of twists, turns, and steep hills on the narrow roads. Those driving should remember to keep to the left and watch out for wandering livestock.

The intersection of Zion Hill Road and North Coast Road, where Sebastian's on the Beach is located, is a good place to start the drive. Heading west, a bumpy road snakes down to the lovely Smuggler's Cove Beach. It has good snorkeling, shade from coconut palms, and an informal shack for drinks and snacks.

Returning east, back to Sebastian's, visitors can break for food at its beachfront restaurant, or spend some

time on the lovely white sands of Apple Bay Beach. Farther ahead is the village of Carrot Bay, home to small restaurants and some more beaches. The trip ends in pleasant Cane Garden Bay.

17

Road Town

🏠 S coast of Tortola 🚗🚢🛫
ℹ️ AKARA Building, de Castro St; 284 494 3134

Road Town bustles on days when cruise ships cast anchor, but even on days when there are none in port, the British territory's main town is active. It is the seat of B.V.I. commerce and home to a large offshore banking industry and other offices. Ferries from Virgin Gorda and St. Thomas in the U.S. Virgin Islands tie up at the Road Town ferry dock, further adding to the town's traffic. It is a working town rather

TOP 5 VIRGIN ISLAND COCKTAILS

Bushwacker
A frozen cocktail similar to a creamy piña colada, made with dark rum.

Painkiller
A refreshing fruity mix, served over ice with a sprinkle of nutmeg.

Limin' de Coconut
A smooth, blended concoction, festively served in half a coconut.

Dark 'n' Stormy
A highball cocktail made with very dark rum and ginger beer.

Cruzan Confusion
This includes banana Cruzan rum, which is produced on St. Croix.

than just a tourist destination, evident from the even mix of locals and visitors dining in the many restaurants. The very heart of Road Town runs from the waterfront one block inland to the narrow Main Street.

East of here, restaurants, shops, and banks overflow on Wickham's Cay I, which is also home to marinas. Farther east sits Wickham's Cay II, base of the huge Moorings charter operations, but with little else.

JR O'Neal Botanic Gardens National Park

Road Town, off Main St
284 494 2060 8:30am–4:30pm Mon–Sat

Road Town's Botanic Gardens provide a pleasant respite from the commotion. Visitors can walk here from the heart of town, but on a hot day a taxi is a better bet. Once here, the gardens offer plenty of shade and benches for resting. The 130,700-sq-ft (12,150-sq-m) gardens feature collections that represent the different plant habitats, exotic species, and a vast collection of palms. Orchids bloom in the gazebo, lilies float in the pond, and cactuses grow in the tropical sun.

Sage Mountain National Park

3 miles (5 km) SW of Road Town 284 494 2069

Established in 1964, the Sage Mountain National Park is B.V.I.'s first national park, founded through a donation from philanthropist Laurance S. Rockefeller. Stretching over 0.1 sq miles (0.3 sq km), the park reaches a lofty 1,716 ft (523 m) and is the highest point on the entire Virgin Islands. It sits so high that Sage Mountain creates rain: as warm moist air rises from the east and south, it cools as it crosses the mountain, falling as rain on the park's northern side.

The park offers wonderful panoramic views to hikers willing to spend some time walking its trails. It is home to many native and introduced species of trees and plants, including mahogany, white cedar, and mamey trees. Hikers on the park's dozen trails, including the popular Mahogany Forest Trail and the Rainforest Trail, might glimpse mountain doves and thrushes flitting among the trees. Much of the vegetation in the area is second growth owing to clearing activity that was carried out by farmers for agricultural purposes, before the establishment of the park.

> **Visitors may enjoy spending part of their day in Tortola driving the North Coast Road for some glorious ocean views and a glimpse into the island's local life.**

VIRGIN GORDA AND OUTER ISLANDS

20

Virgin Gorda

📍 16 miles (25 km) E of Tortola

Reached by ferry from St. Thomas, St. John, and Tortola, Virgin Gorda is a small island that beckon visitors who want to relax with a good book and a frosty drink in hand. It has a handful of restaurants, a bit of nightlife, and some modest shopping, but the real draws are the luscious white beaches and the chance to do nothing but gaze at the glorious sunrises and sunsets.

The southwestern part of the island is known as The Valley, or Spanish Town, which is the heart of the island's activity. Most of it is centered at Virgin Gorda Yacht Harbour, a smallish marina, and the shopping area, while a few restaurants are dotted along the main road of what is not much more than a village.

On the must-see list for nearly every visitor to Virgin Gorda is the Baths National Park, a collection of massive granite boulders on the white-sand beaches that form lovely pools of seawater. Some of the boulders are 40 ft (12 m) in diameter, and were formed when molten rock seeped into existing volcanic rock layers. It is a fair walk from the parking area but the pools are great for swimming and snorkeling. Restaurants and a few shops nearby provide lunch, drinks, and the obligatory T-shirt, as well as other souvenirs.

21

Gorda Peak National Park

📍 North Sound Rd, Virgin Gorda 📞 284 494 2069

The Gorda Peak National Park covers 0.4 sq miles (1 sq km) of land and is one of the last remaining examples of the Caribbean dry forest in the region. It is home to a couple

---

DRIVING AROUND VIRGIN GORDA

Visitors to Virgin Gorda should rent a car for at least a day to get out and about. The 8-sq-mile (21-sq-km) island has just one main road and a handful of side roads, so it is almost impossible to get lost. West on Lee Road from The Valley, a side road leads to Coppermine Point, a ruin of a mine which was originally built in the 1800s. Spring Bay National Park, just before the Baths, sees far fewer people and is an ideal spot to relax at for a few hours. East from The Valley, an unpaved road leads to Savannah Bay, great for sunbathing and swimming. Gorda Peak National Park offers great hiking, and the drive can end at Gunn Creek, where ferry trips to North Sound begin.

↑ A family marveling at the boulders in The Baths National Park, Virgin Gorda

of endangered and threatened plant species, as well as the world's smallest lizard – the Virgin Islands dwarf gecko. Two trails lead up to the Gorda Peak, which at 1,370 ft (417 m) is Virgin Gorda's highest point, and where a lookout tower offers panoramic views of the BVI. On a clear day, it is possible to see all the way to Anegada in the northeast. A picnic table has been placed under the shade of a mango tree where the two trails meet, and provides a pleasant place for lunch or snacks. During the hike uphill, the forest grows more moist with the increasing altitude, and the vegetation changes from species that survive only in dry scrubby areas to those that thrive in slightly damp soil.

↑ A diver exploring the barnacle-encrusted wreck within RMS *Rhone* Marine Park

 22 ⊕

RMS *Rhone* Marine Park

⌂ Off Salt Island 📞 284 494 3904

The Royal Mail Steamer *Rhone* was wrecked here in an 1867 hurricane with more than 100 people on board. Today, it is the only marine national park in the British Virgin Islands, and the main dive destination there. The 310-ft (95-m) vessel sits in two parts at depths ranging from 20 ft to 80 ft (6m to 25m). Much of the ship is intact, with parts such as the propeller, boilers, and more still identifiable. The ship's anchor broke away from the rest of the boat, and this forms the second portion of the marine park.

The *Rhone* is encrusted with marine growth and serves as a home to many types of fish and marine life. Dive trips depart from Tortola and other British Virgin Islands, as well as from St. Thomas and St. John in the U.S. Virgin Islands. Those who wish to dive the site need a permit from the National Parks Trust.

DRINK

Foxy's Bar
Run by legendary Foxy Callwood, this party-like beach bar is the number one draw on Jost Van Dyke, and can be reached only by yacht, water taxi, or on the ferries from West End on Tortola. Visitors on a day trip can enjoy lunch, Foxy's own style of Caribbean rum cocktails, plus beach time and a swim in the warm waters of Great Bay. There are barbecues on Friday and Saturday evenings.

⌂ Great Bay, Jost Van Dyke 🌐 foxysbvi.com

PRACTICAL
INFORMATION

Here you will find all the essential advice and information you will need before and during your stay in the Virgin Islands.

CURRENCY
US Dollar (US$)

TIME ZONE
Atlantic Standard Time, 1 hour ahead of the EST and 4 hours behind GMT. The islands do not observe daylight savings

LANGUAGE
English

ELECTRICITY SUPPLY
The electrical system operates on 110 volts and 120 volts in the British Virgin Islands and US Virgin Islands respectively

EMERGENCY NUMBERS

POLICE & FIRE US VIRGIN ISLANDS	BRITISH VIRGIN ISLANDS
911	**999**

TAP WATER
Outside of resorts, water purity can be unreliable so, to be safe, drink bottled water

When To Go

The Virgin Islands generally have good weather throughout the year, although the hurricane season runs from June to November, reaching its peak in September. Rates tend to be lower during this season, but some hotels may be closed in August and September.

Getting There

Vistors can fly directly from the US mainland to St. Croix and St. Thomas, but will have to change planes in San Juan, Puerto Rico, for Tortola and Virgin Gorda destinations. Flights are offered by Air Sunshine, American Airlines, British Airways, Delta, JetBlue, Spirit Airlines, LIAT, Seaborne Airlines, United Airlines, and Virgin Atlantic.

Personal Security

Use normal precautions to ensure your safety. Avoid dark alleys and deserted beaches. The islands have a low crime rate but it is still advisable to to keep valuables in the hotel safe.

Health

Hospitals are located on the bigger islands including Juan F. Luis Hospital, Myrah Keating Smith Community Health Center, Peebles Hospital, Roy L. Schneider Hospital and the Bougainvillea Clinic. The British Virgin Islands outer islands also have their own smaller health clinics.

Passports and Visas

Citizens of the US do not need a passport to visit the US Virgin Islands, though one is required for all visitors to the British Virgin Islands. More details regarding visa and passport regulations can be obtained from **US State Department** and the tourism websites.

A $20 departure tax is imposed in the British Virgin Islands. This tax is not included in your ticket price and must be paid separately when leaving from the ferry terminal or airport.

You do not have to pay a departure tax in the US Virgin Islands.

US State Department
w travel.state.gov

LGBT+ Safety

The US Virgin Islands shares American principles and is a LGBT+ welcoming destination where there are few objections to public displays of affection. Same-sex marriages were legalized in 2015 and now many LGBT+ friendly resorts, particularly on St. Croix, organize weddings. The British Virgin Islands is tolerant yet islanders are conservative and displays of same-sex affection are uncommon. Same-sex marriages in the territory have not been sanctioned, although this is pending.

Money

Both the US and British Virgin Islands use US Dollars (US$). Banks are located on St. John, St. Thomas, St. Croix, Tortola, and Virgin Gorda. All banks have ATMs, while independent ATMs are found in bars and restaurants. Most hotels, restaurants, and other tourist facilities accept credit cards.

Cell Phones and Wi-Fi

Visitors bringing cell phones should check with their service providers to determine if they will work in the Virgin Islands and if they will be subject to roaming charges. From the US Virgin Islands to the US mainland, calls are inexpensive, but calling the US mainland from the British Virgin Islands is considered an international call. The US-based carrier AT&T has the most cell coverage across the US Virgin Islands. In the British Virgin Islands, it can be accessed from the southeast coast of Tortola and near the ferry dock on Virgin Gorda. Phone cards are available at pharmacies and stores. Some hotels offer Internet access and major towns have cafes with Wi-Fi.

Getting Around

Renting a car is the best way to get around on the Virgin Islands. Car rental agencies have booths at airports and at ferry terminals.

Driving is on the left. There are a number of global rental agencies such as AVIS and Hertz as well as local companies that operate in St. Croix, St. Thomas, Tortola, and Virgin Gorda. A valid driver's license is needed to rent a car on the Virgin Islands. It is advisable to make prior reservations during the high season. Rates are high, particularly on the smaller islands. Fuel is also more expensive than on the US mainland. Taxis meet arriving planes and ferries and are stationed at major hotels. There is a bus service on the main US Virgin Islands, but none on the British Virgin Islands.

Seaplanes, small aircraft and a ferry connect St. Thomas and St. Croix. A ferry service also links St. John and St. Thomas. To Tortola, a ferry is available at Charlotte Amalie or Cruz Bay. Virgin Gorda is reached by ferry from St. John, St. Thomas and Tortola. Ferries also go from Tortola to Jost Van Dyke and Anegada.

Visitor Information

Visitors' centers provide information, brochures, and maps. Opening hours are usually 9am–5pm. More information on where to stay, restaurants, ctivities, and more can be obtained from the various **USVI Tourism** and **BVI Tourism** offices or their websites.

BVI Tourism
w bvitourism.com
USVI Tourism
w visitusvi.com

The breathtaking white sands of Anguilla

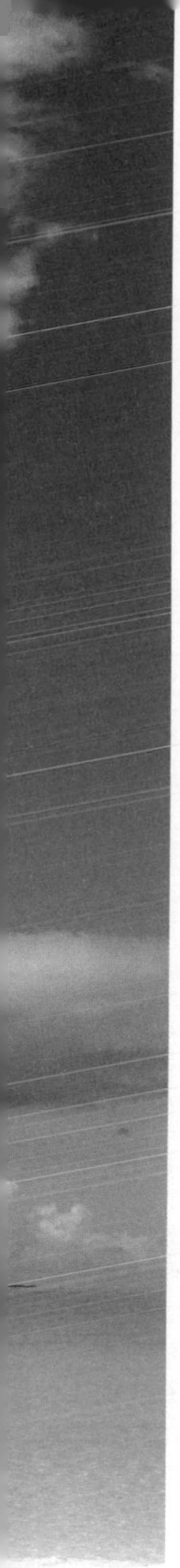

ANGUILLA

Just 16 miles (25 km) from end to end and 3 miles (5 km) across at its widest point, long and thin Anguilla was named after the Spanish or French word for eel. The island is scrubby and fairly flat, but its coral base provides numerous beaches of blindingly white sand. It has a population of around 14,000, with a mere 1,000 inhabitants living in the villagey inland capital, The Valley.

Anguilla was colonized by English settlers from St. Kitts in 1650, though the arid soil and scarcity of fresh water meant that it never became a successful plantation island. In 1967, it was made part of an associated state with St. Kitts and Nevis. This was contrary to the wishes of Anguillans, who revolted against the arrangement; British paratroopers were flown in to restore control in 1969. The island is now a separate, largely autonomous British overseas territory. Since the 1980s, it has established itself as one of the Caribbean's most desirable upscale vacation destinations, and an offshore banking haven. Though Anguilla suffered heavy damage from Hurricane Irma in September 2017, it has recovered fairly quickly.

ANGUILLA

Experience

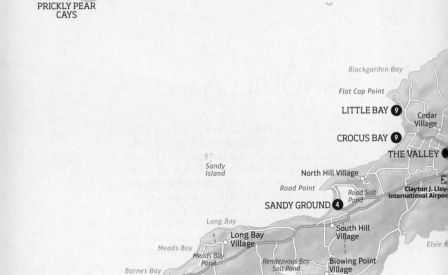

PRICKLY PEAR CAYS **7**

Blackgarden Bay

Flat Cap Point

LITTLE BAY **9** Cedar Village

CROCUS BAY **9**

THE VALLEY

Sandy Island

North Hill Village

Road Point *Road Salt Pond*

Clayton J. Lloyd International Airport

SANDY GROUND **4**

Long Bay

Long Bay Village

South Hill Village

Meads Bay

Meads Bay Pond

Elsie M

Barnes Bay

Rendezvous Bay Salt Pond

Blowing Point Village

West End Bay

Cove Pond

RENDEZVOUS BAY **8**

Lockrum Bay

West End

West End Salt Pond

Pelican Bay

Lower West End Point

COVE BAY **3**

Blowing Point

Anguillita Island

SHOAL BAY WEST **3**

Cap Juluca

Blowing Rock

0 kilometers 2

0 miles 2

N ↑

St. Martin / Sint Maarten

SHOAL BAY EAST ❷

Shoal Bay Village

Little Dix

Bad Cox Pond

Caals Pond

Long Salt Pond

Sandy Hill Bay

Sea Feather Bay

Auntie Dol Bay
Forest Point

Forest Bay

ISLAND HARBOR ❻

Mount Fortune

East End Pond

East End

Grey Pond

HERITAGE COLLECTION MUSEUM ❺

Mimi Bay

Captain's Bay

Snake Point

Junk's Hole Bay

Savannah Bay

Gibbon Point

Goat Cave

Windward Point Bay

Little Scrub Island

Scrub Bay

Scrub Island

Deadman's Cay

ANGUILLA

St. Martin/ Sint Maarten

Île Tintamarre

EXPERIENCE

① The Valley

🏠 Center of Anguilla ➡️🚌
ℹ️ Anguilla Tourist Board,
Coronation Ave.; 264 497
2759; www.ivisitanguilla.
com

Anguilla's capital, The Valley is so small it barely seems like a town. Along the broad Queen Elizabeth Avenue, there are a few civic buildings, including government offices, the post office, and a couple of shopping malls. At the foot of the street is the open-sided People's Market, where fruit and vegetables are sold.

The oldest section of the town is Coronation Avenue, which runs up the hill toward Crocus Bay. Here you'll find a handful of the town's original stone buildings, including the Warden's Place, a former sugar plantation greathouse that has an excellent bakery.

Toward the airport, is St. Gerard's Catholic Church with its three pebble-dashed arches. The adjoining building, **Wallblake House**, is one of the oldest buildings in Anguilla. Built in 1787, this old plantation house has been restored. It has a stone foundation and a clapboard upper set behind a picket fence. The house was donated to a Catholic church in 1959 but proved too small to hold services.

Wallblake House

♿🚻 🏠 Wallblake Road
🌐 wallblake.ai

---

② Shoal Bay East

🏠 4 miles (6 km) NE of The Valley

Extending almost 2 miles (3 km) along the northern coastline, this is Anguilla's best and liveliest beach. Backed by sea grape and coconut palms, Shoal Bay East's swath of powdery white sand shelves into translucent waters, and frequently features in lists of the world's best beaches. A sprinkling of brilliant bars, restaurants, and loungers cater for the handful of hotels and day-trippers from St Martin, but peaceful spots are not hard to find. The protected reef offshore provides opportunities for snorkeling, diving, and glass-bottom kayaking.

"The Fountain," which is the island's most important pre-Columbian site, lies off the eastern end of the beach. A ceremonial Arawak cavern, it is currently closed to the public.

33

The number of idyllic beaches in Anguilla.

> Backed by sea grape and coconut palms, Shoal Bay East's swath of powdery white sand shelves into translucent waters, and frequently features in lists of the world's best beaches.

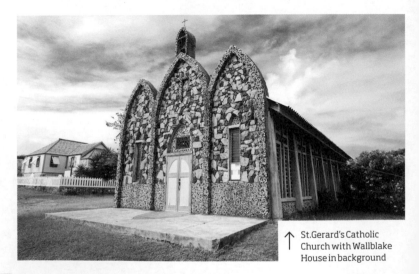

↑ St.Gerard's Catholic Church with Wallblake House in background

A woman examining exhibits included on Sandy Ground's Heritage Tour

3

Cove Bay and Shoal Bay West

SW of The Valley

Around the headland west of Rendezvous Bay *(p248)*, lies the sweeping arc of Cove Bay. It is the base for the island's kitesurfing school, and bobbing offshore is the aqua park – essentially a floating obstacle course – which provides hours of fun for kids.

Two bays farther west lies Shoal Bay West, which is smaller and more secluded than its more famous north-coast namesake. Its most prominent landmark is the ultra-modern Covecastles. Though no longer in operation, these sci-fi-looking villas, designed by award-winning architect Myron Goldfinger, are still a sight to behold.

4

Sandy Ground

2 miles (3 km) W of The Valley

Road Bay is Anguilla's deep-water port, but the sand is as good as the sand on some of the best beaches on the other islands. Set in a cliff-bound bay, the west-facing harbor and its small settlement, Sandy Ground, are well protected. The long stretch of sand is magnificent, backed by beachfront restaurants and bars, houses, and the pier. Offshore, fishing and pleasure boats can be seen anchored in the bay. Around the lagoon, which was once used for salt cultivation, the low mud walls that sectioned the salt pans can still be seen. Salt was once a thriving Anguillan industry and a major export until the 1980s. The **Anguilla National Trust** conducts a Heritage Tour (by appointment) to many heritage sites and places of natural importance. Tours take between 20 minutes and 4 hours and are fully customized.

Anguilla National Trust
 The Valley **8am–4pm Mon–Fri** **axanational trust.com**

5

Heritage Collection Museum

Liberty Rd, East End
264 497 4092 **10am–5pm Mon–Fri**

Restored after being flattened in 2017 by Hurricane Irma, this museum has an interesting, if eccentric, collection of coins, pottery, and photographs that illustrate local life through Arawak and colonial times to recent years.

Opposite the museum lies East End Pond, one of Anguilla's top birding spots. Specialist bird-watching tours to the site and other island wetlands can be arranged through the Anguilla National Trust or Nature Explorer.

TOP 4 **ART GALLERIES IN ANGUILLA**

Cheddie's Carving Studio
0.8 miles (1.3 km) N of Cove Bay
This West End Village location features wonderfully unique driftwood sculptures of local wildlife.

Lynne Bernbaum
Sandy Ground 2640
Caribbean-inspired fine art originals and giclées by this talented, Sandy Ground-based artist.

Devonish Gallery
The Cove, West End Village
Head here for fabulous wood and bronze sculptures and ceramics by renowned artist Courtney Devonish.

Savannah Gallery
Coronation Ave, The Valley 2640
Unique work by local artists using a variety of media is showcased here.

 6

Island Harbor

 4 miles (7 km) NE of The Valley

Some 2 miles (3 km) east of Shoal Bay Village lies Island Harbor, an active fishing community, where brightly colored boats bob at anchor out in the bay. For the adventurous, night excursions in LED-illuminated glass-bottom kayaks are a novel attraction (www.anguillakayak.com).

More conventionally, the Anguilla National Trust (www. axanationaltrust.com) arranges hikes and visits to some of the few archaeological sites in this area, including to "Big Spring." This is the island's second most important Arawak site; a water source and a ceremonial cave, it contains over a hundred petroglyphs, though most are indistinct and in need of restoration.

Beyond the settlement, toward the end of the island, are some remote beaches, including Captain's Bay and Savannah Bay.

7

Prickly Pear Cays

 7 miles (11 km) NW of Sandy Ground ⏰11am-4pm daily 🌐pricklypear anguilla.com

A popular day-trip destination off the north coast of Anguilla, Prickly Pear Cays are two rocky islets separated by a narrow channel. They are home to important colonies of nesting seabirds such as laughing gulls, brown boobies, and the elegant red-billed tropicbird. The critically endangered Lesser Antillean iguana has also been reintroduced here.

It is primarily the gorgeous soft-sand beach and calm clear waters of Prickly Pear East that draw the visitors, however. A couple of laid-back bar-restaurants dish up fresh lobster, offer sun loungers, and even massages. Those craving more action can rent kayaks and snorkel gear.

Restaurants offer transportation to and from Sandy Ground, while the Anguilla National Trust arranges tours to the even more remote seabird colonies of Sombrero Island (Hat Island). The island was so named because it was once shaped like a traditional Mexican hat – but this profile was indelibly altered following the guano mining boom of the mid- to late-1800s.

8

Rendezvous Bay

 5 miles (8 km) SW of The Valley

Anguilla's West End plays host to some of the island's

💬 **INSIDER TIP**
Bankie Banx

Every March, local reggae artist Bankie Banx hosts the annual Moonsplash Festival. Staged in his ramshackle beach bar in Rendezvous Bay, it is the Caribbean's oldest independent music festival.

↑ Brightly painted boats moored off the shore of Island Harbor

swankiest hotels and resorts, as well as more spectacular beaches. Chief among them is Rendezvous Bay, a jaw-dropping crescent of pink sand lapped by sparkling aquamarine waters. The back of the beach is dominated by the neo-Mediterranean architecture of the CuisinArt Resort, a luxurious hotel and spa with pristine white walls that stand out against the sea. The resort features a Greg Norman-designed golf course. A favorite spot among locals, Rendezvous offers impressive views across to St. Martin.

Crocus Bay and Little Bay

📍 1 mile (2 km) NW of The Valley

From the island's highest point at Crocus Hill – a mere 213 ft (85 m) above sea level – a steep descent leads into the delightful Crocus Bay. Historically, this has always been a locals' beach, where Anguillians from The Valley take exercise in the early morning and pelicans glide across the waves in search of fish. But with the arrival of Da'Vida – an award-winning restaurant, bar, and spa – it has become a popular spot with tourists also, who can rent kayaks and standup paddleboards in the area.

Many head for neighboring Little Bay, a diminutive, secluded cove to the north, enclosed by dramatic cliffs and reachable only from the sea. With a mere sliver of a beach, the main attractions lie beneath the sheltered waters, since it is one of the best snorkeling areas on the island, with steeper drop-offs than elsewhere. Little Bay is particularly rewarding in the late afternoon sun, when the cove is at its most serene. For those who like a bit of action, a jump or dive off "The Rock" is a must.

EAT

Blanchard's Beach Shack
The perfect spot to watch the sunset with a cocktail in hand. There is a varied and delicious beach food menu.

📍 Meads Bay 🕑 Sun
🌐 blanchardsrestaurant. com/beach-shack

$$$ⓢ

Da'Vida
Located bang on the beach, with a Caribbean-Asian fusion menu that rivals the views.

📍 Crocus Bay 🕑 Sun & Mon evening 🌐 davida anguilla.com

$$$$

Veya Restaurant
One of Anguilla's finest restaurants, offering creative veggie lunches and nightly live music.

📍 Sandy Ground 🕑 Sun
🌐 veya-axa.com

$$$$

PRACTICAL
INFORMATION

Here you will find all the essential advice and information you will need before and during your stay in Anguilla.

AT A GLANCE

CURRENCY
Eastern Caribbean dollar (EC$)

TIME ZONE
Atlantic Standard Time (AST), 4 hours behind GMT and 1 hour ahead of EST.

LANGUAGE
English

ELECTRICITY SUPPLY
The usual electricity supply in Anguilla is 110 volts AC (60 cycles). Most hotels have two-pin sockets in US style

EMERGENCY NUMBERS

POLICE, FIRE, AND AMBULANCE

911

TAP WATER
It is recommended that you only drink bottled water as Anguilla's water comes primarily from cisterns

When To Go

The best time to visit Anguilla is from December through April, when the island experiences mild temperatures and settled weather. Anguilla's average annual temperature is around 80° F (27° C), with the hottest weather during the hurricane season (July through October). The lightest rainfall occurs from February through April, and the heaviest from August to November.

Getting There

No carriers fly directly from North America into Anguilla, so access is easiest via neighboring St. Martin/Sint Maarten or Puerto Rico. American Airlines offers flights from North Carolina to Puerto Rico. Visitors can then fly to Anguilla with Seaborne Airlines. There are many carriers into St. Martin from where the crossing to Anguilla can be made by ferry or private watertaxi which includes the Link, or by the local airline Winair. Europe is linked to St. Martin from France and Holland. Most UK visitors travel via Antigua, from where Caribbean flights (LIAT and Winair) run up the island chain to Anguilla.

Personal Security

Anguilla is a very safe island. There are hardly any problems concerning personal security and theft is extremely rare. However, it is advisable not to leave any valuables unattended.

Health

Sunburn is the main health hazard. Mosquitoes can be a problem after it rains. No vaccinations are necessary unless visitors are coming from a yellow-fever infected area. There is an accident and emergency department at Princess Alexandra Hospital.

Passports and Visas

Visitors to Anguilla require a valid passport with at least six months' validity remaining, as well as

a return or onward ticket. Visas are not needed by US citizens, Canadians, or EU travelers, but citizens of some other countries do require them. If in doubt, visitors should check with the British High Commission or embassy for details. A departure tax and an airport security charge need to be paid when leaving the island.

LGBT+ Safety

Same-sex sexual activities have been legal in Anguilla, a British overseas territory, since 2001, through an order of the UK's Privy Council. However, marriage and civil unions of same-sex couples have not been legalized and the culture of the island is not very LGBT+ friendly. There are a number of high-end resorts that are non-judgemental and offer luxurious holidays and privacy to LGBT+ visitors.

Money

The currency of Anguilla is the Eastern Caribbean dollar (EC$), which is shared with current and former British territories as far south as Grenada. The US dollar is also widely accepted. Banks follow regular business hours, Monday to Thursday 8am to 3pm, and to 5pm on Fridays. Credit cards are accepted in almost all establishments except in the smallest shops. There are ATMs attached to several banks, and also free-standing in some malls. They give a choice of Eastern Caribbean and US dollars.

Cell Phones and Wi-Fi

The international dialing code for Anguilla is 1 264, followed by a seven-digit island number. When calling out of Anguilla, dial 011 and the international code. When calling locally, all seven digits need to be dialed. The island has complete cell coverage and visitors can use their personal phones, if on roaming. Handsets and SIM cards with local numbers are available at the Digicel and Cable & Wireless offices on the island. Almost all the hotels and villas have Wi-Fi, which is available to their guests.

Getting Around

Car rental companies are not officially permitted to deliver to the airport or ferry port, and will first take visitors to their office to complete formalities. However, they do drop passengers to hotels and villas. Driving is on the left side of the road, and a temporary Anguilla driver's license, in addition to a valid driving license, is mandatory. This can be purchased at any of the car-rental agencies such as AVIS, Island Car Rentals, and Andy's Auto Rentals. The airport and ferry terminals have taxi stands and usually the rate is fixed for two passengers and two pieces of luggage. There are no public buses in Anguilla. Hitchhiking works sometimes, but as is the case anywhere, there is no guarantee of a ride. Island tours are also possible by taxi and take just a couple of hours.

The island's flat terrain is ideal for cycling; however, some unpaved roads can be hazardous. Bikes cost about $25 a day and can be rented from Anchor Miniature Gold and Bou's Cars & Cycle Rentals.

Visitor Information

The **Anguilla Tourist Board** has its main office in The Valley. International offices of the board are located in the UK and the US. There is also an information booth at the Clayton J. Lloyd International Airport. Visitors can pick up maps, brochures and magazines at the airport. The **Official Tourism Website** also has a range of useful information.

Anguilla Tourist Board
w ivisitanguilla.com
Official Tourism Website
w anguilla-vacation.com

ST. MARTIN AND SINT MAARTEN

Columbus sailed past the island of St. Martin/Sint Maarten on November 11 1493, naming it after St. Martin of Tours, whose holy day it was. Lured by its natural salt ponds, Spanish, French, and Dutch colonists jostled for control in the early 1600s, and the island was peacefully partitioned between the French and Dutch in 1648 under the Treaty of Concordia. The division still stands. Covering 37 sq miles (95 sq km), St. Martin/Sint Maarten is the smallest landmass in the world split between two nations. The north side, which accounts for two-thirds of the island, is a *petit morceau* of France (technically an overseas collectivity), whose capital is Marigot. Sint Maarten in the south is an autonomous state within the Kingdom of the Netherlands, with its capital Philipsburg. Together the two halves encompass a hilly, forested interior, lagoons and beaches galore, and form one of the most multicultural spots in the Caribbean, with residents coming from some 90 countries. The island was utterly devastated by Hurricane Irma in September 2017. Visitors are returning, but the effects of the damage are still noticeable and a full recovery will take years.

ST. MARTIN AND SINT MAARTEN

Experience

↑ Anguilla

Baie de Frie

Saba

FALAISE
DES OISEAUX
10
Baie
Rouge

Baie aux
Prunes

Terres
Basses

Pointe du
Canonnier

Baie
Longue

Cupecoy Bay

Mullet Bay

Princess Juliana
International Airport ✈

Maho Bay

Burgeaux Bay

Pelican Key

Agrément

Fort
Saint-Louis

MARIGOT 4

Baie
Nettlé

Baie
Nettlé

Sandy
Ground

Simpson Bay
Lagoon

3
SIMPSON BAY
AND AROUND

Cole Bay

Cole
Bay

0 kilometers   2
0 miles   2

N ↑

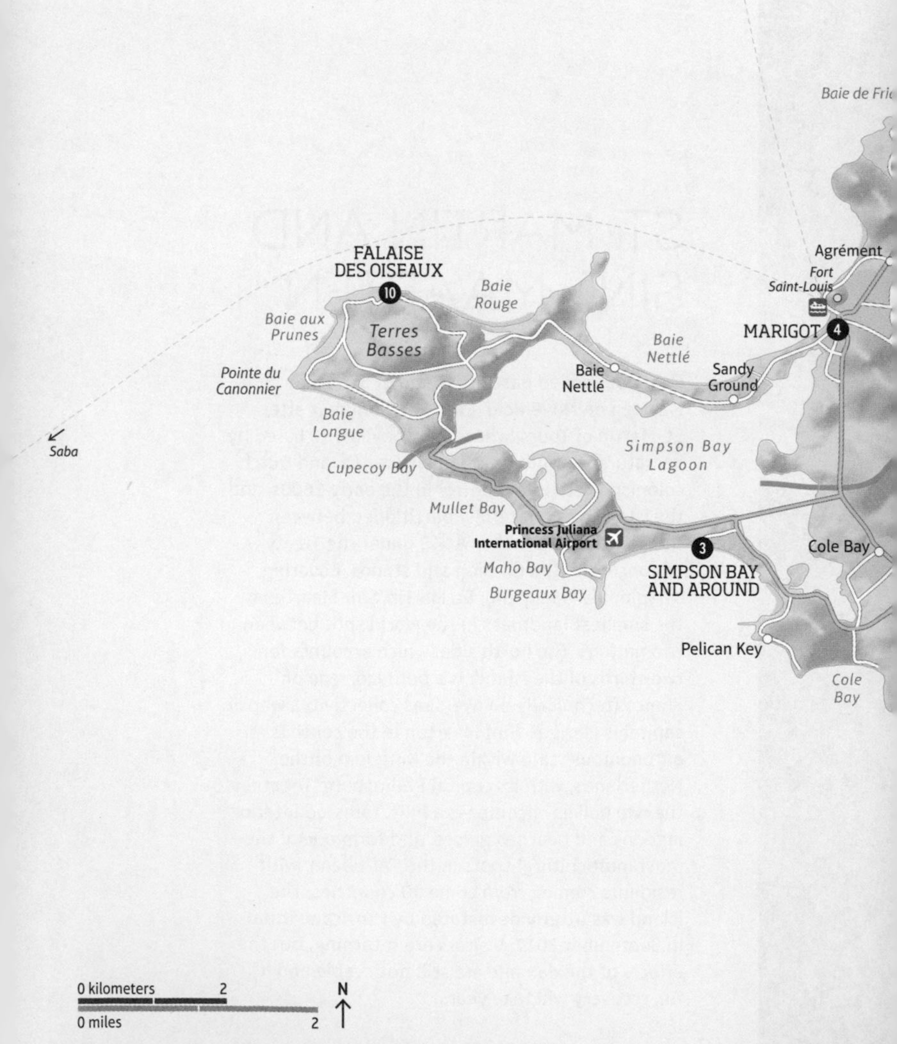

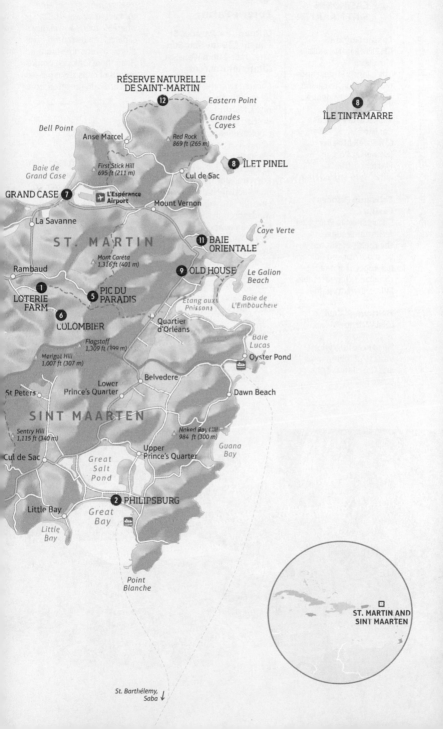

RÉSERVE NATURELLE
DE SAINT-MARTIN

(12) Eastern Point

Grandes
Cayes

Dell Point

Anse Marcel

ÎLE TINTAMARRE (8)

Red Rock
869 ft (265 m)

Baie de
Grand Case

First Stick Hill
695 ft (211 m)

Cul de Sac

(8) ÎLET PINEL

GRAND CASE (7)

L'Espérance
Airport

La Savanne

Mount Vernon

Caye Verte

S T.   M A R T I N

(11) BAIE
ORIENTALE

Rambaud

Mont Caréta
1,316 ft (401 m)

(9) OLD HOUSE

Le Galion
Beach

(1)
LOTERIE
FARM

(5) PIC DU
PARADIS

Baie de
L'Embouchere

Étang aux
Poissons

(6)
COLOMBIER

Quartier
d'Orléans

Flagstaff
1,309 ft (399 m)

Baie
Lucas

Merigot Hill
1,007 ft (307 m)

Oyster Pond

St Peters

Lower
Prince's Quarter

Belvedere

S I N T   M A A R T E N

Dawn Beach

Sentry Hill
1,115 ft (340 m)

Cul de Sac

Great
Salt
Pond

Naked Boy Hill
984 ft (300 m)

Guana
Bay

Upper
Prince's Quarter

Little Bay

(2) PHILIPSBURG

Great
Bay

Little
Bay

Point
Blanche

ST. MARTIN AND
SINT MAARTEN

St. Barthélemy,
Saba

EXPERIENCE

TOP 4 CASINOS IN SINT MAARTEN

Casino Royale
🏠 1 Rhine Road Maho Village, Maho Beach

The island's largest and most glamorous casino, with 400 slot machines.

Tropicana Princess Casino
🏠 Welfare Rd, Cole Bay

Located at Port de Plaisance, this is a glitzy, two-story venue.

Coliseum Princess Casino
🏠 Front Street 74, Philipsburg

As its name suggests, the theme of this busy casino is Ancient Rome. It is known for having the island's highest table limits for many games.

Hollywood Casino
🏠 Billy Folly Road, Simpson Bay

Head here for a wide variety of table games and the island's only bingo facility.

1

Loterie Farm
🏠 Rue du Pic Paradis, St. Martin ⏱ 9am–5pm Sun–Tue, 9am–10pm Wed–Sat 🌐 loteriefarm.com

Located near the foot of Pic du Paradis, the tallest peak on St. Martin, Loterie Farm is nestled in the only area of tropical rainforest left on the island, and opened as a sugar plantation in 1721. Today, the 135-acre (55-ha) estate has been transformed into a multi-activity attraction.

On offer is a hiking trail that winds through the beautiful forest up to about 1400 ft (427 m) above sea level; treetop adventure courses through giant mango and mahogany trees via a series of ropes, cables, and suspended bridges; and, for over 18-year-olds, the Fly Zone Extreme, a high-speed zipline over the forest canopy. Additionally,

Visitors relaxing in the pool and trekking through forest *(inset)* at Loterie Farm ↓

the farm has a superb multi-level swimming pool area connected by waterfalls, where daybeds and luxury cabanas can be rented, and there is a decent restaurant. Head there for lunch before groups of cruise ship passengers arrive in the afternoon.

2

Philipsburg
🏠 S coast of Sint Maarten ✈🚌🚢 ℹ Vineyard Office Park, WG Buncamper Rd

The capital city of Dutch Sint Maarten stretches 1 mile (2 km) across a narrow strip of land that separates the sea from a marshy inland pond. Of the four roads that run from one end of the town to the other, the popular Front Street brims with waterfront cafés, flashy casinos, and

Guavaberry Emporium
🏠8–10 Front St 🕑10am–
6pm daily 🌐guavaberry.com

Sint Maarten Museum
❖🏠 🏠7 Front St ☎721 542
4917 🕑10am–4pm Mon–Fri

↑ Colorful shopping stalls in the middle of
Philipsburg, the capital of Sint Maarten

duty-free shops. Town beautification projects have outfitted new sidewalks with palm trees and decorative lampposts. Sand dredged from the bottom of the sea was spread on Great Bay Beach, which flaunts an impressive boardwalk.

Cyrus Wathey Square on Front Street, across from Captain Hodge Pier, has a striking white courthouse built in 1792 by the Dutch commander Willem Hendrik Rink. The square makes an excellent starting point for a

walking tour since it has a tourist information booth and is at the beginning of the shopping district. Old Street and Sea Street are pedestrian-only walkways lined with pretty flowers, potted palms, and some shops.

The **Guavaberry Emporium** occupies a late 18th-century cedar town house, which was once home to a former governor. Flavored liqueurs from the local guavaberry fruit are the shop's chief product, alongside other island-made goods. Set in a restored 19th-century two-story house, the **Sint Maarten Museum** displays local historic artifacts such as the replica of a typical Arawak *pirogue* (canoe), which stands at the entrance, a photo exhibit of daily island life in the early 1900s, and rescued articles from H.M.S. *Proselyte*, a Dutch frigate that sank off Fort Amsterdam in 1801.

At the far east end of town, locally known as the Head of Town, Bobby's Marina and Great Bay Marina have car rental agencies, a dive shop, and a marine supply store.

THE GREAT DIVIDE

Between 1648, when the French and the Dutch signed the Treaty of Concordia, and 1817, when the borders of the island were set, St. Martin/Sint Maarten changed government 16 times. Legend has it that the Dutch and French settlers decided to partition it by staging a march. The Dutchman stopped for a nap during the walking contest, while the Frenchman trudged on. When the two met, the French had claimed a slightly larger portion of the island.

Simpson Bay and Around

📍2 miles (3 km) W of Philipsburg, Sint Maarten 🚌

The Simpson Bay area includes the bay and beach abutting Princess Juliana International Airport on the island's south coast, and the 11-sq-mile (29-sq-km) Simpson Bay Lagoon. The invisible Dutch-French border runs through the lagoon, so most of the popular resorts, restaurants, and activities on the narrow strip of land separating the lagoon from the sea on the south shore are Dutch. Marigot touches the lagoon on the north (French) side at the trendy Port La Royale. At Cole Bay is Topper's Rhum distillery, where you can learn about rum-making during a comprehensive tour that is followed by tasting the several different flavors in the bar.

→
The turqoise waters
of Simpson Bay
and lagoon

STAY

Oyster Bay Beach Resort

A striking glass-and-concrete resort, with bright rooms and a laidback, beachfront bar.

🏠 10 Emerald Merit, Oyster Pond 🌐 oyster baybeachresort.com

$$⑤

Divi Little Bay Beach Resort

This family-friendly resort is located on a peninsula between two bays. To splurge, opt for the plush Casita Suites.

🏠 Little Bay, Philipsburg 🌐 diviresorts.com

$$⑤

Belmond La Samanna

Overlooking a sandy beach, this resort features airy villas, a spa, and tennis courts.

🏠 Baie Longue, Terres Basses 🌐 belmond.com

$$$

---

④

Marigot

📍 10 miles (16 km) NW from Philipsburg, St. Martin
 ℹ Route de Sandy Ground; 590 875 721

Marigot, the capital of French St. Martin, is a charming town built along the sandy curve of a yacht-filled bay. Contemporary boutiques have moved into colonial buildings and Creole-style houses, and the new blends pleasantly with the old in the center of town. A quaint public square near the harbor is the site of a daily market that offers fresh produce and locally made wares. The largest markets are open on Wednesdays and Saturdays, and mornings are the best time to visit.

Nearby, Fort Saint-Louis overlooks the sea. Built between 1767 and 1789 by the French, the fort was captured and held for two years by the British from 1794 until 1796. The hilltop fortress offers a panoramic view of Marigot and the island's western shore. **Sur les Traces des Arawaks** (On the Trail of the Arawaks) is a history and archaeology museum with exhibits such as tools, pottery, and jewelry crafted by the native tribes who lived on the island as early as 1800 BC. Experts comparing the design of these pieces, have been able to trace the history of the Arawaks to South American

natives and to follow their migration from the Orinoco River basin in Venezuela.

On the waterfront of Simpson Bay Lagoon, Port La Royale marina complex is lined with boutiques and small restaurants reminiscent of those on the French Riviera. Keen shoppers will be pleased to note that all merchandise sold on the island is tax-free. During high season, carnival-like entertainment takes place several evenings a week.

Sur les Traces des Arawaks
 🏠 7 rue Fichot
📞 690 567 892 🕘 9am–5pm Mon–Fri 🚫 Public hols

---

⑤

Pic du Paradis

📍 4 miles (6 km) E of Marigot, St. Martin

Translated as Paradise Peak, the island's highest point at 1,391 ft (424 m) offers great views of Baie Orientale and neighboring islands, and is well worth the effort required to reach the top. A steep, rutted secondary road, off the coastal highway to Colombier, leads inland up

the west side of the mountain to within 1 mile (2 km) of the peak, but only a four-wheel-drive vehicle can manage the trip. Nestled at the foot of the Pic du Paradis, visitors will discover Loterie Farm (p256).

Colombier

📍 3 miles (5 km) E of Marigot, St. Martin ⓣ

Just inland from Friar's Bay, this fertile hilly area at the foot of Pic du Paradis is not known to many visitors. The lush region of Colombier provides the vegetables and fruit sold at the public market in Marigot. At one time, residents produced large crops of sugarcane, mangoes, and coffee. The big plantations no longer exist, and goats now graze along the road that runs past scattered Creole houses.

7 Grand Case

📍 4 miles (6 km) NE of Marigot, St Martin 🚌
🌐 grandcase.com

Called the Gastronomic Capital of the Caribbean, the tiny town of Grand Case has

one main road, a fine beach, and many excellent restaurants – some run by chefs who have trained internationally. The gourmet restaurants are housed in quaint Creole-style houses that sit side by side, allowing prospective diners the opportunity to stroll from one to another comparing menus that are posted outside. In addition, local cooks serve island specialties from open-air lo-los (locally owned – locally operated) set up along the same street. Here, fresh seafood and meats are grilled over oil-drum barbecue pits, and patrons sit at picnic tables to eat their fill.

Although the town is known for fine dining rather than for swimming, the 1-mile- (2-km-) long sandy beach with gentle waters is perfect for swimming and has some great snorkeling spots. The bay also offers a spectacular view of neighboring Anguilla and Creole Rock.

On Tuesday nights in the winter the town hosts Harmony Nights Street Festival. Local bands fill

↑ A buzzing eatery in Grand Case, which is known for its wealth of restaurants

the streets with music using everything from home-made drums to fine brass instruments. Residents also sell traditional art and crafts, and cooks prepare delicious dishes that are local to the island.

One of the best-known shops in Grand Case is **Tijon**, a boutique perfumery that specializes in exquisite hand-crafted products. It also offers perfume-making classes, where visitors can also learn about the art of perfume production and create their own signature fragrance, choosing from over 300 oils at Tijon's Perfume Lab. The European-style shop is well worth a browse, as is the small museum with perfume-related items.

Tijon
🕙 📍 1 Route de L'Espérance, Grand Case, St. Martin
🕙 9:30am–5pm Mon–Fri
🌐 tijon.com

> **The lush region of Colombier provides the vegetables and fruit sold at the public market in Marigot.**

←
Fort Saint-Louis in Marigot, with views across the turquoise ocean

 Paddling in a kayak
on the shallow
waters off Îlet Pinel ↑

8 Îlet Pinel and Île Tintamarre

Îlet Pinel: 0.5 miles (1 km) N of Baie Orientale; Île Tintamarre: 1 mile (2 km) NE of Îlet Pinel

These two undeveloped offshore islands lie within the protected waters of the nature reserve, and their beaches are usually deserted. Both islands are difficult to reach when the wind is strong, but in fine weather each makes an ideal day trip. Pinel is easier to reach by boat, and

↑ A great blue heron, often spotted on the "Cliff of the Birds"

more likely to have visitors, but the north side is isolated and its shore is battered by crashing surf. Water taxis regularly shuttle passengers from the beach at French Cul de Sac, just north of Baie Orientale, to Îlet Pinel. The south coast beaches face St. Martin and have gentle waves, snack shacks, and equipment rentals for watersports.

Île Tintamarre is less visited, but day-sail excursions often make this a snorkeling stop since the area's underwater life is amazing. White-sand beaches ring the island, nick-named Flat Island. Mud from the beach is said to have healing powers, and visitors often slather it on their bodies.

9 Old House

5 miles (8 km) NE of Marigot, St Martin
590 873 267 ◯10am-4pm Tue-Sun

Once the main house of a thriving plantation, this reno-vated Creole-style building has an interesting selection of antique machinery once used in cultivating sugar-cane and producing rum. The manor

> Île Tintamarre is less visited, but day-sail excursions often make this a snorkeling stop, since the area's underwater life is amazing.

house sits at the top of a hill overlooking the Spring Estate, which still belongs to its original owners, the Beauperthuy family. The authentically restored home contains treasures collected by the family over six generations. These include photographs, rare lithographs, and ancient maps arranged among the period furniture as they might have been during the 1700s, when sugar and rum production drove the island's economy. There is also a rum and coffee museum on-site.

10 Falaise des Oiseaux

7 miles (11 km) NW of Philipsburg, St Martin

The high ridge of cliffs that lie along the Simpson Bay

Lagoon, overlooking the Caribbean Sea on the western edge of Terres Basses (Lowlands), is called Falaise des Oiseaux, or "Cliff of the Birds." From here there are fabulous views of St. Martin's coastline, and right across to Anguilla. Many species of both indigenous and migrating bird can be found nesting in the cliff's caves, and keen birdwatchers gather here to observe great blue herons, ospreys, yellow warblers, and bullfinches. Pretty homes and villas are scattered along the *falaise* between Baie Rouge (Red Bay) and Baie aux Prunes (Plum Bay).

 11

Baie Orientale

4 miles (6 km) NE of Marigot, St Martin

Watersports operators, bars, and restaurants line the popular 4-mile (6-km) beach that spreads along this highly developed bay. Calm water and a protective reef make this an ideal spot for swimming and snorkeling, while motorized and wind-powered watercraft add to the fun.

12

Réserve Naturelle de Saint-Martin

Anse Marcel **reserve naturelle-saint-martin.com**

This national nature reserve covers 12 sq miles (31 sq km) – most of which is the Atlantic, but there are land sections on the main coastline too, as well as small offshore islands and rocks. The park features dry coastal forest, mangroves, and ponds in the terrestrial parts, with coral reefs and seagrass beds at sea, and is the habitat of many species of marine life, including humpback whales in season. Dive and boat operators offer tours, or visitors can hike around the northeastern headland. Be sure to stop for a swim midway at the white-sand beach of Petites Cayes.

EAT

Bistro Caraïbes
This stylish restaurant is considered one of the island's best. The menu features French favorites such as frogs' legs, *escargot,* and hearty lamb dishes.

81 Blvd de Grand Case
6–10pm daily
bistrot-caraibes.com

$$$

La Villa Restaurant
A quaint venue serving traditional dishes with some Caribbean twists, and a wide selection of French wines. Those seeking a good deal should opt for the fixed price three-course menu that is also on offer.

93 Blvd de Grand Case
5–10pm daily
Apr–Nov: Wed
lavillasxm.com

$$$

Spiga
Located in an authentic Caribbean Creole-style building, Spiga dishes up creative Italian cuisine alongside an excellent wine list. It's set away from the crowds at the northern end of Grand Case, so is perfect for a dreamily romantic dinner.

4 L'Espérance Rd
6–10:30pm daily
May–Nov: Tue
spiga-sxm.com

$$$

 ←
A colorful beach hut catering for the crowds in popular Baie Orientale

PRACTICAL
INFORMATION

Here you will find all the essential advice and information you will need before and during your stay in St. Martin/Sint Maarten.

AT A GLANCE

CURRENCY
French side:
Euro (EUR)
Dutch side:
Caribbean
guilder (CMg)

TIME ZONE
Atlantic Standard Time
(AST), 4 hours behind
GMT and 1 hour ahead
of EST

LANGUAGE
Dutch on the Dutch side and French on
the French side. Some locals speak in
Papiamento or in a French patois

ELECTRICITY SUPPLY
On the French side,
electricity is 220 volts,
and plugs must fit
French outlets. On the
Dutch side, electricity
is 110 volts

EMERGENCY NUMBERS

DUTCH EMERGENCIES	FRENCH FIRE & POLICE
911	**17**

FRENCH MEDICAL
ASSISTANCE

112

When To Go

While the island of St. Martin and Sint Maarten enjoys sunshine all year round, the best time to visit is December through to April. During this time, Carnival, a two-week fiesta, and the Heineken Regatta take place. Humidity starts to build up in May and does not dissipate until late November. Tropical storms blow through and hurricanes can strike between June through November.

Getting There

The island has frequent flights to and from North America and Europe, as well as other Caribbean islands. All international flights land at Princess (Queen) Juliana Airport (SXM) on the Dutch side. Regional carriers land at both the Dutch airport and the French airport, Aéroport de l'Espérance (SFG). Major carriers flying in include Delta, United Airlines, Corsair, American Airlines, Air Canada, KLM, Air France, Air Caraïbes, Air Antilles, Winair, and LIAT.

Personal Security

Theft is a problem on the island, further complicated by the fact that the Dutch and French police do not readily exchange information. Rental cars are a prime target, as are the valuables left in them so avoid leaving anything in your car.

Isolated beaches and hiking trails are other areas where theft is rampant. Make sure you report all crimes to the police, and get a report of the incident.

Health

The island has two hospitals – St. Maarten Medical Center East of Philipsburg on the Dutch side and the Centre Hospitalier LC Fleming de Saint Martin in Marigot on the French side. Both have 24-hour emergency rooms.

Tap water is generally safe to drink but it doesn't always taste good so locals and tourists often prefer to stick to bottled water.

Passports and Visas

Citizens of the European Union may enter St. Martin and Sint Maarten by presenting a national ID or valid passport. Citizens of all other countries must show a valid passport. All visitors must possess an onward or return ticket off the island. For visitors in general, the maximum uninterrupted stay allowed is 30 days. For visitors from Canada, the European Union, Australia, New Zealand and Japan, it is 3 months. For US and Dutch visitors, it is 6 months. More information can be obtained from the Embassy of France in Washington, DC, Passport Canada, and UK Passport Services. A departure tax is usually included in flight tickets and sometimes in the cost of ferry tickets.

LGBT+ Safety

As territories of liberal European countries, both French St. Martin and Dutch Sint Maarten have been accepting of the LGBT+ community for years. There are laws in place against anti-gay discrimination in both. Same-sex marriage is legal in St. Martin, and while it isn't yet in Sint Maarten, symbolic wedding ceremonies and vow renewals are popular.

Money

The US dollar is widely accepted on both sides of the island, but officially the currency on the French side is the euro (EUR) and on the Dutch side, in Sint Maarten and Curaçao, is the Caribbean guilder (CMg).

Banks and ATMs are located at many locations throughout theisland, with the majority in the capital cities, larger towns, and big resort areas. Most hotels, resorts, restaurants and shops accept major credit cards.

Cell Phones and Wi-Fi

On St. Martin/Sint Maarten, the area code for the Dutch side is 721 and the area code for the French side is 590; calls between the two are considered international. To use a personal cell phone on the island, travelers must check with their service provider to determine if they will work in St. Martin and Sint Maarten and if they will be subject to roaming charges. Hotel reception desks offer information regarding short-term cell phone rental outlets. Phone cards are available at major post offices. Many resorts have wireless Internet service, and Wi-Fi hot spots are scattered around the island.

Getting Around

A rental car is the best way to get around St. Martin/Sint Maarten. A two-lane highway encircles the coast and the secondary roads are in good condition. Most large international agencies such as AVIS and Hertz rent cars on the island, and many local companies such as Paradise meet or beat their rates. Book well ahead during the high season. Several agencies have booths at the airports and large resorts usually have rental cars on-site. Taxis are abundant and charges are government-regulated, with rates posted in each cab. Prices generally increase in the evening, and drivers may charge extra for more than three passengers and any excess luggage.

Public transportation is limited to small daily buses between Philipsburg, Marigot, and Grand Case. Commercial jets arrive at the international airport, located on the Dutch side. Small aircraft fly to nearby islands from L'Espérance Airport on the French side. Island-hopping is possible by high-speed ferry to St. Barths and by catamaran to Anguilla and Saba.

Visitor Information

Visitor information kiosks are located at the airports, main marinas, and cruise ship docks. **Sint Maarten Tourist Bureau** has its office in Philipsburg and **Office du Tourisme de Saint-Martin** has a branch in Marigot. Local weekly and monthly publications listing current events and activities are available free of cost throughout the island.
Office du Tourisme de Saint-Martin
w st-martin.org
Sint Maarten Tourist Bureau
w st-maarten.com

The rugged, mountainous terrain of Saba

SABA AND ST. EUSTATIUS

Until recently part of the Netherlands, Antilles, Saba and St. Eustatius now have the status of special municipalities in the Kingdom of the Netherlands. Some 17 miles (27 km) apart, the islands lie to the south of another Dutch outpost, Sint Maarten. They are tiny places, with rugged coastlines and dramatic interiors rising to volcanic peaks. St. Eustatius – usually referred to as Statia – covers an area of just under 12 sq miles (31 sq km) and has a population of of around 3,200. Saba, dubbed "The Unspoiled Queen", is a mere five square miles, has just one main road called The Road, and some 1,900 inhabitants.

Saba was first colonized by the Dutch in 1640 but due to its inaccessibility and vertiginous terrain, wasn't cultivated like other Caribbean islands. Instead, it became a haven for pirates. Statia, claimed by the Dutch in the 1630s but frequently changing hands between European countries, was, by contrast, prosperous. In its heyday in the 1700s, the regional capital Oranjestad was a major trading hub in the eastern Caribbean for slaves, sugar, and cotton. The island showed its support for the North American colonies during the American Revolution, and in retribution was ransacked by the British. Ties between Statia and the United States remain close.

SABA AND
ST. EUSTATIUS

Must Sees

❶ Mount Scenery
❷ The Quill

Experience More

❸ The Bottom
❹ Fort Bay
❺ Ladder Bay
❻ Zion's Hill
❼ Windwardside
❽ Oranjestad
❾ Lynch Plantation Museum
❿ National Park Visitors' Center
⓫ Miriam Schmidt Botanical Gardens

SABA AND
ST. EUSTATIUS

Saba

St. Eustatius

Saba

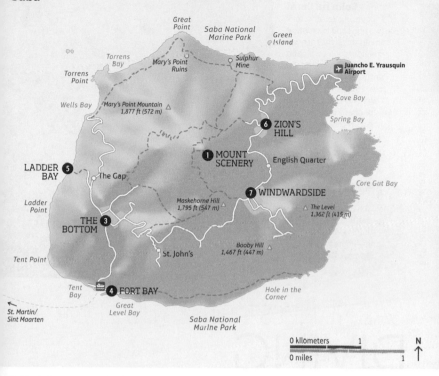

Great Point

Saba National
Marine Park

Green
Island

Torrens
Bay

Mary's Point
Ruins

Sulphur
Mine

**Juancho E. Yrausquin
Airport**

Torrens
Point

Cove Bay

Wells Bay

Mary's Point Mountain
1,877 ft (572 m)

Spring Bay

6 ZION'S
HILL

1 MOUNT
SCENERY

LADDER **5**
BAY

The Gap

English Quarter

Core Gut Bay

Ladder
Point

7 WINDWARDSIDE

THE **3**
BOTTOM

Maskehorne Hill
1,795 ft (547 m)

The Level
1,362 ft (415 m)

St. John's

Booby Hill
1,467 ft (447 m)

Tent Point

Tent
Bay

4 FORT BAY

Hole in the
Corner

St. Martin/
Sint Maarten

Great
Level Bay

Saba National
Marine Park

0 kilometers   1

0 miles   1

N

St. Eustatius

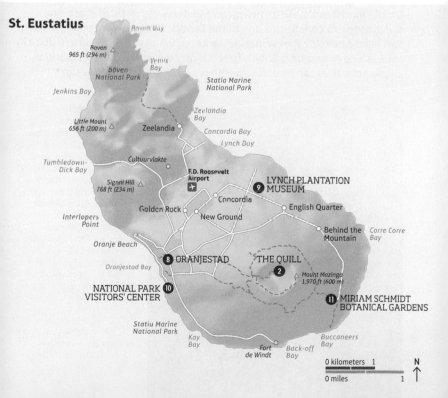

Boven Bay

Boven
965 ft (294 m)

Venus
Bay

Boven
National Park

Statia Marine
National Park

Jenkins Bay

Zeelandia
Bay

Little Mount
656 ft (200 m)

Zeelandia

Concordia Bay

Lynch Bay

Tumbledown-
Dick Bay

Cultuurvlakte

**F.D. Roosevelt
Airport**

LYNCH PLANTATION
MUSEUM

Signal Hill
768 ft (234 m)

9

Interlopers
Point

Concordia

Golden Rock

English Quarter

New Ground

Corre Corre
Bay

Oranje Beach

Behind the
Mountain

8 ORANJESTAD

THE QUILL

Oranjestad Bay

2

Mount Mazinga
1,970 ft (600 m)

NATIONAL PARK
VISITORS' CENTER **10**

11 MIRIAM SCHMIDT
BOTANICAL GARDENS

Statia Marine
National Park

Kay
Bay

Fort
de Windt

Back-off
Bay

Buccaneers
Bay

0 kilometers   1

0 miles   1

N

Colorful Coral

Covering volcanic rock formations and encrusting sunken ships, the thriving kaleidoscopic corals and sponges are dazzling. An unforgettable night dive round Statia's Chien Tong wreck reveals cup coral polyps opening to feed in a blaze of color, while sea turtles bed down inside.

Did You Know?

Saba Bank is the Atlantic's largest submerged atoll and is home to 270 species of fish.

→

Coral and sponges richly hued in orange and shades of green

SABA AND ST. EUSTATIUS FOR
DIVING

Off the tourist radar, the eerie volcanic underwater world of these tiny Dutch outposts constitutes one of the Caribbean's best-kept diving secrets. Each island boasts pristine marine parks brimming with life and a fusion of astonishing colors: from Saba's spectacular pinnacles to Statia's glorious shipwrecks, they can be enjoyed with scarcely another diver in sight.

Otherworldly Marinescapes

The islands' volcanic origins have created stunning underwater scenes out of lava flows including "fingers," bombs, and basalt boulders. Saba's towering seamounts loom up from the seabed, to 90 ft (27 m) below the surface, including the legendary Third Encounter. Piercing the blue void, the jaw-dropping Eye of the Needle is topped with a giant barrel sponge, attracting sharks and rays.

←

The awe-inspiring cluster of pinnacles swathed in coral at Third Encounter

Plunge into the Abyss

Low visitor numbers, well protected marine parks, and professional local operators make for great visibility and healthy reefs teeming with fish. Encircling the entire island, Saba National Marine Park *(sabapark.org)* offers around 30 brilliant dive sites, from the sheltered nursery of Well's Bay to the more exhilarating "bottomless" drop-offs farther out. Statia's surrounding reserve contains 36 sites, including coral gardens, walls, and wrecks, with shallower spots that are accessible to snorkeling novices, too.

→
Longspine squirrelfish, found in Statia

History Submerged

Shipwrecks are a trademark of Statia's underwater world. The star attraction is the Charles ("Charlie") Brown, a vast steel hull sunk in 2003. At Blue Bead Hole, sift the sandy seabed in search of "treasure" – pentagonal blue glass beads, the currency of 17th century Dutch slave traders.

←

Diver exploring the "Charlie" Brown shipwreck in Statia

Did You Know?

Mount Scenery is the highest point on the island, and in the entire Kingdom of the Netherlands.

↑ The impressive cloud- and rainforest-clad Mount Scenery

MOUNT SCENERY

🏛 Saba Trail Shop; 8am–4pm Mon–Fri (to 2pm Sat & Sun); www.sabapark.org

Looming out of the sea just shy of 3,000 ft (887 m), the brooding volcanic bulk of Mount Scenery dominates Saba. Although it is often draped in cloud, on a clear day the views over the glittering Caribbean Sea, studded with islands, are jaw-dropping.

💬 INSIDER TIP
Elfin Trail

In 2018, the new Elfin Trail opened, offering an alternative route up Mount Scenery from above Hell's Gate. It affords great views and more varied vegetation than the staircase as the path also climbs through old plantations.

Even in the mist, the fairytale elfin forest holds plenty of allure, dense with mountain mahogany, laden with bromeliads and orchids, and dripping with moss. Just below, wild plantains, mountain palms, and ferns predominate, while cactuses punctuate the forested landscape. Splashes of color are provided by begonias and raspberries. Wildlife to look out for include the leopard-spotted Saban anole lizard, iguanas, and stray goats. Climbing the Mount Scenery Staircase is the most popular of the island's dozen trails. Precisely 1,064 stone steps climb from the Saba Trail Office in Windwardside to the summit, taking around an hour and a half. The route is mercifully punctuated with benches – ideal spots to have a swig of water and gaze down at Saba. A guided trek with native Saban "Crocodile" Johnson can be organized at the trail shop.

↑ An attractive leopard-spotted Saban anole lizard, unique to the island, perched on a branch

Even in the mist, the fairytale elfin forest holds plenty of allure, dense with mountain mahogany, laden with bromeliads and orchids, and dripping with moss.

↑ Exploring the vast array of flora along one of the many trekking trails

②

THE QUILL

🏠 St. Eustatius 🛈 STENAPA, Gallows Bay; 7am–5pm
Mon–Fri; www.statiapark.org

Towering over Oranjestad, the Quill – Statia's dormant volcano – presides over the southern half of the island, its perfectly formed cone the centerpiece of a national park. It boasts impressive variations in flora and fauna.

The volcano's steep slopes rise to 1,970 ft (600 m) at Mount Mazinga, the highest point on the knife-edge crater rim, cloaked in rare elfin forest, a tangle of gnarled and knotted trees. The Quill's imposing cone "snags" passing clouds, creating a lush seasonal evergreen forest inside the crater, while the drier exterior slopes are coated with thorny woodland. Taking on one of The Quill's trekking trails is a must when visiting Statia, whether strolling with binoculars along the Bird Trail or thrashing through the undergrowth to Mount Mazinga. By far the most walked route is The Quill Trail, which takes you up through verdant vegetation to the crater rim. Though steep, it is an easy, fast climb. The more adventurous may take on the Crater Trail, slithering sharply into the belly of the volcano. The crater floor is truly magical, packed with towering tropical trees and dangling lianas, punctuated with giant volcanic boulders.

RED-BELLIED RACERS

A common sight across trails are red-bellied racers. This slender, dull-colored snake is unique to Statia and Saba. It is most active early morning and late afternoon, and is harmless to humans.

Strip of dry land and glittering sea leading up to The Quill ↑

1 Trekking along the precipitous crater rewards you with stellar views on a clear day.

2 A magnet for nature lovers, the unique Kapok tree with its giant buttress roots can be found here.

3 The crater floor is packed with rare "Daddy-Longlegs" orchids.

Did You Know?

The name Quill comes from the Dutch term "kuil" which means "pit" or "hole."

TOP 5 FLORA AND FAUNA

Lesser Antillean Iguana
Endangered iguana varying in color from green to gray, often seen on rocks.

Kapok Tree
Gigantic tree towering 130 ft (40 m) above the crater floor.

Monarch Butterfly
Vermilion butterfly with veined wings is a sighting year-round.

"Daddy-Longlegs" Orchid
A delicate white flower with trailing tendrils found inside the crater.

Bridled Quail Dove
Generally seen along the forest floor, this attractive bird has an iridescent upper body.

↑ The elaborately painted interior of Sacred Heart Church in The Bottom

EXPERIENCE MORE

STAY

Queen's Gardens Resort & Spa

A luxury hillside resort surrounded by tropical greenery and offering unbeatable island views. Guests will enjoy spacious suites, private Jacuzzis, open-air dining, and a gorgeous spa.

📍 Drive 1, Troy Hill, Saba
🌐 queensaba.com

$$$

The Cottage Club

Ten traditional, self-catering cottages, each with a sea-facing balcony and hotel-level services. There's also a pool and a communal lounge area.

📍 Windwardside, Saba
🌐 cottage-club.com

$$$

3

The Bottom

📍 1 mile (1.6 km) N of Fort Bay, Saba

On the winding road up from Fort Bay, the first town is The Bottom – the largest on the island and the seat of government. Before The Road was built, the main mode for transporting goods from the sea was a walk up steps from Fort Bay or Ladder Bay.

Most buildings are in the typical Saban style with white clapboard houses with red roofs and trimmed lawns, all neatly kept with pride. Among the town's highlights are Sacred Heart Church's sacristy adorned with original paintings by local artist Heleen Cornet, and the **Saba Artisans Foundation**, where Saban lace and other handwork are sold. Other notable buildings include the grand governor's house, and Saba University School of Medicine.

Saba Artisans Foundation

🏛 📍 Matthew Levenstone St 📞 599 416 3260
🕐 8:30am-noon Mon-Fri

4

Fort Bay

📍 SW coast of Saba

Saba's main port, Fort Bay is also the starting point for diving excursions. With a harsh coastline and no sandy beaches or real harbors for boat docking, the island was hard to access. In 1972, the Dutch government built a 277-ft (84-m) deep-water pier at Fort Bay, making it easier for landing cargo and for ferry services. The only gas station on the island is located here, along with the Saba Marine Park Visitor's Center and Hyperbaric Facility.

The adjacent In Two Deep café and Pop's Place are two relaxing eateries with fantastic views of the sea.

5

Ladder Bay

📍 1 mile (1.5 km) NW of The Bottom, Saba 🕐 Dawn-dusk daily

Saba's first port, Ladder Bay, served the island before the

pier was constructed at Fort Bay. More than 800 steps leading up to The Bottom were the major mode of transportation for people and goods until as late as the 1970s.

Today, visitors can climb down to Ladder Bay through the Ladder Trail, the only route to reach the bay. Views to the ocean are impressive, but the hike is strenuous and takes about 40 minutes each way. The highlight of this route is the remains of the old Customs House; it is advisable not to stray off the trail's track as it crosses private land.

The bay has several areas ideal for diving, including Ladder Bay Deep, a sloping reef dropping to a maximum depth of 110 ft (33 m).

To the north lies Wells Bay, where The Road ends. It is sometimes referred to as the "Wandering Beach" since its belt of tan sand is washed away for many months of the year. It usually reappears in spring, when it can lay claim to being the island's only beach.

6
Zion's Hill

⌂ 2 miles (3 km) NE of The Bottom, Saba ⊕⊕

Perched on the little Zion's Hill, Hell's Gate is a small town that can be reached only by The Road. Since many residents did not appreciate the negative name, the town is also known as Zion's Hill.

One of its main highlights is the Holy Rosary Church. Made to resemble a structure from the medieval period, the church was in fact built in 1962. Behind it is the **Saba Lace Boutique**, where some of the best lacemakers on the island exhibit and sell their delicate pieces of art.

Saba Lace Boutique
⊕ ⌂ Zion's Hill ⊕ 9am–noon & 2:30–5pm Mon–Fri

↑ A woman examining the intricate lace embroidery on sale at Saba Lace Boutique in Zion's Hill

7
Windwardside

⌂ 1 mile (1.5 km) NE of The Bottom, Saba ⊕ ⊕ Tourism Office; 599 416 2231

Beyond Zion's Hill, The Road passes through thick forests before reaching the sleepy little town of Windwardside. It is a step back in time, with its quaint shopping area and outstanding examples of typical Saban cottages.

Highlights are the **Harry L. Johnson Museum**, a 160-year-old cottage now used as a museum. It contains original furnishings and a collection of indigenous artifacts. Nearby, the Dutch Museum is also housed in a traditional Saban cottage; its lace collection is of particular interest. Another fine place to visit is **JoBean's Hot Glass Studio**. Visitors can learn to make glass beads or watch Jo Bean at work.

Harry L. Johnson Museum
⊛⊛ ⌂ Windwardside
⊕ 10am–3pm Tue–Sat
⊕ museum-saba.com/ HLJohnson

JoBean's Hot Glass Studio
⊛ ⌂ Windwardside ⊕ 10am–5pm Mon–Sat, 10am–3pm Sun ⊕ jobean-glass.com

8 Oranjestad

⬛ SW coast of St. Eustatius
🔼 ℹ Fort Oranje; www.
statia-tourism.com

The island of St. Eustatius, or Statia, was known during the colonial period as the Golden Rock, because of its importance as a center for international trade. The population during the peak trading years jumped to over 20,000, and the main town of Oranjestad was a thriving, cosmopolitan place. Since 2000, a concerted effort has been made by the St. Eustatius Historical Foundation to restore much of the town area. Now, a stroll through the Upper Town is like stepping back in time, with graceful 17th- and 18th-century wood and stone structures lining the cobblestone streets.

Oranjestad offers the second-largest collection of standing wooden 18th-century buildings in the Americas, exceeded only by Williamsburg in the U.S. The **St. Eustatius Historical Foundation** is housed in the 18th-century home of merchant Simon Doncker. On the

> Oranjestad offers the second-largest collection of standing wooden 18th-century buildings in the Americas, exceeded only by Williamsburg in the U.S.

main level are period rooms filled with authentic furnishings and many household goods from the 18th century. The museum staff coordinate guided walking tours of the town. The Government Guest House is an old stone structure that has been restored and is now in use as an office building. It first served as barracks for the troops at **Fort Oranje**, which sits on a bluff overlooking Lower Town and Gallows Bay. Originally built by the French in 1629, the fort has been fully restored, with the Tourist Office occupying one of the buildings. Just to the south of the fort are the ruins of the **Dutch Reformed Church**, built in the 1750s, and the adjacent cemetery. Another historic site is **Honen Dalim Synagogue**, one of the

oldest synagogues in the Americas. Now in ruins, plans for its restoration are underway with support from St. Eustatius Center for Archaeological Research (SECAR). Built in 1739, the structure and grounds include a cemetery and a *mikvah* – a ritual bath – that was discovered during one of the SECAR excavations.

St. Eustatius Historical Foundation

⬛ Wilhelminaweg 3
📞 599 318 2288 🕐 9am–5pm
Mon–Fri

Fort Oranje

 ⬛ Kerkweg 📞 599 318
2433 🕐 Sunrise–sunset

Dutch Reformed Church

 ⬛ Kerkweg
🕐 Sunrise–sunset

Honen Dalim Synagogue

 ⬛ Breedeweg
🕐 Sunrise–sunset

---

9 Lynch Plantation Museum

⬛ 1 mile (1.5 km) N of
Oranjestad 📞 599 318 2338
🕐 On request

Situated on the northeastern side of St. Eustatius, this small domestic museum was constructed by the Berkel family on their homestead,

and consists of two one-room buildings. The exhibition house, which was constructed by the family in 1916, is a replica of the original house and displays furniture, artifacts, and tools from the plantation. A private school also shares the plantation grounds, which are well maintained with fruit trees as well as the natural flora of the island. An area on the side with a bower is used for weddings and receptions.

National Park Visitors' Center

🅰 Gallows Bay, St. Eustatius 📞 599 318 2884 🕐 7am–5pm Mon–Fri 🌐 statiapark.org

The St. Eustatius National Park Foundation (STENAPA) oversees its many programs from the Visitors' Center in Gallows Bay. It offers exhibits, a small souvenir shop, an internet café, showers, public bathrooms, and a picnic area. Visitors can reserve tours, make taxi reservations, pay fees for park usage or diving, and even purchase plants from the botanical gardens.

Miriam Schmidt Botanical Gardens

🅰 3 miles (5 km) E of Oranjestad 📞 599 318 2884 🕐 🌐 Sunrise–sunset

As one of the national parks under the direction of STENAPA, this site serves to educate locals and visitors about the varied plant life of the island, thus helping to protect and preserve the island's native and endangered flora.

Sited on a former sugar plantation, the gardens were established in 1998, and volunteers work daily on improving various areas. Spaces that have already been completed include the Sensory Garden, Palm Garden, Shade House, Lookout Garden (which offers visitors spectacular views

↑ Diver exploring a coastal area protected by the St. Eustatius National Park Foundation

of St. Kitts and humpback whales), and the Jean Gemmill Bird Observation Trail. Guided tours of the gardens are arranged by the National Park Visitors' Center in Gallows Bay.

The fully restored Fort Oranje on St. Eustatius island, complete with cannons *(inset)*

EAT

The Old Gin House
Head here for ocean-front dining on a lounge deck. The international menu is well prepared, but the irresistable location is the real draw.

🅰 1 Oranjebaai, Oranjestad 🕐 Tue–Wed 🌐 theoldginhouse.com

$$$

Franky's Bar & Restaurant
For a dose of local food and culture in a no-frills setting, this is the place. Saturday is BBQ night, with ribs, lobster, or pork straight off the grill.

🅰 17b Fort Oranjestraat 📞 599 318 0166 🕐 Mon

$$$

PRACTICAL
INFORMATION

Here you will find all the essential advice and information you will need before and during your stay in Saba and St. Eustatius.

AT A GLANCE

CURRENCY
US Dollar (US$)

TIME ZONE
Atlantic Standard Time, 5 hours behind GMT. When the US is on daylight saving , the islands follow the time on the US East Coast

LANGUAGE
Dutch

ELECTRICITY SUPPLY
110 volts. For 220-volt appliances a converter is needed

EMERGENCY NUMBERS

AMBULANCE

913

FIRE SERVICE

912

POLICE

911

TAP WATER
Water purity is unreliable so, to be safe, drink bottled water

When To Go

The climate on both islands is pleasant year-round, and nights can be cool. The summer months are hotter and more humid, and the peak hurricane season is from June through to October. Many people go to Saba in July for the Summer Festival, or in October for the Sea and Learn workshops which cover a range of ecological activities. In St. Eustatius the special days include Carnival in mid-July, and November 16, the designated Statia-America Day.

Getting There

The only way that Saba and St. Eustatius can be reached is by traveling through St. Martin/Sint Maarten. Winair operates several flights daily from Princess Juliana International Airport (SXM) in St. Martin to Juancho E. Yrausquin Airport (SAB) in Saba. It also has daily flights between St. Eustatius and Saba. Ferries, including the Dawn II and The Edge, operate on a weekly schedule between Saba and St. Martin/Sint Maarten. St. Eustatius can be reached via air transport on Winair, with several daily flights from St. Martin to Franklin D. Roosevelt Airport (EUX), daily flights from Saba, and a weekly flight from Golden Rock Airport (SKB), St. Kitts. Great Bay Express runs a ferry service from Sint Maarten to St. Eustatius.

Personal Security

Saba and St. Eustatius have a relatively low crime rate. However, petty theft and street crime can be an issue. The main tourist areas are generally safe, but you should take normal precautions such as avoiding remote areas at night, locking away your valuables and making sure that purses are fnot easy to snatch.

Health

Considering the remoteness of the islands, healthcare on Saba and St. Eustatius is very efficient. For health-related emergencies, there are hospitals such as A. M. Edwards Medical

Center and Queen Beatrix Hospital on both islands, which are staffed by local physicians. Both islands have hyperbaric chambers and well-stocked pharmacies.

Passports and Visas

For both islands, travelers need a valid passport and onward/return ticket. Residents of certain countries are required to obtain a visa to enter the Dutch Caribbean islands; for a list of these countries, it is advisable to consult the website of the tourism bureau. There is a departure fee to be paid just before getting on the plane to return home. The two islands have different departure fees and one can expect a lower fee if the final destination shown on the onward ticket is another Caribbean island.

LGBT+ Safety

Like the other former Dutch colonies in the Caribbean, Saba is an LGBT+ friendly destination. It doesn't have a discernible gay community or entertainment spots but is generally welcoming, and there are a number of tour packages that are promoted to attract LGBT+ visitors. Locals on St. Eustatius can be less tolerant and displays of affection are not recommended. Same-sex marraige was legalised on both islands in 2012 however it is still opposed by locals on St. Eustatius.

Money

The official currency in Saba and St. Eustatius is the US Dollar (US$). There are no limitations on the import and export of currency. Credit cards and traveler's checks are widely accepted. ATM machines are available at the banks in Windwardside and The Bottom in Saba, and in Oranjestad in St Eustatius.

Cell Phones and Wi-Fi

Internet connections are available at most of the hotels, as well as at Island Communication Services. Internet access is available at the Public Library and Computers and More. Visitors bringing cell phones should check with their service providers to determine if they will work and if they will be subject to roaming charges.

Getting Around

Taxis are the favored way to get around both islands, since there is no public transportation. Tourist desks at the airports can connect you with avail-able drivers, and the drivers in their turn give customers their cell phone number so that they can be contacted whenever transport is needed. Sometimes taxis can be scarce, so it is best to contact the tourism offices and make arrangements ahead of time.

Saba has a few car rental agencies while in St. Eustatius there are several, including ARC Car Rental, Brown's Car Rental, Schmidt Car Rental, and Reddy Car Rental, providing small cars capable of navigating the narrow roads.It is easy to find your way, as there is only one main road on Saba, and a limited number of roads in St. Eustatius. Hitchhiking is quite common on Saba and St. Eustatius but visitors should be aware of the potential risks.

Visitor Information

Information on Saba can be obtained from the office of the **Saba Tourist Bureau** located in Windwardside and on St. Eustatius at the **St. Eustatius Tourism Office** in Fort Oranje. Both have their own tourist websites. There are tourist desks at the airports providing maps and brochures, as well as assistance with transportation.

Saba Tourist Bureau
🇼 sabatourism.com
St. Eustatius Tourism Office
🇼 statiatourism.com

View across The Narrows to St. Kitts from Nevis

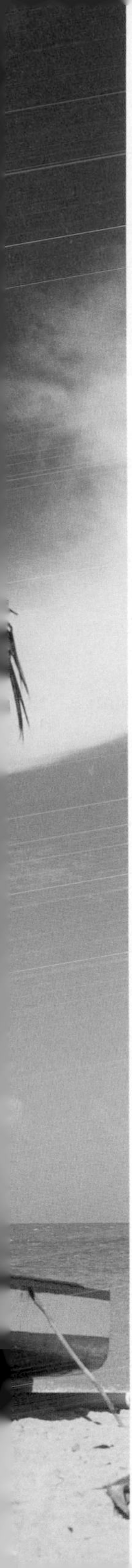

ST. KITTS AND NEVIS

In the 1600s and 1700s, the British and French prized St. Kitts and Nevis. Due to their incredible fertility, the islands were major producers of tobacco, then sugar cane. The importance Britain placed on St. Kitts can be seen in Brimstone Hill Fortress, a colossal fortification dating from 1690, dubbed the Gibraltar of the West Indies. The twin islands became an independent nation in 1983, called the Federation of St. Kitts and Nevis. The sugar industry survived until 2005 – its legacy includes a scenic railway on St. Kitts once used to transport cane from the estates to the capital Basseterre. Tourism, which has grown rapidly on St. Kitts, is now the most important element in the country's economy, along with hosting offshore financial and service companies.

St. Kitts and Nevis are two miles apart, separated by a stretch of water called The Narrows. St. Kitts divides into two halves. The north is mountainous – Mount Liamuiga, a dormant volcano covered in rainforest, rises to 3,972 ft (1,210 m) – and ringed by pretty villages. The south includes the capital Basseterre, the Frigate Bay resort area and popular beaches on the southeastern peninsula. Smaller, circular, and verdant Nevis centers on 3,292 ft (1,003 m) Nevis Peak, another photogenic dormant volcano often topped with clouds. It is possible to drive right around the base of the mountain, stopping off at the villagey Charlestown, plantation inns, and idyllic beaches.

Map labels:
Willet's Bay · Dieppe Bay · *Sandy Bay* · *Convent Bay* · St. Paul's · Sadlers · **St. Kitts** · Newton Ground · *Parson's Ghut* · *Sadler's Ghut* · Tabernacle · Nicola Town · Molineux · *Belle Tete* · *North West Range* · Mount Liamuiga 3,792 ft (1,156 m) · Philips · *Grange Bay* · *Pump Bay* · Sandy Point · Lodge · Cayon · **BRIMSTONE HILL FORTRESS** ❶ · ARAWAK CARVINGS ❺ · Key · *Hermitage Bay* · Half Way Tree · *South East Range* · Olivier Mountain 2,952 ft (900 m) · *Barker's Po...* · Middle Island · *Conaree Bay* · OLD ROAD ❸ · ROMNEY MANOR PLANTATION ❹ · St. Peter's · *Canada Hills* · Upper Conare... · Challengers · **Robert L. Bradshaw International Airport** ✈ · *Half M... Bay* · *Palmetto Bay* · Trinity · Brumaire · BASSETERRE ❷ · FRIGATE BAY ❶❶ · *Frigate Bay South*

Caribbean Sea

ST. KITTS AND NEVIS

Must See
❶ Brimstone Hill Fortress

Experience More
❷ Basseterre
❸ Old Road
❹ Romney Manor Plantation
❺ Arawak Carvings
❻ Southeastern Peninsula
❼ Charlestown
❽ Oualie Beach
❾ Fig Tree Church
❿ Botanical Garden of Nevis
⓫ Frigate Bay
⓬ Nevis Plantation Inns

ST. KITTS
AND NEVIS

*Atlantic
Ocean*

*Sand Bank
Bay*

SOUTHEASTERN
PENINSULA **6**

*Great
Salt
Pond*

Turtle Bay

*Cockleshell
Bay*

*Major's
Bay*

°*Booby Island*

The Narrows

*ite
use
y*

*ana
oint
ast
y*

*ten
y*

*ag's
head*

Vance W. Amory
International Airport

*Newcastle
Bay*

Nisbet Beach

Oualie Bay

Newcastle

OUALIE BEACH **8**

△ *Round Hill
1,014 ft (309 m)*

*Long Haul
Bay*

Cades Bay

Hick's Village

*Pinney's
Beach*

Cotton
Ground

Fountain

Butlers

Vaughans

△ *Nevis Peak
3,232 ft (985 m)*

*Eden Brown
Bay*

Huggins Bay

HARLESTOWN **7**

**NEVIS
PLANTATION
INNS**
12

New River

FIG TREE CHURCH **9**

Taylors Pasture

Figtree

10

Buck's Hill

**BOTANICAL
GARDEN OF NEVIS**

White Bay

Nevis

0 kilometers   4

0 miles   4

N
↑

1 ⟨⟩ ⟨⟩ ⟨⟩

BRIMSTONE HILL FORTRESS

⌂ 10 miles (16 km) NW of Basseterre, St. Kitts ⊤ ⧖ 9:30am–5:30pm daily
ⓦ brimstonehillfortress.org

Standing at 800 ft (243 m), this massive UNESCO World Heritage Site fortress is a vast network of defensive structures and commands an exceptional view over St. Kitts and Nevis.

Using African slave labor, Brimstone Hill was built in stages between 1690 and 1790, when the wars for a British empire were at their fiercest. Known as the "Gibraltar of the West Indies," the fortress was considered impregnable until the French laid siege on it in 1782. Its name is indicative of the hellish smell of sulfur, or brimstone, the result of St. Kitts's volcanic geology. Brimstone Hill became a national park in October 1985, with sanction from the Queen. Many areas within the fortress are now museums featuring interesting displays on the fortifications.

↑ One of the well-preserved rooms within the complex

> **Its name is indicative of the hellish smell of sulfur, or brimstone, the result of St. Kitts's volcanic geology. Brimstone Hill became a national park in 1985.**

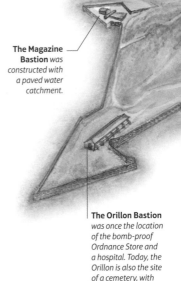

The Magazine Bastion *was constructed with a paved water catchment.*

The Orillon Bastion *was once the location of the bomb-proof Ordnance Store and a hospital. Today, the Orillon is also the site of a cemetery, with tombstones still intact.*

↑ Flag flying on the historic grounds of the fortress

The vast Brimstone Hill Fortress site and its various military structures ↑

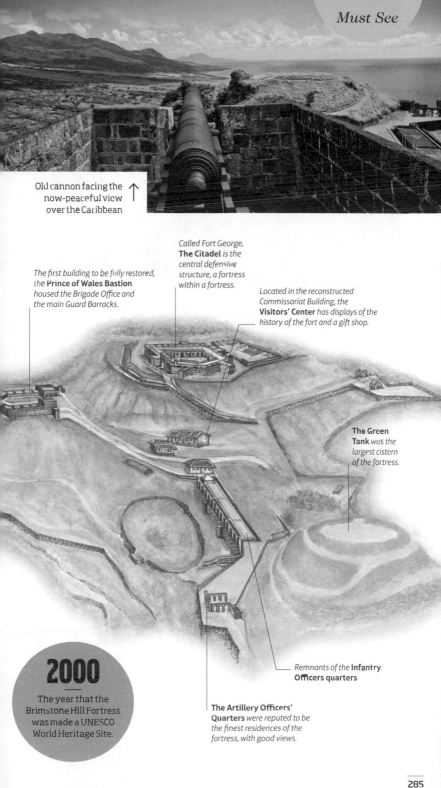

Old cannon facing the now-peaceful view over the Caribbean →

Called Fort George, **The Citadel** is the central defensive structure, a fortress within a fortress.

The first building to be fully restored, the **Prince of Wales Bastion** housed the Brigade Office and the main Guard Barracks.

Located in the reconstructed Commissariat Building, the **Visitors' Center** has displays of the history of the fort and a gift shop.

The Green Tank was the largest cistern of the fortress.

Remnants of the **Infantry Officers** quarters

2000

The year that the Brimstone Hill Fortress was made a UNESCO World Heritage Site.

The Artillery Officers' Quarters were reputed to be the finest residences of the fortress, with good views.

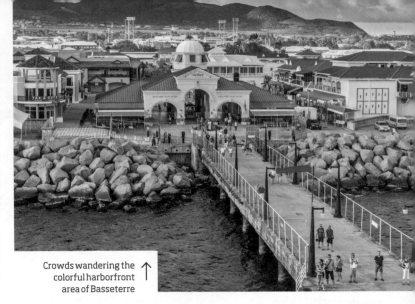

Crowds wandering the colorful harborfront area of Basseterre ↑

EXPERIENCE MORE

 2

Basseterre

🏠 S coast of St. Kitts ✈ 🚌 🚢
ℹ Pelican Mall, Bay Rd

Basseterre sits on the Caribbean, or leeward, coast of St. Kitts – *basse-terre* is French for the sailing term "leeward." The capital of St. Kitts, it is a pretty West Indian town, where many of the original Georgian buildings are still intact.

A century ago all visitors to the island would arrive by sea, passing through the arch of the old colonial Treasury Building, with its rich volcanic stonework, white frames, and a dome. The Treasury Building houses the **National Museum**

Did You Know?

St. Kitts and Nevis is the Western Hemisphere's smallest sovereign state, with a population of 55,000.

of St. Kitts, which displays various artifacts from the pre-Colombian era, including pottery and axe-heads, and colonial military and domestic items such as muskets and irons, as well as maps and prints of plantation life. Nowadays visitors are more likely to arrive via Port Zante, the cruise ship dock, which has a few duty-free shops such as the Amina Craft Market and the Pelican Mall. The port has the capacity to welcome some of the biggest ships in the world.

West from the port, and beyond the Treasury Building, is the Nevis ferry dock, the bus station, and the main market building. The waterfront here is a busy area of the town. Inland from the Treasury Building is The Circus, a popular meeting place in the town. At its center stands the quaint Victorian Berkeley Memorial Clocktower, which dates from 1883. Upstairs a cafe with a balcony offers a view of the bustle below.

Southeast of here is Independence Square, a grassy park surrounded by a

white picket fence overlooked by stone and wooden buildings. Originally the commercial center of Basseterre, when it was named Pall Mall Square, it once held the slave market. The square was renamed upon St. Kitts and Nevis achieving political independence in 1983. At the eastern end of the square is the catholic Co-Cathedral of the Immaculate Conception, which has a barrel-vaulted nave and a distinctive rose window. Next to it is the Court House and, in a pretty wooden Creole building on the north side, the Spencer Cameron Gallery, which exhibits work by Caribbean artists.

Located on Cayon Street is the Anglican St. George's, the main church built by the English in 1706. Fortlands District, on the western edge of the town, has luxurious homes and one hotel, Ocean Terrace Inn, which hosts a lively streetside grill on Friday nights. The northern outskirts of the town have been given over to modern buildings, with supermarkets and light industry. Warner Park, the national stadium, lies on Wellington Road, which runs toward the airport. Built for the Cricket World Cup in 2007, it now hosts cricket matches and the annual music festival.

National Museum of St. Kitts

 Old Treasury Building
869 465 5584 9am–5:30pm Mon–Fri

3

Old Road

6 miles (9 km) NW of Basseterre, St. Kitts

Located at the foot of the concave slopes of the main St. Kitts mountain range, Old Road is a town of clapboard and stone buildings. Settled in 1624 by Thomas Warner who cultivated the islands' bounteous tobacco crop, Old Road was the capital of the English part of St. Kitts. Situated east is Bloody Point, the site of a 15th-century massacre of the Caribs by British and French forces when over two thousand indigenous peoples were killed trying to defend their land and customs.

↑ White-painted carvings by the Arawak, who were early inhabitants of St. Kitts

4

Romney Manor Plantation

4 miles (6 km) NW of Basseterre, St. Kitts 869 465 6253 9am–5pm Mon–Fri

Set in extensive and attractive gardens, Romney Manor is a restored former plantation estate house and a popular port of call for visitors to the island. It was originally owned by an ancestor of Thomas Jefferson, third president of the U.S. The house was then renamed Romney Manor after its acquistion by the Earl of Romney in the 17th century. This plantation was the first in St. Kitts to free its slaves in 1834. Since 1964 the manor has been the home of the Caribelle workshop and store, which produces eye-catching batik textiles.

5

Arawak Carvings

6 miles (9 km) NW of Basseterre, St. Kitts

Before the arrival of the Europeans, St. Kitts – then called Liamuiga, meaning "fertile land" – was inhabited by the Arawak and subsequently the Carib. Inland from Old Road town, in an unassuming setting on a lawn behind a white picket fence, is a small but touching reminder of their life and art. These Arawak carvings, also known as petroglyphs, are depictions of a man and a woman (or possibly male or female gods of fertility), carved in a graphic design into boulders of black volcanic rock. They have been painted white to emphasize their square bodies, waving arms, and antennae.

←

The shuttered facade of Romney Manor Plantation, surrounded by lush greenery

STAY

St. Kitts Mariott Resort & Royal Beach Casino

This sprawling, self-contained resort offers a five-story hotel and a host of delightful villas.

There are several restaurants and bars on site, as well as three swimming pools, a beach, and the Royal St. Kitts Golf Club, which sits just alongside the resort.

🏠 Frigate Bay Rd, St. Kitts ⓦ marriott.com

The Hermitage Plantation Inn

Located on a hillside, this tranquil plantation inn is set in a manor house that dates back to 1670. The gingerbread-style cottages in the garden feature four-poster beds, antique decor, and hammock-strewn terraces.

🏠 Hermitage Rd, Nevis ⓦ hermitagenevis.com

Golden Rock Inn

Cozy cottages combine with 19th-century buildings at this small, friendly hotel – all set within lush tropical gardens. Those looking for a romantic getaway should opt for the two-story Sugar Mill suite. The facilities here are excellent, and include an open-air restaurant and spring-fed swimming pool.

🏠 Gingerland, Nevis ⓦ goldenrocknevis.com

Southeastern Peninsula

🏠 St. Kitts ⓣ

While the north of St. Kitts is characterized by Kittitian villages dotting the flanks of rainforested mountains, the lower-lying hills of the southern part of the island are drier and much less populated. The area is worth visiting because the island's prettiest beaches are located here, along with some excellent beach bars. Unlike the more developed Frigate Bay (p291) to the north, the Southeastern Peninsula is only now being built up. The road along the peninsula leads up and out of Frigate Bay from where it descends into Friar's Bay. The beach at South Friar's Bay is probably the best strip of sand on the island, with beach bars that ply their laid-back trade to day-travelers. The road climbs and falls, sashaying over the hills until it reaches the southern tip of the island. En route, visitors are likely to spot green vervet monkeys. East of Great Salt Pond, on the Atlantic Coast, is the quiet Sand Bank Bay.

On the southern coast, there are several beaches with lovely views across the 2-mile (3-km) The Narrows to Nevis. The liveliest are Turtle Beach, which tends to get a bit crowded due to cruise ship passengers, and Cockleshell Beach. Both have restaurants and bars, and offer stunning views of Nevis. Offshore farther south, the tiny Booby Island has spectacular marine life and is a popular spot for snorkeling and diving.

7

Charlestown

🏠 N coast of Nevis 🚌🚐🚗
ℹ️ Nevis Tourism Authority, Main St; 869 469 7550

Charlestown is a classic, pretty West Indian waterfront town, set on the protected Caribbean

The quaint stone facade and interiors (inset) of the Museum of Nevis History in Charlestown ↓

coast of Nevis. As the small capital of a quiet island, it is never too busy and is a lovely place to spend an hour wandering around.

The ferry port, located at the southern end of the esplanade, is a good place to start any exploration of the network of streets, lined with attractive 18th- and 19th-century stone and wooden buildings, many of which have been restored. These traditional houses are embellished with fret-cut woodwork called "gingerbread trim," and most have massive foundations and walls with a rubble-filled interior space. Also common, the "skirt and blouse" design consists of a stone first story and a light, wooden second story enabling the buildings to withstand high winds and

earthquakes. One such construction is the old Cotton Ginnery, which now houses local craft vendors. The Charlestown Market has local fruit and vegetables on sale in stalls under a pitched tin roof.

The heart of the town, Main Street, has banks, businesses, and the tiny Nevis Sports Museum, with exhibits on Nevisian cricketers and other athletes. Heading south, Main Street cuts diagonally inland, creating two "squares" that are actually triangular; Memorial Square features a small war monument and a clock tower dedicated to soldiers who died in World War I and II, while D.R. Walwyn Plaza is the focal point for the island's buses.

To the north is a pretty stone building called Alexander Hamilton House. Alexander Hamilton, father of the United States' Constitution, and portrayed on the U.S.$10 bill and in the hit musical *Hamilton*, was born here in 1757. The house is home to the Nevis Assembly, the five-member Nevisian Parliament that sits just four or five times a year, and the **Museum of Nevis History**. The museum has displays of Nevis through the ages, with artifacts including Arawak pottery and colonial porcelain. North of here, the

road out of town leads to the serene palm-fringed Pinney's Beach.

On the southern outskirts of town is the Bath Hotel, one of the glories of the island in the late 1700s and one of the first hotels in the Caribbean. Many European visitors came here to treat ailments using the volcanic hot springs nearby. Close by is the **Horatio Nelson Museum**. Dedicated to the British admiral (see box), it has an excellent series of displays, with maps and models of 18th-century ships, and the largest collection of Nelson memorabilia in the world, including portraits.

Museum of Nevis History
⊗🕑 🅰 Alexander Hamilton House 🕘 9am–4pm Mon–Fri, 9am–noon Sat 🆆 nevisheritage.org

Horatio Nelson Museum
⊗🕑 🅰 Belle Vue 📞 869 469 0408 🕘 9am–4pm Mon–Fri, 9am–noon Sat

> **Charlestown is a classic, pretty West Indian waterfront town, set on the protected Caribbean coast of Nevis.**

EAT

El Fredo's
A family-run cafe offering local dishes and fresh juices, such as sorrel and soursop.

 Bay Rd, Basseterre
☎ 869 466 8871
🕐 11am-4pm Tue-Sat

$ $ $

Serendipity Restaurant & Lounge Bar
Enjoy grilled steaks, seafood, and luscious desserts on the terrace overlooking the harbor

 3 Wigley Av, Fortsland
🕐 Sun 🆆 serendipity stkitts.net

$ $ $

Bananas Bistro Restaurant
Tucked away in lush gardens, this eatery offers alfresco dining and good-quality rums.

 International Uppr Hamilton Estates 🕐 Sun
🆆 bananasnevis.com

$ $ $

8
Oualie Beach

📍 4 miles (6 km) N of Charlestown

Oualie was the original name for Nevis. Pronounced as "oo-wah-lee," meaning "beautiful waters," it referred to the freshwater springs on Nevis. Oualie Beach is a lively spot, with pale yellow sands backed by palms and with a great view of St. Kitts across The Narrows. Oualie Bay, formerly known as Mosquito Bay, is well protected, so swimming and other watersports are good here. There is a watersports and mountain biking shop, and a scuba diving outfit. Scuba Safaris Ltd offers diving and snorkeling lessons for both novice and experienced divers. Children aged 8 and over are accommodated for, and those who want to join the scuba safari but stay aboard the boat, affectionately named "bubble watchers," are also welcome.

The bay has a small dock, where visitors from St. Kitts can be dropped

← The charming stone Fig Tree Church, where Horatio Nelson was married

off by water taxis. The Oualie Beach Resort is located on this beach as well, and is run by a family that has been on the island for nearly 350 years. The Annual Nevis Sport Fishing Tournament takes place each year on Oualie Beach, with participants traveling from all over the Caribbean to take part.

Toward the north, the road swings around Nevis Peak before reaching Nisbet Beach. Facing the Atlantic, Nisbet is a pretty beach dotted with coconut trees strung with hammocks, making it a pleasant place at which to relax.

9
Fig Tree Church

📍 2 miles (3 km) E of Charlestown, Nevis

The round-island road that climbs inland from the town of Charlestown passes Fig Tree Church, where Horatio Nelson and Fanny Nisbet were married in 1787 (p289). The original church was built in the 1680s, but the current building actually dates from 1838. It is a stone structure with a bell tower and a red tin roof. Inside, it is possible to see a copy of the marriage certificate that the Nelsons signed at their marriage. Their wedding celebration took place at Montpelier Plantation, where it is commemorated on a plaque on the gates.

10
Botanical Garden of Nevis

📍 3 miles (5 km) SE of Charlestown, Nevis
🕐 9am-4pm Mon-Sat, 10:30am-3pm Sun 🕐 Pub hols 🆆 botanical gardennevis.com

The vast Botanical Garden of Nevis display plants from across the tropical world. They are laid out in several

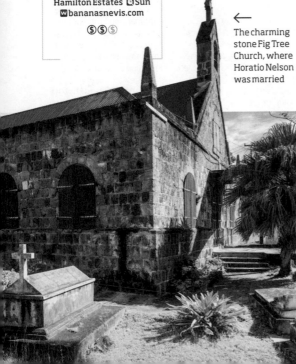

→

Interior structural details and the shaded porch *(inset)* at Montepelier Plantation Inn in Nevis

areas covering a range of environments, including the Tropical Vine Garden, the Orchid Terrace, the Rose Garden, and a Rainforest Conservatory. The conservatory has re-created Mayan temple ruins and a few waterfalls. Other delights include fruit trees and several flowering shrubs and trees. A cafe and a gift shop are set in an attractive Creole building.

Frigate Bay

📍 3 miles (5 km) S of Basseterre, St. Kitts 🚌🚕
🌐 stkittstourism.kn

Frigate Bay is the heartland of tourism in St. Kitts and it has a very different atmosphere from the rural north of the island. From the top of the surrounding hills, there is a panoramic view of the bay itself, and the low-lying sliver of land between the Atlantic Ocean and Caribbean Sea.

On the Atlantic side is Frigate Bay North, where the sandy beach is lined with condominiums and large resort hotels offering an array of entertainment and activities. This is the location of the St. Kitts Marriott Resort *(p288)* with its casino and several restaurants and bars. Just

inland lie the fairways and bunkers of the Royal St. Kitts Golf Course. The course reaches right to the coast, and the onshore ocean winds can have a considerable effect on play.

On the Caribbean side, Frigate Bay South, known as "The Strip," has calmer seas, but a livelier atmosphere. A string of beach bars and watersports operators stand shoulder to shoulder here, giving the beach a party-like, easy-going vibe. It is especially lively at sundown on Thursday and Friday evenings, when there is a bonfire and live music at some of the bars, and on weekends, when the locals descend upon the beach.

Did You Know?

The strait separating St. Kitts and Nevis is known as "The Narrows." A swimming event is held here every year.

🅓

Nevis Plantation Inns

Nevis has some of the loveliest plantation inns in the Caribbean. While they are excellent places to stay, it is also possible to just visit for lunch, afternoon tea, or dinner to get a sense of a long-bygone era.

Dating from the late 1600s, the main house at the Hermitage Plantation Inn *(p288)* is one of the finest wooden buildings in the Caribbean. It has attractive "gingerbread" woodwork, shingle walls, and a red tin roof. Montpelier Plantation Inn was restored in the 1960s and is well worth a stop for a leisurely meal. Other plantation inns include the Golden Rock, above the Atlantic Coast, which has a spectacular view over the coastline, or the inn at Nisbet Plantation, which is the only plantation inn with the advantage of being on the beach. It offers magnificent views from its great house through tall and slender palms to the sea.

PRACTICAL
INFORMATION

Here you will find all the essential advice and information you will need before and during your stay in St. Kitts and Nevis.

CURRENCY
Eastern Caribbean dollar (EC$)

TIME ZONE
Atlantic Standard Time, 4 hours behind GMT and an hour ahead of EST. The islands do not observe daylight savings

LANGUAGE
English

ELECTRICITY SUPPLY
There is a mix of three square-pin sockets in UK style and two-pin sockets in US style

EMERGENCY NUMBERS

POLICE/ AMBULANCE	FIRE SERVICE
911	**333**

TAP WATER
Water purity can be unreliable so, to be safe, drink bottled water

When To Go

The best time to go to St. Kitts and Nevis is between mid-December and mid-April, when the weather is cooler, although this is also the most expensive time to visit. It is humid during August and September.

Getting There

St. Kitts has direct flights from the US on American Airlines, Delta, and Condor Airlines. From the UK, British Airways offers a weekly flight with a stopover in Antigua. LIAT services St. Kitts via Antigua as well. Another hub is St. Martin/Sint Maarten, which is served by Winair. Getting to Nevis is not as easy. Traveling via St. Kitts is one alternative, from where it is possible to cross via ferry from Basseterre to Charlestown or to take a flight (although these are not frequent). If arrival is too late in the day, a water taxi can make the crossing. From within the Caribbean, there are daily flights from San Juan on Puerto Rico with American Airlines. From Antigua there is a hopper service that is scheduled to meet the North American and European flights that land in the mid to late afternoon.

Personal Security

St. Kitts and particularly Nevis are safe islands. There are few problems with personal security (virtually none in Nevis) and theft is very rare, though it is advisable not to leave valuables visible in a car or unattended on the beach.

Health

The main hospitals are Joseph N. France General Hospital in Basseterre and Alexandra Hospital in Charlestown. Vaccinations are necessary if you are coming from a yellow-fever-infected area.

Passports and Visas

All visitors to St. Kitts and Nevis should travel on a valid passport with a valid onward ticket.

Citizens of most European countries and the US do not need a visa. All visitors have to pay a departure tax when leaving the island.

LGBT+ Safety

Same-sex relationships between men are outlawed by "unnatural offenses" laws and are punishable by up to ten years in prison. By contrast no laws exist against relationships between women. However, despite the existence of laws on the books, the government claims there has been no known prosecution of same-sex sexual activity. Nonetheless discretion is advised and there have been incidents against tourists in the past including a gay cruise ship being barred from docking back in 2005.

Money

The currency of St. Kitts and Nevis is the Eastern Caribbean dollar (EC$). On both islands credit cards are accepted in almost all establishments. There are ATMs in Basseterre and Charlestown. Banks follow regular business hours: 8am–2pm Monday to Thursday, 8am–4pm Friday.

Cell Phones and Wi-Fi

Handsets and SIM cards with local numbers for rental are available through Cable and Wireless and Digicel. When phoning out of the islands, dial 011 and the international code. Visitors bringing cell phones should check with their service providers to determine if they will work in St. Kitts and Nevis and if they will be subject to roaming charges. Most of the hotels and some villas have wireless Internet available. There are cafes with internet connection as well.

Getting Around

Car rental companies will deliver to the airport, ferry terminals, hotels, and villas. They will also issue the obligatory local driving license. Car rental companies include TDC Thrifty (both islands), AVIS, and IAS Auto Rentals (St. Kitts) and Nevis Car Rental at the airport in Nevis. Taxis are available at all hotels and at the airport and ferry terminals. Taxi stands include Circus Taxi Stand in Basseterre and Charlestown Taxi Stand in Nevis. Bus services are good on both islands, but, as they are designed for local people, no buses run to Frigate Bay or the Southeastern Peninsula on St. Kitts. They emanate from the main towns, on the waterfront in Basseterre and the two squares in Charlestown. There is no schedule; instead, buses leave when they are full or on the decision of the driver.

The ferry is the most commonly used transportation between the islands. There are car ferries between Major's Bay in the south of St. Kitts and Cades Bay in Nevis. The trip between Basseterre and Charlestown takes 45 minutes and there are about eight or ten crossings each day. For day visits, the car rental agency may allow (with advanced warning) visitors to drop the rented car at the ferry terminal and then pick up another car on arrival in the other island.

Visitor Information

The **St. Kitts Tourism Authority** has offices in the US, Canada, and the UK. On the island, its main office is in Basseterre. The **Nevis Tourism Authority** has its head office and information office in Charlestown.
Nevis Tourism Authority
w nevisisland.com
St. Kitts Tourism Authority
w stkittstourism.kn

English Harbour in Antigua, viewed from Shirley Heights

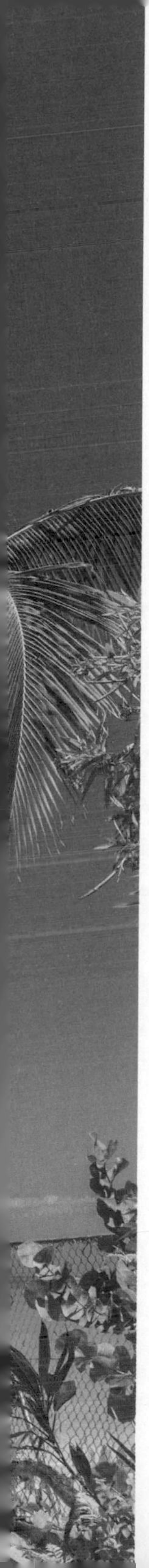

ANTIGUA AND BARBUDA

Antigua's main attraction today is its many fabulous beaches, but in the past it was the fertility of its land, which was ideal for growing sugar cane. The French, Dutch, and English fought over the Island through the 1600s, with the English prevailing, and the island remained in British hands throughout the colonial period. Nelson's Dockyard – so named because the young Horatio Nelson served there – was constructed in the 1700s in English Harbour on Antigua's south coast so Britain could maintain its Royal Navy warships to protect its valuable sugar-producing Caribbean islands.

Fast forward to 1981, and Antigua became an independent nation with smaller and far less populated Barbuda to the north. Barbuda lay directly in the path of category 5 Hurricane Irma in September 2017, and most of its homes were destroyed or severely damaged. The island is welcoming back visitors, but recovery and reconstruction will take time. Southwest of Antigua lies Montserrat, a British overseas territory which, thanks to its Irish heritage, calls itself the Caribbean's Emerald Isle. Here, nature's force – the eruption of Soufrière Hills Volcano in the 1990s, which blanketed the town of Plymouth in ash – has become a major tourist attraction.

ANTIGUA AND BARBUDA

Experience

Barbuda ↑

Antigua

Soldiers Bay

Crosbies

DICKENSON BAY 4

Runaway Bay

McKinnon's Salt Pond

Fort James Bay Fort James

Shipstern Point

←
Montserrat

Deep Bay

Guard Point

Hawksbill Bay

Five Islands Village

ST. JOHN'S

3

Hansons Bay

Golden Grove

Maiden Island

Creekside

Ebenezer

Jennings

Emanuel

JOLLY HARBOUR 9

Bolans

Lignum Vitae Bay

Bendals

MOUNT OBAMA

13

DARKWOOD BEACH 11

FIG TREE DRIVE 12

TURNER'S BEACH 11

Urlings

Johnson's Point

Old Road

Cades Bay

Carlisle Bay

Old Red Bluff

ANTIGUA AND BARBUDA

Barbuda

Antigua

Montserrat

Montserrat

Antigua ↑

Silver Hill
△ 1,173 ft (403 m)

Sweeney's

✈ John A. Osborne Airport

Brades

St. John's

St. Peter's

Woodlands

Old Towne

Salem

20

MONTSERRAT

Iles Bay

Exclusion Zone

Plymouth

Soufrière Hill
3,180 ft (969 m)

0 kilometers   5

0 miles   5

N ↑

Barbuda

Goat Island

Kid Island

Antigua ↖

TWO FOOT BAY AND INDIAN CAVES

18

CODRINGTON LAGOON **17**

11-MILE BEACH **15**

Barbuda Codrington Airport ✈ **16** CODRINGTON

19 MARTELLO TOWER

Palmetto Point

Pink Sand Beach

Cocu Point

Spanish Point

0 kilometers   5

0 miles   5

N ↑

odges Bay

Dutchman's Bay

Cedar Grove

High Point

Long Island

Coolidge

Barnes Hill

V. C. Bird International Airport

5 GILLY GOBINET ART

Crabs Peninsula

Great Bird Island

t. Johnston illage

Piggotts

Guiana Island

Potters Village

Parham

Guiana Bay

Crump Island

Pelican Island

Herberts

Sir Viv Richards Stadium

Seatons

Mercer's Creek Bay

Indian Town Point

7 **8** DEVIL'S BRIDGE

Freemans

Pares

BETTY'S HOPE **10**

Glanvilles

Willikies

LONG BAY

Flat Point

Nonsuch Bay

Green Island

All Saints

Potworks Dam Reservoir

Hughes Point

10 HARMONY HALL

Buckleys

Swetes

ANTIGUA DONKEY SANCTUARY **2**

Newfield

Great Deep Bay

York Island

Liberta

Bethesda

Christian Point

Freetown

St. Philips

Friars Head

n ghes

Christian Hill

Willoughby Bay

6 HALF MOON BAY

Falmouth

Isaac Point

Hudson Point

ENGLISH HARBOUR **1**

Rendezvous Bay

1

Mamora Bay

NELSON'S DOCKYARD

14 SHIRLEY HEIGHTS

0 kilometers   3

0 miles   3

N ↑

EXPERIENCE

English Harbour and Nelson's Dockyard

Dockyard Dr 268 481 5021 8am-6pm daily

On the southern coast of Antigua sits its historic gem: the 15-sq-mile (38-sq-km) Nelson's Dockyard National Park and English Harbour, which is considered the only existing Georgian naval dockyard in the world, and has been a UNESCO World Heritage Site since 2016. Most of the surviving colonial buildings here can be traced to the 18th century, when the dockyard's function was to protect Britain's valuable sugar-producing islands. Additionally, Britain had to keep her ships safe from hurricanes or French naval activity in the Caribbean, in a place where they could be properly serviced and cleaned – and the sheltered, deep-water English Harbour was perfectly positioned.

Admiral Horatio Nelson (*p289*) was stationed at the dockyard from 1784 to 1787, although he did not appear to care for the place, referring to it in letters as "a vile spot" where he was "most woefully pinched" by mosquitoes. After the sugar industry waned in the mid-19th century, Britain turned its attention elsewhere, and the dockyard in its original capacity was closed in 1889.

Now fully restored and quite charming, the buildings – from former pitch, lead, copper, and lumber stores, to officers' quarters and the Admiral's House – function these days as museums, restaurants, cafes, shops, and hotels, and it is easy to spend the best part of a day exploring them.

Also within the boundaries of the site's national park is Galleon Beach. This former burial site for British sailors who fell victim to 18th-century yellow fever outbreaks is now a lovely strand, reached via a short water taxi ride. The ruins of Fort Berkeley, sited at the harbor mouth along a 10-15 minute walking trail, also fall within the park. English Harbour, along with the adjacent Falmouth Harbour, is also known as an international yachting center with many moorings for visiting boats, and it hosts several prestigious regattas and races every year.

Antigua Donkey Sanctuary

Bethesda Village, St. Paul 10am-4pm Mon-Sat antiguaanimals.com

Just a 20-minute drive north of the English and Falmouth Harbours, the Antigua & Barbuda Humane Society (A.B.H.S) runs Antigua's Donkey Sanctuary which currently shelters more than 150 previously abandoned or stray donkeys. Visitors are shown around the site by dedicated staff and introduced to the individual animals. Children will particularly love being able to groom the donkeys, who really enjoy the attention and start to doze off as their coats are brushed.

↑ A neat line of boats in the turquoise water of English Harbour

The rescue center also has numerous cats and dogs waiting to go to new homes; visitors are allowed to take the dogs for walks and play with kittens, soif visitors prefer domestic animals, there is still plenty to enjoy. The site does not charge an entry fee, but visitors are encouraged to donate and "adopt a donkey" in order to help pay for this worthwhile cause.

St. John's

⌂ W coast, Antigua ✈🚌🚐
🛈 Government Complex,
Queen Elizabeth Highway;
268 462 0480

This bustling, historic port city is the governmental and commercial hub of Antigua. At the center is the cruise ship dock at Heritage Quay, lined with upscale duty-free shops and restaurants. Next to this area is the Vendors Mart where visitors can purchase local souvenirs, and Redcliffe Quay, a more quaint shopping and dining area. Other points of interest include the twin-steepled **St. John's Anglican Cathedral**. A wooden church was first built here in 1681 but after a series of earthquakes, the present cathedral was built in 1847. Intended to withstand earthquakes similar to those that destroyed its predecessors, the current building consists of an external stone structure that houses a wooden construction within. Restoration of the church is ongoing, but services are held on Sunday mornings and evenings.

Also worth seeing is the **Museum of Antigua and Barbuda**, which is devoted to the local history of the region, and the Public Market Complex on Market Street, where local farmers sell their produce. Parking is difficult to find, so it is recommended that visitors use taxis or buses to come in for a day of shopping or touring.

On the eastern outskirts of St. John's is the legendary Antigua Recreation Ground, which has seen many cricket matches and records since it opened in 1978. A new stadium was built farther east for the 2007 World Cup, and named after local hero Sir Vivian Richards, a former West Indies cricket team captain.

At the far end of Fort Bay is Fort James, built in the early 1700s. It was the primary fortification to protect the harbor of St. John's. Among the artillery were ten cannons that formed part of the ramparts. When most of the other forts on the island were disassembled, these cannons were left intact. Adjacent to the fort is Russell's, a full-service restaurant installed in a historic building. Pleasant Fort James Beach, which is popular with visitors and locals alike, is also nearby.

St. John's
Anglican Cathedral
⌂ Newgate St 📞 268 462 0820 🕒 daily

Museum of Antigua and Barbuda
💲 🏛 ⌂ Long St 🕒 8:30am–4:30pm Mon–Fri, 10am–2pm Sat 🌐 antiguamuseums.net

↑ St. John's, with the twin steeples of the city's cathedral rising in the distance

Dickenson Bay

⌂ 2 miles (4 km) N of St. John's, Antigua

Located on the northwestern coast of Antigua, and lined with resorts that include the 373-room Sandals Grande Antigua Resort & Spa, Dickenson Bay is by no means the most secluded of the island's 365 beaches – but it is the most popular and appealing, thanks to its soft white sand and calm, clear water. Gently-shelving areas are roped off from watercraft to allow safe swimming for children. The beach faces west, providing the perfect vantage point from which to watch a dramatic sunset (perhaps with a cocktail from one of the several upscale beach bars and restaurants).

Sun loungers and umbrellas can be rented and watersports such as jet- or water-skiing, wakeboarding, parasailing, and banana boating can be arranged at Tony's Watersports Beach Bar and Grill (tonys watersports.com). Snorkeling trips to the coral Paradise Reef off the tiny, uninhabited islands opposite Dickenson Bay can also be arranged.

Just to the south, the beach at adjacent Runaway Bay is quieter, but has few facilities other than a couple of basic bars and trees for shade. A stroll along the powdery sand, however, is always enjoyable.

Gilly Gobinet Art

⌂ Casa Alegre, St. Georges
⌚ Nov-Jun: 9am-1pm Mon-Fri; Jul-Oct: by appt
🌐 gillygobinet.com

Just south of the airport, this lovely gallery showcases one of Antigua's most esteemed and influential artists, Gilly Gobinet. Originally from England, Gobinet lived in France before settling in Antigua in 1984 to become an artist, and now her brightly colored paintings in various sizes and subjects can be viewed at her delightful seafront residence.

Gobinet mainly works in acrylic; pen and ink; oils; and watercolors, and both her figurative and abstract art are inspired by Antigua and other Caribbean islands. Her subjects include birds; trees; flowers, such as hibiscus and bougainvillea; seascapes and marine animals; village scenes that highlight traditional gingerbread houses; and even yachts, as Gobinet is a keen sailor. Artwork is available to be purchased, and Gobinet has taken great care to ensure that it's easily transportable. While perusing, visitors can enjoy a refreshing drink on the verandah and take in the stunning sea views over Fitches Creek Bay.

Half Moon Bay

⌂ 14 miles (22 km) SE of St. John's, Antigua

One of the most beautiful beaches on Antigua, Half Moon Bay's crescent-shaped strand offers two completely different beach experiences: rough surf on the Atlantic side and calm, clear waters at the far eastern end.

Snorkeling is a favorite activity along the reef that forms the bay's breakwater, but there are no watersports operators, so visitors need to bring their own equipment. There is a small bar at the entrance with limited food service, so bringing a picnic basket and cooler is advisable.

← The pristine white curve of Half Moon Bay, a popular Antiguan beach

↑ A large crewed yacht at Antigua's Classic Yacht Regatta

SAILING IN ANTIGUA

An almost circular island with a ragged coastline of deep bays and harbors sitting between the Atlantic Ocean and the Caribbean Sea, Antigua is a yachter's paradise. Among its many offerings are international yachting events, bareboat or crewed charters, and learn-to-sail schools. Marinas equipped to service everything from small monohulls and catamarans to superyachts are located at English Harbour, Falmouth Harbour, and Jolly Harbour. Services at these locations include marine engineering, electronics, and rigging.

REGATTAS AND RACES

For yacht-enthusiasts around the world, Antigua is the place to be in the spring. Among the international yacht racing events held here are the Classic Yacht Regatta in early April, and Antigua Sailing Week in late April. The latter includes classes ranging from large yachts and monohulls to gunboats. The week is filled with beach parties where locals join in the fun.

Ondeck Ocean Racing offers a chance for individuals to become a member of the crew for a day racing on a Beneteau 40.7 or a Farr 40 or 60 yacht.

↑ Yachts taking part in a race during Antigua Sailing Week

OTHER EVENTS AND ACTIVITIES

Antigua has four yacht clubs and hosts an annual inter-club race in January. English Harbour and Jolly Harbour, with their lively clubs, restaurants, and shops, serve as yachting centers. Learn-to-sail programs are offered at many resorts and sailing clubs. Private tuition as well as dinghy sailing classes are available for beginners at Nonsuch Bay (see p326).

Charters are available all around Antigua. Several companies offer crewed or bareboat charters on yachts and will set the itinerary according to preference.

↑ Boats ready for learn-to-sail classes at one of Antigua's resorts

→

A hiker looking down at the crashing waves beneath Devil's Bridge

7
Long Bay

 10 miles (16 km) E of St. John's, Antigua 🚌

The highlights of Long Bay, on the northeast coast (Atlantic side), are the 1,600-ft (488-m) crescent of white sand and the good snorkeling sites on the barrier reef close to shore. The bay accommodates guests from adults-only **Pineapple Beach Club Antigua**, as well as local families with children.

The luxurious Pineapple Beach Club has pools, restaurants, tennis courts, spa, and watersports. Rooms are brightly dressed in white wicker and floral textiles, and most offer gorgeous ocean views out to the Atlantic. Those that are high up on the hill, and the ones down on the beach, offer the most spectacular vistas. Visitors on the Long Bay Beach can get lunch from the Beach House restaurant, which also serves dinner and puts on regular evening barbeques. A range of souvenirs can be purchased from the beach vendors.

Pineapple Beach Club Antigua
📍 🏠 Long Bay 🌐 pineapple beachclub.com

8
Devil's Bridge

🏠 11 miles (17 km) E of St. John's, Antigua 🚌

This natural formation on the Atlantic Coast draws visitors who want to see the dramatic coastline. Devil's Bridge itself is a stone arch over the sea; during high tide the area below becomes a pool with the waves cresting over the top of the bridge. It is said that anyone falling from the bridge is bound to drown, and legend has it that many slaves chose this fate by throwing themselves off the bridge into the sea.

> **Devil's Bridge itself is a stone arch over the sea; during high tide the area below becomes a pool with the waves cresting over the top of the bridge.**

The area, designated a national park, is also the site of the annual Kite Festival, because the very strong winds off the ocean are perfect for aerial kite maneuvers.

Adjacent to Devil's Bridge National Park and sprawling over 1,306,800 sq ft (121,400 sq m) is the eco-friendly **Verandah Resort & Spa**. This pretty hotel features two spectacular protected beaches, a spa and fitness center, children's center, tennis court, and three restaurants. The rooms are spacious and easily accommodate small families, while some can be interconnected for larger families. All rooms have air-conditioning, flat-screen TVs, and small kitchens.

Verandah Resort & Spa
📍 🏠 Long Bay 🌐 verandah resortandspa.com

9
Jolly Harbour

🏠 2 miles (3 km) SW of St. John's, Antigua 🚌 ⛴
🌐 jolly-harbour-marina.com

North of Darkwood Beach (p304), this marina complex has a little of everything: a

great beach, shopping center, tennis courts, and a golf course, as well as a number of restaurants and bars. It also offers a world-class marina for visiting yachts, and is one of the harbors for the annual Sailing Week. Alongside the beautiful beach is Jolly Beach Resort, one of the largest all-inclusives on the island.

Betty's Hope

🏠 5 miles (8 km) SE of St. John's, Antigua 🚌
🕙 10am–4pm Tue–Sat
ℹ Betty's Hope Visitors' Center; www.antigua museums.net

Remains of 17th- and 18th-century sugar plantations are everywhere throughout the Caribbean, but it is unusual to find an actual working windmill of the type used to grind sugarcane on those plantations. Betty's Hope offers that rare find, in one working and one non-working mill surrounded by ruins of a plantation that was a major agricultural contributor to the economy of the island from about 1650 to the 1920s. It was one of Antigua's earliest plantations, and was owned and run by the Codrington family (p307). Exhibits that provide an overview of the island's plantation era are displayed in the visitors' center. An eco-tourism enhancement project aims to continue the conservation of the site.

(p307)

STAY

Nonsuch Bay Resort
Charming cottages and villas are dotted around the bay here, where the steady breezes provide ideal conditions for sailing, windsurfing, and kitesurfing in the azure waters. It's an excellent option for families, as there's also a strong kids' program at the site.

🏠 Hughes Point, St. Philips 🌐 nonsuch bayresort.com

$$$

Sandals Grande Antigua
Regularly voted the "world's most romantic resort," this all-inclusive spot is located on the spectacular beach at Dickenson Bay. There's a wide range of accommodations on offer; choose from elegant butler suites in the high-rise to rondavels with private plunge pools.

🏠 Dickenson Bay, St. John's 🌐 sandals.com

$$$

Jumby Bay Island
This elegant, all-inclusive gem is located on its own secluded island off the north coast of Antigua, reachable only by boat and criss-crossed with winding bicycle paths. The resort features suites and villas dotted along three stunning white-sand beaches.

🏠 Long Island 🌐 oetkercollection.com

$$$

↑ One of the windmills found on the land of an old plantation at Betty's Hope

11

Turner's and Darkwood Beaches

 8 miles (13 km) SW of St. John's, Antigua

Along Antigua's southwestern coast lie these two golden-sand beaches. Both offer good restaurants and beach bars with lounge chair rentals, and are perfect for those not staying at the beach resorts. The snorkeling off Turner's Beach is good, but visitors need to bring their own gear. Cruising yachts often anchor offshore so passengers can enjoy the beach. Darkwood Beach has a lovely stretch of sand and is a great spot for swimmers.

12

Fig Tree Drive

 8 miles (13 km) S of St. John's, Antigua

Heading south from the village of Swetes, the winding road passes through the most thickly forested area on the island – Fig Tree Hill. Ironically there are no fig trees here, but banana and mango trees line the road. A lovely stop on the way is the Fig Tree Culture Shop, where visitors can buy fresh fruits and local food products. A favorite stopover is Wallings Dam, a historic park with a picnic area, hiking trails, and canopy tours. Also in the heart of the rainforest is the Fig Tree Studio Art Gallery, which features the work of local artist Sallie Harker, as well as crafts from the island's artisans. Most local taxi drivers offer tours of the area.

Located along Fig Tree Drive at Old Road Village, **Curtain Bluff Resort** is an elegant, all-inclusive retreat, which features a pool, spa, two beaches, two restaurants, and a beautiful garden setting.

Curtain Bluff Resort
 Morris Bay
w curtainbluff.com

13

Mount Obama

14 miles (22 km) S of St. John's, Antigua

Known as Boggy Peak until August 4, 2009, 1319-ft-

Did You Know?

The "pink sand" beaches in this region take their color from crushed coral.

EAT

Cloggy's Café
A popular spot serving tasty comfort food and specialty cocktails, with excellent views over Falmouth Harbour.

Antigua Yacht Club Marina, Falmouth Harbour, Antigua
268 460 6910
Mon & Sun eve

$$$

Cecilia's High Point Café
This laidback joint offers lovely views of Dutchman's Bay and sun loungers on the beach.

Texaco Dock Rd, St. George, Antigua
Fri-Mon w highpointantigua.com

$$$

The Bay @ Nonsuch
In an open-air setting overlooking the water, the menu here is strong on seafood, with delicacies such as soft-shelled crab, conch, and lobster.

Hughes Point, St. Philips, Antigua w nonsuchbayresort.com

$$$

(402-m-) high Mount Obama is the highest point on Antigua, and is located in the Shekerley Mountains in the southwest of the island. The Antiguan government renamed it after Barack Obama, the 44th President of the United States, on his 48th birthday, in order to salute him as a symbol of black achievement.

The mount has other historical importance too; during the 17th and 18th centuries it served as a refuge for escaped African slaves, also known as "maroons," who often fled from plantations to remote mountainous areas.

The peak can be climbed from its southern or northern side, with the easiest option being from Old Road near Urlings in the south. Here, the Mount Obama Road begins as a dirt track and continues for about a mile before it starts to climb up the hill as a very steep and narrow concrete road, which it is not advisable to drive. Instead, park and hike up, which takes less than an hour and is not overly strenuous. At the summit is a handful of telecommunications

Guests enjoying themselves at one of the renowned BBQ parties at Shirley Heights

towers; unfortunately the gate to this compound is usually locked and unmanned, so you cannot technically stand on the very top of the mountain. Follow the trail around the fence, however, and on a clear day there are wonderful views across to Guadeloupe, St. Kitts, Nevis, and Montserrat.

Shirley Heights

🏠 12 miles (19 km)
S of St. John's, Antigua
🕐 🌐 shirleyheights
lookout.com

High on the hill above English Harbour (p298) sits this renovated historical site, overlooking the sea. It is famous for its panoramic views, and on clear days visitors can see as far as Guadeloupe and the volcanic island of Montserrat. Shirley Heights is especially popular on Sunday evenings, when the place hosts the biggest party on the island for locals and visitors alike. There's a bar at the site, and live music, including steel band and soca band entertainment, plays as the sun sinks below the horizon. The complex also has a restaurant and a band that plays on Thursday evenings.

15

11-Mile Beach

🏠 Barbuda

Making up the southern portion of Barbuda's western coast, 11-Mile Beach, also known as Low Bay Beach, is a dazzling curve of soft pink sand on a flat, narrow spit between the calming waters of the Caribbean and the green-blue Codrington Lagoon.

It is often considered one of the most beautiful beaches in the Caribbean, yet it is isolated and largely empty of people. Most of the strand is accessible only by boat; it's easy for yachts to moor offshore, and catamaran day-trips are available from Antigua, while water taxis can be organized at the jetty in Codrington. Ask the captain to drop you off at a clump of casuarina trees for shade and agree on a time to be picked up again later in the day.

In keeping with the beach's remote location, facilities here are basically non-existent, so visitors should be sure to take plenty of food and drink. For those keen to stay in the area, there is one resort – Barbuda Bay Luxury Beach Hotel – located to the north of 11-Mile. It's a boutique, family-run spot with plush private bungalows.

The picturesque Curtain Bluff Resort located along Fig Tree Drive

16

Codrington

 Eastern edge of the Lagoon, Barbuda

The small town of Codrington is Barbuda's capital and the commercial and government center. Many of the original buildings from the 19th century still exist, and have been enlisted for other uses: the former Ginnery now houses offices, and the stables of the Government House have been converted into a school. The town also has several supermarkets, grocery stores, bars, bakeries, and restaurants; lobster lunches featuring the spiny lobster caught off Barbuda's shores, are a favorite with visitors. On the outskirts of Codrington is a pharmacy, an ice-cream parlor, a souvenir shop, and the Art Café, home of local artist Claire Frank. Here, visitors can browse through her collection of delicate, hand-painted silks.

The town has many small guesthouses, which provide economical overnight lodging.

17

Codrington Lagoon

 4 miles (6 km) W of Codrington, Barbuda

A sheltered waterway separated from the ocean by a narrow spit of land, Codrington Lagoon is home to 170 species of birds, including brown pelicans, herons, and boobies. It is best known, however, as a major habitat for frigate birds, of which roughly 5,000 make their home here in the mangroves. These magnificent birds are famed for their colossal 7-ft (2-m) wingspan and for the males' spectacular show of flirting by puffing out their throats into a bright red balloon during mating season. Many of the birds live all year round in Barbuda, while others travel to and from the

 INSIDER TIP
Speedy Boat

Antigua and Barbuda are connected by the Barbuda Express, a high-speed catamaran that runs six days a week and takes 90 minutes (barbudaexpress.com). The firm also arranges day tours of Barbuda.

Galapagos Islands. Water taxis with knowledgable guides can be arranged at the jetty in Codrington, and it takes about 15 minutes to get to the nesting site on "Man of War Island" – a nickname for the frigates, who have a tendency to harass other water birds fairly violently in order to steal their fish. Mornings are best for bird activity, and from the boat visitors are likely to glimpse the females guarding their young, whose white-tufted heads poke up from the nests.

18

Two Foot Bay and the Indian Caves

 4 miles (6 km) NE of Codrington, Barbuda

As an island composed of limestone, Barbuda has a

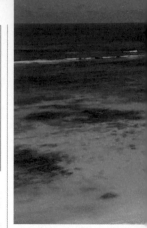

→
The bright waters and golden curve of Two Foot Bay beach in Barbuda

large range of caves to explore. Many are carved into the cliffs on the sea bluffs at Two Foot Bay on Barbuda's northeastern Atlantic coast. These are rich in history from the days when the Arawak, and later runaway slaves, sought the protection of these underground grottoes.

The three-chambered Indian Cave can be visited independently by taxi from Codrington, and the site is also part of a day tour from Antigua on the Barbuda Express ferry. The entrance

---

THE SPINY LOBSTER

In the Caribbean, when a menu includes "lobster" it generally means the spiny lobster, endemic to the warm tropical waters. Unlike the New-England-type lobsters that have the fat frontal claws, these creatures have long, straight spikes coming off the head, great for defense, but not very edible. The lobster meat, however, is delectable. Fishermen bring in large quantities of the catch, and visitors can buy them fresh off the docks, brush with a little butter, and throw them on the heat - making a quick and easy meal fit for a king. They can also be found already grilled at many of the roadside food vendors' stands and, of course, at all the better restaurants.

leads directly into a round chamber and a short narrow passage in which two ancient petroglyphs carved by the Arawak can be seen among the stalagmites and stalactites. These are the only petroglyphs found in Barbuda or Antigua. The second cave has many bats hanging from the ceiling and leads to the third cave, from where it is possible to climb up to its "roof" with the aid of a rope. At the top are gorgeous views over Two Foot Bay's white-sand beach and the crashing Atlantic waves.

Also in the area is the large sinkhole of Darby Cave, which has stalactites up to 8 ft (2 m) long on one side. Palm trees and huge ferns growing round the rim are home to various critters – keep an eye open for iguanas and hermit crabs.

Martello Tower

⚲ 3 miles (5 km) S of Codrington, Barbuda ▭
🕘 6am–8pm daily

Early attempts at settling upon Barbuda by the English were resisted by the fierce Carib people. The island was eventually colonized by John and Christopher Codrington, who came over from Antigua in 1685 to establish a provisioning station and, legend has it, a slave-breeding home for their Antiguan plantations, under a 99-year lease from Queen Anne of England.

Between 1750 and 1800, the British built a fort at a point called River, which included the 32-ft- (9-m-) high observation tower now known as Martello. It was modeled on a tower built on Cape Mortella in Corsica during the Napoleonic Wars.

Apart from defense purposes, the fort was also used as a high vantage point from which to spot shipwrecks on the reefs surrounding the island.

Adjacent to Martello Tower is the laid-back **Pink Sand Beach Bar**, the only beach bar on Barbuda. This restaurant prepares a variety of seafood served alongside traditional Barbudan vegetables and cool drinks. With some spectacular ocean views, the bar is a favorite venue for beach parties.

Pink Sand Beach Bar
⚲ River Beach 🕘 10am–midnight daily

↑ Martello Tower, its bleached bricks now overgrown with local plantlife

MONTSERRAT

⌂ 25 miles (40 km) SW of Antigua ✈🚢 🇮 Montserrat Tourism Division, E. K. Osbourne Building, Little Bay; www.visitmontserrat.com

During the 1990s, the Soufrière Hills Volcano repeatedly roared to life with activity that buried the main town of Plymouth and a significant portion of southern Montserrat in ash. In the years since, the island has developed "volcano tourism," with people coming just to see the devastation and the cloud-shrouded mount. A hardened dome covers the active core of hot lava, quieting the major threat, but there is still significant seismic activity. The island is divided into the Exclusion Zone and the northern hills where the locals have rebuilt their cultural core at Brades.

INSIDER TIP
Visitor Safety

Visitors can pick up a "Guide to Volcanic Hazards" brochure at the tourist board office or the observatory. It outlines the Exclusion Zone, the criteria for entering it, the safety rules to be observed while traveling through it, and emergency protocol advice.

①
The Exclusion Zone

⌂ Southern part of Montserrat ⊙ Daylight hours

In 1995, the Soufrière Hills Volcano erupted, spewing ash that covered the main town of Plymouth and obscured the sun for 15 minutes. A year later, the town was abandoned, buried under layers of ash and mud deposited by pyroclastic activity. Houses on the hills around the center of the island, as well as the W. H. Bramble Airport on the eastern side of the island, were similarly buried and now stand as a modern-day Pompeii for all to observe.

If volcanic activity is at a minimum, people are allowed to go briefly into some areas of the Exclusion Zone to observe the devastation from a closer vantage point. But nobody can enter the zone without a qualified guide, and must follow the restrictions and safety measures. Since no one is allowed near the town of Plymouth, the best places from which to view it are Richmond or Garibaldi hills, where many of the homes remain half-buried in ash. To arrange a tour, contact the Montserrat Tourist Board.

Another interesting way to view the effects of the volcano is aboard a boat tour that embarks from Little Bay. From this vantage point, the

The volcanic landscape of Montserrat, wreathed in clouds

Silver Hill
1,323 ft (403 m) △

Antigua ↑

Caribbean Sea

Little Bay
Gerald's
John A. Osborne Airport
Brades
Bunkum Bay
St. John's
St. Peter's
Woodlands
Jack Boy Hill Viewpoint
Runaway
Salem
Montserrat Volcano Observatory ②
Old Towne
Old Road Bay
Belham
Garibaldi Hill Viewpoint ○
Fox's Bay
Richmond Hill
The Exclusion Zone ①
Gages
Soufrière Hills Volcano △ 3,180 ft (970 m)
Plymouth

White
South Soufrière Hills

0 kilometers 3
0 miles 3
N ↑

LEGEND OF THE RUNAWAY GHAUT

The deep ravines, or ghauts as they are called in Montserrat, are marked by sparkling clear streams carrying fresh water from the hills down to the sea. Visitors are invited to taste the water – which is of astonishingly high quality – at an unassuming little tap at the side of the road near Runaway Ghaut. Legend has it that those who drink from this tap will be drawn back to Montserrat time and again. Since it is not clearly marked, visitors should ask their guide to include it in their tour. Adjacent to the tap is a trail that provides a pleasant and easy walk into a lush picnic and strolling area.

town of Plymouth and the dramatic paths of the volcanic flows are visible.

On the eastern side of the island, the remains of Bramble Airport and the lava dome can be viewed from the lookout at Jack Boy Hill. From this point, the airport, as well as the severely damaged native burial grounds and villages,

can be seen. The specially constructed building offers a viewing platform, a telescope through which to see the volcanic dome (if the clouds have lifted), and picnic areas.

---

②

Montserrat Volcano Observatory

⌂ Flemmings, Montserrat
🕘 8:30am–4:30pm Mon–Fri
🌐 mvo.ms

The Montserrat Volcano Observatory, which is responsible for monitoring the volcano and issuing status alerts, has its own head-quarters at Flemmings, built in 2003. At the Interpretation Center, posters provide an explanation of the techniques used in monitoring volcanic activities, and video shows give a synopsis and examples of the volcano's recent activity, along with a touch screen and displays of rocks, ash, and artifacts. Scientists

are available to answer questions at sessions held on Tuesdays and Thursdays.

The observatory's dedicated website gives the most up-to-date information about the volcano through weekly status reports. Those planning to visit the island should check this site before traveling, since at times it can be too hazardous to visit. Also of interest is the photo gallery, which is updated weekly and has an archive of photographs taken during the periods when the dome was still growing. For those interested in learning more about volcanoes, the site also offers extensive information on volcano-specific events and their monitoring methods. There is a gift shop at the site, where educational and teaching aids on geology, geography, and science for children aged 11 to 18 are available to purchase.

PRACTICAL
INFORMATION

Here you will find all the essential advice and information you will need before and during your stay in Antigua and Barbuda.

CURRENCY
Eastern
Caribbean dollar
(EC$)

TIME ZONE
Atlantic Standard
Time, 4 hours behind
GMT and 1 hour
ahead of EST

LANGUAGE
English

ELECTRICITY SUPPLY
The electricity is mainly
220 volts, though
some hotels have 110
volts as well

EMERGENCY NUMBERS

999 or 911

TAP WATER
Water purity is
unreliable, so, to be
safe, drink bottled
water

When To Go

While Antigua and Barbuda are warm year-round, the heat can get sticky from June through October, which is also the hurricane season. Peak times for visitors to Antigua – other than the winter holidays – are late April (Sailing Week), August (Carnival), and November (Independence Day); March (St. Patrick's Day – the only one on the islands) in Barbuda; May (Caribana); and July (Calabash) in Montserrat.

Getting There

V. C. Bird International Airport (ANU) in Antigua is served by major airlines such as British Airways, Air Canada, Delta, United Airlines, US Airways, American Airlines, and Virgin Atlantic as well as regional airlines such as LIAT and Caribbean Airlines. The smaller regional airlines, Winair and Montserrat Airways, have flights from Antigua to Barbuda and Montserrat. The larger islands are also linked by a Barbuda Express Ltd. daily ferry, and the port of St. John's on Antigua welcomes large cruise ships on a regular schedule. There are three protected harbors on Antigua, with marinas and immigration checkpoints for yachts wanting to tour the coastline and visit Barbuda. Caribbean Helicopters also operates from Antigua to Montserrat.

Personal Security

While not idyllically crime-free, these islands are relatively safe for visitors. However, it is advisable to take the normal precautions of keeping valuables guarded, sticking to well-populated areas, and not roaming around alone at night.

Health

The primary health facility for Antigua and Barbuda is Mount St. John's Medical Centre Located at Michael's Mount, St John's. Glendon Hospital, in Montserrat, offers emergency services to both locals as well as visitors.

Passports and Visas

Travelers are required to have a valid passport to enter Antigua, Barbuda, and Montserrat. Visitors also need to have return tickets and confirmed accommodations. Visas are not required for citizens of the US, some European, and certain other countries. Check with your nearest embassy or high commission for details. Montserrat has a departure tax of $21 which can only be paid in cash. Departure tax for Antigua and Barbuda is included in flight costs.

LGBT+ Safety

Same-sex unions in any form are illegal in Antigua and Barbuda and could entail a punishment of up to 15 years in prison. An unfortunate recent development was in 2016 when Antigua and Barbuda refused to sign a UN agreement, which 85 other states signed, requesting legislation against discrimination on account of sexual orientation or gender identity. However, the islands are popular with LGBT+ couples, and it's unlikely they will receive any prejudice in tourist resorts and restaurants, but discretion is generally advised.

Money

The currency for all three islands is the Eastern Caribbean dollar (EC$). Antigua has a number of banks and cash can be obtained (as EC$) at most ATMs. Credit cards are accepted in Antigua and many vendors also accept US dollars (but not euros or UK pounds). In Barbuda and Montserrat, credit cards are not as commonly accepted and vendors prefer EC dollars.

Cell Phones and Wi-Fi

In Antigua and Barbuda, Cable & Wireless and Digicel offer inexpensive phones with prepaid minutes and local SIM cards. Cable & Wireless also provides cell services in Montserrat. Some US cell phone services such as Cingular work on Antigua. Montserrat and Antigua have Internet cafes and most hotels offer high-speed Internet connections. Visitors bringing cell phones should check with their service providers to determine if they will work and if they will be subject to roaming charges.

Getting Around

Car rentals on Antigua and Montserrat are plentiful and easy to arrange either in advance or at the airport, but in Barbuda there are no cars for hire. AVIS and Hertz Rent-A-Car in Antigua, and Neville Bradshaw Agencies and Equipment & Supplies Ltd. in Montserrat are popular car rental agencies. Driving in Antigua can be dangerous at times as roads are narrow, street lights are not consistant and potholes and speed bumps can suddenly appear. As road conditions can be poor, be sure to check the vehicle you are hiring for marks from the previous user before you leave the agent. Take photographs of any damage.

The public bus system runs on an unscheduled basis. In Barbuda, a popular way to get around this flat island is by bike and rentals can be arranged. Taxi drivers on the islands double as tour guides. In Montserrat, drivers can also arrange for a guided trip into the Exclusion Zone if the volcano is not threatening.

Visitor Information

For Antigua and Barbuda, visitors can contact the tourism offices located in the US, Canada, and the UK. The **Antigua and Barbuda Ministry of Tourism** also operates an information kiosk at Heritage Quay in downtown St. John's and has information available at the V. C. Bird International Airport. The Montserrat Tourist Board has its main office at Farara Plaza in Brades, as well as offices in London. Useful information for visitors is also available at the island's Gerald's Airport.
Antigua and Barbuda Ministry of Tourism
w antigua-barbuda.org

A church spire overlooking the island of St. Barthelemy

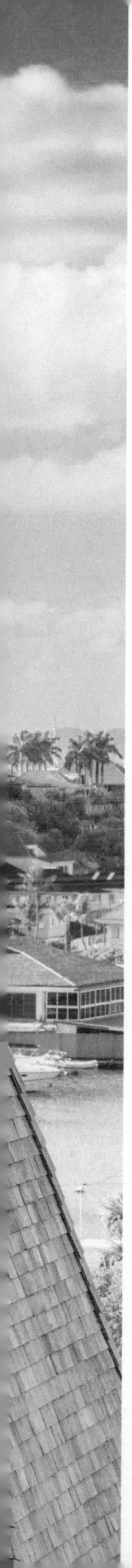

ST. BARTHELEMY

Christopher Columbus named St. Barthelemy after his brother, Bartolomé, although the island was first settled by French colonists from St. Kitts. Their first attempt to settle there, in 1648, ended when they were massacred by the indigenous Caribs. But other countrymen returned, and the island became a base for buccaneers. France sold St. Barthélemy to Sweden in 1784. Its capital, Gustavia – named after the then Swedish king, Gustav III – became a prosperous free port. Sweden returned the island to France in 1878 after a referendum.

In recent times, St. Barths, as it's casually known, was a commune within the overseas *département* of Guadeloupe. But in 2007 it became a stand-alone French Overseas Collectivity, giving it more autonomy. Covering an area of just nine sq miles (23 sq km), St. Barths is hilly and ringed with fine beaches. Because its rocky and arid soil never supported slave plantations, the population is mostly of European descent (Swedish as well as French). Upscale tourism is the driving force of the economy on this chic and exclusive bolt hole.

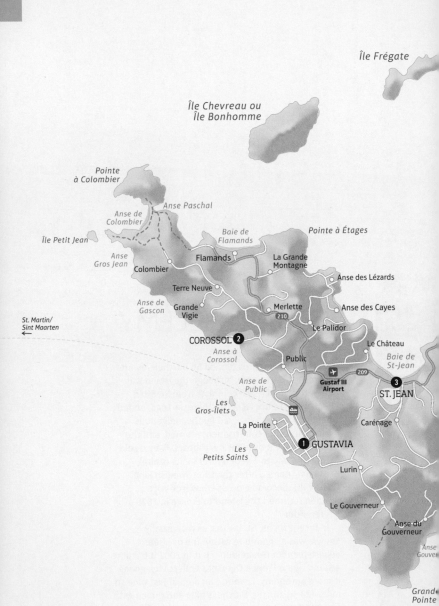

Île Pelé

Île le Boulanger

Île Frégate

Île Chevreau ou
Île Bonhomme

Pointe
à Colombier

Anse Paschal

Pointe à Étages

Anse de
Colombier

Baie de
Flamands

Île Petit Jean

Anse
Gros Jean

Flamands

La Grande
Montagne

Anse des Lézards

Colombier

Terre Neuve

Anse des Cayes

Anse de
Gascon

Grande
Vigie

Merlette

210

Le Palidor

St. Martin/
Sint Maarten
←

Le Château

COROSSOL 2

Anse à
Corossol

Baie de
St-Jean

Public

209

ST. JEAN 3

Anse de
Public

Gustaf III
Airport

Les
Gros-Îlets

La Pointe

Carénage

1 GUSTAVIA

Les
Petits Saints

Lurin

Le Gouverneur

Anse du
Gouverneur

Anse
Gouve

Grande
Pointe

0 kilometers   1

0 miles   1

N
↑

ST. BARTHELEMY

Experience

1 Gustavia
2 Corossol
3 St. Jean
4 Anse de Grande Saline
5 Anse du Grand Cul-de-Sac
6 Anse du Petit Cul-de-Sac

Île Toc Vers

Les Grenadines

Pointe Milou

Pointe Lorient

Pointe Milou

La Tortue

Pointe Mangin

Mont Jean

ANSE DE GRAND CUL-DE-SAC

5

ANSE DU PETIT CUL-DE-SAC

6

Baie de Lorient

Marigot

Grand Cul-de-Sac

rient

209

211

Camaruche

Vitet

209

Petit Cul-de-Sac

Petite Saline

Montagne du Vitet 938 ft (286 m) △

Morne de Grand Fond 899 ft (274 m) △

211

Toiny

Anse de Toiny

Grande Saline

La Grande Saline

Grand Fond

Morne Rouge 528 ft (161 m) △

Pointe de Toiny

Anse de Grand Fond

4

ANSE DE GRANDE SALINE

Anse de Chauvette

ointe u Gouverneur

Fourmis

Île Coco

Îlot sud de l'Île Coco

ST. BARTHELEMY □

Locally made

With a vast array of goods made on the island, you can be sure to take home unique gifts. Artists, designers, and skilled craftspeople have galleries, boutiques, and studios, and their items range from clothing and jewelry to paintings and sculptures. Discover the traditional woven straw work made by the women of Corossol and Colombier who intricately weave the native latanier palm straw into delightful baskets, handbags, and broad-brimmed hats. You can purchase these at stalls along Gustavia's harbor.

↑ Locally made, traditional straw products hanging outside a boutique

ST. BARTHELEMY FOR
SHOPPERS

The best place in the Caribbean for tax-free shopping, St. Barths offers a great selection of designer shops and chic boutiques. The highest concentration of shops is in Gustavia, followed by St-Jean, and a pleasant way to spend half a day is strolling between the two.

Raise a Glass

The best place to buy French wines, spirits, and champagnes, Le Cellier du Gouverneur (*cellierdugouverneur.com*) on Rue de la République in Gustavia sells everything from a great vintage to an affordable but refreshing rosé. Head to Marché U in St-Jean, the biggest supermarket on St. Barths, for fine French groceries and wines.

←

French wines, spirits and champagne

Did You Know?

Ligne St. Barth is St. Barths' own skincare line, made naturally from the island's plants and fruits.

← Charming upscale boutiques in the main town of Gustavia

Chic Boutiques

Adjacent to Rue de la République, Rue de la France and Rue du Général De Gaulle have a number of locally owned boutiques and specialty stores to explore. There are also some charming cafes and bars, along with French and English bookstores, leather goods shops, and pharmacies selling luxurious French beauty products. Another of the island's centers of shopping action is along the main road at St-Jean going toward Lorient. Several of the shopping malls here, including Les Galeries du Commerce, La Villa Creole, La Sodexa, and L'Espace Neptune, are filled with boutiques selling the trendiest beachwear and chicest clothes.

💬 INSIDER TIP
Schedule your Shopping

As in France, many shops close at noon for a long 2–3 hour *déjeuner* but often stay open as late as 8pm for evening browsing. Many are also closed on Sundays and Wednesday afternoons.

Luxury Fashion

Right on the harbor in Gustavia and also known as Quai de la République, this premier shopping area rivals London's Bond Street and New York's Fifth Avenue. Nicknamed "Rue du Couturier", designer outlets include Louis Vuitton, Bulgari, Chopard, Longchamp, and Dolce & Gabbana. Vanita Rosa *(vanitarosa.com)* showcases unique, playful fashion inspired by the vibrant colors of the St. Barths landscapes.

→ A selection of designer fashion found on the "Rue du Couturier"

EXPERIENCE

Gustavia

🏠 W coast of St Barthélemy
➕🚌 ℹ Quai Général de
Gaulle; 590 278 727

Gustavia is one of the prettiest harbor towns in the Caribbean. Its steep bay walls tumble to a rectangular waterfront, with attractive red-roofed buildings overlooking the harbor from three sides. Much of the waterfront itself is a boardwalk, where tenders moor at the restaurants and bars, which gives the bay a very pleasant ambience. At Christmas and New Year, Gustavia harbor is one of the most fashionable places in the world. Luxury yachts sit anchored, sterns to the boardwalk, hosting parties for celebrities.

Onshore, the streets are steep and narrow, but full of character. There is often a lively buzz around the many bars and shops, particularly on the boardwalk. The streetfronts are lined with serious names in the world of fashion: Armani, Dolce & Gabbana, and Bulgari. On the waterfront at the head of the bay is the small St. Bartholomew's Anglican Church, which is built from white-painted stone and dates to 1855, and sits in a pretty garden full of palm trees. Services are held in both French and English, and it's a popular wedding venue for tourists. The church also hosts occasional performances by the local choir group, La chorale Aux Bons Chœurs. Look out for the enormous iron anchor across the road that is believed to come from an 18th-century English warship. It was discovered in 1981, when it was accidently picked up by a tugboat. Behind St. Bartholomew's is the Catholic church, and up a flight of stairs above both of them, the Swedish clock tower can be seen from several points around the harbor. It can be recognized by its small triangular roof.

At the far point of the bay's outer arm, beneath the fort, are two notable buildings. The Mairie de St. Barth (town hall) is a modern version of the mayoral buildings that are seen all over France and its dominions. Adjacent to it, and housed in the Wall House, an old stone Swedish warehouse, is the **Wall House Museum**. This displays an eclectic series of artifacts, photographs, and

---

SWEDISH HISTORY IN ST. BARTHS

The island of St. Barths was Swedish for a century. In the late 1700s, King Gustav III of Sweden decided to capitalize on the growing global seaborne trade and looked for an outpost in the Caribbean. A deal was struck with France and the island was loaned to Sweden in return for a French presence in Gothenburg and trading rights in the Baltics. For a while, the free port of St. Barths was very successful and the population rocketed, but in the mid-1800s, trade tailed off and the island went into a decline. In 1878 King Oskar II of Sweden put nationality to a referendum and the islanders voted to return to France.

→ Strolling past colorful houses on the Rue Jeanne d'Arc in Gustavia

paintings illuminating the island's history, including the Swedish period. The exhibits include models of traditional St. Barthian houses (low buildings that face away from the prevailing wind), household items, and articles woven from the local latanier palm.

Just a few elements of Swedish heritage remain in the small town, which took its name from King Gustav III, the Swedish ruler at the time when the island became Swedish. Only a handful of the pretty stone buildings date from this era, as sadly most were destroyed in a devastating hurricane in 1850 and a great fire in 1852. Dinzey House, on Rue Jeanne d'Arc, dates to the 1820s and is one of the few houses to have survived the fire. It was built by and named after Sir Richard Dinzey, the son of the

governor of Saba, and has been meticulously restored by its current owner, who is also the Honorary Consual of Sweden. Several streets carry Swedish names, however, including Prinsgatan and Kungsgatan.

Wall House Museum

⊗ 🏛 La Pointe, Gustavia Harbor 🕐 8:30am–noon & 2:30–6pm Mon–Fri, 9–11am & 2:30–5pm Sat 🌐 st-barths. com/museum

> At Christmas and New Year, Gustavia harbor is one of the most fashionable places in the world. Luxury yachts sit anchored, sterns to the boardwalk, hosting parties for celebrities.

↑ The pictureque skyline of Gustavia harbor, beginning to light up as dusk falls

EAT

Bonito Saint Barth
With a lovely terrace overlooking Gustavia's harbor, this restaurant is a celebrity favorite and has a menu to suit.

🏠 4 Rue Lubin Brin
🕐 6:30pm–1am Mon–Sat
🌐 ilovebonito.com

$$$

L'Isola Ristorante
Head here for Italian classics; with an elegant, minimalist menu and a chef from Rome, it's considered by many to be the island's best spot.

🏠 Rue Roi Oscar II
🕐 6:30–11pm daily
🌐 lisolastbarth.com

$$$

Crêperie
A traditional French crêperie in the heart of Gustavia, offering both sweet and savory options alongside burgers, paninis, and other tasty staples.

🏠 Rue Roi Oscar II
🌐 creperiestbarth.com

$$$

2
Corossol

📍 **1 mile (2 km) N of Gustavia** 🚌

The pretty village of Corossol, situated on a protected bay to the north of Gustavia, is one of the distinctly local areas of St. Barths. Corossol is home to many "Barthéleminois" families and has a slightly more local character than other areas of the internationally popular island. It is an excellent destination for those who wish to experience some of the traditional culture of St. Barths, from fishermen mending their nets on the beach to villagers weaving intricate straw baskets. On special occasions, the local women don traditional costumes and bonnets. At sunset, head to Corossol Beach, just off the main road, to take a few atmospheric pictures.

3
St. Jean

📍 **1 mile (2 km) NE of Gustavia** 🚗

The second and only other sizable town in St. Barths, St. Jean sits on the island's north shore on Baie de St. Jean, just over the hill from Gustavia, overlooking a spectacular blue bay. St. Jean's small airport is set at one end of the bay, on the aptly named Plaine de la Tourmente (Plain of Torment), a very difficult runway to land on. There are several hotels and bars along the beach, the most fashionable on the island. At the center of the beach, essentially splitting it into two separate strands, stands the iconic Eden Rock Hotel, set on its own promontory. Behind the beach is the small town, which has two rows of shops and several restaurants and bars. Roads lead inland past a couple of hotels to many of St. Barths' numerous villas.

4 🍴
Anse de Grande Saline

📍 **3 miles (5 km) SE of Gustavia**

This remote, white sandy beach is wrapped by rocky cliffs at each end and takes its name from the large salt pond nearby. Perhaps the most photogenic of St. Barths' many beaches, Anse de Grande Saline lies in a beautiful secluded cove on the southern coast. It is reached by

following Rue Lubin Brin from Gustavia, or by taking the D209 road east from Baie de St-Jean, followed by a 10-minute clamber over dunes from the parking lot.

All visitors need on Anse de Grande Saline are sunglasses and a smile. While topless subathing is common on St. Barths beaches, this unspoiled stretch of sand is known for its entirely nude – though discreet – sunbathers (although this practice is not at all mandatory). The water here is clear and warm with minimal current, which provides good snorkeling conditions. There are a couple of restaurants near the parking lot, but no concessions at the beach itself. Day-trippers should

↑ The red-roofed resort of Eden Rock Hotel, a world-renowned venue in St. Jean

> **INSIDER TIP**
> ### St. Barths on a Budget
>
> To keep prices low, visit off-season (mid-April–mid-December) for good discounts on accommodation. Opt to stay in places with a kitchen, and shop for picnics at the supermarchés. Make beach-going your main activity, since they are all public and free.

↑ The stunning, crescent-shaped beach of Anse du Grande Cul-de-Sac

bring water and snacks, and, if possible, chairs and umbrellas since there is little shade to be found throughout the day.

Anse de Grand Cul-de-Sac

📍 5 miles (8 km) E of Gustavia

Located at the northeastern and Atlantic side of the island, Anse de Grand Cul-de-Sac is reached by taking the D209 road east from Gustavia or Baie de St-Jean. The crescent-shaped beach here is narrow, and there are few areas of sand to lounge on, but it is set on a warm, shallow reef-protected bay that is often referred to as a lagoon. You can wade almost the entire way across the water at low tide, so it's a popular spot for families with small children and islanders on weekends.

The lagoon is also a favorite area for watersports, offering excellent wind- and kite-surfing, kayaking, stand-up paddle boarding, and snorkeling excursions to see rays and turtles. Local centers rent out equipment and can organize lessons.

The surrounding hotels offer great views across the lagoon, or you can use sun-loungers for the afternoon at a number of restaurants and beach bars offering tasty French and Creole food.

Anse du Petit Cul-de-Sac

📍 6 miles (10 km) E of Gustavia

Also accessed from the D209 road and roughly a mile east of Anse du Grand Cul-de-Sac, is the similar lagoon-shaped bay and white-sand beach of Petit Cul de Sac. As its name suggests, it's tiny, but incredibly beautiful and very secluded with only a few villas on the hillsides above.

The Atlantic is quite hard to enter here, due to rocks along the shoreline. However, once successfully past the rocks, this area is good for snorkeling. Turtles can also be glimpsed on the left side of the cove, while the small tidal pools on the tip to the right of the beach are perfect for young children to splash around in.

TOP 5 SCENIC BEACHES OF ST. BARTHS

Plage de St-Jean
Sitting in a bay of aquamarine water, this popular spot boasts a few toes-in-sand bars.

Anse de Grande Saline
Capped at both ends by rocky hillsides, this stretch has an isolated, undeveloped appeal.

Anse du Gouverneur
Brilliant turquoise water hemmed in by green hills.

Anse de Colombier
Reached via a steep hike, this is a favorite for catamaran trips.

Baie des Flamands
The longest walkable beach on the island.

> St. Jean's small airport is set at one end of the bay, on the aptly named Plaine de la Tourmente (Plain of Torment), a very difficult runway to land on.

PRACTICAL
INFORMATION

Here you will find all the essential advice and information you will need before and during your stay in St. Barthelemy.

AT A GLANCE

CURRENCY
Euro (EUR)

TIME ZONE
Atlantic Standard Time, 4 hours behind GMT and 1 hour ahead of EST

LANGUAGE
French

ELECTRICITY SUPPLY
The St. Barths electrical system delivers 220 volts at 60 cycles through standard French sockets

EMERGENCY NUMBERS

POLICE, FIRE, AND AMBULANCE

18

TAP WATER
Water comes from a variety of sources and is generally safe to drink but if in doubt, stick to bottled water

When To Go

The weather in St. Barths is generally good year-round. The dry season lasts from December through May, while heavier rains are expected between June and November during the hurricane season. Most visitors arrange a trip during the winter season from January to April, when there are also a handful of cultural and sporting events.

Getting There

There are no direct flights to St. Barths and a change of planes will be necessary. From neighboring St. Martin/Sint Maarten, there are islandhopping flights into Aéroport Gustave III, St. Barth's only airport. Scheduled flights are offered by Winair and St Barth Commuter, and Air Caraïbes. Tradewind Aviation flies from San Juan, Puerto Rico. Visitors can also charter a plane through these companies. Travelers from Britain may choose to fly via Antigua, from where chartered planes to the island are available. It is also possible to make the link from St. Martin/Sint Maarten by boat. Daily ferries are also available, but can be quite unreliable and taking one of these might entail an overnight stay on St. Martin. The Voyager offers daily ferry service between St. Martin, Saba, and St. Barths. Though expensive, boats are available for private charter.

Personal Security

Crime is extremely rare in St. Barts but it's still worth taking sensible precautions such as securing your valuables.

Health

No vaccinations are needed to enter St. Barths. For medical emergencies there is an Accident and Emergency department at the Hôpital de Bruyn in Gustavia. However, it does not have enough facilities to handle complicated procedures and patients are transferred either to St. Martin or farther afield to Puerto Rico.

Passports and Visas

Entry regulations are the same as in France and the European Union. EU travelers are permitted entry without a visa. US and Canadian citizens can also enter on a passport without a visa. Other nationalities should check with their local French embassy. An onward or return ticket is needed.

LGBT+ Safety

Glamorous St. Barths is a favourite destination for all sexualities and LGBT+ visitors are welcomed due to the accepting nature of the French culture. Discrimination based on sexual orientation is banned and same-sex marriage has been legal and recognised since 2013.

Money

The official currency of St. Barths is the euro. Banks are located in Gustavia and St-Jean, while ATMs are found around the island. Some American cards may not work in the local ATMs so visitors must check with their bank beforehand. Credit cards are accepted at all establishments connected with tourism, and some restaurants may offer a choice of either paying in euros or US dollars.

Cell Phones and Wi-Fi

The telephone system in St. Barths is overseen by France Telecom and other providers such as Orange Caraïbe, which offer good cell-phone coverage and Internet in addition to landlines. Cell phones can be hired through a handful of shops. St. Barths' International Direct Dialing code is 590. This is followed by a nine-digit number that begins with 590 for landlines and 690 for cell phones. Local calls can be made by dialing 0 before the nine-digit number. Visitors bringing cell phones should check with their service providers to determine if they will work in St. Barths and if they will be subject to roaming charges.

Getting Around

Although quite expensive, hiring a car is the best option in St. Barths. Vehicles can be delivered to the respective hotels and returned at the airport on departure. Most car rental companies, such as Europcar and Turbe Car Rental, are at the airport. A local driving license is not required here. Taxis are not readily available, particularly after dark, and during high season they may have to be booked days in advance. However, many hotels have their own cars that pick up guests arriving at the airport or the ferry dock. There are taxi stands at the airport and at the municipal parking in Gustavia. There are no buses or other forms of public transportation.

Visitor Information

There is an efficient tourist office, the Office du Tourisme, on the waterfront in Gustavia. Abroad, the publicity for St. Barths is handled through the various **Atout France** offices around the world. Many publications on St. Barths offer useful information on facilities and activities available here. Visitor information can also be found on the useful **St. Barths Online** website.

Atout France
🆆 atout-france.fr
St. Barths Online
🆆 st-barths.com

GUADELOUPE

Guadeloupe is a French archipelago whose two largest islands are hinged together like an open oyster shell. Grande-Terre, the eastern half, is flat, covered in sugar cane, dotted with resort towns, and has Guadeloupe's main commercial hub, Pointe-à-Pitre. Basse-Terre, the western half, is mountainous, rainforested, and home to La Grande Soufrière, an active volcano that is the Lesser Antilles' highest peak. The two halves are joined by bridges over the Rivière Salée (Salt River). Smaller outer islands float nearby like spilled pearls. On Marie-Galante, sugar cane and rum production are still important. Les Saintes comprise a cluster of nine islands, just two of which are inhabited. La Désirade (The Desired), so-named by Columbus for being the first sight of land on his second voyage in 1493, has minimal tourist facilities but great natural appeal.

Guadeloupe was much sought after by colonial powers. It was first settled by the French in 1635. At times during the 1700s and early 1800s the British occupied the land, but it finally ended up in French hands in 1816. In 1946, Guadeloupe became an overseas department of France, a status which, despite several independence movements, remains today. In its cuisine, music, and language, Guadeloupe displays a blend of French and creole traditions. Though French is the official language, French creole is used by many locals in everyday conversation.

GUADELOUPE

Anse-Bertran

Port-Louis

Grande Anse
Deshaies
Sofaïa
Sainte-Rose
Îlet à Fajou
Grand Cul-de-Sac Marin

Basse-Terre

Lamentin
Baie-Mahault
Pointe-à-Pitre International Airport

Baille-Argent

POINTE-À-PITRE
①

Pointe-Noire
Acomat
ROUTE DE LA TRAVERSÉE
⑦
Versailles
Bas du-Fo

Parc Zoologique et Botanique des Mamelles
Cascade aux Ecrevisses
Petit-Bourg
Vernou
Petit Cul-de-Sa Marin

JACQUES COUSTEAU UNDERWATER RESERVE ⑧
Pigeon
Piton de Bouillante 3,569 ft (1,088 m)
Goyave

Bouillante
Matéliane 4,258 ft (1,298 m)
Sainte-Marie

Caribbean Sea

Marigot
PARC NATIONAL DE LA GUADELOUPE ⑥

Vieux-Habitants
La Soufrière 4,813 ft (1,467 m)
Capesterr Belle-Eau

Baillif
Baillif Airport
Saint-Claude
Saint-Sauveur
Bananier

Basse-Terre
Monts Caraïbes 2,254 ft (687 m)
Trois-Rivières

Vieux-Fort

TERRE-DE-HAUT
⑨ Les Saintes Airport

Grande Anse
La Savane

Terre-de-Bas
La Coche
Grand Îlet

Les Saintes

GUADELOUPE

Experience

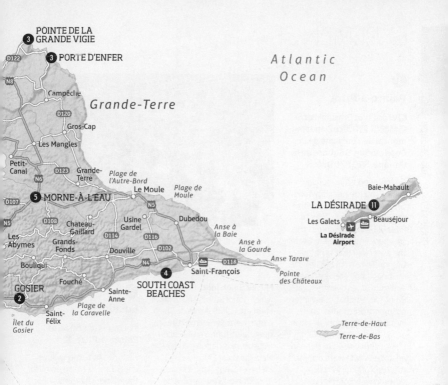

POINTE DE LA GRANDE VIGIE ③

③ **PORTE D'ENFER**

D122

N8

Campêche

Grande-Terre

D120

Gros-Cap

Les Mangles

Petit-Canal

N6

D123

Grande-Terre

Plage de l'Autre-Bord

⑤ **MORNE-À-L'EAU**

Le Moule

Plage de Moule

N5

D107

D108

Chateau-Gaillard

Usine Gardel

Dubedou

D114

D116

Anse à la Baie

Les Abymes

Grands-Fonds

Douville

D102

Anse à la Gourde

GOSIER ②

Fouché

N4

④ **SOUTH COAST BEACHES**

Saint-François

D118

Anse Tarare

Sainte-Anne

Pointe des Châteaux

Saint-Félix

Plage de la Caravelle

Îlet du Gosier

Atlantic Ocean

Baie-Mahault

LA DÉSIRADE ⑪

Les Galets

Béauséjour

La Désirade Airport

Terre-de-Haut

Terre-de-Bas

Ménard

Vieux-Fort

Caye Plate

D205

Saint-Louis

Dorot

Desruisseaux

D206

⑩ **MARIE-GALANTE**

Grande Anse

Le Haut du Morne

N9

Capesterre

Grand-Bourg

D203

Moulin des Basses

Marie-Galante Airport

0 kilometers 10

0 miles 10

N

Dominica ↓

EXPERIENCE

① Pointe-à-Pitre

🏠 W coast of Grande-Terre
❌➕🚌🚢 ℹ️ Office Départe-mental du Tourisme de la Guadeloupe, 5 Square de la Banque; 590 820 930

↑ A school group pressing their noses to the glass at L'Aquarium de la Guadeloupe in Gosier

Guadeloupe's commercial center and the main town on Grande-Terre, Pointe-à-Pitre sits on the eastern shore of Petit Cul-de-Sac Marin, at the southern end of Rivière Galée, the waterway that separates Grande-Terre from Basse-Terre.

Though battered by fires and hurricanes over the years, Pointe-à-Pitre has many interesting historical sites. These include the atmospheric Place de la Victoire, which once held the guillotine used to behead aristocrats who were opposed to a revolutionary French government. South of the square is the silvery mesh of the **Mémorial ACTe**, which is built on Darboussier, once the largest sugar factory in the Lesser Antilles. This thought-provoking site opened in 2015 and is dedicated to the history of the slave trade.

To the west, the Sougues-Pagès House is a lovely example of 1800s French Caribbean architecture, and now houses the

Musée Saint-John-Perse, which honors the island's Nobel Laureate (1960), Alexis de Saint-Léger, better known as the poet Saint-John Perse. Place Gourbeyre is dominated by the Neo-Classical Église Saint-Pierre et Saint-Paul. Its open interior is a fine example of the hurricane- and earthquake-resistant metal construction popularized by Gustave Eiffel.

Mémorial ACTe

 🏠 Rue Raspail 🕐 9am–7pm Tue–Sat, 10am–6pm Sun 🌐 memorial-acte.fr

Musée Saint-John-Perse

🏠 9 Rue Nozières 📞 590 900 192 🕐 9am–5pm Mon–Fri, 8:30am–12:30pm Sat

---

VICTOR SCHOELCHER

Statues honoring Victor Schoelcher stand throughout the French Antilles. Born in 1804, he began publishing anti slavery articles in 1833, founded an abolition society in 1834, and led the commission that emancipated slaves in all French colonies in 1848. Guadeloupe and Martinique then credit him with beginning the republican political movement on the islands. He served as their representative to the French National Assembly in 1848–1851 (when he was forced into exile for opposing Napoléon's coup d'etat), and again in 1871, and was declared senator for life in 1875. He died in 1893.

---

② Gosier

🏠 4 miles (6 km) SE of Pointe-à-Pitre 🚌

Historically, Gosier was an important defense point for the island. The ruins of Fort Louis, built in 1695, still sit atop a hill above a waterway that divides the eastern and western parts of Guadeloupe. The fort was renamed Fort l'Union during the French Revolution. Another citadel, Fort Fleur d'Épée, was built by the British in 1756. Below the ruins, **Musée Fort Fleur d'Épée** is located in the trendy Bas-du-Fort area. It displays a fine repertoire of objects from the 18th-century war between France and Britain. For marine life enthusiasts there is **L'Aquarium de la Guadeloupe**, which showcases sea life, corals, and mangroves of the French Caribbean region.

The town's beach is lined with outlets offering offshore trips and watersports. Vendors sell colorful clothes, spicy aromas waft from cafes, and there are budget hotels close by. The best strip of sand is along Pointe de la Verdure.

Musée Fort Fleur d'Épée

🏠 Bas-du-Fort 📞 590 909 461 🕐 9am–5pm daily

L'Aquarium de la Guadeloupe

  ⬜ Place Créole, Bas-du-Fort Marina ⏲ 9am–6:30pm daily 🌐 aquarium delaguadeloupe.com

---

③

Porte d'Enfer and Pointe de la Grande Vigie

⬜ 13 miles (21 km) N of Pointe-à-Pitre ⓣ

Two of Guadeloupe's dramatic natural sites lie on the north coast of Grande-Terre. At land's end, Pointe de la Grande Vigie provides great views. Cliffs along this shoreline tower more than 250 ft (76 m) above the rocky coast. Two lookouts reached by driving south down the east coast are Pointe du Piton, a signed viewpoint, and Porte d'Enfer, a sheltered lagoon guarded by two majestic cliffs that form "The Gate of Hell." Chemin de la Grande Falaise is a 7-mile (11-km) path that runs south along the coastal ridge to Pointe Petit-Nègre and takes a 2-hour hike to complete.

Did You Know?

The shape of the Guadeloupe archipelago resembles that of a butterfly.

④

South Coast Beaches

Gosier marks the western edge of a string of sandy beaches that run along the south coast of Grande-Terre to Saint-François and the narrow peninsula of Pointe des Châteaux, together forming Guadeloupe's most popular tourist area. Hotels, restaurants, and snack bars are set on the sand, while dive shops and watersport centers offer equipment and trips. Plage de la Caravelle, and Plage de Bois Jolan are two gorgeous beaches to the east. Between Sainte-Anne and Saint-François, the coast road leads through a rural area dotted with isolated coves. The hills above, known as Les Grands-Fonds, offer a splendid view of the coast. The D118 coast road leading to Pointe des Châteaux is flanked by excellent small unnamed beaches, reached by cutting through wild vegetation that grows between the road and the water. On the Atlantic side, Anse à la Gourde is a beach popular with locals, while Anse Tarare is a sheltered cove favored by naturists.

---

⑤

Morne-à-l'Eau

⬜ 11 miles (18 km) N of Pointe-à-Pitre ⓣ ⓘ Town Hall, Place de la Mairie, 590 242 709

This fishing and agricultural village was once a major sugar-producing town. Today, the only reason to visit is to see the famous cemetery that sits on a hillside above the intersection of highways N5 and N6. This unique above-ground graveyard has ornate shrines dedicated to deceased islanders. On All Saints' Day, people come here to honor the dead, and thousands of candles illuminate the site.

↑ Checkered monuments at the unusual cemetery in Morne-à-L'Eau

6

Parc National de la Guadeloupe

⌂ 3 miles (5 km) S of Vernou
ℹ Habitation Beausoleil,
Montéran, 97120 Saint-
Claude; www.guadeloupe-
parcnational.com

La Soufrière, a 4,813-ft
(1,467-m) active volcano,
towers over the tropical
forest at the southern end
of Basse-Terre that makes up
Guadeloupe's national park.
In 1992, UNESCO designated
115 sq miles (300 sq km)
around the volcano as a
biosphere reserve because

> La Soufrière, a 4,813-ft (1,467-m) active volcano, towers over the tropical forest at the southern end of Basse-Terre that makes up Guadeloupe's national park.

of its importance as a diverse
habitat – comprising tropical
rainforest, coastal forest, and
mangrove – for more than
300 interesting species of
trees and bushes.

Most days, the top of the
volcano, the highest peak in
the Lesser Antilles, is hidden
by clouds and rain, but several
maintained hiking trails lead
to the summit and other
viewpoints. Parc National
operates an office in the town
of Saint-Claude, which is the
base for many guided and
independent tours of
the park. You can
pick up maps,
brochures, guide

recommendations, and other
information from here before
heading into the park.

The biosphere reserve
extends outside the park to
include 14 sq miles (37 sq km)
of coral reefs, mangrove
forests, freshwater swamps,
and sea-grass beds in and
around Grand Cul-de-Sac
Marin, the northern lagoon
that separates Grande-Terre
and Basse-Terre. This area
has turtles, giant sponges,
soft corals, sea urchins,
and many fish species. The
mangrove forest also shelters
kingfishers, terns, pelicans,
herons, and other migratory
and native birds.

❼

Route de la Traversée

🅰 1 mile (2 km) W of
Versailles, E Basse-Terre
ℹ La Maison de la Forêt,
Route de la Traversée

The cross-island roadway
D23, known as Route de la
Traversée, cuts east to west
across Basse-Terre through
the mountains and rainforest
of the Parc National de la
Guadeloupe. While the drive
itself is a pleasant shortcut
from one coast to the other,
the stops along the way are its
true appeal. Beginning at the
eastern end, the Route leaves
Highway N1 near the commune
of Versailles. After traveling for
approximately 7 miles (11 km),
a turn south on a small road
leads to the settlement of
Vernou and Sault de la Lézarde
(Lizard's Leap), a magnificent

← Access trail through
the biosphere reserve
to the Soufrière volcano
(inset), Basse-Terre

waterfall that cascades into
a rocky pool that is safe for
swimming. Visitors are advised
to wear shoes with good
traction, and to carry a
bathing suit for a dip in the
waterfall's pool. From the
parking lot on the outskirts
of Vernou, the hike leads
through resplendent green
fields and forest along
a groomed, but steep trail to
the falls. West of Vernou, after
about 5 miles (8 km), the
Route leads to Cascade aux
Écrevisses (Crayfish Waterfall),
which is one of the most
popular attractions on Basse-
Terre, as well as the easiest
to reach. The walk from the
parking lot takes less than 15
minutes, which explains why
visitors flock here. Two paths
lead up to the top of the falls,
and the one on the left is used
as a 20-ft (6-m) slide into the
Corossol River. Stop at the
visitors' center, La Maison de
la Forêt (Forest House), to pick
up information and explore
the three interpretive trails,
then continue along the
Route through the Col des
Deux Mamelles (Pass of Two
Breasts), which sits between
two lofty peaks – Mamelle de
Petit-Bourg and Mamelle de
Pigeon – before sloping back
toward sea level.

The final stop is at the **Parc
Zoologique et Botanique des
Mamelles** (Zoo and Botanical
Gardens). Besides the flora
and fauna (the zoo is home
to around 85 animal species
native to the Caribbean and
Guyana) the park also offers
an elevated rope bridge and
zipline through the treetops

**Parc Zoologique et
Botanique des Mamelles**
🅰 Route de la
Traversée, D23 ⏰ 9am–
6pm daily 🔲 zoode
guadeloupe.com

↑ A shoal of fish at the
Jacques Cousteau
Underwater Reserve

❽

Jacques Cousteau
Underwater Reserve

🅰 W coast of Basse-Terre
📞 590 988 172

The dark-sand beaches of
Malendure and Pigeon, just
north of Bouillante, are the
gateway to the Jacques
Cousteau Underwater
Reserve, a protected sea
park that pays homage to
the legendary "Man-Fish,"
recognized as the father of
underwater exploration.

The reserve, which extends
from the steep-sided coast
to nearby Îlets Pigeon, teems
with marine life and shelters
two sunken ships that provide
excellent conditions for scuba
divers. For less experienced
divers, the shallow waters are
brimming with colorful
coral, tropical fish and even
turtles. Glass-bottom boats
allow non-divers to view the
tropical fish living along the
park's pristine coral reef. In
January 2004, the town of
Bouillante honored Jacques-
Yves Cousteau, who died in
1997, by commissioning a bust
of the underwater pioneer
and submerging it 39 ft (12 m)
deep in Coral Garden off Îlets
Pigeon. Cousteau developed
the first scuba in 1943 and
declared the west coast of
Guadeloupe as one of the
world's ten best dive sites.

RUM IN GUADELOUPE

Produced for more than three centuries, rum is more than just a drink – it is an essential part of Guadeloupe's history, economy, and culture. There are two types: *rhum agricole* ("agricultural rum") is the most prestigious and obtained by distilling sugar cane juice; and "industrial" or "traditional" rum, derived from the fermentation of molasses. Both produce a tasty clear liquid in light or dark varieties – if you prefer it sweet, add sugar, or tartness, add lime.

THE HISTORY OF GUADELOUPE RUM

Rum production has been a Guadeloupe tradition since the first sugarcane fields were cultivated by the French from 1635. Jean-Baptiste Labat (1663-1738), some-times simply called Père Labat (Father Labat) was a Parisian clergyman, botanist and scientist who was sent there in 1696. When he arrived it is said that he contracted brucellosis (a highly contagious fever caused by ingestion of unpasteurized milk or undercooked meat) and was miraculously cured by a bitter, foul-smelling tonic he created called taffia; a fermented and distilled by-product of sugar cane. After a few changes to the method and ingredients, he then went on to design copper stills to produce a much more agreeable-tasting liquor from the juice.

HOW GUADELOUPE RUM IS MADE

Rum is produced by fermenting either straight sugarcane juice, or molasses, which is made by boiling the sugarcane into a dark syrupy liquid. Distillery machines press up to 22 lb (10 kg) of cane to obtain 2 pints (1 liter) of rum, which is then aged with yeast for at least six months in oak barrels a minimum of three to four years to earn the name "Old".

↑ Old machinery used for distilling pure cane juice at the Distillerie Bielle on Marie-Galante

Harvesting the sugarcane, ↑ a process which takes place between February and June

RUM DISTILLERIES FOR TOURS AND TASTINGS

Le Domaine de Séverin
At this property dating to 1928, a tractor-pulled train takes visitors to the distillery, a sugar cane field, plantation home, and spice and rum factories. The distillery, located in Sainte Rose, produces several varieties of white and old *rhums agricoles* which can be purchased in the shop *(severinrhum.com)*.

Distillerie Damoiseau
This authentic, family-run distillery opened in Le Moule in 1948 and now has a 50 per cent market share in Guadeloupe. Visitors can take a self-guided tour around the property and signboards explain each process from extracting the cane to bottling *(damoiseaurhum.com)*.

Distillerie Bologne
This small traditional distillery, located up a steep road in the scenic cane fields of Basse-Terre and dates back to 1897. A variety of rums are available to taste and purchase including one made from black sugarcane juice *(rhumbologne.fr)*.

Distillerie de Poisson
Also known as Distillerie du Père Labat, *rhum agricole* is produced at this traditional sugar estate in Grand-Bourg dating to 1860. Visitors can walk over the large conveyor where sugar cane is fed into a grinder before sampling the signature white rum under the shade of an old grove of mango trees *(rhumdu perelabat.com)*.

La Distillerie Reimonenq
Reimonenq, founded in 1916, is home to an interesting museum displaying farming artifacts, distillery machinery, and a barrel-making workshop. There is also a tropical collection of insects on the top floor. La Distillerie Reimonenq is located near the coast in Sainte Rose *(rhum-reimonenq-musee.com)*.

① The train at Le Domaine de Séverin in Basse-Terre

② A worker filling bottles of old rum at Distillerie Bologne

③ The variety of rums on offer at Distillerie de Poisson (also known as Distillerie du Père Labat)

⑨
Terre-de-Haut

🏠 9 miles (15 km) SE off
Basse-Terre's coast 🚗🚌🚤
ℹ️ Tourist Office, 39 Rue
Jean Calot, Terre-de-Haut;
590 943 061

Of the eight islands that make
up Les Saintes, only Terre-de-
Haut and Terre-de-Bas are
populated. Terre-de-Haut
attracts more visitors given its
harbor, natural beauty, picturesque fort, and easy access.
The compact island is ideal for
exploring on foot, although
group tours by minibus are
available from the harbor.

The main town is Le Bourg,
which sits in the curve of a bay
midway along the western
coast. Brightly painted houses,
boutiques, and restaurants
line the narrow streets. An old

↑ The lovely scenery
and harbor streets
(inset) of Terre-
de-Haut

cemetery with graves of
the island's first French
settlers is located in the
center of the town. The fortified summit of Morne du
Chameau is the island's highest point (1,014 ft/309 m), and
offers great views of the sea
and nearby islands.

Fort Napoléon is the biggest tourist attraction on the
island and offers spectacular
views in all directions. Though
it was never fired upon or
called on to defend the region,
a section of the fort houses a
museum featuring pictures,
maps, drawings, and artifacts
attesting to the violent period

of Caribbean history during
the 17th and 18th centuries.
Other parts of the fort have
been renovated as a modern
art museum. Directly across
the bay sit the ruins of Fort
Joséphine, named in honor of
Emperor Napoléon's first wife.

Most visitors spend their
time on the island's splendid
beaches or taking a diving
trip. In town, Baie du Bourg is
a UNESCO World Heritage Site
and listed as one of the world's
most beautiful bays. Plage de
Pompierre is a popular, palm-
shaded beach that is connected by a hiking trail to Grande
Anse, a beautiful but unsafe-
for-swimming beach midway
down the east coast. Anse
Crawen, on the west coast,
allows topless sunbathing and
swimming. However, snorkelers prefer the nearby Plage

> ### DAY TRIPS TO THE OUTER ISLANDS
>
> A day trip to one of the outer islands is an opportunity to
> explore a less populated area, scuba or snorkel unspoiled
> reefs, and enjoy a solitary picnic or a meal with the locals.
> Overnight accommodations are basic, but charming. The
> islands are accessible from Guadeloupe by air and by sea.
> Organized guided tours are the best way to take in a day
> trip; you can also arrange your own transportation and
> activities through the various tourist board offices.

Figuier. Equipment for watersports can be rented at Plage de Marigot.

Fort Napoléon

🕙 🅰 Le Chameau 📞 690 610 151 🕓 Times vary, call ahead 🚫 Public hols

---

Marie-Galante

🅰 27 miles (44 km) SE off the coast of Grande-Terre 🚢🚌🚕🚆 🚹 Office du Tourisme de Marie-Galante, Rue du Fort; www.ot-mariegalante.com

Marie-Galante is called the Island of a Hundred Windmills, though only 72 of the 19th-century stone structures remain, giving the flat isle a nostalgic ambience. Ox-drawn carts, once the chief means of transportation, are not an uncommon sight. Sugar production remains an important part of the economy, but tourism is gaining ground due to the island's superb beaches and old-fashioned appeal.

Among the most interesting sights, **Murat Plantation** stands out. Once a huge sugar plantation with more than 200 slaves, its Neo-Classical mansion has been restored to its original state and is now an eco-museum, featuring colonial memorabilia. It also houses the Museum of Arts and Popular traditions. Three rum distilleries offer tours and tastings. Of these, **Distillerie Bielle** is the largest producer and turns out well-known rums in various flavors, such as the gold-medal-winning Shrubb, which tastes of oranges. Close to the fishing village of Saint-Louis, the **Ecolambda** is a bio-climatic house with medicinal and flowering plants. Several hiking trails are maintained by the Office National des Forêts, and there are a dozen lovely beaches along the west coast.

Murat Plantation

🕙 🅰 Section Murat 97112, Grand-Bourg 📞 590 974 868 🕓 9am–noon & 2:30–5:30pm Mon-Fri, 9am-1pm Sat & Sun

Distillerie Bielle

🕙 🅰 Section Bielle 97112, Grand-Bourg 🕓 9:30am-1pm Mon-Sat, 10am-noon Sun (Nov-May) 🌐 rhumbielle.com

Ecolambda

🕙🕙 🅰 Section Saragot 97134, Saint-Louis 📞 590 973180 🕓 By reservation

---

La Désirade

🅰 6 miles (10 km) off Grande Terre's east coast 🚢🚌 🚹 Tourist Board of La Désirade, Capitainerie; 590 200176

La Désirade is the most off-the-beaten-track island of Les Saintes. Most visitors consider it perfect for a day trip, but there are also many places to stay overnight. Only the south coast is populated and a single road links Beauséjour, the principal town, with smaller settlements that dot the reef-sheltered shore. White-sand beaches are protected by a long strand of pristine coral reefs, and the island is home to an astonishing variety of plants and rare animals. Development is catching up as more visitors discover the untouched beauty of the beaches and hiking trails. Inland trails run across the central plateau and hikers are rewarded at the end of a steep climb with panoramic views from the 895 ft (273 m) Grande Montagne. You can also see the abandoned lepers' colony at Baie-Mahault and explore the ruins of a cotton factory.

EAT

La Touna
Superb grilled options, French-style desserts and lovely views to Pigeon Island; what's not to like?

🅰 Pigeon-Galets 🕓 Mon, Sun eve 🌐 la-touna.com

$$$

Le Mabouya dans La Bouteille
This romantic restaurant blends French fare with Caribbean ingredients, offered alongside an extensive wine list.

🅰 17 Salines Est, Saint-François 🕓 Tue 🌐 lemabouya.fr

$$$

Le Reflet de L'île
A welcoming spot offering Creole cuisine and delicious fruit rum cocktails.

🅰 3 Rue Marine, Capsterre 📞 590 974130 🕓 Mon

$$$

PRACTICAL
INFORMATION

Here you will find all the essential advice and information you will need before and during your stay in Guadeloupe.

AT A GLANCE

CURRENCY
Euro (EUR)

TIME ZONE
Atlantic Standard Time, 4 hours behind GMT and 1 hour ahead of EST. Guadeloupe does not observe daylight savings

LANGUAGE
The official language is French, but Creole is widely spoken and recognized as a language

ELECTRICITY SUPPLY
Guadeloupe uses 220 volts AC, 50 cycles, and most places have French-style outlets so adaptors might be necessary

EMERGENCY NUMBERS

AMBULANCE	FIRE SERVICE
15	**18**

POLICE
17

When To Go

While air temperature varies little from one month to another, February through June is the driest period and the best time to visit. Rain and humidity picks up in July and lingers through early January. Carnival begins the Friday after Epiphany Sunday and ends on Mardi Gras (Fat Tuesday). Following the French tradition, businesses close for several weeks during August and September.

Getting There

Guadeloupe has only one international airport, Guadeloupe Pôle Caraïbes in Pointe-à-Pitre, and seven regional airstrips, including Marie-Galante Grand-Bourg, Terrede-Haut Airport, and La Désirade Airport. The outer islands of the archipelago may be reached by ferry service. Both air and sea service change seasonally, but Air Canada, American Airlines, and Delta offer flights from North America, at least weekly during high season. Air France provides non-stop service from Paris, and Air Caraïbes and LIAT connect the islands within the Antilles. The ferry companies between these islands are L'Express des Iles, Comatrile, and Jean's Ferry Service.

Personal Security

Crime is rare in Guadeloupe and the outer islands, but take simple precautions and do not leave valuables in rental cars.

Health

There are several modern medical facilities located throughout the islands, including the Centre Hospitalier Universitaire de Pointe-à-Pitre with a 24-hour emergency room.

Passports and Visas

Other than the French, the citizens from all countries within the EU must present a valid passport to enter the island. Citizens of France

may show a passport, an official identity card, or a valid French residence permit. Immigration officials may ask to see an onward or return ticket, proof of sufficient funds for the planned stay and an address where visitors will be staying.

LGBT+ Safety

Like France, Guadeloupe legalized homosexuality in 1791, and today Guadeloupe's LGBT+ community are protected under French anti-discrimination legislation and same-sex marriage was legalized in 2013. However there have been incidents of prejudice against local LGBT+ individuals, so discretion is advised away from hotels and the gay-friendly nudist beaches of Anse Tarare and Anse Saline.

Money

The legal currency is the euro, and other currencies can be exchanged at 24-hour ATMs and banks, which are open in all the main towns from 8am to 4pm Monday to Friday. Most major credit cards are accepted, but may not be welcome at small cafés, especially on the outer islands. Some US cards may not work in the local ATMs.

Cell Phones and Wi-Fi

Visitors bringing cell phones to Guadeloupe should check with their service providers to determine if they will work and if they will be subject to roaming charges. Cell phones can be purchased from Orange Caraïbe offices. Hotels may offer Internet service, and Wi-Fi hotspots are scattered around the island. Internet cafes are located in larger towns.

Getting Around

Guadeloupe has a well-maintained network of highways and secondary roads that connect every part of the main island, and a rental car is the best way to travel from one point to another. Most large international agencies rent cars on the island. Book well ahead during high season. Large hotels may have rental cars on-site for daily or weekly rental. Several agencies such as AVIS, EuropCar, QuickRent, Budget, and Voitures

des Îles have booths at the airport. Taxis are abundant at the airports, ferry docks, and cruise ship terminals. They have meters and legally add a hefty surcharge to fares between 9pm and 7am and on Sundays and holidays. The operators for taxis are Taxi Art, Taxi Guadeloupe, C.D.L Taxi, Taxi Les Saintes Travel, Satevan, and Taxi: La Désirade. There are frequent bus services throughout the island, but it is best to know some French to communicate with the drivers.

The outer islands, connected to the main islands via ferry, can be navigated on foot or by bicycle. Marie-Galante has a minivan service between towns, but most visitors take group tours or rent a car.

Visitor Information

Tourist information kiosks are located at the arrival area of the airports and other tourist-oriented sites on all islands. Comité du Tourisme des Îles de la Guadeloupe maintains tourism offices on each of the Guadeloupen islands. The **Guadeloupe Islands Tourist Board** also has a very informative website.

Guadeloupe Islands Tourist Board
w visitguadeloupe.co.uk

The pier and Catholic church at Les Anses-d'Arlet

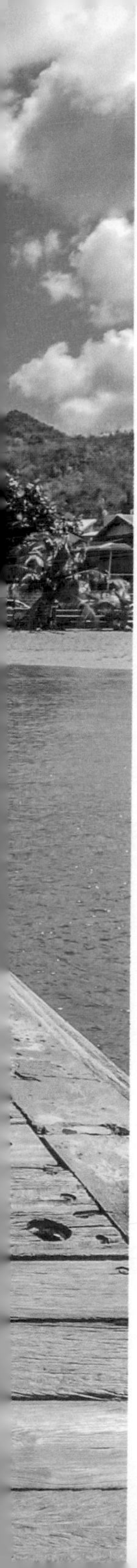

MARTINIQUE

Often referred to as the Isle of Flowers from its pre-Columbian name, Martinique served as an inspiration for the post-Impressionist artist Paul Gauguin, who visited in 1887. It's easy to see why. The landscapes of this French Caribbean island are beautiful and dramatic, particularly in the lush and mountainous north. Around a fifth of the island's 400,000-strong population live in the capital Fort-de-France.

Martinique's colonial past followed a similar pattern to Guadeloupe's. "Discovered" by Columbus, it was claimed by the French in 1635, and, after various struggles with the British, became French for good in 1815. Martinique's plantation economy was based on slave labor. Slavery was declared illegal on the island and elsewhere in the French West Indies in the late 1700s, but was reinstituted by Napoléon Bonaparte and continued until 1848. Napoleon's empress Joséphine was born and spent her childhood on Martinique. The biggest event in the island's history was the eruption of Mont Pelée in 1902, which destroyed the town of Saint-Pierre, killing some 30,000 people.

Nowadays, Martinique is an overseas *département* of France, with a Franco/Caribbean creole culture. As well as tourism, banana farming and rum (or *rhum* in French) production are important aspects of the economy. Rum bottles here carry the Appellation d'Origine Contrôlée designation, more commonly applied to fine wine.

Grand'Rivière
Macouba
D10
Basse-Pointe

Anse Couleuvre
Anse Céron
N1
Le Lorrain

Gorges de la Falaise
L'Ajoupa-Bouillon
Le Marigot

Mont Pelée
4,586 ft (1,398 m)
Fond Saint-Jacques

LE PRÊCHEUR 6

Tombeau
des Caraïbes
Le Morne Rouge

Morne Jacob
2,900 ft (884 m)
D15

Morne-des-Esses

SAINT-PIERRE 1
D1
Fonds-Saint-Denis

Observatoire du
Morne des Cadets
D1

Anse Turin
Pitons du Carbet

Le Morne-Vert

Le Carbet
Piton Lacroix
3,925 ft (1,196 m)

D20
Verrier
Saint-Joseph

Bellefontaine
N3
Cap Enragé
N2
Balata

Case-Pilote

Fond Lahaye
Schoelcher
A1

FORT-DE-FRANCE 2

*Caribbean
Sea*

Baie de
Fort-de-France

Pointe du Bout

Anse à l'Âne
3

Gallochat
TROIS-ÎLETS
AND AROUND
POINTE DU BOUT

Morne Gardier
1,309 ft (399 m)

Les Anses-d'Arlet

Grande-Anse-d'Arlet
D7
Le Diamant

Morne Larcher
1,570 ft (478 m)
Grand
Anse d
Diama

Rocher
du Diamant

MARTINIQUE

Must See
1 Saint-Pierre

Experience More
2 Fort-de-France
3 Trois-Îlets and Around Pointe du Bout
4 Sainte-Marie
5 Caravelle Peninsula
6 Le Prêcheur

MARTINIQUE

4 SAINTE-MARIE

Reserve Naturelle
de la Caravelle

Tartane

Château
Dubuc

La Trinité

5
CARAVELLE
PENINSULA

*Atlantic
Ocean*

Gros-Morne

D1

N1

Îlet Chancel

Le Robert

D1

N1

Le Lamentin

N6

Le François

Îlet Metrente

Îlet Long

Martinique Aimé Césaire
International Airport

Ducos

N5

Saint-Esprit

Montagne du Vauclin
△ *1,653 ft (504 m)*

D5

Petit-Bourg

Le Vauclin

Rivière-Salée

N8

*Pointe
Faula*

La Mauny

Anse Macabou
Macabou

Rivière-Pilote

N8

N6

Le Marin

N5

Sainte-
Luce

N5

△ *Piton Crève-Cœur*
656 ft (200 m)

Pointe Marin

Sainte-Anne

Îlet Chevalier

*Étang des
Salines*

Baie des Anglais

å
Anse Trabaud

*Grande Anse
des Salines*

*Savane des
Pétrifications*

0 kilometers   5

0 miles   5

N
↑

❶

SAINT-PIERRE

🏠 12 miles (20 km) NW of Fort-de-France 🛈 Office Municipal de St. Pierre, Rue Victor-Hugo; 596 783 405

Located in northern Martinique, Saint-Pierre was once a thriving cosmopolitan city. This changed following a volcanic eruption at the start of the 20th century.

Founded in 1635 as the island's first capital, Saint-Pierre was the economic hub of Martinique when it was devastated by the eruption of Mont Pelée in 1902. It was rebuilt, and today is a prosperous and modern urban area, constructed around ruins left by the volcano's fury. The town never recovered its former status, but is a picturesque and tranquil place to visit.

①

Musée Vulcanologique et Historique

🏠 Rue Victor Hugo 📞 596 781 516 🕘 9am–5pm daily

Also known as Le Musée Franck Perret, this small but interesting museum was created by American geologist and volcanologist Franck Perret in the 1930s. It displays relics that he collected from the rubble after the disaster – deformed clocks that stopped at 8am, a melted church bell, and photographs from the region's heyday when the city was known as the Little Paris of the West Indies. Guides are on hand at the site, and there are graphic displays explaining the volcanic development of the Caribbean's islands.

A documentary film about the eruption is shown in both French and English.

---

②

Ruins

🏠 Rue Bouillé

Glimpses of the prosperous original city can still be spotted throughout present-day Saint-Pierre, in the ruins that can be visited around the town.

Église du Fort

The first stone church was built on this site around 1680 and administered by the Jesuits. On the morning of the eruption, the fort was filled with townspeople celebrating Ascension Day and all in attendance died. Now overgrown

> 💬 INSIDER TIP
> **All Aboard**
>
> The best way to get an overview of the city and its volcanic remains is to take the Cyparis Express, a mini-train that travels through the narrow streets, stopping at interesting sights (cyparisexpress.com).

Map:

③ Centre de Découverte des Sciences de la Terre

Distillerie Depaz 1 mile (1.5 km) ④

Centre de Nautique de Saint-Pierre

RUE DE LA REINE
RUE D'ORLÉANS
ALLÉE PÉCOUL
RUE HURTAULT
RUE DU DR DESCHIENS
RUE SCHOELCHER
RUE CASTELNAU
RUE ISAMBERT
RUE DE L'ÉGLISE
② Église du Fort
RUE DES BONS ENFANTS
RUE MACARY
RUE LFVASSOR
RUE PERRINON
La Roxelane
RUE SAVANE DU FORT
RUE DE L'ABBÉ GRÉGOIRE
BOULEVARD LAIGRET
Caribbean Sea
RUE ISAMBERT
② Cachot de Cyparis
RUE DENFER
② Ancien Théâtre
Musée Vulcanologique et Historique ①
VICTOR HUGO
RUE PASSET
RUE BOUILLÉ
BOULEVARD LAIGRET
RUE LONGCHAMP
Plage de St-Pierre
RUE DU PETIT VERSAILLES

0 meters 300 N ↑
0 yards 300

↑ The scenic coast of Saint-Pierre, overlooked by the bulk of Mont Pelée

with vegetation, the church's stone ruins, toppled columns, and blackened foundations remain a haunting reminder of that fateful day. Note the thickness of the overturned walls, which testify to the violence with which the church was struck.

Ancien Théâtre

The staircases leading to the lobby of the Ancien Théâtre still stand as a symbol of the grandeur of the city's 800-seat theater, which was built in 1786 to resemble the performance hall in Bordeaux in France.

↑ A tourist exploring the atmospheric ruins of the Ancien Théâtre

Cachot de Cyparis

Built in 1660, the thick walls of this prison saved inmate August Cyparis, the sole survivor of the volcano. The prison was named for him

Centre de Découverte des Sciences de la Terre

🏠 Habitation Périnelle
🕐 Jul-Aug: 10am-5pm; Sep-Jun: 9am-4pm
🌐 cdst.e-monsite.com

Opened in 2004, the Discovery Center of Earth Sciences is located at the foot of Mont Pelée. Allow around two hours to explore the scientific exhibitions, which include a mineral gallery, a giant aerial photo of Martinique, and a cinema showing films on the Caribbean volcanoes as well as on tsunamis and cyclones.

Distillerie Depaz

🏠 Plantation de la Montagne Pelée 🕐 10am-5pm Mon-Fri, 9am-4pm Sat 🌐 depaz.fr

Located on the northern outskirts of Saint-Pierre, this

> ### MONT PELÉE ERUPTION 1902
>
> A few days before the 1902 eruption, Mont Pelée emitted large clouds of volcanic ash. Although Saint-Pierre's residents had experienced many natural disasters, they ignored these signs of imminent danger. At 8am on May 8, 1902, Mont Pelée erupted, spewing molten ash over the city. All but one of the 30,000 residents were killed. The sole survivor, an inmate of the local jail, was rescued three days later by sailors.

rhum agricole distillery sits in pretty gardens surrounded by sugarcane fields, from where there is an exceptional view of the top of Mont Pelée. A free self-guided tour – with signs in French and English – touches on the estate's history from 1651, the mechanics of distilling, and visits a water-driven crushing wheel and a museum of artifacts from the eruption. Afterwards you can sample and purchase the *rhums*.

EXPERIENCE MORE

Fort-de-France

⬛ West coast of Martinique
✈🚢 ℹ️ 29 rue Victor Hugo
97200; www.tourisme-centre.fr

The capital of Martinique is a lively city with French flair, wrapped in tropical colors. Next to the harbor in Baie des Flamands is the Place de la Savane, full of palm trees and flowers and an ideal starting point for a walking tour.

Fort Saint-Louis occupies a peninsula on the east side of Place de la Savane. The fortress was built in 1638 during the rule of Louis XIII. Part of the fort is still used by the military, and guided tours (in French and English) are available from La Savanne tourist info kiosk across the street. East of Fort Saint-Louis is Fort Desaix (built 1768–1771), now the military headquarters.

On the west side of the park, the **Musée d'Archéologie et de Préhistoire** is set up in a historic building with well-organized relics and exhibits of the island's pre-Columbian inhabitants and its early European colonists.

Among the most impressive artifacts are the ceramics and stone tools used in pre-Columbian times. The museum also has an interesting display of clay figureheads used by the Arawaks for decoration.

Just a short distance from here is the **Cathédrale Saint-Louis**. Built in the late 1800s on the site of six earlier churches and renovated in 1978, it is the masterpiece of Henri Picq, a renowned French architect. The church has a 187-ft (57-m) steeple and stunning stained-glass windows. The town's largest market is located just north of the cathedral on Rue Antoine Siger. Each morning farmers lay out their produce under the building's metal roof as the city wakes up. Products on offer include spices, vanilla, peppers, flavored rums, and an array of fresh produce.

The most outstanding building in Fort-de-France, also designed by Picq, is the **Bibliothèque Schoelcher**, which pays homage to the French abolitionist writer Victor

Schoelcher (p328). The domed library houses more than 130,000 books, many of which were donated by Schoelcher himself. The collection ranges from old texts to crime novels.

North of La Savane is **Musée Régional d'Histoire et d'Ethnographie**. Housed in a Neo-Classical villa, the museum is decorated with mahogany furniture and fine lattice-work and is an interesting recreation of a 19th century bourgeois home.

The striped facade of Bibliothèque Schoelcher in Fort-de-France ↑

EXPERIENCE Martinique

→ Slave memorial by Laurent Valère, near Le Diamant, Anse Cafard

Musée d'Archéologie et de Préhistoire

🏛️ 9 Rue de la Liberté 📞 596 715 705 🕐 9am–4pm daily

Cathédrale Saint-Louis

🏛️ Cnr of Rue Victor Schoelcher and Rue Antoine Siger 📞 596 735 978 🕐 6:15–10:30am & 2:30–5:30pm daily

Bibliothèque Schoelcher

🏛️ 1 Rue de la Liberté 📞 596 556 830 🕐 1–5:30 pm Mon, 8:30am–5:30pm Tue–Thu (to 5pm Fri), 8:30am–noon Sat

Musée Régional d'Histoire et d'Ethnographie

🏛️ 10 Boulevard Général de Gaulle 📞 596 728 187 🕐 8:30am–5pm Mon, Wed–Fri, 2–5pm Tue, 8:30am–12:30pm Sat

 3

Trois-Îlets and Around Pointe du Bout

🏛️ 18 miles (28 km) S of Fort-de-France 🚌 ℹ️ Office du Tourisme des Trois-Îlets, Place Gabriel Hayot, 596 684 763; Marina de la Pointe du Bout, 596 634 879

Martinique's prime tourist district lies just across the water from the capital. Frequent ferries connect Fort-de-France to the marina at Pointe du Bout, on the north shore of a curved peninsula.

In Trois-Îlets, **L'Église Notre Dame de la Bonne Délivrance** (Our Lady of Good Deliverance) dominates the square. This church was where the future Empress Josephine, Napoléon's wife, was baptized in 1763. Now designated a historic monument, the lovely white church is open to visitors who wish to see the baptismal font.

Musée de la Pagerie, in nearby La Pagerie, has mementos of the empress in the old kitchen block of her former home.

On the outskirts of Trois-Îlets is Le Village de la Poterie, home to potters and other craftspeople who sell their wares here. East of the village lies **La Savane des Esclaves**, which offers insight into the history of slavery on Martinique. It features a museum, a reconstructed slave settlement from the 19th century, and a medicinal garden. Farther west is La Maison de la Canne, part of an 18th-century plantation that includes the old Vatable rum distillery.

Heading south, the drive to the town of Le Diamant is one of the most picturesque areas on Martinique. Le Diamant is a charming hamlet of pretty houses with colorful facades. It is also the starting point of the 3-hour hike to Morne Larcher, which is the island's highest point. In 1804, during the Napoleonic wars, the British Navy fortified it with cannons, and registered it as the warship HMS *Diamond Rock*. From this unsinkable ship, the British blockaded Martinique for 17 months, before the French floated barrels of rum to the rock, got the sailors drunk, and captured the stronghold.

L'Église Notre Dame de la Bonne Délivrance

🏛️ Place Centrale de la Commune, Trois-Îlets 🕐 9:15–11:45am daily

Musée de la Pagerie

🏛️ La Pagerie, D7 📞 596 683 834 🕐 9am–4:30pm Tue–Fri, 9:30am–2:30pm Sat 🚫 Sun & public hols

La Savane des Esclaves

🏛️ Quartier La Ferme 🕐 Times vary, check website 🌐 lasavanedesesclaves.fr

---

DRINK

La Zinc du Nord Caraïbes

Evenings at this unpretentious and friendly bar can get loud thanks to the live music and karaoke.

🏛️ 145 Rue Bouille, Saint-Pierre 📞 596 896 029 🚫 Mon

Wahoo Café

Set on the beach with chairs in the sand, this is the perfect spot for sundowners.

🏛️ Plage de Grande Anse 📞 596 746 995

Garage Popular

Always lively, with Creole-style snacks, "car part decor," and plenty of cocktails and beer.

🏛️ 121 Rue Lamartine, Fort-de-France 📞 059 679 8676 🚫 Sun

EAT

Restaurant 1643

Located in one of the oldest Creole houses on the island, this upscale eatery offers an ever-changing menu of meat and seafood éntrees, superbly flavored with French herbs.

◨ Anse Latouche, Le Carbet ◷ Mon & Wed, Sun dinner ⓦ restaurant 1643.com

$$$

Restaurant L'Hibiscus

A dinner-only restaurant, known for its fusion of Creole and French cuisine. Expect beautifully-presented main courses and deliciously gooey desserts to linger over on the sea-facing terrace.

◨ 23 Lotissement Panoramique, Trois-Rivières, Sainte-Luce ☎ 596 625 569 ◷ Tue, Wed & Sun

$$$

Pura Vida

Classic French dishes are given a Caribbean twist at this popular establishment. It's particularly strong on seafood - try the coconut conch stew. The attractive terrace with lounge sofas is the perfect place to sip a couple of cocktails after your meal.

◨ Villa B14, Gros Raisin, Sainte-Luce ◷ Mon ⓦ restaurantpura vida.fr

$$$

↑ Visitors exploring the intriguing Musée du Rhum in Sainte-Marie

❹

Sainte-Marie

◨ 21 miles (34 km) NE of Fort-de-France ⓘ Office Samaritain du Tourisme, Town Hall, Coast Rd; www. sainte marie-martinique.fr

The town of Sainte-Marie, an officially designated Ville Fleurs (Flower Town), is the largest urban area on the Atlantic side of the island, and Martinique's fourth-largest city. Most of the daily activity takes place along the pretty waterfront, which faces Îlet de Sainte-Marie, a scrap of land 1,320 ft (400 m) offshore. This is accessible by foot via a *tombolo* (sandbar) when the tide is low, usually from January through April. The island's hiking club organizes guided walks along the *tombolo* when sea and weather conditions permit. The sandbar is also a popular destination for cyclists and ATV riders. While the rare geological formation is worth seeing, and a highlight of the town, strong ocean currents usually make swimming dangerous in the coves carved into the sediment strip, and hiking on the Îlet can be extremely arduous.

The **Musée du Rhum** is located on the edge of town at Distillerie Saint-James. Set in a colonial house on the former Sainte-Marie Sugar Plantation, the museum holds a fine collection of antique machinery, photographs, documents, and a tasting bar.

The **Habitation Fond Saint-Jacques**, 1 mile (1.5 km) north of town, is one of the best preserved estates on Martinique. Self-guided tours include a visit to the renovated chapel, warehouses, kitchen, and ruins of other buildings where Père Jean-Baptiste Labat developed a rum still and oversaw

the profitable production of the liquor by Dominican priests in the late 1600s.

Musée du Rhum

 Distillerie Saint-James, Le Bourg-Sainte-Marie **C** 596 693 002 **O** 9am–5pm Mon–Sat

Habitation Fond Saint-Jacques

 194 Rue du Pavé, 97230 **O** 10am–4pm Mon–Fri **W** domainedefondsaint jacques.com

---

5

Caravelle Peninsula

A 17 miles (27 km) NE of Fort-de-France **i** Office de Tourisme de Trinité, Centre Commercial le Galion; 596 586 998

Jutting into the Atlantic Ocean off the east coast of Martinique, Caravelle Peninsula, a sheer strip of steep cliffs descending to picturesque beaches, looks almost like an independent islet. The tip of this ragged peninsula is protected within the **Réserve Naturelle de la Caravelle**, which is intersected by several hiking trails. The lighthouse here is the island's oldest working one and has great views over Tartane, a popular beachfront village.

The ruins of **Château Dubuc** lie within the reserve and visitors can explore its grounds and stone relics. Built in about 1770 by the legendary Dubuc de Rivery family, the estate, in the guise of a sugar plantation, was allegedly used for smuggling operations and acquired great wealth from selling slaves and valuables from looted ships.

Réserve Naturelle de la Caravelle

C 596 644 259

Château Dubuc

Caravelle Peninsula **C** 0596 580 900 **O** 9am–4:30pm daily

---

6

Le Prêcheur

A 40 km (25 miles) NW of Fort-de-France **i** Le Syndicat d'Initiative du Prêcheur, Le Bourg; 596 529 145

The coast at the base of Mont Pelée was the first area of the island to be settled during the 17th century, and the villages

> **The tip of this ragged peninsula is protected within the Réserve Naturelle de la Caravelle, which is intersected by several hiking trails.**

of Le Prêcheur and Saint-Pierre became the center of Martinique's thriving sugar and cocoa industries.

Once home to an elite society that included French aristocrats, Le Prêcheur is now a simple fishing village. Just south of town, the coastal road passes steep cliffs known as Tombeau des Caraïbes, where, according to legend, a band of native Kalinagos jumped to their death to avoid being captured or defeated by French settlers in the 1600s.

Distillerie Neisson is one of the last producers to grow its own sugarcane, and connoisseurs claim the rum made from this cane is one of the best in the world.

Distillerie Neisson

Domaine Thieubert **O** 8am–5pm Mon–Fri, 8:30am–noon Sat, 9am–noon Sun **W** neisson.fr

← The Réserve Naturelle de la Caravelle, a protected area on the picturesque peninsula

A DRIVING TOUR
ROUTE DE LA TRACE

Length 24 miles (39 km) **Difficulty** The main road is paved and well maintained. Various tour operators offer guided excursions to the more rugged areas of the national park

A scenic drive through the interior rainforest, Route de la Trace or N3 climbs from Fort-de-France, on the Caribbean coast, to Le Morne Rouge, the highest village on the Martinique at 1,500 ft (457 m). Flanked by lush vegetation, the route follows an old path laid by Jesuit priests in the 1700s. Visitors now drive on the road winding through the mountain range and professional guides lead 4WD excursions off-road and through rugged terrain. Some areas can only be navigated on foot. A popular hiking trail is the Trace des Jésuites, which runs along a ridge above the Route de la Trace and offers sweeping views of Mont Pelée.

Locator Map
For more detail see p340

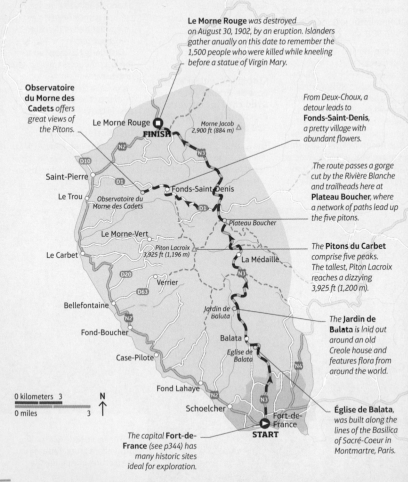

Le Morne Rouge *was destroyed on August 30, 1902, by an eruption. Islanders gather anually on this date to remember the 1,500 people who were killed while kneeling before a statue of Virgin Mary.*

Observatoire du Morne des Cadets *offers great views of the Pitons.*

From Deux-Choux, a detour leads to **Fonds-Saint-Denis**, *a pretty village with abundant flowers.*

The route passes a gorge cut by the Rivière Blanche and trailheads here at **Plateau Boucher**, *where a network of paths lead up the five pitons.*

The **Pitons du Carbet** *comprise five peaks. The tallest, Piton Lacroix, reaches a dizzying 3,925 ft (1,200 m).*

The **Jardin de Balata** *is laid out around an old Creole house and features flora from around the world.*

Église de Balata, *was built along the lines of the Basilica of Sacré-Coeur in Montmartre, Paris.*

The capital **Fort-de-France** *(see p344) has many historic sites ideal for exploration.*

Le Morne Rouge
FINISH

Morne Jacob 2,900 ft (884 m)

Saint-Pierre
Le Trou
Observatoire du Morne des Cadets

Le Morne-Vert

Le Carbet

Piton Lacroix 3,925 ft (1,196 m)

Verrier

Bellefontaine

Fond-Boucher

Case-Pilote

Fonds-Saint-Denis

Plateau Boucher

La Médaille

Jardin de Baluta

Balata

Église de Balata

Fond Lahaye

Schoelcher

Fort-de-France
START

0 kilometers 3
0 miles 3

N ↑

↑ The lush flora and
fauna surrounding the
Pitons du Carbet

PRACTICAL
INFORMATION

Here you will find all the essential advice and information you will need before and during your stay in Martinique.

AT A GLANCE

CURRENCY
Euro (EUR)

TIME ZONE
Atlantic Standard Time, 4 hours behind GMT and 1 hour ahead of EST

LANGUAGE
French is the official language but Creole is also widely spoken

ELECTRICITY SUPPLY
Martinique uses 220 volts AC, 50 cycles. Most places only have French-style outlets

EMERGENCY NUMBERS

AMBULANCE	FIRE SERVICE
15	**18**

POLICE
17

TAP WATER
While tap water in the main towns is safe, it is best to stick to bottled water in rural areas

When To Go

Temperatures vary little from one month to another, but February through June is the driest period, with rain and humidity picking up in July and lingering through to the end of the year. The annual Carnival often begins in January and runs non-stop into late March. Budget travelers and students prefer the summer months, when prices are lower and crowds are lighter, but tropical storms regularly pass over the region and sometimes develop into hurricanes. Following the French tradition, some businesses close for several weeks during August and September.

Getting There

Martinique has a modern international airport, Airport Aimé Césaire in Lamentin. Air services change seasonally, but airline companies, including Delta, Air Canada, and American Airlines, offer flights from North America at least weekly during high season. Air France has direct flights from Paris and Air Caraïbes connects Martinique with several nearby islands. There are no direct flights to Martinique from the UK. The largest ferry companies, with frequent services between Martinique and Guadeloupe, Les Saintes and Marie-Galante, are Express des Îles and Compagnie Maritime West Indies. Martinique's main port is in Fort-de-France and there is a cruise ship terminal within walking distance of the capital.

Personal Security

Crime is relatively rare on Martinique, with crimes against tourists even more uncommon. However, visitors are advised to take precautions, especially against theft from rental cars. Report any crime to the police and request a written report.

Health

Medical facilities are modern and conveniently located throughout the island. The main hospital is Hospital Pierre Zobda Quikman.

Passports and Visas

Citizens of countries other than France must present a valid passport to enter Martinique. Citizens of France may show a passport, an official identity card, or a valid French residence permit. In addition, immigration officials may ask to see a return ticket, proof of sufficient funds for the planned stay, and an address where visitors will be staying on the island.

LGBT+ Safety

France in fact legalized homosexuality in Martinique in 1791, and today the LGBT community is protected by anti-discrimination legislation and same-sex marriage was legalized in 2013. Attitudes towards public displays of affection by all sexes are relaxed in tourist resorts and beaches, but are ill-advised in the mostly conservative Catholic local areas.

Money

The legal currency is the euro, and other currencies are exchanged at banks in the main towns. Bank hours are Monday to Friday, 8am–4pm. Most major credit cards are widely accepted, but may not be welcome at small cafés and shops, especially in rural areas. Most major towns have ATMs.

Cell Phones and Wi-Fi

Orange Caraïbe provides the network on the island. Some hotels have wireless Internet, most large towns have Internet cafes, and Wi-Fi hot spots are scattered around the island. Visitors bringing cell phones should check with their service providers to determine if they will work in Martinique and if they will be subject to roaming charges.

Getting Around

Most large international agencies and many local companies including AVIS, Europcar, and Budget Rent-a-Car hire cars on Martinique. Book well ahead during the high season, when rates are higher. Large hotels may have rental cars on-site. Agencies either have booths or deliver to the airport. It is advisable to have insurance that covers rentals, especially for theft and damage. Check the vehicle for preexisting damage. Taxis are abundant at the airports, cruise ship terminals, and ferry docks. Hotels also arrange taxis for guests. Taxis are equipped with meters and legally add a hefty surcharge to fares 8pm–6am and on Sundays and holidays. If the taxi does not have a working meter, a rate and surcharges should be agreed upon beforehand.

Visitor Information

Tourist information kiosks with maps and brochures are found at the airports and near the ferry docks. The **Office de Tourisme in Fort-de-France** and the **Martinique Tourism Authority** offices provide valuable information. Tourism offices are also found in the US, Canada, and UK. Websites run by the official tourism offices have photographs, maps, details about vacation planning, and links to a large number of tourist-oriented businesses. Much of the information is in French.

Martinique Tourism Authority
W martinique.org
Office de Tourisme in Fort-de-France
W tourisme-centre.fr

DOMINICA

The Caribbean's so-called Nature Island is the most mountainous of the Lesser Antilles. Its peaks reach over 4,600 ft (1,402 m), and tropical forests blanket over two-thirds of the interior. Geologically, the Island is one of the youngest in the Caribbean and volcanic in origin, hence the presence of the world's second largest thermally active lake (The Boiling Lake) and bubbling mud pools. The island's soil is incredibly fertile; coffee, cocoa, bananas, and tropical fruits are grown.

Like many Caribbean islands, Dominica was inhabited by the Caribs when the Europeans arrived. They called the island Waitukubuli – meaning "tall is her body." The island still has a pre-Columbian population, most of whom live in the Kalinago Territory. The French and British tussled over Dominica during the 1600s and 1700s, but from the early 1800s the island remained in British hands until it gained independence in 1978. While English is the official language, many people speak a French-based creole dialect. Following the rapid decline of its once all-important banana trade in the 1990s, Dominica began to turn to eco-tourism. In September 2017, Hurricane Maria hit the island, damaging thousands of homes and stripping the landscape bare. Though natural and man-made regeneration continues, the forests are green again, and most trails and sights are open.

DOMINICA

Must See
① Morne Trois Pitons National Park

Experience More
② Roseau
③ Soufrière
④ Trafalgar Falls
⑤ Emerald Pool
⑥ Cabrits National Park
⑦ Kalinago Territory
⑧ Morne Diablotin National Park

Guadeloupe ↗

Capucin Cape

Car Poi

Pennville

Clifton

Morne aux Diables
2,824 ft (861 m)

Cottage

CABRITS NATIONAL PARK

Douglas Bay

⑥

Fort Shirley

Portsmouth

Indian River

Prince Rupert Bay

Picard

Picard River

Dublanc

Bioche

Colihaut

Batalie Bay

Coulibistri

Salisbury

Macoucherie Rum Factory

Méro

Saint Joseph

Layou

*Caribbean
Sea*

DOMINICA ▣

Martinique ↓

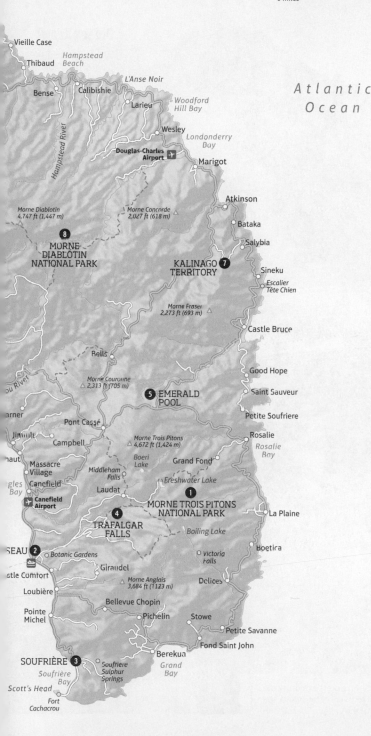

Atlantic
Ocean

Vieille Case
Thibaud
Hampstead
Beach
L'Anse Noir
Bense
Calibishie
Woodford
Hill Bay
Larieu
Hampstead River
Wesley
Douglas-Charles
Airport
Londonderry
Bay
Marigot
Atkinson
Morne Diablotin
4,747 ft (1,447 m)
Morne Concorde
2,027 ft (618 m) △
Bataka
Salybia
8
MORNE
DIABLOTIN
NATIONAL PARK
KALINAGO
TERRITORY
7
Sineku
Escalier
Tête Chien
Morne Fraser
2,273 ft (693 m) △
Castle Bruce
Bells
Good Hope
Morne Couronne
△ *2,313 ft (705 m)*
Saint Sauveur
5 EMERALD
POOL
Petite Soufriere
ou River
Pont Cassé
arner
Morne Trois Pitons
4,672 ft (1,424 m) △
Rosalie
Rosalie
Bay
Jimmit
Campbell
Boeri
Lake
Grand Fond
haut
Massacre
Village
Middleham
Falls
Freshwater Lake
Canefield
gles
Bay
Canefield
Airport
Laudat
1
MORNE TROIS PITONS
NATIONAL PARK
La Plaine
4
TRAFALGAR
FALLS
Boiling Lake
2
SEAU
○ Botanic Gardens
Boetica
stle Comfort
Giraudel
○ *Victoria*
Falls
Loubière
△ *Morne Anglais*
3,684 ft (1123 m)
Delices
Pointe
Michel
Bellevue Chopin
Pichelin
Stowe
Petite Savanne
SOUFRIÈRE **3**
Berekua
Fond Saint John
Soufrière
Sulphur
Springs
Grand
Bay
Soufrière
Bay
Scott's Head
Fort
Cachacrou

Trekkers exploring the sparsely vegetated landscape of the Valley of Desolation ↑

ⓘ ⓧ ⓨ ⓓ

MORNE TROIS PITONS NATIONAL PARK

🏠 8 miles (13 km) E of Roseau 🚌Ⓣ 🄵 Dominica Forestry and Wildlife Division; 767 266 5852/5856

Containing the crown jewels of Dominica's natural treasures, Morne Trois Pitons National Park is justifiably on every visitor's itinerary. Soaring peaks smothered in a tropical canopy create a rugged, luxuriant landscape, cleft with dramatic ravines and crater lakes.

The largest of Dominica's three national parks, Morne Trois Pitons dominates the southern half of the island and contains many of the country's most spectacular geological attractions, including the three-peaked mountain after which it is named, which tops 4,672 ft (1,424 m). But more accessible scenic lakes and waterfalls are also set within this pristine rainforest, with plenty of birdlife, including two rare parrots. The main access point is the mountain village of Laudat.

Active Volcanic Wonders

Volcanic activity is at its most dramatic in the Boiling Lake. The endpoint of a challenging day-trek, this steep-sided cauldron of bubbling grayish-blue water lurks beneath an eerie veil of steam. On the way here, trekkers pass through the equally otherworldly Valley of Desolation, a mass of sulfurous fumaroles, mud pools, and curiously colored streams.

Sparkling Freshwater Features

A less ambitious trek takes in the park's two main bodies of water. Freshwater Lake is Dominica's largest, located 2,500 ft (762 m) above sea level, where kayaks and rowing boats can be rented. More atmospheric, Boeri Lake is usually brooding beneath mist, though it sparkles in the sunlight. Titou Gorge is also worth seeking out. Formed by solidified lava formations and fed by a waterfall, it makes for an unusual and bracing swim. Northeast of Laudat, lie the impressive Middleham Falls.

> 💬 INSIDER TIP
> ## Time Your Tickets
>
> It's cheaper to buy a weekly national park pass ($12) rather than to pay entry fees for Dominica's individual attractions ($5).

① One of the wettest parts of the island, often covered in cloud, Freshwater Lake affords great views of the surrounding peaks when clear.

② Another park highlight is the spectacular Emerald Pool, where waters plunge from the 50 ft (15 m) falls and provide a refreshing dip after trekking.

③ The world's second largest hot lake, Boiling Lake ranges from 180-197° F (82-91° C). The lake sits inside a deep basin, always covered in steam, with its center emitting hot gases.

EXPERIENCE MORE

2

Roseau

⚑ 36 miles (58 km) SW of Douglas-Charles Airport ⬛⬛⬛ 🛈 Marpin House, 5-7 Great Marlborough St; 767 448 2045

The capital of Dominica, Roseau, is a busy, colorful, and noisy town during the day and very quiet at night. The town is small enough to be explored on foot.

The oldest part of town is around Old Market Square, formerly the original slave market, and has several interesting old buildings and many specialty craft stores. Also near the Old Market Square is the Dominica Museum, which has a small collection of artifacts tracing the island's history. The newer part, along the southern banks of the Roseau River, has offices, shops, and bazaars where goods of all kinds spill out onto the sidewalks. The New Market on Bay Front is best visited early in the morning, when it is at its busiest and liveliest.

Also worth visiting is the **Roman Catholic Cathedral of Our Lady of Fair Haven**, built of volcanic stones gathered from the banks of the river. Its construction started in 1841, but the building was not completed until 1916, when the west steeple was added. The cathedral has been undergoing renovation work and is closed to the public. The **Botanic Gardens**, on the site of an old sugar plantation, cover 1,742,400 sq ft (161,850 sq m), and comprise the largest open space in the city.

Roman Catholic Cathedral of Our Lady of Fair Haven

⚑ Virgin Lane ⏰ Dawn to dusk

Botanic Gardens

⌖ ⚑ Bath Rd, Morne Bruce ⏰ 6am–7pm daily 🌐 dominicagardens.com

Did You Know?

Champagne Reef in Soufrière is named for the bubbles that pour from the rocks due to geothermal activity.

TOP 4 **DOMINICAN DIVING SITES**

Champagne Reef
⚑ Scott's Head Marine Reserve
A great spot for novices.

Scott's Head Pinnacle
⚑ Scott's Head Marine Reserve
This spectacular site features a "Swiss cheese" rock formation.

Point Break
⚑ Capucin Cape
Atlantic and Caribbean currents meet here; for seasoned divers only.

Five Finger Rock
⚑ Cabrits Marine Park
A fist-like boulder, known for beautiful spotted eagle rays.

3

Soufrière

⚑ 7 miles (11 km) S of Roseau ⬛

Soufrière is a small village noted for its palm-fringed

beach, fishing boats, and waterside church with its murals of village life. It was named by early French settlers for the sulfur that belches out from the ground nearby. Visitors can walk up to the sulphur springs and hot pools along the Soufrière river valley through huge stands of towering bamboo.

Heading south from the village, the land arches round a picturesque bay to the island's southwestern tip, the Scott's Head (also known as Cacharou) Peninsula. The bay itself comprises the Soufrière Scotts Head Marine Reserve, one of the Caribbean's premier diving destinations. The reserve contains coral-encrusted pinnacles, an impressive drop-off, and the renowned Champagne Reef – all teeming with colorful and curious sealife.

↑ Bright green waters and surrounding vegetation of the Emerald Pool

Trafalgar Falls

🏠 5 miles (8 km) E of Roseau
🚌 🕐 🗓 Daily

Trafalgar Falls are the easiest to reach of the island's many water falls. Visitors should still be careful, since the rocks can sometimes be slippery. There are two falls cascading down a gorge into pools littered with huge black rocks and surrounded by lush vegetation. The larger of the falls, on the left, is known as "father" and the other as "mother." Left of "father" there is a hot pool to relax in.

Close to the falls is the **Papillote Wilderness Retreat and Nature Sanctuary**. This small eco-resort is set in magnificent tropical gardens with many rare orchids, and has its own mineral pools, natural hot springs, and waterfalls.

←
A diver exploring the stunning coral reefs off the shore of Soufrière

The resort was destroyed by Hurricane Maria in 2017, but is being rebuilt.

Papillote Wilderness Retreat and Nature Sanctuary
🕐 🗓 🗺 🏠 Trafalgar Falls Rd, Roseau 📞 767 295 9564
🗓 Daily

Emerald Pool

🏠 8 miles (13 km) NE of Roseau 🚌

Located midway between Canefield and Castle Bruce, Emerald Pool is one of the most visited sites on the island. It is a short walk through montane rainforest about 3 miles (5 km) northeast from Pont Cassé. The pool is a grotto with its own waterfall and surrounded by tropical plants, flowers, and ferns. The thick canopy prevents too many ground-hugging plants from flourishing. The rich birdlife includes jaco parrots, hummingbirds, and the elusive mountain warbler. A section of the trail is paved with rock slabs laid by the Kalinagos centuries ago. The pool gets crowded at times and a morning visit is best.

HIKING IN DOMINICA

The best way to see Dominica is on foot, along one of the many hiking trails. In fact, hiking is the only way to reach some of the island's hidden treasures - emerald pools, cascading waterfalls, and bubbling lakes. The island's best trails are found in the magnificent Morne Trois Pitons National Park *(see p383)*. Hikes range from the less strenuous routes to the spectacular Trafalgar Falls to the more arduous climbs to Boiling Lake. Some require an experienced guide's assistance and a local guide will ensure that hikers get much more out of their trip.

On the opposite page you will find some of the best hiking routes in Dominica. Many of the hiking trails are designated easy, which means they are of short duration and can be tackled by most people. Moderate level walks take longer to hike and involve more difficult terrain that may require some scrambling. Difficult level are strenuous but exhilarating hikes for experienced hikers.

Did You Know?

In July 2007, George Kourounis became the first person to cross Boiling Lake from above, suspended by ropes.

Group of hikers among the
fumaroles and hot springs
of Desolation Valley ↑

1 Hiker scaling the boulders at Trafalgar Falls

2 Swimming in the pool at the base of Middleham Falls

3 Hikers and a guide on the trail to Boiling Lake

HIKING TRAILS IN DOMINICA

EASY LEVEL

Trails to Emerald Pool and Trafalgar Falls can be very busy on days when cruise ships are in port. The earlier visitors set out on a hike, the greater are their chances of spotting wildlife.

Emerald Pool is a well-signposted, family-friendly 15-minute hike which allows visitors to explore the lush vegetation of the tropical rainforest and wildlife on the way to the pool. Those who bring swimwear can also take a dip in the very cool water.

Trafalgar Falls is one of Dominica's most popular natural attractions. The twin falls are only a short hike from the visitors' center just outside Trafalgar. Hikers can swim in the pool below the smaller waterfall to cool off.

Titou Gorge can be reached by a short hike which passes through a series of pools, surrounded by solidified lava formations and tree canopy. A hot spring outside the entrance is ideal for a dip.

MODERATE LEVEL

It is best to begin the Middleham Falls hike from Laudat. The initial hike is a little steep, but the path levels out before descending to the falls.

Middleham Falls is one of Dominica's highest waterfalls, it takes about 1 hour to hike through the beautiful rainforest to reach these high-altitude falls. The forest is home to numerous bird species including the Sisserou Parrot.

DIFFICULT LEVEL

It takes at least 6 hours for the round-trip to Boiling Lake and the Valley of Desolation, and about the same time to scramble up to the summit of Morne Diablotin and back.

Boiling Lake is the world's second-largest actively boiling lake and is enveloped in a vaporous cloud.

Syndicate starts at the Syndicate Visitors' Center and passes through spectacular scenery. It takes 2 hours and follows the gorge of the Picard River, which runs into the sea at Portsmouth.

Cabrits National Park

Established in 1986, Cabrits National Park covers over 2 sq miles (5.5 sq km) of upland and 1.5 sq miles (4.5 sq km) of the surrounding underwater park, Cabrits Marine Reserve. The site contains the ruins of the 18th-century Fort Shirley – often considered Dominica's most important historic site – the volcanic peaks of East and

West Cabrits, tropical forest, the largest swamp on the island, sandy beaches, and coral reefs just offshore to the north. *Cabri* is a French word for "young goat." The place was so-named because French sailors would leave goats on the peninsula so that they would have fresh meat when they returned.

Fort Shirley and the garrison were largely built by the British, but the French added to it during their years of occupation (1778–84). Altogether there were more

than 50 major buildings, although many of them were covered by vegetation after the fort was abandoned in 1854. At its height, the fort had seven gun batteries. Today, cruise ships dock at the pier in Prince Rupert's Bay to visit the park. There are fabulous views from Fort Shirley across the bay and inland to the mountains.

Kalinago Territory

Kalinago Territory occupies 6 sq miles (15 sq km) of the island with an extensive coastline and agricultural land behind. The U.K. gave the land back to the descendants of the island's original inhabitants in 1903. Today, the Kalinagos engage mostly in agriculture and fishing, still making their canoes by hand. They are also expert potters and weavers, using traditional methods that have been passed down for centuries to create baskets so tightly woven that they are watertight. Traditional music, dance, and

---

KALINAGOS AND MAROONS ON DOMINICA

Indigenous to South America, the Kalinagos (Caribs) are said to have been fierce people. They began to migrate north to the islands in about AD 1000, ousting the Taínos and Arawaks, who had arrived 1,000 years earlier. Their war canoes, holding more than 100 men, were fast enough to catch a sailing ship. The Kalinagos built villages and cleared land to farm. About 3,000 Kalinagos, direct descendants of those early settlers, still live on Dominica, which they call Waitukubuli, meaning "tall is her body." In the late 18th century, Dominica became the home for large numbers of Africans who had escaped slavery in the surrounding islands. They took refuge in the mountainous terrain and were known as Maroons, and fought a guerrilla war against the British troops until they were defeated in 1814. After Emancipation in 1848, however, the island again became a refuge for Africans escaping from the nearby French islands, where slavery was still practiced.

A visitor photographing the overgrown ruins at Fort Shirley, Cabrits National Park

herbal medicine are still practiced here. There are more than 16 arts and crafts shops in the territory selling various handicrafts made by the locals. Experience the heritage of Dominica's indigenous people at the Kalinago cultural village – Kalinago Barana Aute. This is a full-scale reproduction of a Carib village, with traditional thatched buildings by Crayfish River. Guided tours of the site are available from mid-October through April.

Morne Diablotin National Park

⌂ 14 miles (23 km) N of Roseau

The Morne Diablotin National Park is the island's third national park, having been formally established in early 2000. It is home to the "Little Devil" Mountain, Dominica's highest peak at 4,747 ft (1,447 m) and covers 34 sq miles (88 sq km) of oceanic rainforest, including the area known as Syndicate, which is home to the Jaco and rare Sisserou parrot. Both species are endemic only to Dominica, and their protection was a key factor in the inauguration of the park. Morne Diablotin is not named for the devil but for the devilish call of the black-capped petrel that used to breed on the higher slopes of the mountain. The park is part of the vast Northern Forest Reserve and teems with birdlife and hundreds of species of towering trees, plants, and exotic flowers.

Visitors need to allow themselves 6–7 hours to climb the mountain, have a picnic lunch at the top, and descend after that. The trail starts at a height of about 1,700 ft (518 m) and becomes progressively steeper, and can be wet in places. The Syndicate Nature Trail, on the edge of the park, is much easier and ideal for the less adventurous. It takes about 30 minutes, but it is best to allow for more time in order to fully enjoy everything there is to see along the way.

A short distance away, the trail runs through a section of forest that contains most of the avian species to be found on the island. There are three stunning lookout points along the trail.

↑ A Sisserou parrot, a rare bird found within Morne Diablotin National Park

EAT

Old Stone Grill
Located inside a rustic stone house, head here for tasty and affordable Caribbean cuisine.

⌂ 15 Castle St, Roseau
☎ 767 440 7549 ⏰ Mon & Sat lunch; Sun

$⑤$⑤$

Pearl's Cuisine
A long-running local favorite that dishes up delicious, authentic Caribbean fare.

⌂ Sutton Place Hotel, 25 Old St, Roseau
☎ 767 448 8707 ⏰ Sun

$⑤$⑤$

Riverside Café
Meals at this popular lunch spot are served on the delightfully shady verandah.

⌂ Citrus Creek Plantation, La Plaine
⏰ 10am–5pm daily; dinner by appt
🌐 citruscreekplantation. com/restaurant

$⑤$⑤$

↑ Kalinago Barana Aute, a traditional cultural village within Kalinago Territory

PRACTICAL
INFORMATION

Here you will find all the essential advice and information you will need before and during your stay in Dominica.

AT A GLANCE

CURRENCY
Eastern Caribbean dollar (EC$)

TIME ZONE
Atlantic Standard Time, 4 hours behind GMT and 1 hour ahead of EST

LANGUAGE
English is the official language, although many people speak Kweyol, a dialect that is based on French, as well as African and indigenous Kalinago languages

ELECTRICITY SUPPLY
Dominica operates on 220-240 volts and US visitors need to carry adaptors and transformers for their appliances

EMERGENCY NUMBERS
AMBULANCE, POLICE, AND FIRE

999

TAP WATER
Water purity is unreliable so, to be safe, drink bottled water

When To Go

The best time to visit the island is between January and June when it is generally dry. The rainy season is between August and October, when hurricanes can occur.

Getting There

There are no direct international flights from North America or Europe to Dominica. Airlines fly into Puerto Rico, Antigua, Sint Maarten, Saint Lucia, Barbados, Martinique, and Guadeloupe. From these islands there are connecting flights on Air Antilles, LIAT and Seaborne Airlines to the Douglas-Charles Airport. While Canefield is 15 minutes from Roseau, Douglas-Charles is a 90-minute drive from the capital. There is a highspeed catamaran ferry service between Dominica and Saint Lucia, Guadeloupe, and Martinique, and cruise ships regularly dock at the island. The main ferry operator is L'Express des Îles. Check the timetables before traveling.

Personal Security

Dominica has a low crime rate but it is better not to wear expensive jewelry or carry large sums of money. It is also sensible not to leave valuables unattended on the beach or in view in parked rental cars.

Health

Dominica has three major hospitals, Portsmouth Hospital and Princess Margaret Hospital in Roseau, both of which have intensive care units, and the smaller Marigot Hospital which is being rebuilt. Princess Margaret Hospital has the island's only hyperbaric chamber. Visitors should have adequate personal insurance and medical cover. Most big hotels also have a doctor on call in case of minor medical emergencies.

Passports and Visas

Visitors are required to show a valid passport on arrival in Dominica to immigration officials. They

need to show a return ticket and have to pay a departure tax when leaving. Visitors from North America and Europe do not require a visa. Customs officers may ask visitors to open their luggage for a quick inspection. It is a good idea to carry a copy of proof of ownership, such as receipts for expensive items.

LGBT+ Safety

Both male and female same-sex sexual activity is illegal in Dominica, and, unlike in most Caribbean islands where it is illegal only in the law books, men and women have been arrested, tried and given fines and sometimes lengthy jail sentences. In 2011, the government signed a US-backed UN statement calling for an end to violence and other human rights abuses "based on sexual orientation and gender identity," which is a sign that officially progress is being made. Evangelical leaders have opposed the arrival of gay tourists to the island so LGBT+ visitors should be careful about straying from recommended areas and activities.

Money

The local currency is the Eastern Caribbean dollar. However, most places on the island accept US dollars, pounds Sterling and euros. All major credit cards are widely accepted, although some restaurants take only cash, so check in advance. Banks are open from 8am to 2pm from Monday to Thursday and 8am to 4pm on Fridays.

Cell Phones and Wi-Fi

The island's area code is 767. To call from and to the US, dial 1 and then the number. For calls to the UK, dial 011 44 and then the number (omitting the first 0). For phone services, contact FLOW. Visitors bringing cell phones should check with their service providers to determine if they will work in Dominica and if they will be subject to roaming charges.

Getting Around

The best way to explore the island is to hire a car and there are several rental agencies such as Valley Car Rental and Best Deal Rent-a-Car.

Most rentals are based in the capital, Roseau. Visitors need to buy a month's valid license and have to be over 25 years of age. Most of the roads are paved and much of the island is now accessible by car even if the last leg of the journey may have to be made on foot – for example, to the start of a hiking trail or to a deserted beach. Heavy rains can cause sudden landslides so watch out for potholes. If lost, it is best to ask one of the locals for directions.

Public buses can be flagged down on the road and ply dawn to dusk. Taxis are also vailable from the airports and Roseau but are usually expensive.

Visitor Information

Discover Dominica Authority in Roseau helps visitors find their way around the island. It guides them on where to stay, activities, and more. There are overseas offices in the US, UK, Germany, and France. **A Virtual Dominica** also has a comprehensive tourist information site.
A Virtual Dominica
w avirtualdominica.com
Discover Dominica Authority
w discoverdominica.com

Soufriére Bay at twlight, overlooking Petit Piton

SAINT LUCIA

Saint Lucia has been called the Helen of the West Indies. For like Helen of Troy from Greek mythology, it has a peerless beauty and has been fought over with great passion. From the mid-1600s to early 1800s, the island changed hands between the French and British 14 times. The British eventually won, and controlled Saint Lucia until independence was granted in 1979. However, the Gallic influence is still very strong. Places bear French names and while the official language is English, a French creole dialect, kweyol, is widely spoken. Sugar cane and more recently bananas were the backbones of Saint Lucia's economy, but tourism is now the main source of income.

From a visitor's perspective, Saint Lucia comes in two halves. Much of the south is mountainous wilderness coated in rainforest. Near the languid town of Soufrière in the southwest you'll find the towering green fangs that are the Pitons, Sulphur Springs Park, which is billed as the world's only drive-in volcano; and historic plantation estates growing cocoa and citrus fruits, several of which have been turned into memorable hotels. The beaches in the southwest are mostly of volcanic dark sand; superb snorkeling and diving awaits just offshore. The more developed north has beaches of golden sand, and encompasses the bustling capital Castries, along with Rodney Bay Village, the island's only resort area. At nearby Pigeon Island, you can learn all about Saint Lucia's military colonial history.

SAINT LUCIA

Must Sees

1 Pigeon Island National Landmark
2 The Pitons

Experience More

3 Soufrière
4 Marigot Bay Resort & Marina
5 Choc Bay
6 Gros Islet
7 Rodney Bay
8 Castries
9 Vieux Fort and East Coast

*Caribbean
Sea*

Marigot Ba

Massacré

Anse la Raye

Canaries

Canaries Rive

*Anse la
Liberté*

Belvedere

Bouton

*Anse
Couchon*

SOUFRIÈRE

*Soufrière
Estate*

3

*Soufrière
Bay*

*Soufrière
Volcanic Are*

Pitot Falls

PETIT PITON 2

*Anse des
Pitons*

*Fond Doux
Plantation
and Resort*

GROS PITON 2

Fond Gens Libre

*Choiseul
Bay*

Choiseul

River
Dorée

SAINT LUCIA ☐

↑ *Martinique*

PIGEON ISLAND
NATIONAL LANDMARK ❶
Cap
Estate
Cas-en-Bas

Plantation Beach

GROS ISLET ❻
RODNEY BAY ❼

△ *Mount de Feu*
823 ft (144 m)

A t l a n t i c
O c e a n

Monchy

Labrelotte Bay

Corinth

△ *Mount Gaiac*
472 ft (251 m)

CHOC BAY ❺

Grande
Rivière

Marquis Bay

Vigie Bay

Malabar
Beach
La Toc
Bay

George F.L.
Charles Airport

Paix Bouche

Grande
Anse

CASTRIES ❽

Babonneau

Desbarras

The Pink
Plantation House

Monkey
Town

Incommode

Forestierre

MARIGOT BAY RESORT
AND MARINA ❷

Bexon

Marc

Derniere Riviere

acmel

L'Abbayee

La
Belle Vie

Ravine Poisson

△ *Mount La Combe*
1,442 ft (439 m)

Dennery

Dennery
Island

Millet

△ *Morne Gimie*
3,118 ft (950 m)

Praslin

Praslin Bay

Mamiku Gardens

Mon Repos

Patience

Anse
Patience

Fond
St. Jacques

△ *Mount Grand Magazin*
2,031 ft (619 m)

Latille
Gardens

Escape

Fond
Bay

Micoud

Blanchard

❾ EAST COAST

Desruisseaux

Fargue

Grace

Savannes

Hellene

Savannes
Bay

lenbouche
tate

Laborie

Laborie
Bay

Mankote
Mangrove

Hewanorra
International Airport ✈

Pointe Sable

VIEUX FORT ❾

Maria Islands

Barre de l'Isle Ridge

Dennery River

Mamiku River

Troumassee River

Anse la Riche River

0 kilometers   5

0 miles   5

N
↑

❶ 🏃 🏍 🍴 🍽 🛍

PIGEON ISLAND NATIONAL LANDMARK

🏠 8 miles (13 km) N of Castries 📞 758 452 5005 🚌🚌 🕐 9am–6pm daily
ℹ️ Interpretive Center, near the entrance gate

With remnants of military barracks and encampments, Pigeon Island is a fascinating historical landmark. Despite its rocky coastline, a number of excellent, white-sand beaches around the island provide good swimming opportunities.

↑ Ruins of the barracks scattered around the eastern side of the island

Covering an area of 44 acres (18 ha), the Pigeon Island National Landmark was first fortified by the French in 1778, who were ousted the following year by a British naval force. It was from here that English Admiral Rodney attacked the French fleet in 1782. The ensuing Battle of Saintes ended French domination in the Caribbean. Pigeon Island remained one of the most formidable forts for decades but was abandoned in 1861. Since then it has been a whaling station and served as a U.S. Naval Air Station during World War II. In 1972 the island was joined to the mainland by a man-made causeway built from dirt excavated to form the Rodney Bay Marina.

↑ Pigeon Island National Landmark jutting out into the sea

Covering an area of 44 acres (18 ha), the Pigeon Island National Landmark is connected to the mainland by a causeway.

↑ The Interpretive Center and museum, which displays items of historical interest

SAINT LUCIA JAZZ & ARTS FESTIVAL

From humble beginnings in 1991, the Saint Lucia Jazz & Arts Festival has grown into the Caribbean's most successful jazz festival. For many years the program included more R&B, soul, and pop, attracting international superstars such as Diana Ross, UB40, and even Rihanna. More recently, the event has returned to its jazz roots, showcasing overseas stars alongside local and regional talent. The annual weeklong musical extravaganza takes place in May, with Pigeon Point National Landmark the main venue, but with events sprinkled across the island, accompanied by plenty of partying.

THE PITONS

⌂ 20 miles (32 km) S of Castries 🚌

Saint Lucia's most iconic landmark, the twin sugarloaf peaks of the Pitons rise majestically from the sea on the southwest coast. A challenging but rewarding climb, the Caribbean's most photographed rocks can be admired more easily from a handful of viewpoints across the island, or from a boat bobbing in the bay.

Located south of Soufrière, the towering Pitons are omnipresent in Saint Lucia, featuring on the country's flag, as well as giving their name to the local beer. Dramatic remnants of volcanic lava domes that formed between 200–300 thousand years ago, they were revered as Gods by the indigenous Arawaks. Later they provided hideouts for escaped plantation slaves in the "Brigand Wars." Petit Piton, the more northerly peak, is 2,437 ft (743 m) high, while Gros Piton reaches 2,529 ft (771 m) and has a much larger base. From various angles, they appear side by side, whereas they are actually almost 3 miles (5 km) apart, connected by a volcanic ridge fronted by dazzling (imported) white-sand beaches that shelve into the coral-rich sea.

HIDDEN GEM
Piton Falls

These beautiful waterfalls are on the way to Petit Piton along the Jalousie Plantation road. The cascading warm water makes for a refreshing shower and the two pools are ideal for bathing.

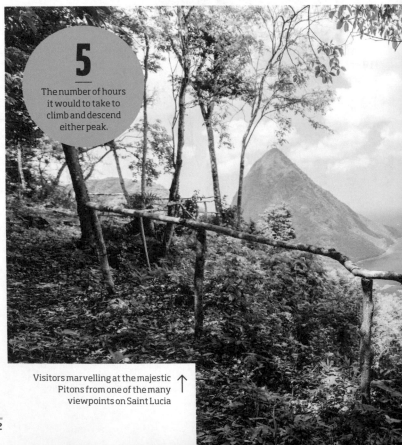

5

The number of hours it would to take to climb and descend either peak.

Visitors marvelling at the majestic Pitons from one of the many viewpoints on Saint Lucia ↑

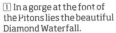

1 In a gorge at the foot of the Pitons lies the beautiful Diamond Waterfall.

2 Idyllic secluded beaches wait to be explored at the base of Gros Piton.

3 A spectacular panoramic vista of the Pitons across the Soufrière Valley can be seen from the road to Castries.

EXPLORING THE PEAKS

If you're planning on climbing and trekking both peaks, guides are necessary and available from the community tour guide association in Fond Gens Libre, at the base of Gros Piton, or can be organized in advance through a tour operator. From the interpretive center in Fond Gens Libre, the first half of the two-hour Gros Piton Nature Trail is a steady ascent, before becoming a steep incline with many tricky steps cut into the rock. Several resting places punctuate the climb. Wear sturdy shoes, come armed with water and snacks in a day sack, and make an early start for cooler temperatures and a likely cloudless sky at the summit.

EXPERIENCE MORE

3

Soufrière

📍 15 miles (24 km) S of Castries 🚌🚐

Saint Lucia's first settlement and former capital during French rule, Soufrière is now a charming fishing town. During the French Revolution, the Revolutionary Council ordered that all French names must be changed, so Soufrière briefly became La Covention.

The town, which has a beach fringed with coconut palms, is divided into two by the Soufrière River. Most of the shops, restaurants, craft centers, and guesthouses are located in the few streets inland from the jetty. Traditional Creole homes with their ornate filigree friezes and elaborate balconies stand out, and the market is decorated with colorful murals.

According to local history, Malmaison, situated on the outskirts of town, is where Napoléon Bonaparte's wife Joséphine spent her childhood. Other estates in the area include the Diamond Estate, famous for its gardens and therapeutic mineral baths, and visitors can see coconuts, copra and cocoa being processed at the Morne Coubaril Estate.

The Soufrière Volcanic Area is located just south of town. There is a giant crater, formed during an eruption 40,000 years ago, as well as 24 cauldrons of bubbling mud that boil at around 340° F (171° C) within the 304,900 sq ft (28,350 sq m) site. It is advisable to keep to the marked paths; guides can be booked at the entrance.

STAY

Coco Palm Resort

These gabled blocks contain spacious, well-appointed rooms; bag one on the ground floor and step straight from the patio to the pool.

📍 Rodney Bay Blvd
🌐 coco-resorts.com

⑤⑤⑤

Ladera

Set high above the sea, this unusual luxury resort's open-sided rooms make the most of the jaw-dropping views.

📍 Rabot Estate, Soufrière 🌐 ladera.com

⑤⑤⑤

Anse Chastanet

A romantic resort nestled into the hillside, with an on-site spa and easy beach access.

📍 Old French Rd
🌐 ansechastanet.com

⑤⑤⑤

4

Marigot Bay Resort & Marina

📍 Marigot Bay 📞 758 458 5300 🌐 marigotbayresort.com

Marigot Bay is about 7 miles (11 km) south of Castries. Surrounded by lush foliage-covered hills, it is considered among the most beautiful anchorages in the Caribbean and has been the setting for several movies, including the original *Dr. Dolittle* (1967) and *Firepower* (1979). The busy marina here is full of local craftsmen at work.

Marigot Bay Resort & Marina is a luxury resort with accommodations nestled in the hillside overlooking the bay. Some of the suites have private plunge pools and most units offer fabulous views of the palm-fringed cove. There are excellent restaurants and a spa on-site, all of which are open to non-guests, too.

Fishing Boats on the shore at Soufrière ↑

5

Choc Bay

📍 3 miles (5 km) N of Castries 🚌

Choc Bay, a popular tourist area, boasts a tree-lined stretch of sand with gentle waves lapping the shore.

Inland from the bay, Union Trail is a self guided nature walk. It is an easy looped walk through the rainforest, where the rare multi-hued Saint Lucia parrot can be spotted.

Nearby, **Fond Latisab Creole Park**, in the Fond Assau community, is part of Saint Lucia's Heritage Tourism Program. It offers a glimpse of the Creole traditions of preparing cassava bread, cooking on macambou leaves, catching crayfish, and log-sawing to the rhythms of a traditional *chak chak* (musical instrument) band.

Fond Latisab Creole Park
🐾 🏠 Babonneau 📞 758 450 5461 🕐 9am–4pm daily

CHOCOLATE IN SAINT LUCIA

Artisanal chocolate is on the up in the Caribbean, and Saint Lucia is no exception, with a local industry focused on controlling the whole process, from bean to bar. The rich volcanic soil, high altitude and rainforest water combines to create the ideal environment for cocoa production. Topping the list is global brand Hotel Chocolat (www.hotelchocolat.com), which owns the 140-acre Rabot Estate and a fabulous restaurant with a cacao-infused menu. Anse Chastanet (www.ansechastanet.com) produces Emerald Estate chocolate and boasts a chocolate laboratory. Both offer tours with tastings, and sell their products on site.

FRESH COCOA BEANS

A buzzing street in Gros Islet during the village's weekly Friday "Jump Up"

the busy harbor. It has suffered four major fires over the last 200 years, but the last one enabled the planners to rebuild the city on a grid, making it very easy to explore. The colorful market on Peynier Street is full of interesting local produce that can be explained by a market guide, available for a small tip at the entrance.

Built in 1899, the **Roman Catholic Cathedral of the Immaculate Conception** contains many paintings with biblical scenes in which all the characters are black. The cathedral is located on the eastern side of Derek Walcott Square, named for the island's 1992 Nobel Laureate for Literature. A hill to the south of town, the Morne, offers a breathtaking aerial view of Castries. Given its strategic position, the French built Fort Charlotte near its summit in the late 18th century, which was later added to by the British.

Gros Islet

📍 8 miles (13 km) N of Castries 🚌

Across Rodney Bay is Gros Islet, a small fishing village and home to the famous Friday night "Jump Up." This huge open-air party fills the streets and lasts until the early hours of the morning. Tables and chairs are placed outside and loud music booms from huge speakers, as revelers move from one bar to the next, drinking beer and dancing the night away. It is also a great place to try local specialties from the many street vendors.

Rodney Bay

📍 6 miles (10 km) N of Castries 🚌

One of the most popular yachting destinations in the Caribbean, Rodney Bay has a beautifully landscaped marina with restaurants, bars, shops, and galleries. It is also one of the leading charter centers in the Caribbean. Visit during the day to browse the shops and enjoy a waterside lunch, or at night, when its nightlife venues grow lively.

Castries

📍 NW coast of Saint Lucia
✈🚌🚢 🛈 Pointe Seraphine; 758 452 3036

Castries is a bustling little city of gingerbread houses that hug the hillsides surrounding

The area is now a protected historic sight and has many restored military buildings.

Roman Catholic Cathedral of the Immaculate Conception

📍 Laborie St 📞 758 452 2271
🕐 8am–4pm daily

Vieux Fort and East Coast

📍 25 miles (40 km) S of Castries 🚗🚌

Vieux Fort is close to the southern tip of the island and commands fine views across to St. Vincent. Once the island's capital and main harbor, and named after a fort built here in the 17th century, Vieux Fort is now the island's windsurfing center. On its outskirts, the **Mankote Mangrove** is a favorite spot with bird-watchers.

Farther north along the eastern coast is Savannes Bay, known for its bird reserve. While the west coast is sheltered, the rocky east coast is often battered by Atlantic breakers, making it popular with surfers. Farther ahead from Micoud are the **Latille Gardens**, which present a blaze of tropical color, exotic fruits, and waterfalls.

Dennery, farther north, is one of the island's prettiest villages and has a long history of fishing and boatbuilding.

Some of the boats are still constructed by hand from trees felled in the rainforest.

Mankote Mangrove
🐦 📞 758 454 5014
🕐 Dawn to dusk daily

Latille Gardens
🌿🐦 📞 758 489 6271

> Once the island's capital and main harbor, and named after a fort built here in the 17th century, Vieux Fort is now the island's windsurfing center.

 ←
Vendors and shoppers flocking to the bustling local market in downtown Castries

SAINT LUCIA'S PLANTATIONS

French settlers established Saint Lucia's first plantations in the mid 18th century along the fertile southwest coast. Cotton was the main crop, though cacao and coffee also featured. But by 1765, sugar had arrived and by 1815 it had taken over. The commercial success of the sugar estates was due to African slave labor, a colonial legacy that has had a lasting impact on Saint Lucia and the Caribbean as a whole.

PLANTATION LIFE

For the European plantocracy, life was privileged, but for the slaves it was brutal. Inadequately housed and fed, they endured long days of back-breaking work and were frequently flogged or even executed. Unsurprisingly, many slaves rebelled. Following the French Revolution, slaves in Saint Lucia were freed by Republicans. Sensing a threat to their freedom in a British take-over, they formed freedom-fighting groups and attacked plantations.

AFTER EMANCIPATION

Slavery was abolished on Saint Lucia in 1834 and 14,000 slaves were freed, though they were made to serve a four-year "apprenticeship" before fully gaining their liberty. The end of slave labor, and the rise of sugar beet production in Europe spelled the beginning of the end for sugar cane, although it remained Saint Lucia's main export until the mid-20th century.

PLANTATIONS TODAY

From bijou restaurants to boutique hotels, chic eco-resorts and organic farms to adventure parks, Saint Lucia's plantations have left their dark histories behind and embraced tourism. They tend to play down the brutality of slavery and focus instead on crafts, skills, and produce (such as cacao) or on their stunning natural surroundings.

→
A worker grinding the cacao beans using his feet at a plantation in Soufrière

↑
Ruins of the old sugar mill on the Balenbouche Estate

PLANTATION ESTATES

Diamond Falls Botanical Gardens and Mineral Baths (Soufrière Estate)
Part of the Soufrière Estate – one of the island's oldest plantations – was transformed into delightful botanical gardens. Crammed full of colorful tropical plants frequented by hummingbirds, they also contain a small waterfall and hot mineral baths to soak in (diamondstlucia.com).

Balenbouche Estate
A major sugar plantation for almost two hundred years, the estate is now both an organic farm, and an eco-friendly guesthouse and retreat. Guided tours take in the old plantation house and sugar mill (balenbouche.com).

Fond Doux Plantation and Resort
This 19th-century plantation estate-turned environmentally friendly resort is also a working organic farm. It offers activities galore, from Zumba to tree-planting, cacao processing to cocktail making, or simply lolling by the pool. Guests stay in restored Creole cottages (fonddouxresort.com).

Mamiku (Estate) Gardens
Formerly home to French aristocrats, a British military post and then a sugar plantation, Mamiku is rich in history. Today, the estate grows cacao, bananas, and coconuts. Enjoy a stroll through the gardens, a spot of bird-watching or hike up to Rainforest Ridge (mamikugardens.com).

The Pink Plantation House
This late 19th-century former colonial estate mansion once hosted British government officials. Now it's painted pink and is a top lunchtime restaurant, with three artistically designed rooms for rent (pinkhousestlucia.com).

1 One of the buildings at the Fond Doux plantation in Soufrière

2 Tourists learning about the cacao industry at Fond Doux

3 The striking Pink Plantation House, now a restaurant

PRACTICAL
INFORMATION

Here you will find all the essential advice and information you will need before and during your stay in Saint Lucia.

AT A GLANCE

CURRENCY
Eastern Caribbean dollar (EC$)

TIME ZONE
Atlantic Standard Time, 4 hours behind GMT, and 1 hour ahead of EST

LANGUAGE
English is the official language, although many people speak a French-based patois

ELECTRICITY SUPPLY
The usual electricity supply is 220 volts, but most hotels also have 110-volt sockets, which are suitable for US appliances

EMERGENCY NUMBERS

AMBULANCE AND FIRE	POLICE
911	999

TAP WATER
Water is generally safe to drink

When To Go

Saint Lucia has year-round good weather (average daytime temperatures are around 85° F (29° C) but the high season is between mid-November and March, which are the driest months. Most rain falls between May and October. Hurricane season lasts from June through November.

Getting There

The international airport is at Hewanorra just outside Vieux Fort, about 40 miles (64 km) south of Castries. It receives regular scheduled non-stop services from British Airways and Virgin Atlantic from the UK, American Airlines, JetBlue, United Airlines and Delta from the US, and Air Canada and WestJet from Canada. Visitors from Europe and Australia have to connect with one of these carriers. The smaller George Charles Airport at Vigie, just north of Castries, has some international connections, but mostly serves other Caribbean destinations.

Saint Lucia is visited almost daily by cruise ships, and the main terminal is at Pointe Seraphine, just outside Castries. L'Express Des Iles is a great way to explore nearby islands, and runs a high-speed ferry service between Saint Lucia, Martinique, Guadeloupe, and Dominica.

Personal Security

Saint Lucia has a low crime rate but stick to well-lit, popular areas, and avoid wearing expensive jewelry or carrying large sums of money. It is a good idea to keep valuables in the hotel safe. Vendors are likely to pester visitors, especially on the beach or in town, but a firm "No thanks" should do the trick.

Health

All hotels have doctors on call. Victoria Hospital, St. Jude Hospital, Dennery Hospital, and Soufrière Hospital are the island's main medical facilities. Insect repellent is essential, as mosquitoes can be a problem.

Passports and Visas

A passport is required to visit Saint Lucia. An immigration form has to be filled in, one part of which is stamped and returned, and must be handed back at the time of departure. Citizens of the US and of specific Commonwealth nations do not require a visa to enter. Check with your nearest embassy or high commission for details. Luggage is often checked, so in case of jewelry or expensive cameras, travel with a copy of the purchase receipt. A departure tax for passengers over the age of 12 is applied at the time of ticket purchase.

LGBT+ Safety

Same-sex activities are illegal for men but legal for women. Government and religious organisations have recently indicated that it's time for a review of antiquated laws that discriminate against LGBT+ people and make them vulnerable to hate and violence. Though there have been incidents in the past, the island is cautiously promoting itself as a friendly destination and LGBT+ tourists can discreetly blend in at entertainment venues and resorts.

Money

The official currency is the Eastern Caribbean dollar (EC$), but US dollars are accepted almost everywhere. Banks are open Monday to Thursday 8am to 2pm, and to 5pm on Fridays. Banks offer a fixed rate of exchange, usually better than the rates offered in hotels and shops. There are ATMs throughout the island and all major credit cards are widely accepted. When arranging for a taxi, guide, or charter, visitors should check which currency they are dealing in.

Cell Phones and Wi-Fi

The international dialling code for Saint Lucia is 1 758. To call the UK, dial 011-44 and the number, and for the US, dial 1 followed by the number. Card and coin-operated public phones are found easily. Cards can be purchased through FLOW offices, which also rent cell phones. Internet access is available at most large hotels, at Pointe Seraphine, and at cafes with Wi-Fi. Visitors bringing cell phones should check with their service providers to determine if they will work in Saint Lucia and if they will be subject to roaming charges.

Getting Around

Car rental is the best way to explore the island. Renters should be over 25 of age and have a valid driver's license. If they do not have an international driver's license, a temporary one can be purchased from rental firms such as AVIS, Hertz, and Island Car Rental. In Saint Lucia driving is on the left side of the road. Road signs are rare and some side roads may be pot-holed. In case of an accident or breakdown in a hired car, call the hire company or the police. Taxis and island buses are easily available and cheap. Taxi drivers attend special courses so they make excellent guides; they can be hired for a trip, by the hour or by the day, but always negotiate a price first.

There are regular bus services between the main towns, but evening services are less frequent, and smaller towns and villages may not be served. There are frequent services between Castries and Gros Islet and less frequent services to Soufrière and Vieux Fort. The southern-bound buses do not run late in the evening.

Boat services run between Castries and Soufrière. An exhilarating means of moving around the island is by helicopter, available at Saint Lucia Helicopters.

Visitor Information

The Saint Lucia Tourist Board has its main office at Castries, and overseas offices in the UK, US, Canada, France, and Germany. Tourist Information centers are located at La Place Carenage, Pointe Seraphine, Soufrière, and at both airports. In-depth information is located on **Saint Lucia Tourism Authority's** website.
Saint Lucia Tourism Authority
🆆 stlucia.org

Vibrant fruit and vegetable stall in the Grenadines

ST. VINCENT AND THE GRENADINES

SVG, as it is often abbreviated to, is a diverse nation made up of 32 islands, just nine of which are inhabited. It gained independence from Britain in 1979. St. Vincent includes the capital Kingstown, along with black-sand beaches, rainforests, and waterfalls, and at its top La Soufrière volcano. European settlers were kept at bay longer on St. Vincent than on most other Caribbean islands. In 1675, a Dutch ship carrying enslaved Africans was shipwrecked off the southern coast. The survivors were welcomed by the native Kalinagos, or Caribs. They intermarried and their children were known as "Black Caribs" by the British. During the wars of possession between the British and French in the 1700s, they favored the French. When St. Vincent was ceded to Britain under the Treaty of Versailles of 1783, the Caribs resisted, leading to the Carib Wars. Finally defeated in 1796, most Black Caribs were deported to Roatan off the coast of Honduras, while the rest were sent to Sandy Bay near Owia in northeastern St Vincent, where their descendants still live. The chief of the Black Caribs, Joseph Chatoyer, died in the revolt and is a national hero.

South of the mainland of St. Vincent lie the Grenadines. Stretching down toward Grenada, this string of small islands and cays includes friendly Bequia, jet-set Mustique, crescent-shaped Canouan, Mayreau, Union Island (a transportation hub for the southern Grenadines), and the Tobago Cays, a cluster of uninhabited islets in a coral reef lagoon.

ST. VINCENT AND THE GRENADINES

ST. VINCENT AND THE GRENADINES

Must See

❶ Tobago Cays

Experience More

❷ Kingstown
❸ Botanical Gardens
❹ Villa
❺ Mesopotamia Valley
❻ Owia
❼ Canouan
❽ Mustique
❾ Bequia
❿ Mayreau
⓫ Union Island

St. Vincent

Bequia

Mustique

Southern Grenadines

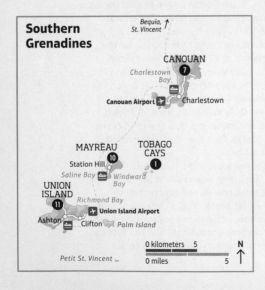

Southern Grenadines

Bequia, St. Vincent ↑

CANOUAN ❼

Charlestown Bay

Canouan Airport ✈ ○ Charlestown

MAYREAU ❿
Station Hill
Saline Bay *Windward Bay*

UNION ISLAND ⓫
Richmond Bay
✈ **Union Island Airport**

Ashton ○ Clifton *Palm Island*

TOBAGO CAYS ❶

Petit St. Vincent

| 0 kilometers | 5 |
| 0 miles | 5 |

N ↑

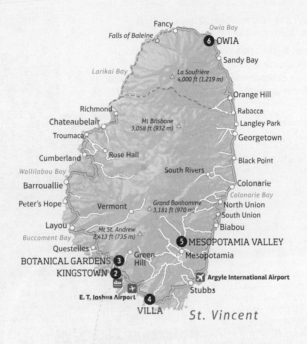

Fancy

Falls of Baleine

Owia Bay

6 OWIA

Sandy Bay

Larikai Bay

△ La Soufrière
4,000 ft (1,219 m)

Orange Hill

Richmond

Rabacca

Chateaubelair

*Mt Brisbane
3,058 ft (932 m)* △

Langley Park

Troumaca

Georgetown

Cumberland

Rose Hall

Black Point

Wallilabou Bay

South Rivers

Barrouallie

Colonarie

Peter's Hope

Vermont

Colonarie Bay

North Union

Layou

△ Grand Bonhomme
3,181 ft (970 m)

South Union

Buccament Bay

*Mt St. Andrew
2,413 ft (735 m)*

Biabou

Questelles

5 MESOPOTAMIA VALLEY

Green Hill

Mesopotamia

3 BOTANICAL GARDENS

2 KINGSTOWN

✈ **Argyle International Airport**

E. T. Joshua Airport ✈

4

Stubbs

VILLA

St. Vincent

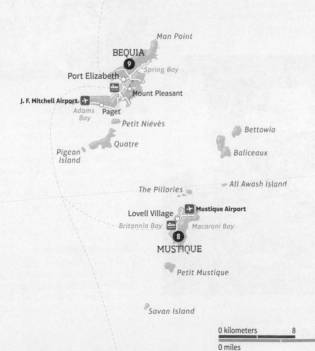

Man Point

BEQUIA

9

Spring Bay

Port Elizabeth

Mount Pleasant

J. F. Mitchell Airport ✈

Adams Bay

Paget

Petit Niévès

Bettowia

Quatre

Pigeon Island

Baliceaux

The Pillories

All Awash Island

Lovell Village

✈ **Mustique Airport**

Britannia Bay

8

Macaroni Bay

MUSTIQUE

Petit Mustique

Savan Island

| 0 kilometers | 8 |
| 0 miles | 8 |

N
↑

Canouan ↓

❶

TOBAGO CAYS

🏠 1 mile (1.5 km) E of Mayreau 🚢 Day trips from the other Grenadine islands 🌐 tobagocays.org

Sheltered by the aptly named Horseshoe Reef, the Tobago Cays are a group of uninhabited isles. The waters are exceptionally clear, and the diverse marine life includes squirrel fish, angelfish, and grouper.

Five magical islets make up the Tobago Cays, which lie just off Mayreau, the smallest inhabited isle in the Grenadines. The 2-mile-(4-km-) long Horseshoe Reef encloses four of the cays (Petit Bateau, Jamesby, Petit Rameau, and Baradal) within a sandy-bottomed aquamarine lagoon. The fifth cay, palm-topped Petit Tabac, is the perfect desert island fantasy, and was even chosen for such a role in the first *Pirates of the Caribbean* movie.

To protect these delicate ecosystems, the islands were declared a marine park in 1997 by the Vincentian government, though their popularity is putting them under increasing pressure. Comprising a mere 1.5 sq miles (4 km sq), the cays are the favorite stop on any tour of the Grenadines, attracting thousands of visitors annually on visiting yachts, cruise ship excursions, or day-trips from the populated neighboring islands.

Wonderful Wildlife

In addition to the abundant shoals of fish supported by the reefs, the park's other highlight is a turtle sanctuary off the rocky outcrop of Baradal. Here, it's possible to snorkel among the seagrass watching green turtles feed, with stingrays and eagle rays even making the odd appearance. Anchoring dinghies and fishing is prohibited.

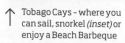

↑ Tobago Cays - where you can sail, snorkel *(inset)* or enjoy a Beach Barbeque

> 💬 INSIDER TIP
> ### Beach Barbecue
>
> If anchored overnight in the cays, ask the boat captain to reserve a spot at the nightly fresh lobster BBQ (except in the closed season, May through August). It's held on Petit Bateau beach and run by local fishermen.

There's wildlife of interest on land too: a stroll along the short trails of the larger cays takes you through rare dry tropical forest peppered with the occasional flowering shrub that supports a surprising amount of birdlife. Resident seabird populations include bridled terns and brown pelicans, but plenty of migratory birds stop over here too.

→

Huge prehistoric-looking iguana, a resident of Tobago Cays

TOP 5 ACTIVITIES ON TOBAGO CAYS

Swim with Turtles
It's a heavenly experience to swim silently alongside the turtles as they forage in the seagrass.

Picnic on the Beach
The dazzling soft sands of Petit Tabac make for a lovely picnic spot while gazing out at the sea.

Seek out Iguanas
Basking in the sun or lurking in the under-growth, green iguanas are widespread on the cays.

Snorkel on the Reef
Seek out puffer fish, barracuda, and nurse sharks around Horseshoe Reef.

Birdwatch
A keen eye through a pair of binoculars can pick out scores of roosting and nesting seabirds on Catholic Rock Bird Sanctuary.

EXPERIENCE MORE

Kingstown

🏠 SW coast of St. Vincent
➕🚌🚕 ℹ️ Upper Bay Street;
784 457 1502

A busy port city nestled in a sheltered bay, Kingstown is known as the City of Arcades, thanks to the many arched walkways scattered across its tiny downtown area. This area features some of the town's main attractions, including the three churches on Grenville Street: the Anglican St. George's; the more flamboyant St. Mary's Cathedral, and the Methodist Church; which was built in 1841 with money raised by freed slaves. Not far from downtown is a market area known as Little Tokyo, so named because its fish market was built with Japanese aid.

Situated on a 630-ft (192-m) ridge, north of the capital, Fort Charlotte offers expansive views of the island's leeward coast and the Grenadines. It's a steep 40-minute walk from town, but the resulting vistas are worth the effort. Built in 1805 to repel invasions from the sea, the fort stationed many of its 34 cannons pointing inland, since the British felt their greatest threat came from the local people. A few of the cannons still exist, and oil murals displayed in the fort depict aspects of the island's history.

Botanical Gardens

🏠 2 miles (4 km) E of Kingstown 📞 784 457 1003
🌐 ⏰ 6am–6pm daily

The oldest in the Western Hemisphere, these Botanical Gardens were created in 1765 by General Robert Melville, then-governor of the Windward Islands. The gardens were founded as a station to propagate plants from all parts of the British Empire, and they feature a wide variety of native and exotic plants. One particularly famous specimen is a thriving descendant of a breadfruit tree, brought here by the British naval officer Captain William Bligh (whose notorious first voyage to obtain the flowering tree ended in mutiny). There is a breeding program for rare plants and the endangered national bird, the St. Vincent parrot.

EAT

The French Verandah
Extensive meat and seafood options are available at this gourmet waterside restaurant.

🏠 Mariner's Hotel, Villa Bay Beach 🌐 mariners hotel.com/menu

💲💲💲

Paradise Beach Hotel Restaurant
Choose from local or international flavors in a stunning beachside setting. Friday night is BBQ night.

🏠 Villa Beach, St. Vincent
📞 784 457 479

💲💲💲

Sparrow's Beach Club
A supremely chilled location. Sink back on a lounger with your toes in the sand, while tucking into a plate of lobster fresh from the sea.

🏠 Big Sands, Union Island
📞 784 458 8195

💲💲💲

↑ Visitors strolling through the lush Botanical Gardens

The palm-fringed coastline of Owia, in eastern St. Vincent

The Mesopotamia Valley, or "Mespo," regarded as the breadbasket of St. Vincent, is a luxuriant valley teeming with cultivated vegetation.

4

Villa

3 miles (5 km) SE from Kingstown, St. Vincent

The liveliest strip in St. Vincent, Villa is the place for great nightlife. Villa and nearby Indian Bay offer good restaurants, bars, and clubs. Some of the best known hotels can be found here as well, while the Young Island Resort is just offshore.

5

Mesopotamia Valley

8 miles (13 km) NE of Kingstown, St. Vincent

The Mesopotamia Valley, regarded as the breadbasket of St. Vincent, is a luxuriant valley teeming with cultivated vegetation. Encircled by mountains, including Grand Bonhomme, the island's highest at 3,181 ft (970 m), it is a unique sight in the southern Caribbean. Just north, the colorful **Montreal Gardens** are worth visiting for the range of flowers and plants grown here.

Montreal Gardens

Near Richland Park, Windward Hwy 784 458 1198 9am–4pm Mon–Fri

SAILING IN THE GRENADINES

There's no better way to explore the varied cays, coves, and islands of the Grenadines than by chartering a boat. Sharing a catamaran or monohull among four to six people makes the operation more affordable than you might think. Services can include a captain and a cook, although dining options will vary according to your preferred budget. The captain can help plan the itinerary.

6

Owia

30 miles (48 km) NE of Kingstown, St. Vincent

On the north side of La Soufrière *(p390)*, Owia is one of the few Kalinago villages on the island's rugged northeastern coast. It is known for a series of beautiful tidal pools in an area called Salt Pond. The scenery here is quite dramatic, as waves of the feisty Atlantic dash against the surrounding volcanic rocks.

A LONG WALK
LA SOUFRIÈRE HIKE

Distance 5 km (3 miles) **Time** 4 hours **Getting There**
Minibus from Kingstown to Orange Hill; 4WD from Orange
Hill to Bamboo Ridge.

The hike up the 4,000-ft- (1,219-m-) high La
Soufrière is a moderately strenuous, approximately
four-hour climb. It is advisable to take a guided tour
as novices can get lost. The active volcano can be
approached from either side of St. Vincent, though
the easier trek is via the Atlantic Coast. The trail
leads through varied vegetation such as arrowroot,
banana, and coconut plantations, tropical rainforest,
and then cloud forest with its stunted growth. The
view from the summit is absolutely breathtaking.

Locator Map
For more detail see p384

*The highest peak on the island, **La
Soufrière** dominates the northern part
of St. Vincent. In 1970, a new island was
formed in its crater lake.*

*A dry riverbed,
Jacobs Well
is surrounded
by pristine
tropical
rainforest.*

Fancy

Beleine Bay

Falls of
Baleine

Owia Bay

Owia

Big Bay

Tucker Bay

Sandy Bay

Trois Loups Bay

Big Sand
Bay

Larikai Bay

La Soufrière
4,000 ft (1,219 m)

Orange Hill

Jacobs Well

**START/
FINISH**

Bamboo Ridge

Rabacca

Langley Park

*A short walk from Bamboo Ridge, the
dry **Riverbed** is full of lava flow and
rocks and is a popular picnic spot.*

*A four-wheel-drive
through plantations
ends at **Bamboo Ridge**,
where the foot-trail
begins. At 1,300 ft
(396 m), this is the point
where the mountain
climb starts.*

0 kilometers   3

0 miles   3

N

← Magma dome in the crater
of La Soufrière volcano

↑ A walker on the uphill climb to the summit of La Soufrière

7
Canouan

🏠 14 miles (22 km) S of
St. Vincent ✈️🚢
🌐 canouan.com

Stretching over no more than 5 sq miles (13 sq km), Canouan is home to some of the Caribbean's most spectacular beaches. Its powder-white sands, clear waters, and an impressive coral reef make it excellent for sailing, swimming, and snorkeling. The main town, Charlestown, is in Charlestown Bay, the island's primary anchorage with its long beach. The exclusive Canouan Resort with its 18-hole Trump International Golf Course and stylish casinos draw many famous guests.

8
Mustique

🏠 7 miles (11 km) SE of
Bequia ✈️🚢 🌐 mustique-island.com

Mustique has long been associated with British royalty and celebrities. This tiny 2-sq-mile (5.5-sq-km) island was acquired by a single proprietor, Scottish landowner Colin Tennant, in the 1960s. He developed it into a private resort for the rich and famous. Today, apart from private residences, there are villas available for weekly rental. Visitors can explore the island by scooter or car, or partake in the watersports that are on offer, including swimming, sailing, scuba diving, and snorkeling. Day trips from St. Vincent to the island are organized by the Mustique Company. The island is also known for the world-famous Basil's Bar, which first gained renown as a favorite haunt of Princess Margaret.

9
Bequia

🏠 9 miles (14 km) S of
St. Vincent 🄸✈️🚢
🄸 Bequia Tourism Association, Port Elizabeth; www.bequiatourism.com

The second largest of the Grenadine islands, Bequia is the northernmost in the Grenadine chain. Its capital, Port Elizabeth, is a pretty waterfront town set in the natural harbor of Admiralty Bay. Lined with hotels, restaurants, bars, and shops, it is a popular stop. Bequia's famous model boat-builders have their workshops here and can

↑ A shaded pier in Port Elizabeth, Bequia's capital town

be seen crafting intricate, traditional double-ended whalers as well as other contemporary boats.

Bequia has a long tradition of fishing and whaling, and the International Whaling Commission allows the island to kill a quota of four humpback whales a year as a way to continue important local customs. The Whaling Museum at Paget chronicles the island's whaling history. The aptly named Mount Pleasant near the east coast offers panoramic views of Bequia's golden beaches, coves, and sparkling waters. On the northeastern side of the island, the Old Hegg Turtle Sanctuary is worth visiting. It is run by conservationist Orton King, who lovingly tends to hawksbill turtles.

10
Mayreau

🏠 6 miles (10 km) SE of
Canouan 🚢

An essential stop on a sailing day trip, Mayreau is the

↑ Sunrise over the water, as seen from the veranda of a villa in Mustique

smallest inhabited island in the Grenadines. Most of its population lives at Station Hill, which has a handful of restaurants and bars. Built of stone in 1929, the old Roman Catholic Church is a short uphill walk from Station Hill. It offers great views of the island, across Salt Whistle Bay with its private resort, and the Tobago Cays.

Union Island

🏠 1 mile (1.5 km) SE of Mayreau 🚤🚌

In the southern part of the island chain, Union Island is the commercial center of the

Did You Know?

Many scenes from the first *Pirates of the Caribbean* movie were filmed in St. Vincent and the Grenadines.

Grenadines, and also the hub of yachting and airport traffic. Measuring around 3 miles (5 km) long, it is fringed with gorgeous bays, lagoons, and reefs with perfect swimming and sailing waters.

Though many people visit Union Island to catch a yacht charter, there is also a lot to do for those who decide to stay on the island itself. The main town, Clifton, has a few good restaurants, small hotels, main harbor and anchorage, and an open-air market where visitors can buy crafts and fresh produce. Clifton also offers a cheerful, unpretentious atmosphere that can be lacking on some of the area's more-visited islands. At 1,000 ft (305 m), Mount Taboi is the highest point in the Grenadines, and hiking the mountain or any of the island's numerous nature trails is a good way to explore the terrain. The island is also known for its Big Drum dance which is performed in times of disaster, but also on joyous occasions such as weddings, or the launching of a new boat.

STAY

Beachcombers Hotel

This family-run hotel offers colorful rooms, villas, or cottages, set within a tropical garden. Facilities include a pool and a charming beach-side bar-restaurant.

🏠 Villa Beach, St. Vincent 🌐 beachcombers hotel.com

$$$

Young Island

A private island just a hop from St. Vincent, with cottages sprinkled amid leafy grounds. A strip of white sand is strewn with hammocks, and yacht charter is available.

🏠 1 Island Crossing, St. Vincent 🌐 young island.com

$$$

Sugar Reef

Set in a coconut plantation, this intimate resort offers either rustic-chic rooms or colonial splendor across its two sites.

🏠 Crescent Beach, Bequia 🌐 sugarreef bequia.com

$$$

David's Beach Hotel

Head here for a handful of gorgeous airy suites, with large balconies overlooking a pristine, soft-sand beach. Rates are all-inclusive, with daily boat or island tours available.

🏠 Delmont Bay, Union Island 🌐 davidsbeach hotel.com

$$$

PRACTICAL
INFORMATION

Here you will find all the essential advice and information you will need before and during your stay in St. Vincent and the Grenadines.

AT A GLANCE

CURRENCY
Eastern Caribbean dollar (EC$)

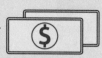

TIME ZONE
Atlantic Standard Time, 4 hours behind GMT and 1 hour ahead of EST

LANGUAGE
English

ELECTRICITY SUPPLY
Voltage is 220 volts, 50 cycles, but Petit St. Vincent has 110 volts, 60 cycles

EMERGENCY NUMBERS

POLICE, FIRE, AND AMBULANCE

999 or 911

TAP WATER
Water purity is unreliable so, to be safe, drink bottled water

When To Go

The average annual temperature in St. Vincent and the Grenadines is 81° F (27° C). The rainy season lasts from May to November, while the coolest months are from November to February. A good time to visit is between December and February, when some of the islands' biggest events and festivals take place.

Getting There

International flights arrive in St. Vincent and the Grenadines via Argyle International Airport. which opened in 2017 to replace the E. T. Joshua Airport in St. Vincent. A 15-minute drive to the capital, Kingstown, the airport is the second in the Caribbean to be solar powered. Interational and domestic services from the US, Canada and other Caribbean islands arrive via Air Canada Rouge, American Airlines, Caribbean Airlines, Leeward Islands Air Transport or LIAT, Mustique Airways, One Caribbean, Sunwing Airlines and SVG Air. There are also a number of smaller airports in the Grenadines, J. F. Mitchell Airport in Bequia, Canouan Airport, Mustique Airport and Union Island Airport, which run domestic flights.

Personal Security

The beaches do not have lifeguards. It is advisable not to leave personal belongings unattended and to avoid walking in unlit areas.

Health

Milton Cato Memorial Hospital is the largest of the six public hospitals on the islands, with smaller ones in Georgetown, Chateaubelair, and Bequia and clinics throughout the islands. Maryfield Hospital in St. Vincent is a fully private hospital.

Passports and Visas

Visitors must have a valid passport, with the exception of citizens of the Organization of Eastern Caribbean States (OECS), who only need

proof of citizenship (driver's license or voter's registration card). Visas are required from citizens of various nations, so check with your nearest embassy or high commission. All visitors must have an onward or return ticket as well. Jewelry, cameras, and other expensive items are allowed if they are for personal use only. Passengers 18 years and over are allowed free import of 200 cigarettes or 50 cigars and 1 liter of wine or spirits. Drugs, firearms and ammunition, and spear fishing equipment are prohibited. A departure tax is to be paid when leaving the island.

LGBT+ Safety

In close-knit, strongly Christian St. Vincent and the Grenadines, gross-indecency laws have remained on the books since the British colonial era, making homosexual activity illegal. Socially also, the islands are not the most LGBT+ friendly, though attitudes are slowly changing, with young people more tolerant than previous generations. Still, LGBT+ visitors would be best advised to be discreet in public.

Money

The official currency is the Eastern Caribbean dollar (EC$). Bank hours are Monday to Thursday 8am to 1pm and Friday 8am to 5pm. A few ATMs are located in St. Vincent, Bequia, and Union Island. Major credit cards are accepted everywhere.

Cell Phones and Wi-Fi

Cell phone service is available in most places, and visitors can receive and make calls through their roaming service. Local telephone operators include FLOW and Digicel SVG Ltd. Visitors bringing cell phones should check with their service providers to determine if they will work in St. Vincent and the Grenadines and if they will be subject to roaming charges.

Getting Around

If visitors do not have an OECS or international driver's license, a local one can be obtained. Taxis and minibuses are readily available and vehicles can be hired at rental agencies,

including AVIS, B&G Jeep Rental, Rent and Drive, and Greg's Auto Care and Rental Services. There are also a number of reliable tour services for sightseeing trips around the islands. On St. Vincent, public buses link major towns and villages. The fit and adventurous can opt for bike and scooter rentals.

If you want to travel between the islands, inter-island ferries are a cheap and popular way to see St. Vincent and the Grenadines.

Visitor Information

St. Vincent and the Grenadines Ministry of Tourism has its main office on Upper Bay Street in Kingstown and there is an information booth at the airport as well. **Bequia Tourism Association** has an office in Port Elizabeth. Overseas, tourist offices are located in the UK, Canada, and US.

Bequia Tourism Association
w bequiatourism.com
St. Vincent and the Grenadines Ministry of Tourism
w discoversvg.com

GRENADA

During the 1600s the European powers fought over Grenada with the indigenous population. To avoid surrendering to the French, in 1651 the last remaining Caribs hurled themselves off a cliff on the north coast at a spot called Caribs' Leap. In 1783, under the Treaty of Versailles the island passed to British control, and remained so until 1974 when it became a sovereign state. It is proudly independent. As you drive around, you cannot fail to notice how many roadside kerbs and buildings are painted in the red, gold, and green colours of the national flag.

Grenada is lush and mountainous, with much of the land forested or agricultural. The so-called Spice Isle is famous for its production of nutmeg. Though the crop was devastated by Hurricane Ivan in 2004, it has made a comeback. That said, many farmers are now focusing on cacao; the island has five chocolate factories. Many of Grenada's 110,000-strong population live in the southwest. Here you'll find the pretty capital St. George's, along with Grand Anse – Grenada's tourist hub and location of its most popular beach – and a number of other fine strands and deeply indented, yacht-dotted bays. Grenada is in fact a tri-island state encompassing Carriacou and Petite Martinique. These much smaller and less visited sister isles lie to the northeast of Grenada itself, in the Grenadines chain.

Carriacou ↗

GRENADA

Must See

① St. George's

Experience More

② Leapers Hill
③ Grand Étang Forest Reserve
④ The Tower Estate
⑤ Underwater Sculpture Park
⑥ Belmont Estate
⑦ Petite Martinique
⑧ Carriacou
⑨ Nutmeg Processing Cooperative

Sauters Bay

LEAPERS HILL ②

Duquesne Bay

Duquesne — Sauters

Crayfish Bay

St. Mark Bay — Samaritan

Victoria — Waltham

Maran Bay

NUTMEG PROCESSING COOPERATIVE ⑨

Maran — ○ *Victoria Falls*

Peggy's Whim

Gouyave

Rosemont — △ *Mt. St. Catherine 2,757 ft (840 m)*

Mt Home

Palmiste Bay

Marigot Bay — Grand Roy — △ *Mt. Granby 2,240 ft (682 m)*

Marigot

○ *Concord Falls* — Beauregard — *Harford Village*

Woodford — St. Margaret — *Plaisance*

Brizan — *Grand Étang Lake* — ○ *Seven Sisters Falls* — *Royal Mt. Carmel Falls*

Granton — ○ *Annandale Falls*

Moliniere Bay

UNDERWATER SCULPTURE PARK ⑤ — Moliniere — △ *South East Mountain 2,348 ft (715 m)*

Constantine — **GRAND ÉTANG FOREST RESERVE** ③

Fontenoy — ○ La Mode — *Felix Park*

Tempé — Vincennes

ST GEORGE'S ① — St Paul's — Bellevue

Belmont — **THE TOWER ESTATE** ④ — St. David's

Grand Anse Beach — Laborie

Grand Anse — Marian — B. Bacolet

Morne Rouge Bay — Morne Rouge — Calvigny — Confer — Petit Bacaye — *La Sagesse Beach*

Calliste

Point Salines — ✈ Maurice Bishop International Airport — *Hog Island* — *Calvigny Island*

Glover Island — L'Anse aux Épines — *True Blue Bay*

0 kilometers 4 / 0 miles 4 — N ↑

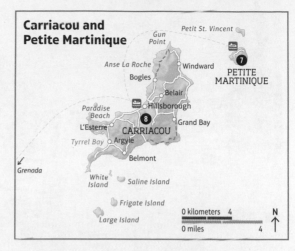

Carriacou and Petite Martinique

Diamond Island

Ronde Island

Caille Island

Petit St. Vincent

Gun Point

Anse La Roche

Windward

Bogles

Belair

Hillsborough

7

PETITE MARTINIQUE

Paradise Beach

8

L'Esterre

CARRIACOU

Grand Bay

Tyrrel Bay

Argyle

Grenada

Belmont

White Island

Saline Island

Frigate Island

Large Island

0 kilometers   4

0 miles   4

N

Sugar Loaf

Green Island

Sandy Island

La Fortune

△ Levera Hill
848 ft (258 m)

River Sallee

High Cliff Point

6 **BELMONT ESTATE**

Tivoli

Conference

Pearls

Paradise

Great River Bay

Grenville

Telescope Point

Grenville Bay

Soubise

Marquis Island

St. Andrews Bay

Gt Bacolet Pt

Menere Bay

GRENADA

Carriacou and Petite Martinique

Grenada

↑ Houses in St. George's, dotting the hillside around its pretty harbor

ST. GEORGE'S

⌂ SW coast of Grenada ✈🚢🚌 *i* Burns Point (east end Carenage); 473 440 2279

Grenada's quaint capital, St. George's, is renowned for its attractive, horseshoe-shaped harbor. It is surrounded by pastel warehouses and old Georgian buildings rising up the hills, with distinctive red-tiled roofs that were once the ballasts of ships. What's more it is only a short hop south to impressive Grand Anse, a mile-long gently curving belt of sand that is undeniably the island's most magnificent beach.

① Carenage

The inner harbor, called the Carenage, is the center of St. George's marine activity, filled with colorful Carriacou sloops, fishing vessels, and tourist boats. Rimming this harbor is

Did You Know?

The waters off St. George's are home to cruise liner *Bianca C,* the Caribbean's largest diveable wreck.

Wharf Road, which is lined with shops and restaurants. Visitors can stroll along the Carenage waterfront and into the hills to capture stunning views. Lowther's Lane is the perfect vantage point for watching boats coming into the harbor, especially in the morning.

Facing the Carenage are the exquisite Georgian-style Houses of Parliament and three of the city's prominent churches, still roofless after the devastation of Hurricane Ivan in 2004: St. Andrew's Presbyterian Kirk, St. George's Anglican Church, and St. George's Roman Catholic Cathedral. Built in 1818, the

cathedral's Neo-Gothic tower is the city's most visible landmark. The church itself dates to 1884 but it was built on the site of an older church.

Built in 1894, the Sendall Tunnel connects the Carenage to the Esplanade, which is home to a duty-free mall, located at the cruise terminal.

EAT

Patrick's Homestyle Cooking
For a fixed price, diners can indulge in a 20-dish tapas-style feast.

⌂ Lagoon Rd 📞 473 440 0364 ⏰ Fri–Sun pm

$⑤$⑤$⑤

Umbrellas Beach Bar
A relaxed favorite with tourists and locals alike, this eatery offers delicious, well-priced specialties.

⌂ Grand Anse Beach ⓦ umbrellas.gd

$⑤$⑤$⑤

② Fort George

📍 St. George Point ⏰ 9am-5pm Mon-Fri

Fort George is another ideal point from which to photograph the Carenage and the city. Sitting high atop St. George Point with its battery of cannons pointing out to sea, it towers above its surroundings. Built in 1706 by the French, it is now the police headquarters. The site where politician Maurice Bishop and many cabinet members were executed in 1983, this fort was bombed by American troops in the infamous military intervention that followed.

③ Grande Anse

📍 2 miles (3 km) S of St. George's 🚌🚤

Reigning over Grenada's southwest tip, Grand Anse is a splendid sight. Backed by palms and sea-grape, this majestic, silky stretch of sand extends roughly 1.5 miles (2 km) around a sheltered bay. With spaces to play, picnic, or snooze, the beach is popular with locals and tourists alike. The busier northern end offers umbrellas and loungers for rent, as well as a craft and spice market – perfect for

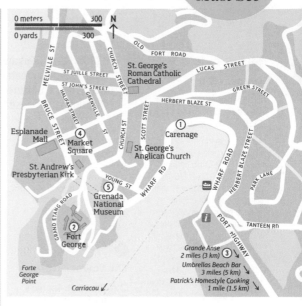

souvenir-shopping. Further along the sand, past the dive operators, the vibe gets progressively more mellow.

④ Market Square

Not far from the Esplanade, the Granby Street leads to Market Square (also called Spice Market). Outdoors, women in traditional Grenadian attire sell spices and produce. In the new, cooler indoor market, a range

↑ A woman wearing bright, traditional attire at a stall in Market Square

🄾 PICTURE PERFECT
Fort George

Lofty Fort George provides the perfect vantage point for pictures of the Carenage, with the city's pastel-colored buildings stacked up on the hillside and miles of lush vegetation beyond.

of souvenirs and products made in Grenada are sold.

⑤ Grenada National Museum

📍 Corner Young & Monkton sts 📞 473 440 3725 ⏰ 9am-4:30pm Mon-Fri; 10am-1pm Sat

Just off Young Street is the Grenada National Museum. Housed in a former army barracks and prison, this interesting museum covers many aspects of the island's history and culture, from the Caribs to the more recent Hurricane Ivan.

EXPERIENCE MORE

2
Leapers Hill

🏛 23 miles (37 km) N of St. George's 📞 473 444 3222 🕐 10am-4pm daily

A historic landmark also known as Carib's Leap, this is where the Carib Indians leaped off a 100-ft (30-m) cliff into the sea, rather than surrender to advancing French colonists in 1651. This unhappy site is a good pit stop while touring the island. There is a cemetery, as well as some recreated petroglyphs on the rocky wall, and travelers can enjoy a scenic view of the Grenadine islands.

3
Grand Étang Forest Reserve

🏛 7 miles (11 km) NE of St. George's 🕐 9am-4pm Mon-Fri ℹ Grand Étang Visitors' Center; 473 440 6160

Located high in the central mountains, this reserve protects a lush rainforest and several ecological sub-systems, and is popular for sightseeing and hiking, with trails leading to its many waterfalls (p404). The forest was greatly damaged by Hurricane Ivan in 2004, but has quickly regrown. The visitors' center's walkway is lined with spice vendors and musical entertainers, and visitors may also get a chance to spot mona monkeys, although they

largely remain deeper in the area's mountainous rainforest. The center has some interpretive displays, and provides a good view of Grand Étang Lake in the extinct volcanic crater.

4
The Tower Estate

🏛 St. Paul's, St. George's 🕐 10am-6pm Fri 🌐 the towerestategrenada.com

The Tower Estate centers around a historic stone plantation house that has remained in the same family since the 1940s. It sits atop a hill in the community of St. Paul's, which is a short drive from the capital. The Tower is open for guided tours, which take in the house itself and its history, and the beautiful grounds filled with flowering trees and shrubs, a spice garden, and an organic farm. The addition of afternoon tea following the tour makes the experience extra-special. Although these tours run only on Fridays, private bookings may be made for alternative days.

← A mona monkey resting in the branches of a tree within Grand Étang Forest Reserve

> **In 2006, British-Guyanese sculptor Jason de Caires Taylor created the world's first underwater sculpture park in Moliniere Bay, following hurricane damage to the region.**

5
Underwater Sculpture Park

🏛 Molinere Beauséjour Marine Protected Area 🌐 puregrenada.com

This series of 75 eerie underwater human sculptures forms one of Grenada's more unusual attractions. In 2006, British-Guyanese sculptor Jason de Caires Taylor created the world's first underwater sculpture park in Moliniere Bay, following hurricane damage to the region. The concrete, life-size figures are gradually becoming encrusted with coral, thus acting – very successfully – as artificial reefs, and attracting ever-increasing numbers of fish.

Famous figures in the collection include *The Lost Correspondent*, a man seated hunched over a typewriter; *Man on a Bike*, which shows a figure cycling; and *Vicissitudes*, in which a circle of children from a variety of backgrounds hold hands in a symbol of resilience and unity.

Additional sculptures have been added by local artist Troy Lewis since the park's inauguration. This powerful group of statues is based on indigenous art and culture, and demonstrates intricate, ceremonial carving.

The sculptures, which lie between 6 and 26 ft (8 m) below the water, can be accessed by walking south along the coastal path from Dragon Bay and then swimming, or by taking a snorkeling, scuba, or glass-bottom boat tour from Grand Anse Beach.

↑ *Vicissitudes*, within Grenada's Underwater Sculpture Park

Belmont Estate

📍 20 miles (32 km) N of St. George's 🕐 8am–4:30pm Sun–Fri 🌐 belmont estate.net

It is possible to get a glimpse of traditional Grenadian plantation life at this 0.5-sq-mile (1.5-sq-km) estate dating back to the late 1600s, and owned by the Nyacks since 1944. Originally a coffee plantation, the estate has changed crops over the years; today, primarily cacao and nutmeg are grown here.

Touring the cacao operation, visitors learn about the traditional processing of a cacao bean, from its beginning as a pod on the tree through fermenting to drying on wooden trays in the sun. It is possible to sample delicious cacao tea and organic dark chocolate, produced by the Grenada Chocolate Company nearby. There is also a small museum on site, which documents island history and houses estate memorabilia. The plantation's lunch buffet of Creole dishes, including estate-grown fruits and vegetables, is a feast.

Another plantation house in this area well worth a visit is **Helvellyn House**, located at the northern tip of the island and dating from 1939. This is a good spot to enjoy an alfresco lunch of authentic, home-cooked Caribbean dishes served in a lovely setting of gardens with a view of the Grenadines. The pottery workshop here also offers lessons.

Helvellyn House
📍 La Fortune, St. Patrick 📞 473 442 9252 🕐 Pottery workshop: 9am–5pm Mon–Sat

↑ Cocoa beans drying out, part of the process at Belmont Estate

WATERFALLS OF GRENADA

With its mountainous terrain and lush tropical rainforest, Grenada boasts some of the most beautiful waterfalls in the Caribbean. Grand Étang Forest Reserve *(see p402)*, has the highest number in any one geographic region. Rosemount Falls, in the parish of St. John, is privately owned and open only to visitors lunching at Rosemount Plantation House. Farther north, Victoria Falls (also called Tufton Hall) is the island's tallest waterfall, and is relatively difficult to reach. Visiting one or all of these cataracts is a highlight of a trip to the island.

WATERFALLS OF GRAND ÉTANG FOREST RESERVE

Grand Étang harbors five waterfalls within the reserve or on its fringes: Concord, Honeymoon, Annandale, Seven Sisters, and Royal Mt. Carmel. Trails pass through rainforest, citrus groves, and plantations growing fragrant spices and fruits.

Annandale Falls is one of the easiest waterfalls to reach. A delightful garden of labeled trees, such as nutmeg, and flowering plants, line the path to the falls.

Concord Falls consists of three waterfalls, Concord, Au Coin, and Fontainbleu, of which the first is the most accessible and popular.

↑ Concord Falls in the Grand Étang Forest Reserve

↑ The stunning natural pool formed at the Seven Sisters waterfall

FLORA AND FAUNA

Trails around the waterfalls are lined with huge mahogany and gommier trees, and endemic plants such as Grand Étang fern. Wildlife includes nine-banded armadillos and iguanas. The mona monkey, introduced from Africa three centuries ago, is one of the most easily spotted animals near Rosemount Falls. Water hyacinths, among other plants such as balisier, wild fuchsia, and hibiscus, thrive near Grand Étang's waterfalls. Selaginella and fungi are widespread in the forest around Victoria Falls.

① A dazzling red Hibiscus flower in full bloom.

② The pretty pale lilac flowers of the Water hyacinth thrive near Grand Étang's waterfalls.

③ The Nine-banded armadillo is just one of the species that live in the habitat of Grenada's falls.

↑ Victoria Falls, Grenada's tallest waterfall

A lone figure walking on one of Petite Martinique's beautiful beaches at sunrise →

❼ Petite Martinique

 3 miles (5 km) NE of Carriacou

Dominated by a 738-ft (225-m) volcanic cone, the tiny island of Petite Martinique is roughly 1 mile (1.6 km) across. It is sparsely populated and most residents know each other. The sea is the source of livelihood here and boat-building is the main occupation of most islanders.

Travelers arrive at the jetty in Paradise, the sole village. There is only one main road, so a taxi tour takes under an hour. While Paradise has a white-sand beach, Petit St. Vincent, a 5-minute boat ride away, and other surrounding cays, have a few good strands and offer excellent snorkeling.

❽ Carriacou

 23 miles (37 km) N of Grenada 🚢🚌 ℹ Main St, Hillsborough; 473 443 7948

Although covering an area of just 13 sq miles (34 sq km), Carriacou is the largest of the Grenadine islands. Carriacou is the Carib word for "Land of Reefs," and it is ringed by many exquisite reefs. The Osprey Lines ferry arrives daily from Grenada to the main town, Hillsborough. Here, the **Carriacou Museum**, set in a restored cotton gin mill, exhibits Carib and African artifacts, and traces early British and French occupation. It also pays tribute to Canute Caliste (1914–2005), the acclaimed Grenadian artist.

For a panoramic view of Hillsborough Bay, head northeast to the 640-ft (195-m) site of Princess Royal Hospital in Belair, framed by cannons.

Farther south down the west coast, **KIDO Ecological Research Station** arranges guided eco-tours, including hiking through High North National Park and turtle-watching. Nearby, the secluded and scenic Anse La Roche beach can be reached by water taxi or on foot.

South of Hillsborough on L'Esterre Bay is the famous Paradise Beach, easily accessible with plenty of amenities. Just offshore, Sandy Island is popular for snorkeling and picnics.

Farther south, Tyrrel Bay is a yachters' haven. Heading east, water-taxis are available in Belmont to ferry visitors to White Island, an islet with pristine stretches of sandy beach and great snorkeling.

Carriacou Museum

Paterson St, Hillsborough 473 443 8288 9:30am–4pm Mon-Fri Public hols

KIDO Ecological Research Station

Sanctuary, Carriacou w kido-projects.com

❾   Nutmeg Processing Cooperative

Central Depradine St, Gouyave 473 444 8337 8am–4:30pm Mon-Fri

You can smell the island's most important export before you see it being processed in the uninviting warehouse in the center of Gouyave, a west-coast fishing village. Although a tour of the processing plant is short, it's inexpensive and fascinating. Nutmeg harvesting goes on all year, although there are peak seasons. Trees do not produce fruit for the first six years, and only reach maturity after 25 years.

> ## Did You Know?
>
> Grenada is the world's second largest producer of nutmeg after Indonesia.

SPICE ISLE

More spices are grown in Grenada per square mile than anywhere else in the world. With the fragrant aromas of cinnamon, ginger, and vanilla wafting through the air, the island has been dubbed the "Isle of Spice." The most important crop is nutmeg, coined "black gold" by former Prime Minister George Brizan. Spice estates offer tours highlighting the various stages of spice production, and also sell fresh spices and spice products.

NUTMEG AND MACE

Grenada regained its position as the second-largest producer of nutmeg in the world, after recovering from the damage it suffered during Hurricane Ivan in 2004. Nutmeg production has been the backbone of Grenada's economy and agriculture since 1843, when it was brought here from Indonesia. Along with its twin spice, mace, which grows around the shell of the nutmeg, it is one of the isle's top export crops.

↑ The fleshy pericap contains nutmeg and mace

→ A nutmeg seed pod covered in lacy, scarlet mace

Workers carrying out quality control at a processing plant ↑

OTHER SPICES

Grenada's spices include cloves, ginger, pepper, pimento, cinnamon, and bay. All over the island, there are plantations and processing plants.

The cinnamon bark is peeled during the rainy season. When dried in the sun, it curls to form cinnamon sticks.

Bay leaves have a distinct aroma. They are found on the evergreen bay tree, native to the Windward Islands.

Black pepper berries grow on creeping vines. Reddish in color when picked, they turn black after drying.

Clove buds when picked are deep red.

PRACTICAL
INFORMATION

Here you will find all the essential advice and information you will need before and during your stay in Grenada.

CURRENCY
Eastern Caribbean dollar (EC$)

TIME ZONE
Atlantic Standard Time, 4 hours behind GMT and 1 hour ahead of EST

LANGUAGE
The official language is English, but a French-African patois is also spoken

ELECTRICITY SUPPLY
Grenada operates on 220 volts, but 110-volt appliances also work if used in conjunction with adaptors

EMERGENCY NUMBERS

AMBULANCE, POLICE, AND FIRE

911

TAP WATER
Water purity is unreliable so, to be safe, drink bottled water

When To Go

Most people visit Grenada between December and April. Year-round temperature ranges from 75° to 85° F (24° to 30° C), with November through February being the coolest and January through May the driest season. June through December is humid, although there are hardly any prolonged spells of rainfall. Hurricane season lasts from June through November, with September the peak month.

Getting There

All flights arrive at Maurice Bishop International Airport (GND). From the UK, British Airways and Virgin Atlantic have weekly direct flights to Grenada. US airlines with flights to Grenada are American Airlines, Delta, and JetBlue. Caribbean Airlines (CAL) also has flights from North America. From Toronto, weekly direct flights between December and April are offered by Air Canada, which also has year-round flights to Barbados, with LIAT connections. Condor has flights between Frankfurt, Germany and Grenada during the winter. CAL and LIAT also connect Grenada to other Caribbean islands.

Personal Security

Grenada is generally safe for traveling. However, muggings and purse snatchings may occur after dark, so it is best to keep valuables in the hotel safe and to exercise caution when walking and traveling in local buses or taxis.
  Often found on beaches, the tiny green fruit of the manchineel apple trees contains poison, which can blister the skin.

Health

The General Hospital in St. George's, Princess Alice Hospital in St. Andrew's Parish, and Princess Royal Hospital in Carriacou are public hospitals. Visitors should have medical insurance. All hotels have doctors on call. In case of hurricanes and other emergencies, evacuation to a larger center is common.

Passports and Visas

A valid passport for UK and US citizens, or a proof of citizenship bearing a photograph for Canadians, and a return ticket are required. The citizens of the US, Canada, British Commonwealth, Japan, South Korea, most Caribbean and European countries, do not require a visa. Contact the Immigration Department or visit the Grenada Tourism Authority website (www.puregrenada.com) for a list of countries requiring, and those exempt from, visas. There is a departure tax, but it is included in the price of airline tickets.

LGBT+ Safety

Grenada criminalizes consensual sexual relations among people of the same-sex through laws tabled since the British colonial era. Socially, the community is not receptive to LGBT+ activity, and though there are friendly resorts and places to hang-out, same-sex travellers, especially male, should be discreet while in public.

Money

The official currency is the Eastern Caribbean dollar (EC$). Most places accept US dollars, but banks have the best currency exchange rates. Traveler's checks are accepted everywhere, and major credit cards are accepted by most hotels, car rental companies, and shops.

Banking hours are usually Monday through Thursday 8am to 3pm, and Friday 8am to 4pm. ATM machines are available on Grenada and Carriacou.

Cell Phones and Wi-Fi

The country code for Grenada is 473, followed by a seven-digit number. Cell-phone service is available from FLOW and Digicel. Visitors bringing their own cell phones should check with their service providers to determine if they will work in Grenada and whether they will incur roaming charges. Roaming service is available to AMPS-compatible cellular owners. Local cell phones can also be rented from the FLOW and Digicel offices. Most hotels have wireless and/or business centers with Internet. There are a few Internet cafes dotted around the island.

Getting Around

Taxis and minibuses for hire are readily available and are denoted by an "H" license plate. Between 6pm and 6am, there is an additional charge. Private minibuses provide an inexpensive service. Buses display route numbers, and fares are fixed according to distance. The bus terminus is on Melville Street in St. George's. In Carriacou, buses run from about 7am to 5pm. Water taxis are available in St. George's, Carriacou, and Petite Martinique. To hire cars, visitors need to be over 21, with a driving license and a local driving permit, issued by car rental firms such as AVIS, Y&R Car Rentals, J&B Auto Rentals and Wayne's Auto Rental. Grenada has about 650 miles (1,050 km) of paved roads in decent condition. However, most have blind corners, with narrow or no shoulders. Driving is on the left and all occupants must wear seat belts.

Osprey Lines Ltd. has a daily ferry service connecting Grenada, Carriacou, and Petite Martinique. SVG Air has a daily 20-minute flight from Grenada to Carriacou's Lauriston Airport.

Visitor Information

The **Grenada Tourism Authority** has offices in Canada, Carriacou, Germany, the US, and the UK. Its head office is in Grenada. The **Carriacou and Petite Martinique Tourism Association** also provides information concerning transportation and accommodations on Grenada's sister islands.
Carriacou and Petite Martinique Tourism Association
🌐 carriacoupetitemartinique.com
Grenada Tourism Authority
🌐 grenadagrenadines.com

The pristine sand and azure waters at Hilton Beach

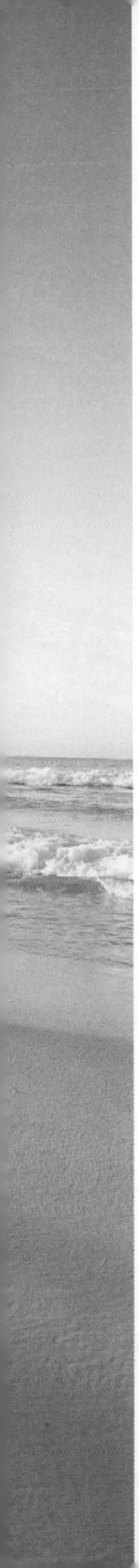

BARBADOS

The Caribbean's most easterly landmass was first colonized by the English in 1627. It soon became one of the region's most important islands for sugar cane cultivation, with the labor carried out on plantation estates by slaves brought over from West Africa. Following emancipation in 1834, many workers lived in moveable, timber chattel houses, which are still common sights today. The Garrison area was the Caribbean's largest British military establishment in colonial times, and is now on UNESCO's World Heritage List.

After more than 300 years as a colony, Barbados gained its independence in 1966. However, it retains some English characteristics, with cricket played on village greens and Anglican churches everywhere. The island has many of its own cultural features though, from road tennis to local dishes such as pudding and souse (pickled pork mixed with steamed sweet potato). The big annual event is Crop Over, a colorful carnival that runs from June through August and dates back to celebrations marking the end of the sugar cane harvest.

The island divides into distinctive parts. Bridgetown, in the southwest, is Barbados's busy, commerce-driven capital. The west coast is lined with luxury hotels and villas and centered on Holetown, where the English settlers first landed. Down on the south coast it's more developed and livelier, while the unspoiled, wave-pummelled east coast couldn't be more different – the beauty spot of Bathsheba is a magnet for serious surfers. The rural interior is dotted with historic plantation houses, and areas are still covered by swathes of sugar cane.

North Point

Archer's Bay

Flatfield

Salmond

River Bay

Stroud Bay

Hope

Cuckold Point

1C

Cave Hill

Bromefield

Half Acre

Alexandra

Cove Bay

1B

Maycock's Bay

Church Hill

Boscobelle

Fustic

Rose Hill

1 ST. NICHOLAS ABBEY

1

Six Men's Bay

Mile and A Quarter

11 BARBADOS WILDLIFE RESERVE

Shorey Village

2

SPEIGHTSTOWN **10**

Sedge Pond

Belleplaine

Bawdens

1

Gibbes Beach

Gibbes

Chalky Mount

2A

Apes Hill

BATHSHEBA

Alleynes Bay

Mount Standfast

2

9

Andromeda Gardens

Porters

Orange Hill

Surinam

Folkstone Beach

Welchman Hall Gully

Hunte's Gardens

Easy Ha

HOLETOWN **8**

3A

Wilson Hill

Paynes Bay Beach

HARRISON'S CAVE

12

3

Hoytes Village

2A

Hopewell

Four Cross Roads

2

Appleby

Market Hill

3

1

Warrens

Jackson

3B

GUN HILL SIGNAL STATION

6

Black Rock

Charles Rowe Bridge

Brighton Beach

1

Bank Hall

4

Boarded Hall

5

BRIDGETOWN **4**

Belleville

Pebbles Beach

3 GARRISON HISTORIC AREA

Newtor

Needham's Point

Hastings

OISTINS

St. Lawrence Gap

2

5

SOUTH COAST

Enterprise

0 kilometers 4
0 miles 4

N

BARBADOS

Must See

❶ St. Nicholas Abbey

Experience More

❷ South Coast
❸ Garrison Historic Area
❹ Bridgetown
❺ Oistins
❻ Gun Hill Signal Station
❼ Sunbury Plantation House
❽ Holetown
❾ Bathsheba
❿ Speightstown
⓫ Barbados Wildlife Reserve
⓬ Harrison's Cave

Atlantic Ocean

Martin's Bay

Glebe Land

Bath

Conset Bay

Ashford

Sealy Hall

Skeete's Bay

Ragged Point

Mount Pleasant

Blades Hill

Coles

Kendal

River Land

Bottom Bay

❼ SUNBURY PLANTATION HOUSE

Long Bay

Brereton

Six Cross Roads

Long Bay

Crane Beach

Rices

Foul Bay

St. Patricks

❼

St. Martins

✈ Grantley Adams International Airport

Long Beach

Sayes Court

BARBADOS ☐

❶ ⟨⟩ ⟨⟩
ST. NICHOLAS ABBEY

🏠 17 miles (27 km) NE of Bridgetown 🚌 🕐 10am–3:30pm Sun–Fri; distillery and syrup factory sometimes closed on weekends 🌐 stnicholasabbey.com

Set in a former sugar plantation, St. Nicholas Abbey is a magnificent house built in the mid-17th century by wealthy planter, Colonel Berringer. The spectacular grounds feature a croquet lawn and a herb garden.

Constantly expanding its repertoire for tourists, St. Nicholas Abbey provides the island's most interesting diversion away from the beach. Tours of the oldest existing building in Barbados take in the slave ledger on the wall, a reminder of the forced labor, which enabled the plantation to thrive. The daily risk to life for black laborers is depicted in a film from the 1930s. Arguably the tour's highlight, it was shot by former owner Colonel Cave and is shown in the former chapel.

The complex also features a recently restored sugar syrup factory and a local rum distillery. Demonstrations of the historic syrup factory are given during the cane harvest, which runs from January through to May. The distillery offers regular tours, which also include a complimentary rum punch.

In 2019, a restored heritage steam railway opened, which takes visitors on a scenic tour of the plantation estate. The train truddles down a picturesque avenue of mahogany trees to Cherry Tree Hill, where a breathtaking view of the coastline awaits.

↑ Antique mahogany furniture in the interior rooms of the abbey

↑ Bottles of local rum on display at the St. Nicholas Distillery

 HIDDEN GEM
A mill down the hill

Just downhill from St. Nicholas Abbey, Morgan Lewis Mill (open daily 10am–5pm; T6224039) is the Caribbean's most intact sugar windmill. Visitors can admire it for free from outside, or pay for a short informative guided tour of the interior.

←

The historic Morgan Lewis sugar mill, a short walk from the abbey

Did You Know?

The imposing sandbox tree in the center of the great house's courtyard is over 400 years old.

↑ The stunning Jacobean Great House, the oldest building in Barbados

↑ A surfer returning from catching some sunset waves in St. Lawrence Gap

EXPERIENCE MORE

❷ South Coast

 5 miles (8 km) SE of Bridgetown 🚌

The south coast is built up all the way from Bridgetown to Oistins, but still has some marvelous stretches of sand. A well-signposted detour off the main coast road leads to St. Lawrence Gap, which is the party capital of Barbados. It has restaurants offering a wide range of cuisines, but the local Bajan dishes, especially the fresh fish, are superb. Toward the evening, cheap but delicious fast-food stalls spring up along the road. Local vendors also set up stalls selling handmade jewelry and other crafts. Bars play live music and the nightlife continues until the early morning hours. St. Lawrence has a small police post but late-night revelers should still take care and avoid walking in areas with poor lighting.

The Gap is also worth visiting during the daytime, for the impressive Chattel House Village, a collection of shops selling tropical fashions, handicrafts, and souvenirs.

---

❸ Garrison Historic Area

📍 2 miles (3 km) SE of Bridgetown ⓣ

The first garrison in the West Indies was located in the Garrison Historic Area. More than 70 original buildings and forts still stand, most of which date from 1789 onward, when Barbados became the British army's headquarters in the Leeward and Windward Islands. Today, Garrison Savannah hosts the island's horse-racing track and is used for parades and celebrations. Races are held almost every Saturday, and provide great entertainment for visitors and Bajans alike.

Barbados Museum is set in what was the garrison's prison. Built around 1818 and an example of West Indies Georgian architecture, it is a great place at which to learn about the island's history, culture, and people. The exhibits are displayed in a series of galleries, set in former cells.

Northwest of the Garrison Historic Area is **Mount Gay Distilleries**, which has been officially producing rum since 1703, making it the world's oldest. Guided tours take visitors through the process of rum-making and end in the tasting room.

On the northern side of the Garrison Savannah stands the elegant George Washington House, where the American founding father lodged for six weeks when he was 19. Upstairs is a small museum, and in the grounds is the entrance to the underground Garrison Tunnels.

STAY

Atlantis Historic Inn
Comprising four charming rooms, this boutique hotel is nestled along the rugged Atlantic coast, so guests fall asleep to the sound of crashing waves.

📍 Bathsheba 🌐 atlantis hotelbarbados.com

 $ $ $

CRICKET IN BARBADOS

Cricket is big in Barbados - played with passion on the beach and on virtually every patch of grass across the island on weekends. Sir Frank Worrell - the first black captain of the West Indies cricket team - features on the Barbados five-dollar note while Sir Garfield Sobers, one of the sport's best ever batsmen, is the country's only living National Hero. His statue stands outside Kensington Oval, the home of Barbados cricket since 1982, and the Caribbean's premier cricketing stadium. Located on Spring Garden Highway, just north of Bridgetown, it hosts regional and international fixtures. When the Windies (West Indian team) are in town, the place takes on a carnival atmosphere, which even non-aficionados of the sport can enjoy. Die-hard enthusiasts will also want to visit the nearby Cricket Legends of Barbados museum (cricketlegendsbarbados.com).

↑ Statue of Sir Garfield Sobers outside Kensington Oval Cricket Ground

↑ Barbadians playing a game of cricket on the beach

Barbados Museum
⊛⊚ 📞 246 538 0201
🕐 9am–5pm Mon–Sat, 2–6pm Sun

Mount Gay Distilleries
⊛⊛⊚ 🅰 Exmouth Gap, Spring Garden Hwy
🕐 9:30am– 3:30pm Mon–Fri
🌐 mountgayrum.com

4
Bridgetown

🅰 SW coast of Barbados
❎🚌🚢 ℹ Barbados Tourist Office, Bridgetown Harbor Rd; 246 427 2623

Founded in 1628, Bridgetown is a fascinating combination of the old and new. The town center is compact and any walking tour typically starts in the National Heroes Square with its statue of Lord Nelson. Adjacent is the Careenage, where in the early days ships would be careened – turned over to have barnacles scraped off their sides. A busy marina today, it is packed with luxury yachts and surrounded by bars, restaurants, and shops.

At the end of Broad Street, the main shopping street in Barbados, are the Italian-Renaissance style **Parliament Buildings**, the third oldest in the English-speaking world, and a U.N.E.S.C.O. World Heritage Site. The Parliament was founded in 1637 and has met regularly since 1639. The west wing houses the Museum of Parliament and the National Heroes Gallery.

Nearby is the **Bridgetown Synagogue** and cemetery. Founded in 1654, the synagogue is the oldest in the Western Hemisphere. It is open to the public, and contains the **Nidhe Israel Museum**.

Bridgetown Harbor hosts the modern cruise-ship terminal. Along the waterfront is the Pelican Village, an arts and crafts center set amid beautiful gardens.

Parliament Buildings
⊛ 🅰 Broad St 📞 246 310 5400 / 5401 🕐 10am–4pm Mon–Fri

Bridgetown Synagogue and Nidhe Israel Museum
⊛ 🅰 Synagogue Lane
📞 246 436 6869 🕐 9am–4pm Mon–Fri

→
A bronze statue of Lord Nelson, erected in 1813, stands in Bridgetown

Did You Know?

The name "Barbados" comes from the Spanish word for beard, due to the island's many bearded fig trees.

Oistins

📍 **7 miles (11 km) SE of Bridgetown** 🚌

Named after the Austin family, the area's first landowners, Oistins is the island's main fishing port and is home to a modern jetty and busy fish market. It has a long history, and in 1652 a treaty was signed here that led to Barbados accepting the authority of Oliver Cromwell, the Lord Protector of England, Ireland, and Scotland.

The village has many historic buildings that are now protected, as well as several rum shops. Visitors can watch the fishing boats return at the end of the day and unload their catch. Oistins is famous for its annual Fish Festival (Easter weekend), during which street stalls are set up to sell salt fish cakes and fried fish amid music and dancing.

Gun Hill Signal Station

📍 **5 miles (8 km) NE of Bridgetown** 🚏 🕐 **9am–5pm Mon–Sat**

Gun Hill Signal Station is part of a chain of signal stations built across the island by the British in 1818. Mirrors were used to flash warnings from one station to the next about approaching enemy ships. Standing at 700 ft (213 m) above sea level, the station has been carefully restored by the Barbados National Trust. It offers great views over most of the island and has a small museum housing military memorabilia. From its tower, the statue of a white lion is visible below the station. This British military emblem was carved in 1868 by Henry Wilkinson, a British officer.

Sunbury Plantation House

📍 **10 miles (16 km) E of Bridgetown** 🚌 🕐 **10am–5pm daily** 🌐 **sunbury plantation.com**

Built around 1660 by one of the island's first settlers, Matthew Chapman, Sunbury Plantation House is among the oldest and grandest of the great houses in Barbados. It was built to withstand hurricanes with walls more than 30 inches (76 cm) thick.

Restored after a fire in 1995, the Great House re-creates the ambience of the 18th and 19th centuries. Its original furnishings have been replaced by antiques from across the island – look out for the Barbados mahogany furniture, some of which has been made from trees grown on the plantation. It is the only great house with all rooms open for viewing, and guests are able to have dinner here and then tour the house. A unique collection of carriages is displayed in the cellars, and plantation machinery is scattered around the landscaped grounds. There is also a bar, restaurant, and gift shop on-site.

TOP 5 GOLF COURSES IN BARBADOS

Old Nine, Sandy Lane
An intimate nine-hole meander, this is the resort's oldest course.

Royal Westmoreland
A championship course overlooking the island's Platinum Coast.

Green Monkey, Sandy Lane
Carved out of a quarry, this Tom Fazio-designed course is ultra-exclusive.

Apes Hill
Challenging holes in a stunning clifftop site.

Barbados Golf Club
A popular, good-value option for the average club golfer.

←

Cooks frying fresh fish on a barbeque during Oistins's annual Fish Festival

↑ The palm-shaded facade and sumptuous interiors *(inset)* of Sunbury Plantation House

Farther east, Crane Beach nestles beneath cliffs that overlook the fabulous white and pink sands. In olden times, ships would anchor in the bay and a clifftop crane would load or unload their cargo. Protected by a coral reef, the bay provides safe swimming.

a stretch of the Thames called the Limehouse Hole.

St. James Parish Church is one of the oldest churches on the island, with some parts believed to date from 1660. The south entrance and porch are more than 300 years old.

Today, Holetown is a busy center with some bars and shops. During the Holetown Festival (Feb), the place comes alive with street parades.

Driving out of Holetown, you will see long expanses of palm-fringed, white-sand beaches along the west coast with its safe, shallow turquoise Caribbean waters. This stretch of coastline is home to many of the island's upscale resorts and private homes.

Just north of Holetown, the Folkstone Marine Park was created in 1976, when a Greek freighter, previously destroyed by fire, was deliberately sunk to create an artificial reef. The deep site is suitable only for experienced divers, but the shallow waters off Folkstone Beach feature a marked underwater trail that can be tackled by all.

⑧ Holetown

🏠 6 miles (10 km) N of Bridgetown 🚌

Located on the west coast, Holetown was first named Jamestown (for the British monarchs, James VI and I) by Captain John Powell in 1625. Two years later, the first English settlers arrived and began calling the place Holetown; the inlet where they anchored reminded them of

RUM PRODUCTION

Forever associated with pirates and sailors, rum has a dark history, built on the back of slavery and the sugar cane industry. Light or white rums, which can be bottled immediately or aged for only a few months, are popularly used in cocktails. Dark or gold rums are usually aged for many years in wooden casks as they develop their color and flavor, and are drunk neat or over ice. Three of the island's distilleries produce some of the world's best aged rum and can be toured - try Mount Gay, the slick Foursquare Rum Distillery & Heritage Park, or St. Nicholas Abbey *(p414)*.

9 Bathsheba

11 miles (18 km) NE of Bridgetown

As travelers approach this small, pretty fishing village on the rugged Atlantic coast, they are met with spectacular views of the huge boulders offshore that line its dramatic landscape. The crashing waves – known as the Soup Bowl – make Bathsheba a popular spot for surfers, and it hosts many international surfing events. Though it's too dangerous to swim here, low tides reveal several rock pools in which to take a sea bath.

On the outskirts of Bathsheba is Andromeda Gardens, one of the most remarkable and varied botanical gardens in the Caribbean. Created by Iris Bannochie in 1954, it was bequeathed by her to the Barbados National Trust. The gardens showcase spectacular botanical displays including hibiscus, orchids, bougainvillea, and heliconia.

A couple of miles southwest of Bathsheba, are the smaller but beautifully landscaped Hunte's Gardens. They're a labor of love for Bajan horticulturalist Anthony Hunte, who greets many visitors personally.

10 Speightstown

10 miles (16 km) NE of Bridgetown

Just over 10 miles (16 km) from Bridgetown lies Speightstown (pronounced "Spikestown"), the island's second town. Formerly a whaling center and the first commercial port in Barbados, these days it exudes a feeling of tranquil nostalgia. Queen Street, the main thoroughfare, retains some of its original architecture, characterized by residential wooden balconies hanging above commercial operations below. Combined with the renovated esplanade, boardwalk, and a sprinkling of appealing eateries, this makes Speightstown a pleasant place to stroll. Midway along the main street, the Arlington House Museum is housed in a restored gabled merchant's home. It chronicles the town's history across stories floors of interactive exhibits.

Heading north of the town takes travelers to the clifftops at windswept North Point, which offers stellar views down the rugged East coast. Between January and March, migrating humpback whales may be spotted from here.

BEACHES IN BARBADOS

Bottom Bay
A favorite for wedding shoots, with azure waves and cream sands.

Crane Beach
Head here for pink sands and boogie-boarding.

Pebbles Beach
Despite the name, expect super-soft sand and gentle waters here.

Paynes Bay
Easily accessible, this is the west coast's biggest beach.

Gibbes Beach
This slender, palm-shaded strip of sand is blissfully secluded.

11

Barbados Wildlife Reserve

14 miles (22 km) NE of Bridgetown ⏰10am–5pm daily 🌐barbadoswildlifereserve.com

The Barbados Wildlife Reserve is a great place at which to see the island's wildlife in its natural surroundings. The reserve was founded in 1985 by Canadian primatologist

Jean Baulu to protect the Barbados green monkey. These monkeys originally came from West Africa in the mid-17th century, but are now found throughout the island. Over time, other native animals such as iguanas, agoutis, armadillos, and the rare red-footed tortoise, have also been introduced into the reserve's mahogany woods.

There are several imported animal species, a walk-through aviary, a collection of snakes, and an education center, built from coral stone gathered from the nearby fields.

Harrison's Cave

🗺 7 miles (11 km) NE of Bridgetown 🚌
🕙 9am–3:45pm Wed–Sun
ℹ Welchman Hall, St. Thomas; www.harrisons cave.com

A magnificent attraction, this cave was carved out over millions of years by seeping surface water. It comprises a series of crystallized limestone subterranean caverns with underground rivers, waterfalls, and uniquely shaped stalagmites, stalactites, and columns. The cave is named for Thomas Harrison, who owned the land in the 1770s. Although several expeditions ventured into the caves, it took almost 200 years before it was fully mapped by Danish engineer and cave adventurer Ole Sorensen. Conducted tours through the caverns aboard electric trolleys are available.

Just north of Harrison's cave, the Old Richmond Plantation is the setting for the sprawling Flower Forest. It was planted by a group of islanders who wanted to preserve an area of tropical beauty for future generations. The area is also rich in wildlife and includes chattering birds and green monkeys, and there is an information center on-site.

Home to 200 species of tropical plants, flowers, and fruits, the Welchman Hall Gully, 2 miles (3 km) north of Harrison's Cave, is owned by the Barbados National Trust. There used to be an entrance from the gully into Harrison's Cave. General William Asygell, the gully's original owner, introduced tropical plants from around the world in 1860, and today there are mature trees and towering bamboo groves. The grapefruit, once called the forbidden fruit of Barbados, is said to have originated here. The aim is to introduce more native plants so that the gully's flora and fauna resembles that of the island in the 18th century.

←
Waves rolling into picturesque Bathsheba bay

↑ The dramatic rock formations inside Harrison's Cave

EAT

Waterfront Café
This popular, semi-open restaurant serves up delicious Caribbean fare with an emphasis on Bajan specialties.

🗺 Careenage, Bridgetown 🗓 Sun 🌐 water frontcafe.com.bb

The Tides
West coast dining at its finest, with inventive seafood dishes and particularly mouthwatering desserts.

🗺 Holetown 🗓 Sat lunch 🌐 tidesbarbados.com

Shakers Bar & Grill
A buzzing rum shop-cum-restaurant, offering a mix of tasty local dishes and North American comfort food. Blackened fish with fries washed down with a rum sour is a winner.

🗺 Brownes Gap, Hastings
📞 246 228 8855
🕙 Tue–Sat, dinner only

PRACTICAL
INFORMATION

Here you will find all the essential advice and information you will need before and during your stay in Barbados.

AT A GLANCE

CURRENCY
Barbados dollar (BDS$)

TIME ZONE
Atlantic Standard Time, 4 hours behind GMT and 1 hour ahead of EST

LANGUAGE
English, but a local Bajan patois – a combination of old English and West African languages – is widely spoken

ELECTRICITY SUPPLY
The electricity supply is generally 110 volts/50 cycles; All European appliances will need adapters

EMERGENCY NUMBERS

AMBULANCE	FIRE SERVICE
511	**311**

POLICE
211

TAP WATER
Tap water is safe to drink

When To Go

The high season is from December to April, but Barbados has year-round good weather with an annual average temperature of 80° F (27° C). The best time to visit is from January to April, which are the coolest months. It tends to get very hot between July and September. There are lots of activities throughout the year, but the Holetown Festival in February and Crop Over Festival in July and August are always exciting times to visit.

Getting There

Grantley Adams International Airport is 8 miles (13 km) east of Bridgetown and is served by several major airlines from the US and Europe, including American Airlines, Air Canada, JetBlue, British Airways, LIAT, Virgin Atlantic, and Caribbean Airlines.

Personal Security

Barbados has a low crime rate but it still pays to take sensible precautions. It is advisable not to wear expensive jewelry or flash large sums of money. Keep valuables out of sight in parked cars or when on the beach, and avoid straying into unfamiliar areas late at night. In case of theft or any crime, report to the police.

Health

There are no serious health problems, but visitors should protect themselves from the sun and insects. Tap water is generally safe to drink. The main hospital is Queen Elizabeth on the outskirts of Bridgetown. The island also has a number of private, modern health centers such as Bayview Hospital and Sandy Crest Medical Centre.

Passports and Visas

All visitors need a valid passport and a return ticket to enter Barbados. A visa is not required from citizens of the US, Canada, UK, most

Caribbean and European countries, and Japan. Travelers should contact the Ministry of Foreign Affairs and Foreign Trade for a list of countries requiring, and exempted from, visas. Officials may also ask travelers to show adequate funds to cover their visit.

LGBT+ Safety

In conservative Barbados, same-sex activity is frowned upon and can draw derisive attention, so public displays of affection are best avoided. The island's LGBT+ and human rights activists have been challenging the anti-homosexuality laws which, though rarely invoked, currently carry a maximum penalty of life imprisonment. Barbados is, however, a popular destination with LGBT+ visitors and the island is gradually becoming more relaxed in its attitude to same-sex relationships.

Money

The official currency is the Barbados dollar (BDS$) which is tied to the US dollar at US$1= BDS$2. It comes in bills of 2 (blue), 5 (green), 10 (brown), 20 (purple) 50 (orange) and 100 (gray) dollars.

Most major credit cards are widely accepted in all the island's cities but may not be welcomed in small places such as cafes. There are 24-hour ATM facilities at a number of locations around the island. However, ATM machines dispense only local currency. Bridgetown, Holetown, and Speightstown have many banks and they also have branches scattered across the island. Banks are open from 8am to 3pm Monday to Thursday and from 8am to 1pm and 3pm to 5pm on Friday. The airport bank is open from 8am to midnight daily.

Cell Phones and Wi-Fi

The international dialling code for Barbados is 246. There is direct international dialing from hotels and payphones, which also accept phone cards. Visitors bringing their own cell phones should check with their service providers to determine if they will work in Barbados. Digicel and FLOW are among the most popular phone operators on the island. Most large hotels offer Internet. Internet cafes are found in most towns.

Getting Around

Buses are a great way to get around and a good way to meet the locals. They operate throughout the island and there is a set fare irrespective of distance. It is advsiable to carry the exact fare or use tokens, which can be bought at bus stations.

Taxis are easily available as well and they are identifiable by "Z" on their license plates. There are no meters, so visitors are advised to agree a fare before the trip. Taxi drivers also make knowledgeable guides for either a half-day or a one-day tour.

A rental car is the best way to explore the island independently. Visitors must have a valid driver's license or international license and purchase a temporary Barbados one. The license is valid for a year. There is a government tax of 12.5 percent on all rentals. Rental cars have an "H" on the license plate. Check the condition of the car, especially the tires, before accepting it and make sure there is a good spare. Cars drive on the left and the speed limit is 25 mph (40 kph) in towns, 40 mph (60 kph) on rural roads, and 50mph (80 kph) on sign-posted highways. Many service stations only accept cash. The main operators are ABC Rentals, Courtesy Car Rentals, Double J Car and Moke Rentals, and Drive-A-Matic Car Rentals.

Visitor Information

All tourist information, including brochures and maps, is available from the **Barbados Tourism Authority**, which has an office in Warrens, St. Michael, as well as two smaller branches at the Bridgetown Port and at Grantley Adams International Airport.

Barbados Tourism Authority
🔳 barbados.org

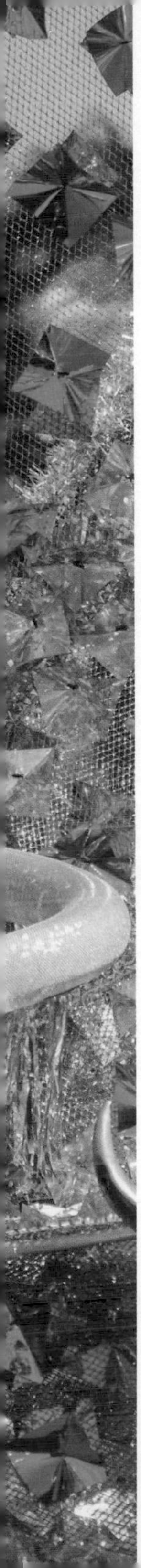

TRINIDAD AND TOBAGO

Often shortened to T&T, the twin-island nation of Trinidad and Tobago Is as physically varied as it is culturally diverse. Lying at the southerly end of the Caribbean chain, the islands have wild Atlantic beaches, calm Caribbean shorelines, and rainforested interiors. Due to their proximity to South America, the islands host an incredibly rich array of wildlife, in particular birds. Trinidad is partly industrialized, its southern half characterized by the trappings of the oil and natural gas industries that have long ensured the country's thriving economy. Unspoiled Tobago, 22 miles (35 km) northeast of Trinidad and, at just 25 miles (40 km) long, tiny compared with its far bigger brother, focuses on tourism, with an emphasis on eco-tourism.

After colonization by the Spanish, Dutch, and French in the 1600s and 1700s, the two islands came under British rule in the early 1800s. Tobago in fact changed hands between the colonial powers some 31 times up to 1814, when it was ceded to the British. In 1962, Trinidad and Tobago became an independent country. Due to centuries of influx of African slaves, European colonial settlers, and indentured laborers from India, brought to work on plantations after slavery was abolished, Trinbagonians are an incredibly multicultural lot. Trinidad's famous pre-Lenten carnival is the ultimate expression of the Trini identity, and a showcase of calypso and steel pan music, which originated on the islands.

TRINIDAD AND TOBAGO

Experience

1. Port of Spain
2. Chaguaramas and the Bocas
3. Blanchisseuse
4. Maracas Bay
5. Asa Wright Nature Centre and Lodge
6. Central and South Trinidad
7. The Northeast Coast
8. Pigeon Point Beach
9. Crown Point
10. Buccoo
11. Mount Irvine
12. Kimme Museum
13. Castara
14. Englishman's Bay to Bloody Bay
15. Tobago Cocoa Estate
16. Scarborough
17. The Windward Coast
18. Tobago Forest Reserve
19. Charlotteville
20. Speyside
21. Little Tobago

Tobago

Turtle Beac

MOUNT IRVINE **11**

BUCCOO **10**

PIGEON POINT BEACH **8**

Bon Accord

CROWN **9**
POINT

ANR Robinson
International
Airport

Trinidad

TRINIDAD
AND TOBAGO

Bocas

CHAGUARAMAS **2**
AND THE BOCAS

Tobago

Trinidad

Point Fortin

Cedros
Point

Bonasse   Chatham

Columbus
Bay

Icacos

San
Francique

St. Giles
Islands

L'Anse
Fourmi

Man
O'War Bay

19 CHARLOTTEVILLE

Cambleton

SPEYSIDE **20**

21
LITTLE
TOBAGO

Bloody
Bay

Parlatuvier

Delaford

ENGLISHMAN'S BAY
TO BLOODY BAY **14**

Parrot Hall

King's
Bay

CASTARA **13**

King Peter's Bay

18
TOBAGO FOREST
RESERVE

Roxborough

Culloden
Bay

Moriah

TOBAGO
COCOA ESTATE

17 THE WINDWARD COAST

Plymouth

15

Mason Hall

Glamorgan

Belle Garden

Goodwood

Pembroke

2 KIMME MUSEUM

Mount St George

Goldsborough Bay

Bethel

16 SCARBOROUGH

Lambeau

Bacolet
Point

Little
Rockly
Bay

0 kilometers   6
0 miles   6

N

↙ Port of Spain

↗ Scarborough

San
Souci

Toco

MARACAS
BAY

Blanchisseuse
Bay

Matelot

Grande
Rivière

Maracas **4**

3 BLANCHISSEUSE

7 THE NORTHEAST
COAST

Las
Cuevas

Maraval

El Tucuche
3,071 ft (936 m)

5 ASA WRIGHT NATURE
CENTRE AND LODGE

Salybia

**PORT OF
SPAIN** **1**

Matura

Tunapuna

Piarco
International
Airport

Arima

Valencia

Gulf of
Paria

Coroni
Swamp

St. Helena

Sangre Grande

Cunupia

Coroni Arena
Reservoir

Cunaripa

Upper Manzanilla

Longdenville

Talparo

Lower
Manzanilla

Carapichaima

Todd's Road

Biche

Manzanillo
Bay

Couva

Navet
Reservoir

Nariva
Swamp

California

Tabaquite

Point Lisas

Tortuga

6 CENTRAL AND
SOUTH TRINIDAD

Guctuaro
Point

Claxton Bay

Point Radix

Marabella

Rio Claro

Ortoire River

San Fernando

Tableland

Mayaro

La Brea

Princes
Town

Vessigny

Preau

Fyzabad

Penal

Basse
Terre

Guayaguayare

os Bajos

Siparia

Sadhoowa

Rushville

Galeota
Point

Palo Seco

Moruga

Trinity Hills

Palo Seco
Bay

Moruga
Point

0 kilometers   20
0 miles   20

N

Swamps and Wetlands

The sky floods a deep pink as thousands of scarlet ibis return to roost – the main draw of an afternoon boat ride through Caroni Swamp *(p430)*. Beyond the birdlife, boas coil round branches, caiman and anacondas lurk in the shallows, while crab-eating racoons and silky anteaters skulk in the undergrowth. Over in Nariva Swamp *(p432)*, capuchin and red howler monkeys steal the show in the canopy. A paddle through the wetlands may also result in a rare sighting of the elusive manatee.

→

Embarking on a boat tour through the Caroni Swamp

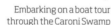

TRINIDAD AND TOBAGO FOR
WILDLIFE ENCOUNTERS

Due to Trinidad and Tobago's proximity to South America, the islands' tropical wetlands, forests, and coastline are teeming with exotic wildlife. A birdwatcher's paradise, the country hosts around 470 species, while its protected areas are home to a wealth of other fascinating creatures.

Around the Coast

Witnessing turtles lumbering up the sands to deposit their eggs from March through August, or the hatchlings making their perilous dash toward the sea, is a poignant experience. Community guides organize responsible turtle-watching tours.

←

Leatherback sea turtles approaching the sea

TURTLE WATCHING

Visitors need to be quiet and maintain a distance behind the nesting turtle, which can easily be spooked. Torches/flashlights must be turned off (unless infrared) and flash photography should not be used. It's also imperative not to block the female's path up the beach, nor impede her retreat back into the sea.

TOP 5

BIRDS OF TRINIDAD AND TOBAGO

Channel-Billed Toucan
The blue and black bill of this toucan can be seen in the rainforest canopy.

Scarlet Ibis
Look out for flocks of these deep pink birds in Caroni Swamp.

Red-Billed Tropicbird
Dreamy tail feathers make this the poster bird of Little Tobago.

Ruby Topaz Hummingbird
One of T&T's 17 species of hummingbird, this sports a golden breast.

Cocrico
The national bird of Tobago is a noisy pheasant-shaped fowl.

← Bats flying from Mount Tamana

Rainforest-clad mountains

Trinidad is home to the world-renowned Asa Wright Nature Centre *(p432)* with its remarkable array of colorful birds. In contrast, the twilight mass exodus of hungry bats from the caves of Mount Tamana is a spectacular sight, while the Tobago Forest Reserve *(p438)* is a magnet for bird-lovers, and home to the rare sabrewing hummingbird.

→ A queen angelfish swimming in the waters of Tobago

Beneath the Waves

Marine wonderlands lie round the protected reefs off Tobago, offering the chance to swim along with shoals of psychedelic fish while on the lookout for lobster and eels, hidden in the crevices. Thrilling drift dives in the nutrient-rich current off the Atlantic coast offer large manta rays and schools of huge barracuda and jacks. Speyside *(p439)* highlights include the Caribbean's largest brain coral – 15 ft (5 m) across – and the exquisitely hued soft and hard corals of the Japanese Gardens.

Costumed dancers taking part in Port of Spain's carnival parade ↑

EXPERIENCE

 1

Port of Spain

⌂ NW coast of Trinidad ✈⛴
🛈 29 Tenth Ave, Barataria;
868 675 7034

Gridlocked with traffic but bubbling with life, Trinidad's capital is home to the island's best restaurants and nightlife, as well as a vibrant cultural scene. Downtown's centerpiece is Independence Square, a shop-lined boulevard with the Brian Lara Promenade – named after Trinidad's greatest ever cricketer – in the middle. A short walk from here is the state-of-the-art **Central Bank Museum**, with interactive exhibits including the history of money, local currency, and works from the Bank's extensive art collection. To the north, busy Frederick Street threads up past Woodford Square, a grassy park that is home to an impromptu speakers' corner known as the University. On the square's western side stands the Red House, the imposing Neo-Renaissance parliament building. At the northern end of Frederick Street, the **National Museum and Art Gallery** houses a collection on local history and geology, an art gallery, and the imposing National Academy for the Performing Arts (NAPA), the venue for concerts and other cultural events. Past the museum are the wide spaces of Queen's Park Savannah, the focal point of the annual Carnival parade. At its northern edge, the **Royal Botanic Gardens** are home to some 700 trees and exotic plants that attract plenty of birds. The avifauna is even more prolific at the nearby **Caroni Swamp Bird Sanctuary**, where the main draw is the stunning scarlet ibis. Daily boat tours leave around 4pm – in time to witness thousands of ibis returning to roost.

→

Silhouetted palm trees as the sun sets on Maracas Bay

Central Bank Museum
 Eric Williams Plaza
🕒 9am–3pm Mon–Fri
🌐 central-bank.org.tt

National Museum and Art Gallery
🕒 Cnr Frederick & Keate sts 📞 868 623 0339 🕒 10am–6pm Tue–Sat, 2–6pm Sun

Royal Botanic Gardens
Circular Rd 📞 868 622 4221 🕒 6am–6pm daily

Caroni Swamp Bird Sanctuary
Off Uriah Butler Hwy 🕒 9am–4pm daily 🌐 caroni birdsanctuary.com

---

②
Chaguaramas and the Bocas

📍 6 miles (10 km) W of Port of Spain 🚌 ℹ Chaguaramas Development Authority (CDA), off Western Main Rd; www.chaguaramas.com

Port of Spain's playground, and a haven for yacht owners, the Chaguaramas area occupies the island's western tip. To the north is a national park centered around Tucker Valley, with its bamboo groves, rainforests, and hiking trails. On the southern coast, where U.S. troops built a base during World War II, the **Military History and Aerospace Museum** chronicles the island's military history. Spreading into the Gulf of Paria, the Bocas islands are a favored spot for palatial holiday homes. Gaspar Grande holds the **Gasparee Cave**, a huge cavern with some impressive stalactites and a pool at its base.

Military History and Aerospace Museum
 Western Main Rd, Chaguaramas 📞 868 634 4391 🕒 9am–5pm Tue–Sun

Gasparee Cave
Gasparee Island

---

③
Blanchisseuse

📍 17 miles (27 km) NE of Port of Spain 🚌

The closest thing to a resort on Trinidad's northern coast is Blanchisseuse. With its upper and lower villages, this rural area is backed by a string of wild beaches that are favored by surfers. It offers peace and quiet, a few appealing places to stay and dine, and swimming in the sea and the sparklingly clean Marianne River. The river also has a number of waterfalls upstream, reached by an easy 30-minute walk. It is possible to hike from Blanchisseuse along the undeveloped coastline to the east, toward spectacular Paria Bay without a guide.

④
Maracas Bay

📍 7 miles (11 km) NE of Port of Spain

Trinidad's most popular beach, Maracas Bay is a palm-lined sweep of fine yellow sand, backed by forested hills. Quiet during the week, it becomes the place to be on weekends, when locals set up camp under beach umbrellas and enjoy drinks and food, such as the must-try Bake 'n' Shark.

East of Maracas is another lovely spot for swimming: Las Cuevas, the north coast's longest beach. Quieter than Maracas but with the same facilities – its only downside is the sandfly population.

Asa Wright Nature Centre and Lodge

📍 Arima Valley, Arima-Blanchisseuse Rd, Trinidad
🕐 9am–5pm daily
🌐 asawright.org

High in the rainforested hills of the Northern Range, this center is a renowned ecolodge that offers some of the best bird-watching in the Caribbean. Spread out around a colonial great house, the 2-sq-mile (5-sq-km) pristine forest is home to a multitude of birds and animals. Bird-watchers can see up to 159 species of birds, some with stunning plumages. Non-guests can visit during the day to tour the immediate grounds and for lunch.

Central and South Trinidad

Home to the majority of the island's East Indian population, Central and South Trinidad have some stunning natural attractions. Lining the east coast is the spectacular 14 mile (22 km) Manzanilla Beach, backed with a dense coconut plantation that gives the area its name, The Cocal. Inland from here, the threatened Nariva Swamp extends across 23 sq miles (60 sq km). A mix of reed-lined marshes, mangroves, and the Bush Bush Island Forest Reserve, this wetland area – Trinidad and Tobago's largest – is best visited during the rains. Guided tours can take nature-lovers in boats or kayaks along channels where caiman, anacondas, and peaceful manatee lurk.

Southern Trinidad is oil country, and roadside derricks and offshore rigs have become part of the scenery. The geological richness bubbles to the surface at La Brea, site of the world's largest **Pitch Lake.** Covering an area of around eight soccer pitches, it contains an estimated 10 million tons of

Asa Wright Nature Centre and Lodge, home to many bird species *(inset)* ↓

↑ A guided boat tour through the Bush Island Forest Reserve

> 💬 **INSIDER TIP**
> **Turtle-Watching**
>
> Visitors on a turtle watch need to maintain a respectful distance and should not use flash photography. It is also imperative not to block the female's path up the beach or back to the sea.

asphalt. A guide from the visitor center will ensure that you experience the lake's disconcerting hissing in a safe way without being sucked under in gooey, more liquid sections.

On the northern outskirts of Trinidad's second city, San Fernando, visitors can observe rare birdlife at the **Point-a-Pierre Wildfowl Trust**. Also in the area is the **Maha Sabha Indian Caribbean Museum**, stuffed full of documents, artifacts, and photos chronicling the country's Indian-Trinidadian experience.

Pitch Lake

🕒 🏠 Southern Trunk Rd
📞 868 651 1232 🕘 9am–5pm daily

Point-a-Pierre Wildfowl Trust

⬡ ⬡ 🏠 Off the Southern Main Road 📞 868 658 4200
🕘 10am–5pm daily
🌐 papwildfowltrust.org

Maha Sabha Indian Caribbean Museum

🏠 Waterloo 🕘 10am–5pm Wed–Fri 🌐 icmtt.org

---

⑦
The Northeast Coast

🚌 To Arima

The northeast coastline is among Trinidad's most beautiful. Matura, a wind-swept stretch of beach, is favored by leatherbacks as an egg-laying site. For a number of years a community turtle conservation project has been running (turtlevillagetrust.org). The community also offers visitors responsible guided turtle-watches, during the turtle season (March through August). Matura is also a great spot for beachcombing, but the waters are too rough to swim. Visitors can take a dip some 2 miles (3 km) north at

Salybia, where Rio Seco Waterfall, surrounded by greenery, tumbles down into a wide, deep pool. Kayaking on the Salybia River is also offered in this area.

For proper beachlife, it is best to head another 12 miles (19 km) along the main road to Toco, a peaceful fishing village whose calm waters are protected by a reef.

The only good resort along the northeast coast is Grande Riviere, a laid-back spot by the rugged beach with a few staying and eating options. To the west, Shark River offers freshwater bathing.

> **Did You Know?**
>
> There is enough asphalt in Pitch Lake to pave around 3,100 miles (5,000 km) of highway.

Colorful seaside huts on
Pigeon Point Beach

Pigeon Point Beach

⌂ Pigeon Point Rd,
Crown Point

Hyped as Tobago's best beach, Pigeon Point is certainly the island's most quintessentially Caribbean seashore, with its white sand overhung by palm trees, and turquoise waters lapping at the base of its thatched-roof jetty. Controversially, it is also the only beach on the island to charge an entrance fee, which is used to maintain the excellent facilities. Pigeon Point is a great place to spend the day, especially for families with kids, since there is a play ground and the calm waters remain shallow almost up to the distant reef. There are stalls selling food and drinks, while jet skis and Hobie Cats buzz around offshore.

Crown Point

⌂ SE coast of Tobago
✈ 🚌 ℹ️ ANR Robinson
International Airport;
868 639 0509

Tobago's most touristy area, Crown Point holds a wealth of restaurants and hotels, as well as some great beaches.

Within walking distance of the airport, **Store Bay Beach** is a compact stretch of white sand with gentle surf, clear waters, and several craft shops. There is also a line of restaurants that serve some delicious takeaway lunches and breakfasts.

Store Bay Beach
⌂ Store Bay Local Rd
🕙 Lifeguards and changing facilities: 10am–6pm daily

Buccoo

⌂ 4 miles (6 km) NE of Crown Point, Tobago 🚌

Northeast of Crown Point, Shirvan Road shoots off the main Milford Road toward Buccoo, a faded fishing village

STEEL PANS

The sound of sweet steel pan is synonymous with Trinidad and Tobago, and visiting a panyard (where pan bands practice) can be an exhilarating experience. Made from oil drums, pans vary in size and musical range from the tenor pan to the bass, which consists of a set of six full-size oil drums. Band sizes also vary, with some containing over 100 pannists. Every year, soloists and bands compete for prizes and bragging rights in the annual Panorama competition in Queen's Park Savannah just before Carnival.

that plays host to the Sunday School outdoor party each Sunday night. This vibrant street party begins every week with music from a local steel band orchestra.

Just offshore, Buccoo Reef is the island's most heavily visited patch of coral, with double-decker glass-bottom boats making regular sorties from all the beaches in the area. Though the 40-odd species of coral have suffered a lot of damage from storms and human encroachment, there is still some color to be seen alongside a host of gorgeous tropical fish such as butterfly and parrot fish. If leaving the boat to snorkel during a tour, it's important

Did You Know?

The steel pan is said to be the only acoustic instrument that was invented in the 20th century.

not to put your feet down, in order to avoid causing any further damage to the fragile environment.

To the south of the reef is the crystal-clear water of the Nylon Pool sandbar, where swimming is a thoroughly refreshing treat.

 11

Mount Irvine

🏠 5 miles (8 km) NE of Crown Point, Tobago 🚌

Past Buccoo is Mount Irvine, a coastal village that is home to Tobago's first golf course, the 18-hole **Mount Irvine Golf Course.** Slight farther along is Mount Irvine Bay Beach, a stretch of yellow sand overhung by sea grape and palm trees, and with covered gazebos for picnicking. Other amenities include washroom facilities and a handful of appealing restaurants and bars. The waves here are some of the best in Tobago, making it a surfers' paradise between November and April. At the other side of the beach is a sandy area that offers lovely swimming and good snorkeling over the rocks and coral. Beyond Mount Irvine, the coast road sweeps past two more excellent places to swim, Grafton and Turtle Beaches. Both have long, wide strands, crystal water, and are perfect for a day by the sea.

Mount Irvine Golf Course
⏱ ➄ 🏠 Shirvan Rd
🌐 mtlrvine.com

← A tour boat cruising through the calm waters off the shore of Crown Point

12

Kimme Museum

5 miles (8 km) NE of Crown Point 10am–2pm Sun, or by appt luisekimme.com

Just past the Mount Irvine Golf Course (p435), Orange Hill Road leads up into the hills and to the intriguing Kimme Museum, the turreted, mural-decorated former home and studio of German sculptor Luise Kimme, who lived in Tobago for some 30 years, until her death in 2013. Inspired by local life and folklore, her stunning pieces are each sculpted from a whole oak trunk, and depict everything from the mythical La Diablesse to Nijinsky dancers, and dancing couples.

13

Castara

18 miles (29 km) NE of Crown Point

Castara is the first point of interest along this stretch of inaccessible coastline; a beautiful mini-resort that has grown up around a placid fishing village and a gorgeous curve of beach. It is a laid-back and attractive spot, and is ideal for spending some time relaxing, with a couple of great beachside eateries and a sprinkling of guesthouses overlooking the bay. There is enough space so it rarely feels crowded; however, if need be, it is possible to seek some solitude in the adjoining Little Bay. Castara is also one of the points from which boat tours are available for the various excellent beaches and snorkeling spots located nearby.

14

Englishman's Bay to Bloody Bay

20 miles (32 km) NE of Crown Point

The countryside beyond Castara becomes noticeably less developed, with the

↑ Colorful boats littering the golden sands of Castara's beach

Northside Road twisting through jungle-smothered hillsides with hardly a building in sight. The first place to stop is Englishman's Bay, a stunning horseshoe of yellow sand that lies between untouched rainforest on one side and emerald waters on the other. The offshore reef here offers good snorkeling opportunities.

Just above the fishing village of Parlatuvier, people can stop at a roadside parking spot for some pretty views of the bay below, with fishing boats bobbing in the water and terraced smallholdings rolling up the hillside.

Beyond this village is Bloody Bay, which offers some fine coastal views, with the spectacular Sisters Rocks lying just offshore. At the bay's rough, yellow-sand beach, a turnoff swings inland leading to the Tobago Forest Reserve (p438). Moving east along the coast, visitors finally reach Charlotteville (p439) at the island's northeast tip.

15

Tobago Cocoa Estate

Cameron Canal Rd, Roxborough tobago cocoa.com

The scenic views are a bonus during the informative tours of this small cocoa estate,

↑ The dramatic curve of Englishman's Bay, backed by one of the world's longest protected rainforests

where visitors can learn about the whole chocolate-making process from bean to bar, finishing up with a tasting. Although the business was established in 2006, it took five years for the first bar to be produced. The plantation grows the organic cacao, which is turned into award-winning artisanal chocolate by a chocolatier in France. The popular estate tours run weekly from December to April; outside of this they are by advance appointment only (email to book), and will be run only for a minimum of ten people.

16

Scarborough

🚗 7 miles (11 km) NE of Crown Point, Tobago 🚌
ℹ️ Cruise ship complex; 868 635 0934

Tobago's capital, Scarborough, is a hotbed of activity compared to the rest of the island, with taxis and shoppers crowding the streets, vendors setting up their stalls at the roadside, and plenty of traffic streaming to and from the busy ferry port. The best place for shopping is the market, set back from the seafront and accessed from Gardenside Street. It is busiest on Fridays and Saturdays, but visitors will always find piles of exotic fruits and vegetables and other assorted general goods.

On the other side of Gardenside Street is the vast Botanical Garden, its smooth lawns and fishponds offering quiet respite from the clamor. It is open every day.

Scarborough's other main draw is Fort King George. A collection of handsome, restored colonial-era brick buildings surrounding the modern lighthouse, the complex features many cannons and offers sweeping views down the windward coast and over Scarborough. The fort is also home to the small but interesting **Tobago Museum**, which has some absorbing exhibits on the island's local history.

Tobago Museum
♿ 🏛️ Fort King George
📞 868 639 3970 🕐 9am–4:30pm Mon–Fri

> The first place to stop is Englishman's Bay, a stunning horeshoe of yellow sand that lies between untouched rainforest on one side and emerald waters on the other.

EAT

Veni Mangé
This hospitable restaurant has a lively vibe, with painted wooden tables and walls laden with local art. The Creole-influenced menu is delicious – try the grilled fish with tamarind or *chadon beni* sauce.

📍 67A Ariapita Ave, Port of Spain 📞 868 624 4597 🕐 Sat & Sun

Makara
Creative modern Caribbean cuisine is beautifully presented and served in style at this sophisticated eatery that overlooks Buccoo's bay. Sample elegant cocktails as the sun goes down, and the waves wash gently over the rocks below.

📍 55 Auchenskeoch Rd, Buccoo 🕐 Tue 🌐 makaratobago.com

Kariwak Village
The ambience is relaxed and rustic at this open-sided, thatched-roof restaurant. The menu is set daily, based on whatever is freshly available, with a *prix fixe* menu featuring plenty of local vegetables. On weekends, a dinner buffet is served, accompanied by live music.

📍 Store Bay Local Rd, Crown Point 🌐 kariwak.com

17

The Windward Coast

📍 15 miles (24 km) NE of Scarborough, Tobago 🚌

In comparison with the tranquil leeward side of the island, bordered by the calm Caribbean Sea, the windward coast is more rugged, washed by pounding Atlantic waves and with strong currents that make some beaches out of bounds to swimmers. The best place to experience the sea is King's Bay, fringed by a forest of palms and with calm water and fine volcanic sand. To the southwest there is another chance to get wet at **Argyle Waterfall**, the island's highest three-tiered cascade with several pools. Otherwise, the windward coast is best appreciated as a scenic – if winding – drive, its pretty villages with board houses teetering at the edge of the cliffs or spreading out on either side of the coastal road.

Argyle Waterfall

⊗ ⊗ ⊜ 📍 Windward Rd ⏰ 9am–5pm daily; last tour 4pm

↑ Visitors exploring the lush, thickly packed greenery of Tobago Forest Reserve

18

Tobago Forest Reserve

📍 17 miles (27 km) NE of Scarborough, Tobago 🚇

The Tobago Forest Reserve, which is the oldest protected rainforest in the Western Hemisphere, comprises approximately 22 sq miles (57 sq km) of land in the northern half of the island, accessible via a scenic road. Much of the area cannot be reached, but from Gilpin Trace – marked by a huge rock by the roadside – visitors can follow a trail into the close-packed forest, with its towering trees and greenish light filtering through the thick canopy. Traveling with a guide is recommended and you can hire one at the entrance to the reserve.

Did You Know?

The red color of the scarlet ibis - Trinidad's national bird - comes from carotene in its diet of shellfish.

Charletteville

🏠 **27 miles (43 km) NE of Scarborough, Tobago** 🚌

Tucked into a protected bay at Tobago's extreme north-east tip, Charlotteville is a slow-paced place, with tourism and fishing coexisting easily as the main industries. Tumbling down a steep hillside, the village meets the sea at the yellow sands and calm waters of Man O' War Bay.

Overlooking the bay to the west is the Cambleton Battery, while to the east, via a rough track around the headland, is Pirate's Bay – perhaps Tobago's prettiest beach, entirely unde-veloped and with excellent snorkeling spots.

Speyside

🏠 **20 miles (32 km) NE of Scarborough** 🚌 **From Scarborough**

On the island's east coast, Speyside offers some of Tobago's best diving and snorkeling. The viewing area on the Scarborough road gives a bird's-eye view of the brightly painted village and the offshore islands, including Little Tobago rising from the blue seas.

It's possible to see some incredibly diverse marine life among Speyside's reefs, while above ground there is also some great bird-watching.

Little Tobago

🏠 **2 miles (3 km) NE of Speyside in Tyrrel's Bay**

As one of the Caribbean's main seabird sanctuaries, Little Tobago is a highlight for bird-watchers – though this protected islet will enthrall even the most casual nature lover, thronging as it does with colonies of brown and red-footed boobies, terns, and magnificent frigate birds (especially impressive when the males inflate their scarlet pouches). But the stars of the show are the red-billed tropicbirds, with their trade-mark scarlet bills, dazzling

TOP 4 VIEWPOINTS IN TOBAGO

Flagstaff Hill
A former military lookout, offering views across both Atlantic and Caribbean waters.

Glasgow Bar
It's hard to beat this breezy cliffside setting above Parlatuvier Bay.

Caribbean Kitchen
An open-sided veranda that offers unmatched views of the sunset.

Fort King George
The steep climb from Scarborough is worth it; look out for the rugged landscapes to the east.

white plumage tinged with black, and trailing tail feathers. During the nesting season (December through March) their aerial acrobatic displays are captivating. Glass-bottom boats are easily rented in Speyside, taking tourists out to the island on a guided trip that may also include a spot of snorkeling at the delightful Angel Reef, though serious bird-watchers can engage a naturalist guide and focus on the avifauna.

The main viewpoint sits at the top of the small island, affording great views back to Pigeon Peak on the mainland. Though the birds are the main draw, the steep-sided forested outcrop is home to plenty of intriguing reptiles – such as green iguanas and a host of geckos and lizards – and curious plants, such as giant anthuriums and Texas madrones, the bark of which exfoliates to reveal colorful smooth underlayers.

A diver hovering above an impressive reef formation off the shore from Speyside

PRACTICAL
INFORMATION

Here you will find all the essential advice and information you will need before and during your stay in Trinidad and Tobago.

CURRENCY
TT dollar (TT$)

TIME ZONE
Atlantic Standard Time, 4 hours behind GMT and 1 hour ahead of EST

LANGUAGE
English is the main language spoken on both islands, but French Creole (or patois) is still spoken among elders in Trinidad

ELECTRICITY SUPPLY
The electric current is 110 or 220 volts, 60 cycles. Plug sockets take two flat prongs

EMERGENCY NUMBERS

FIRE AND AMBULANCE	POLICE
990	**999**

TAP WATER
Tap water is safe to drink

When To Go

The best time to visit is between January and May, when the weather is most pleasant. By May, the dry season has parched the landscape. June through December is the rainy season. Visitors also come during September, when there is a dry spell known as the Indian summer and the air fares dip.

Getting There

The islands are served by international flights that land at Piarco International Airport and ANR Robinson International Airport in Trinidad and Tobago, respectively. The main airlines are American Airlines, JetBlue, Caribbean Airlines, Continental, Delta, Condor, British Airways, Virgin Atlantic, and WestJet. Ferries and cruise ships dock at King's Wharf in Trinidad, and Scarborough in Tobago.

Personal Security

Crime is a problem in inner city areas of Port of Spain, and visitors have been victims of robberies in both Trinidad and Tobago. Be especially alert if leaving Piarco International Airport after dark, as travelers have been accosted in the airport parking lot, on the highway, and outside residences on arrival. Avoid maxi taxis and arrange a taxi pickup through your hotel. To stay safe, avoid walking alone at night in deserted areas, and lonely beaches.

Health

There are no major health hazards on the islands. Both islands have good hospitals, such as the Port of Spain General Hospital and Scarborough General Hospital.

Passports and Visas

Citizens of the European Union (plus Switzerland and Norway), the US, and Canada do not need a visa for stays of less than three months. Citizens

of other countries must apply for a visa from the nearest Trinidad and Tobago embassy or consulate.

LGBT+ Safety

In 2018, a legal challenge to the country's law against consensual homosexual sex was upheld in court. Though appealed by the Government, the judge's ruling that the law was unconstitutional gave a boost to the LGBT+ community. Although it remains on the books, at least for now, the law is not enforced and there's a very lively and activist LGBT+ community, with public events during Pride month and other activities during the year. However, as the general population is at best tolerant and can be hostile, it is wise to be cautious, especially with public displays of affection.

Cell Phones and Wi-Fi

Visitors bringing cell phones should check with their service providers to check if they will work in Trinidad and Tobago and whether they will be subject to roaming charges. Both islands' code is 1 868. Tri-band mobiles will work in the two islands, and local pay-as-you-go SIM cards are also widely available. Wi-Fi is accessible in most hotels and restaurants, shopping centers and at various hotspots throughout the islands.

Money

The local currency is the TT dollar (TT$). Banks, found in all towns and cities, offer the best exchange rates. ATMs are widespread; those at Crown Point and Piarco airports dispense US dollars and local currency. Credit cards are widely accepted.

Getting Around

Apart from a reliable bus service connecting the major towns on both islands, transportation is run privately. All buses in Trinidad leave from the City Gate terminus in downtown Port of Spain, as do maxi taxis (20-seater buses), color-coded yellow (Port of Spain and the west), red (east west corridor), green (central and south), black (around Princes Town), and brown (San

Fernando). In Tobago, buses depart from the depot on Sangster Hill Road in Scarborough. Route taxis running on set routes are great for short trips. It is best to ask locals for help with the routes. A water taxi connects the Port of Spain to San Fernando, as well as Chaguaramas in the Western Peninsula.

However, the easiest way to get around the islands is to take a tour or rent a car. There are numerous car rental companies on both islands. Visitors renting a car need to be over 25 and should hold a valid driving license. Major international companies such as Thrifty and Hertz have franchises on both islands. Other car rental companies include Econo-Car, Auto Rentals, Rattan's, and Sheppy's. It is advisable to check the condition of the vehicle before hiring it.

The two islands are also linked by air and ferry. Airports are at Piarco and Crown Point, while ferries run between Port of Spain and Scarborough.

Visitor Information

The **Tourism Development Company**, Trinidad and Tobago's tourist board, operates booths at both international airports.
Tourism Development Company
 gotrinidadandtobago.com

ARUBA, CURAÇAO, AND BONAIRE

Lying just north of Venezuela, the so-called A.B.C. islands have a dry climate and are located outside the hurricane belt. They are part of the Kingdom of the Netherlands, with Aruba and Curaçao largely autonomous countries, and Bonaire a "special municipality."

The Dutch West India Company took over the islands in the 1630s, established plantations and imported African slaves, training them for domestic and farm labor, then reselling them throughout the Caribbean and the Americas. During these years, the creole Papiamentu language began to evolve, incorporating Dutch, Spanish, Portuguese, and some Arawak and African dialects. Today, it is still widely spoken, though the official language is Dutch. When Venezuela discovered oil off its northern coast in the early 1900s, Aruba and Curaçao became distilling centers, and immigrant workers arrived from around the world. The Dutch developed Curaçao into one of the Caribbean's most important ports, and today it is a valuable petroleum refining center. Tourism, however, is also a vital part of the economy, on all three islands.

While the Dutch heritage is a strong presence on the A.B.C.s, it's mixed with classic Caribbean elements. The islands hold annual carnivals showcasing their music, a combination of traditional calypso and drum-pounding tumba that produces spirit-lifting beats, as well as street dances called jump-ups.

ARUBA, CURAÇAO AND BONAIRE

Experience

① Oranjestad
② California Dunes and Lighthouse
③ Palm Beach
④ Arikok National Park
⑤ Eagle Beach
⑥ Christoffel National Park
⑦ Museum Kura Hulanda
⑧ Curaçao Maritime Museum
⑨ Willemstad
⑩ Flamingo Sanctuary
⑪ Washington Slagbaai National Park
⑫ Kralendijk
⑬ Kaminda Goto
⑭ Rincón
⑮ Pekelmeer

ARUBA, CURAÇAO, AND BONAIRE

Aruba   Bonaire   Curaçao

Aruba

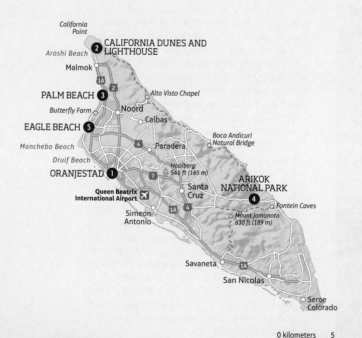

California Point
CALIFORNIA DUNES AND LIGHTHOUSE ②
Arashi Beach
Malmok
1A
②
Alto Visto Chapel
PALM BEACH ③
Butterfly Farm
Noord
Calbas
EAGLE BEACH ⑤
④
Boca Andicuri Natural Bridge
Manchebo Beach
Paradera
Druif Beach
Hooiberg 541 ft (165 m)
⑦
ORANJESTAD ①
ARIKOK NATIONAL PARK ④
Queen Beatrix International Airport
Santa Cruz
④
Fontein Caves
Simeon Antonio
1A
△ Mount Jamanota 630 ft (189 m)
Savaneta
1A
San Nicolas
Seroe Colorado

0 kilometers   5
0 miles   5

N

Curaçao

Sabana Westpunt

CHRISTOFFEL
NATIONAL PARK

6

Barber

Soto

*Santa
Marta Bay*

Dokterstuin

Tera Kora

Sint Willibrordus

10

**Curaçao
International Airport**

FLAMINGO SANCTUARY

*Playa
Kanoa*

Meiberg

Hato

Sint Michiel

Muizenberg

MUSEUM KURA HULANDA **7** **8** CURAÇAO MARITIME MUSEUM

9 WILLEMSTAD

Seru Grandi

*Mambo
Beach*

Oostpunt

0 kilometers 10

0 miles 10

N

Bonaire

WASHINGTON SLAGBAAI
NATIONAL PARK

Playa Funchi

11

Boca Cocolishi

Boca Slagbaai

Lake Goto

KAMINDA GOTO **13** **14** RINCÓN

Karpata

Santa Barbara

Hato

Antriol

*Klein
Bonaire*

12 KRALENDIJK

Bonaire International Airport

Belnem

*Lac
Bay*

*Sorobon
Beach*

Pink Beach

15 PEKELMEER

Lacre Point

0 kilometers 10

0 miles 10

N

Pastel-painted buildings
within the port town of
Oranjestad

Archaeological Museum

Schelpstraat 42 297 582
8979 For renovation

②

California Dunes
and Lighthouse

7 miles (11 km) N of
Oranjestad, Aruba

The main west coast highway
leads north to the California
Lighthouse at the tip of the
island. Just past the town of
Malmok is an elevated
stretch of isolated land
known locally as
hudishibana (in the
native language
once spoken by
the Caiquetio), but
often called the
California Dunes.
Here, rolling
mounds of white
sand spread across
a desert landscape,
surrounding the
lighthouse that was
constructed on the
island between
1914 and 1916. The
name comes from
the S.S. *California*, a
wooden-hulled
ship that sank just
offshore in the late
1800s, and is now
a popular dive
site. The light-
house is closed to

EXPERIENCE

①

Oranjestad

W coast of Aruba
L G Smith Blvd.; 297 582
3777

At the center of Aruba's
capital, Oranjestad, lies the
Yacht Basin and cruise-ship
port, fronted by brightly colored shops and restaurants
built in Dutch colonial style.
Lloyd G. Smith Boulevard, the
main roadway, runs along the
waterfront and connects the
town to popular tourist areas
along the northwest coast.
Although the town lacks major
attractions, it offers a pleasant
diversion from the beach.

At the south end of the
town lies Fort Zoutman, constructed in 1796 and named
for an admiral in the Dutch
navy. Adjoining the fort is
Willem III Tower, which
was built in 1868. It is well-
preserved and used to serve
as a lighthouse. Across from
the fort, is the Renaissance
Mall and marketplace, with
more than 100 upscale shops.
A couple of blocks inland, the
small **Archaeological
Museum** displays stone tools
from 4,500 years ago found at
Arikok and Sero Muskita, and
human bones unearthed from

the settlements of the
island's first Arawak
inhabitants,
the Caiquetio.

Near the main hotel
area is Aruba Aloe Balm
N.V., the oldest company
in the world to use the
therapeutic aloe vera
plant in its skin, hair, and
cosmetic products. The
company grows its own
high-quality Aruba aloe
vera, and visitors can
tour the factory to learn
about the process, from
preparing the plant to
the finished products,
as well as the history of
the company.

→

California Lighthouse,
sitting atop a golden
stretch of beach

TOP 4 SAILING TRIPS FROM THE A.B.C. ISLANDS

Luxury on the Seas
Champagne and a gourmet lunch are part of this elite experience (pelican-aruba.com).

Ships Ahoy
Board a pirate-themed schooner to explore dive sites (jolly-pirates.com).

Bonaire Kayak
Kayak or snorkel among protected mangrove forests (clearbottom bonaire.com).

Head to Klein Curaçao
With a spectacular reef and white sand beaches, "Little Curaçao" is great for snorkeling and diving (mermaidboattrips.com).

---

visitors, but the views from its elevated base are spectacular and include the dunes, beaches, and the greens of Tierra del Sol Resort & Golf Club. Late in the afternoon, the view gets even more breathtaking as the sun sets.

3

Palm Beach

🅰 4 miles (6 km) N of Oranjestad, Aruba

Ranked among the best beaches in the world, Palm Beach is a long stretch of white sand lined with luxurious upscale resorts, restaurants, beach bars, and watersports operators. Among the extravagant resorts, three Marriott complexes sprawl across landscaped grounds at the north end of the beach, which provide a flowering habitat for tropical birds. At the southern end, Divi Aruba Phoenix Beach Resort occupies the last bit of sand before a rocky outcrop that separates Palm from Eagle Beach (p448).

Just opposite the resort is the **Butterfly Farm** featuring 40 species of butterfly. There are guided walks exploring the life cycle of a butterfly. Just south of the high-rise Palm Beach hotels is an open marsh where birds are protected in Bubali Bird Sanctuary, which attracts hundreds of migratory birds.

Butterfly Farm
  J E Irausquin Boulevard 🕘 9am–4pm daily 🌐 thebutterflyfarm.com

---

Arikok National Park

🅰 8 miles (13 km) E of Oranjestad, Aruba 🚇
🕘 Entrance hut: 7am–5pm daily; park: 24hr daily
ℹ National Park Office, Santa Cruz; 297 585 1234

The entrance to this ecological park is east of the town of Santa Cruz. The park protects a large portion of land bordered on the east by the sea. Within its boundaries are 21 miles (33 km) of marked hiking trails that wind through native flora. Wildlife includes *conejos* (rabbits), indigenous *kododo blauw* (whiptail lizards), and the *cascabel* (rattlesnake).

A walking path leads to Cunucu Arikok, a semi-restored farm at the foot of Cero Arikok, a 500-ft- (150-m-) tall hill that is the base of the airport's radar station. The farm has a typical country house made of mud-and-grass adobe and protected by the remains of a cactus fence and stone wall.

Heading east from the road at the entrance is a trail that leads to the highest point on the island, Mount Jamanota at 630 ft (189 m). This road leads visitors to the coastline, which begins with sand dunes. The Dos Playa beach here is not ideal for swimming due to strong currents, but photographers will enjoy snapping shots of the unique landscape.

From the beach's snack bar, a road leads to the Fontein Caves, where beautiful Indian rock paintings decorate the walls and ceilings. Nearby is the Fontein Garden, which has a 19th-century plantation house. It is also the site for a museum displaying old tools.

Did You Know?

Crushed coral and shell in Aruba's powdery white sand keeps it cool underfoot, even in the midday heat.

↑ Christoffel National Park in Curaçao, home to many unusual species of plant (inset)

5
Eagle Beach

📍 2 miles (3.2 km) N of Oranjestad, Aruba

The picturesque Eagle Beach is separated from Palm Beach (p447) by a rocky overgrown stretch of coastline. While Palm Beach is known for non-stop action, Eagle Beach is more relaxed; motorized water-sports are banned offshore and picnic tables draw both local families and guests from nearby resorts. The white-sand beach is wide, and the calm water is perfect for swimming. There are fewer restaurants and bars than there are on Palm Beach and the hotels reach no higher than the palm trees. Many pro-perties participate in the Green Globe Program, signifying that they adhere to environment-ally-friendly policies and sustainable tourism standards.

6
Christoffel National Park

📍 25 miles (40 km) NW of Willemstad, Curaçao 📞 599 9864 0363 🕐 7am–4pm Mon-Sat, 6am-3pm Sun

Spread over what was once three plantations, Christoffel National Park now serves as Curaçao's prized eco preserve. At its entrance, the Savonet Museum showcases the island's natural features and history through geological and archaeological exhibits.

The museum is housed in the former Savonet Plantation great house, and preserves the story of the various peoples who came, or were brought, to the island. Exhibits bring to life information about the first inhabitants of the area – the indigenous Arawack people who reached the island from Venezuela over 4,000 years ago – alongside displays that consider the plantation colonial era, and move into modern times.

Four marked hiking trails wind through the 7-sq-mile (18-sq-km) park. Hikers take on the challenge of the hulking 1,240-ft (370-m) Mount Christoffel, which offers views of the rugged countryside. Color-coded driving routes lead to various areas of the sprawling park including the windward coast, noted for its ancient rock drawings and cave-riddled cliffs. Another route begins at Piedra de Monton, from where it winds past hillsides covered with wild orchids, to the coves of Santa Marta Bay and Seru Bientu.

> While Palm Beach is known for non-stop action, Eagle Beach is more relaxed; motorized watersports are banned offshore and picnic tables draw both local families and guests from nearby resorts.

7

Museum Kura Hulanda

📍 Klipstraat 9, Otrobanda, Curaçao ⏰ 9:30am-4:30pm Mon-Sat 🌐 kurahulanda. com/museumx

This intriguing museum, which stands adjacent to the Kura Hulanda Village & Spa hotel, is dedicated to an important aspect of Curaçao history: the Transatlantic Slave Trade. Near the entrance is an open area featuring a huge sculpture of Africa, which is also a profile of a woman's face. This is the visitor's first glimpse of what is to come in this unique and sometimes harrowing collection of artifacts, which tells the story of nearly two centuries of African slavery.

In the 17th and 18th centuries, Africans were captured from their native villages and brought to the Dutch Caribbean to work on plantations. Between 1630 and 1795, the Dutch brought over 477,000 enslaved Africans to the New World – around 5 per cent of all the slaves brought by the combined European nations of Britain, Holland, Spain, Portugal, and France. Exhibits at the museum also include a small but fascinating collection of African, Antillian, and South American cultural artifacts and art, which neatly showcases the influence exerted by Africa upon Caribbean culture. Audio guides (Dutch and English versions available) can be rented at the entrance.

The museum was created by Dutch entrepreneur and philanthropist Jacob Gelt Dekker, who also renovated an eight-block area of the then-shabby section of Otrobanda in downtown Willemstad (p450).

8

Curaçao Maritime Museum

📍 N van den Brandhofstraat 1 Scharloo Abou, Wilemstad, Curaçao ⏰ 9am-4pm Mon-Sat (hours may vary Nov-Apr, check website) 🌐 curacao maritime.com

The Curaçao Maritime Museum has a permanent exhibit that comprises many artifacts from the island's 500-year history, including models of ships; nautical charts; navigation equipment; a mini oil refinery; and information on the colonial era, when Curaçao was a highly prized possession, fought over by the Spanish and Dutch.

An extremely informative 20-minute video gives visitors a broad history of the island and its value as a major commercial hub, given its proximity to the South American coast and its natural deepwater harbor. The museum building itself is a restored 17th-century beauty that melds the old and the new architectural styles of Curaçao. The museum also offers guided tours that teach visitors about the country's oil industry, as well as –twice a week – a tour of the harbor, taking a route beneath the famed Queen Juliana Bridge that winds past dry docks, naval dock, and the oil refinery on one of the Queen Emma pontoon bridge's ferries.

→

An old cannon, which sits outside the Curaçao Maritime Museum

STAY

Bucuti & Tara Beach Resort
This romantic, adults-only resort is a stunning retreat with an eco-friendly culture.

📍 L. G. Smith Blvd., Eagle Beach, Aruba 🌐 bucuti.com

💲💲💲

Eden Beach Resort
Choose rest, relaxation, and family fun at this friendly resort and spa. With plenty of activities on offer, it's a great choice for bigger groups.

📍 Bulevar Gob. N Debrot 73, Bonaire 🌐 edenbeach.com

💲💲💲

Santa Barbara Beach & Golf Resort
This remarkable spot offers pure luxury, Caribbean-style. The large estate overlooks a spectacular beach, and offers what is easily one of the best golf courses in the region.

📍 Santa Barbara Plantation, Nieuwpoort 🌐 santabararesort curacao.com

💲💲💲

↑ Dutch-Caribbean colonial-style buildings along Willemstad's waterfront

Willemstad

📍 SW coast of Curaçao
✈ 🚌 🚕

Designated a UNESCO World Heritage Site in 1997, historic Willemstad is the capital of Curaçao. Its older area is made up of distinct districts, with their architectural styles reflecting the 17th-century Dutch colonization of the islands. Sint Annabaai ("St. Anna Bay"), a channel linking the sea to the inner harbor, divides the central city into Otrobanda, a primarily residential area, and Punda, the commercial hub.

No visit to Willemstad is complete without a stroll over the Queen Emma Bridge, which was designed by U.S. business-man Leonard B. Smith in 1888. Sometimes referred to as Our Swinging Old Lady, the much-photographed floating pon-toon bridge spans the Sint Annabaai channel and swings open and closed according to boat traffic on the river. When the bridge is open for ships,

residents can cross via free ferries. Also straddling the channel is the city's other iconic bridge: the Queen Juliana, which at 185 ft (57 m) is the highest bridge in the Caribbean.

One great way to see the city is to set aside a couple of hours to take a walking tour of the historic district, which takes in Willemstad's main sights. A typical tour would start and end at the **Rif Fort Village** in Punda. This fort was built in the 19th century to protect the entrance to Sint Annabaai and is now part of a shopping and entertainment mall.

The fort is just a short walk from the Queen Emma Bridge, across which in Otrobanda is Kura Hulanda, a village-like boutique hotel and spa, and the Kura Hulanda Museum, which details the history of slavery in the New World.

Nearby is the 17th-century Fort Amsterdam, which once served as part of the primary defense system for the city, and as headquarters of the Dutch West India Company.

It is now the home of the Governor, with government offices also located here. Another colonial-era fort in the area is Waterfort. Though only its original walls remain, it is a pleasant spot for dining and nightlife.

One of the great wonders of Willemstad is the **Mikvé Israel-Emanuel Synagogue**. Consecrated over 285 years ago, it is the oldest synagogue in continuous use in the Western Hemisphere. Its unique sand floors symbolize the desert that Moses and his people had to cross to freedom, and the silence that the Jewish settlers had to maintain about their religion before they fled the Spanish Inquisition to Curaçao. The site also hosts a museum exhibiting religious and cultural artifacts, historical information about the Jewish community, and a gift shop.

For those interested in the history of philately, the small Postmuseum in Punda has an impressive collection of historic and modern stamps. Another piece of Willemstad color is the floating market of Venezuelan vendors, who come over to the city in boats to sell fresh fish, fruit, and vegetables at the market at Sha Casprileskade in down-town Punda. This tradition, which has been in place for over 100 years, has fluctuated recently due to the political tensions in Venezuela but is still operating.

Most visitors to Willemstad enjoy the atmosphere and hearty local fare of Plasa Bieu (Old Market). Here, locals and tourists rub shoulders at big

Did You Know?

Iguana soup is a local delicacy on Curaçao, with the reptile's meat and eggs considered an aphrodisiac.

wooden tables, while chefs serve up a variety of specialties, including the classic *kabrito stofi* (goat stew) and *giambo kadushi* (cactus soup), as well as more familiar Caribbean dishes like fried plantains and okra, and fresh local fruit juices.

Rif Fort Village
🅰 Gouverneur van Slobbeweg 📞 599 9435 5000

Mikvé Israel-Emanuel Synagogue
🅰 Hanchi Snoa 🕙 9am–4:30pm Mon–Fri (services: 6:30–7:45pm Fri, 10am–noon Sat) 🌐 snoa.com

↑ Merchants unloading fresh produce at Willemstad's floating market

↓ This walking route takes in the main sights in the center of Willemstad

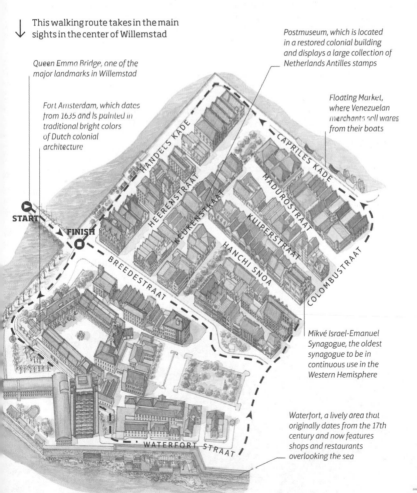

Queen Emma Bridge, one of the major landmarks in Willemstad

Fort Amsterdam, which dates from 1635 and is painted in traditional bright colors of Dutch colonial architecture

Postmuseum, which is located in a restored colonial building and displays a large collection of Netherlands Antilles stamps

Floating Market, where Venezuelan merchants sell wares from their boats

START

FINISH

HANDELS KADE

HEERENSTRAAT

KEUKENSTRAAT

CAPRILES KADE

MADUROSTRAAT

KUIPERSTRAAT

HANCHI SNOA

BREEDESTRAAT

COLOMBUSTRAAT

Mikvé Israel-Emanuel Synagogue, the oldest synagogue to be in continuous use in the Western Hemisphere

Waterfort, a lively area that originally dates from the 17th century and now features shops and restaurants overlooking the sea

WATERFORT STRAAT

10

Flamingo Sanctuary

⌖ 15 miles (24 km) NW of Willemstad, Curaçao

The salt flats near Landhuis Jan Kok and Landhuis Hermanus are one of the best places in Curaçao to spot flamingos. Visitors arrive at this protected area on the way to the little town of Sint Willibrordus, en route to Playa Porto Mari. The pink long-legged birds, so evocative of the relaxed tropical life, can be seen in their natural habitat, standing in the water, skimming the shallows for food, or flying majestically above its glassy surface. Their diet of brine shrimp, other small crustaceans, and blue-green algae gives them their distinctive bright pink color; the young birds are gray and become pink later in their lives.

There are other birds at the sanctuary as well, such as herons and egrets, but the flamingos are by far the most impressive. The site's bird population can vary quite dramatically from day-to-day, but it's always worth a stop on the way to the beach to see what you can spot. Watch from afar, with binoculars if possible, and don't venture too near the flamingos as they will get nervous and fly away.

> **Extending over 25 sq miles (66 sq km), the Washington Slagbaai National Park covers about 20 per cent of the northern part of the island of Bonaire.**

11

Washington Slagbaai National Park

⌖ 16 miles (25 km) NW of Kralendijk, Bonaire ⓣ
⊙ 8am–5pm daily ✕ Jan 1 & Dec 25 ⓘ Park entrance; www.washingtonpark bonaire.org

Extending over 25 sq miles (66 sq km), the Washington Slagbaai National Park covers about 20 per cent of the northern part of the island of Bonaire. Dive sites, hiking trails, salt pans, a lake, and driving routes are within the boundaries of what originally comprised two of the largest plantations on the island, Washington and Slagbaai. The plantations, called *kunukus* in the local Papiamentu language, grew the distinctive divi-divi trees for their pods, which were processed into tannin for use in tanning animal hides; and aloe plants for their sap, which was used as a laxative.

The Washington *kunuku* became a public park in 1969, and when the Slagbaai property was added in 1979, the area became the first nature sanctuary in the A.B.C. Islands. Parrots, flamingos, iguanas, and parakeets are just a few of the many endemic species that live within the park. The beaches provide nesting grounds for all four species of Caribbean sea turtle, and the park is part of the Ramsar Convention, an international treaty that protects wetlands and their inhabitants. The visitors' center, located at the park entrance, has many of the original plantation-era structures still intact and is a good place to pick up maps and other useful site information. A museum, set in the former main house, displays historical, archaeological, and geological information about the island and its native plants and wildlife. Highlights of the park include the 784-ft (238-m) Brandaris Hill, the highest point on the island; Pos di Mangel, a key area for bird-watching; Boca Chikitu, a rocky cove backed by sand dunes; and Wayaka and Boca Slagbaai, the prime snorkeling beaches. Two dirt driving tracks wind through the park: yellow, making a 21-mile (33-km) sweep along the north coast, and green, a 14-mile (23-km) stretch connecting sites in the middle of the park. Nature lovers will

A shady, colonnaded plaza located at the edge of the ocean in Kralendijk

want to spend time on the walking paths that start at the visitors' center, and the hiking-biking trails up to Brandaris and Pos di Mangel. The freshwater lake at Pos di Mangel attracts large flocks of birds.

 Kralendijk

🏠 W coast of Bonaire 🚗🚤
🛈 Tourism Corporation Bonaire 2; 599 717 8322

Bonaire's capital, Kralendijk, is a large, easygoing village about midway along the island's sharply curved lee-ward coast. The town's main road runs parallel to the sea, so orientation and navigating is simple. The best way to get around is on foot.

When a cruise ship is in port, the narrow streets transform into an outdoor arts and crafts marketplace with booths offering a variety of local artwork. A daily produce market takes place in an open-air building near the town pier. Most of the permanent shops and restaurants line the two main roads, Kaya Craane –

 Turquoise water and rugged terrain within Washington Slagbaai National Park

with its pretty waterfront promenade – and Kaya Grandi, a block inland.

Fort Oranje stands guard at the southern end of the town center. It is one of the oldest structures on Bonaire, built by the Dutch in 1639, and allotted four cannons to defend against the English, Spanish, and French. The stone tower was added in 1932, and the fort now houses government offices. Next door, the lovely two-story golden-yellow building also dates from the 19th century and is a fine example of Dutch Caribbean architecture. The raised front porch and staircase is particularly attractive. Various government offices are also located in the building, known as the Bestuurskantoor (government office). Unfortunately, neither of these two historic buildings is open to the public.

The **Terramar Museum**, located close to the cruise docks on the Kralendijk oceanfront, is an archaeological museum, which showcases over 7,000 years of the history of Bonaire and the Caribbean through various interesting artifacts, 3D reconstructions, and interactive presentations. Housed in a bright-yellow historic building, well-known as Van der Dijs, the museum is surrounded by an upscale residential and shopping complex.

Terramar Museum
🏠 Kaya J.N.E Craane 24, Kralendijk ⏰ 9am–5pm Mon-Fri, 10am–4pm Sat
🌐 terramarmuseum.com

EAT

2 Fools and a Bull
An exquisite five-course meal, with wine pairing, is served at this intimate venue – only 17 (adult) guests can be seated per session. The menu is not suitable for vegetarians.

🏠 Palm Beach 17
⏰ Sat & Sun
🌐 2foolsandabull.com

$$$

La Cantina Cerveseria
This relaxed restaurant features an in-house brewery that always has something new to offer. Expect delicious cocktails and great international cuisine.

🏠 Kaya Grandi 12, Kralendijk ⏰ 6–10pm Wed-Sun 🌐 lacantina bonaire.com

$$$

Kome
With a name meaning "eat" in the local Creole language, it's no surprise that the cuisine here is inspired by all the great traditions of classical and modern cooking.

🏠 Johan van Walbeeckplein 6, Curaçao ⏰ Sun
🌐 komecuracao.com

$$$

 A graceful group of pink flamingos, gathered in the waters of Lake Goto

 13

Kaminda Goto

📍 9 miles (15 km) NW of Kralendijk, Bonaire

Kaminda Goto is a road that follows the shores of Lake Goto (Gotomeer), on the southwest border of the national park. The road up to the landlocked saltwater Lake Goto offers excellent close-up views of flocks of flamingos that nest and feed around the water. The birds are shy, but are most interested in food and preening, so patient watchers have a good chance of getting a proper look at these fascinating creatures. Benches at the paved Salina Grande viewing area provide a good place to sit and watch the birds.

14

Rincón

📍 11 miles (18 km) NW of Kralendijk, Bonaire

The oldest town on the island, Rincón (Spanish for "corner"), is rich in local flavor. It was founded by the Spanish late in the 1500s as an inland safe haven hidden from view of pirate ships. Later, the village became a community of former slaves and is the birthplace of many of the island's political and business leaders. The town annually hosts a jubilant Dia di Rincón (Rincón Day) to celebrate the official birthday of the King of the Netherlands on April 27. The day-long party features music, local craft, and *crioyo* food. At the center of the town, the impressive San Luis Bertran Church is considered a historical monument, even though the present structure was completed in 1984. Originally built in 1861, the church was destroyed by a hurricane in October 1907. The present church was rebuilt around the ruins beginning in 1977.

Rincón is also the site of two other places well worth visiting: the **Echo Conservation Centre** and the **Cadushy Distillery**. The former protects Bonaire's endangered yellow-shouldered Amazon Parrot through research, conservation management, and public

Did You Know?

Bonaire's airport is called Flamingo Airport – and is painted pink – in honor of the local birds.

outreach. There are tours every Wednesday at 5pm at the conservation centre.

The Cadushy Distillery makes a unique liqueur from one of the species of cactus found on the ABC islands. The Cadushy cactus is combined with traditional lime drink at the only distillery on Bonaire. Visitors can take a free tour of the distillery before relaxing in the courtyard to enjoy a drink under ancient trees that are alive with birdlife.

Echo Conservation Centre
 Kunuku Dos Pos
🕐 5pm Wed; by appt
🌐 echobonaire.org

Cadushy Distillery
🎫 Kaya Cornelis D. Crestian 8 & 10 🕐 10am–5pm Mon, Wed & Fri 🌐 cadushy.com

15

Pekelmeer

📍 13 miles (21 km) S of Kralendijk, Bonaire

At the south end of Bonaire, Pekelmeer is a protected sanctuary for Southern Caribbean flamingos. Many of them come from Venezuela, 50 miles (18 km) away, to breed and tend their young. During hatching season, as many as 2,500 chicks are born here.

Other birds also nest and feed at Pekelmeer including heron, osprey, and other marine birds. Morning and late afternoon are the best times to see the birds in flight, but visitors are advised to stay in their cars to avoid disturbing the birds.

> The town annually hosts a jubilant Dia di Rincón (Rincón Day) to celebrate the official birthday of the King of the Netherlands.

DIVING OFF BONAIRE

Bonaire's National Marine Park protects some of the healthiest reefs in the world, and scuba divers enjoy exploring more than 86 named sites. Water off the leeward side is sheltered by the island's reverse-C-curve shape, providing excellent conditions for learners and novice divers, while the more exposed sites near the north and south coasts present plenty of challenges for experienced divers.

UNDER THE SEA

Thriving coral formations grow close to the shore in fairly shallow water, which allows snorkelers fabulous opportunities to observe a wide variety of tropical fish, rays, and other marine life including Caribbean reef octopuses and frog fish. The octopuses are easy to spot at night, as their blue-green skin is reflective, and they feed in shallow coastal seagrass beds. The frog fish changes color to camouflage itself as it crawls along the sea floor using its bottom fins as feet.

↑ The impressive Elkhorn coral, named for its antler-like branches

DIVING RESORTS

Diving resorts serve as one-stop destinations for vacationers who want to spend most of their time in or under water. Diving lessons begin in shallow water near the shore. Even beginners may dive with an instructor during a discovery class. Buddy Dive Resort is one of several hotels in Bonaire that cater to divers with packaged vacations and tailored dive classes for both adults and children (buddydive.com).

↑ The jetty at the Buddy Dive Resort in Bonaire

← Strikingly colored queen angelfish

A DRIVING TOUR
ARUBA

Length 19 miles (31 km) **Difficulty** The main roads are paved, but secondary roads can be rough and some pass through rugged terrain

Aruba, Curaçao, and Bonaire are each small enough to tour by car in a single day. Tour operators offer around-the-island excursions and many of the local taxi drivers make knowledgeable guides. However, one of the best ways to discover the islands' unique features is on a self-guided driving tour. Aruba is a two-faced beauty with glamorous west coast beaches and a high-energy downtown area while its interior is strewn with curious rock formations. The following driving route showcases the best of the island.

Locator Map
For more detail see p444

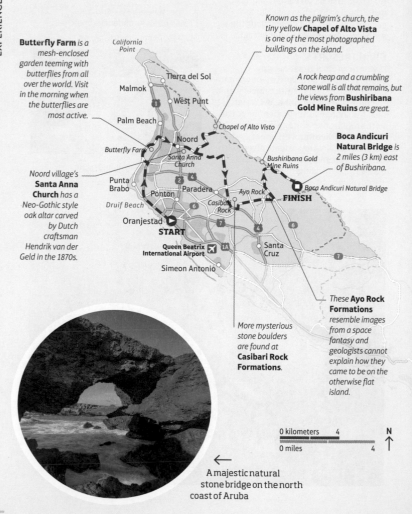

Known as the pilgrim's church, the tiny yellow **Chapel of Alto Vista** is one of the most photographed buildings on the island.

Butterfly Farm *is a mesh-enclosed garden teeming with butterflies from all over the world. Visit in the morning when the butterflies are most active.*

A rock heap and a crumbling stone wall is all that remains, but the views from **Bushiribana Gold Mine Ruins** are great.

Boca Andicuri Natural Bridge is 2 miles (3 km) east of Bushiribana.

Noord village's **Santa Anna Church** *has a Neo-Gothic style oak altar carved by Dutch craftsman Hendrik van der Geld in the 1870s.*

California Point

Tierra del Sol

Malmok

West Punt

Palm Beach

Noord

Chapel of Alto Visto

Butterfly Farm

Santa Anna Church

Punta Brabo

Paradera

Ayo Rock

Bushiribana Gold Mine Ruins

Boca Andicuri Natural Bridge

FINISH

Ponton

Druf Beach

Casibari Rock

Oranjestad

START

Queen Beatrix International Airport

Santa Cruz

Simeon Antonio

These **Ayo Rock Formations** *resemble images from a space fantasy and geologists cannot explain how they came to be on the otherwise flat island.*

More mysterious stone boulders are found at **Casibari Rock Formations**.

0 kilometers 4
0 miles 4

N

A majestic natural stone bridge on the north coast of Aruba

ARUBA, CURAÇAO AND BONAIRE

Aruba

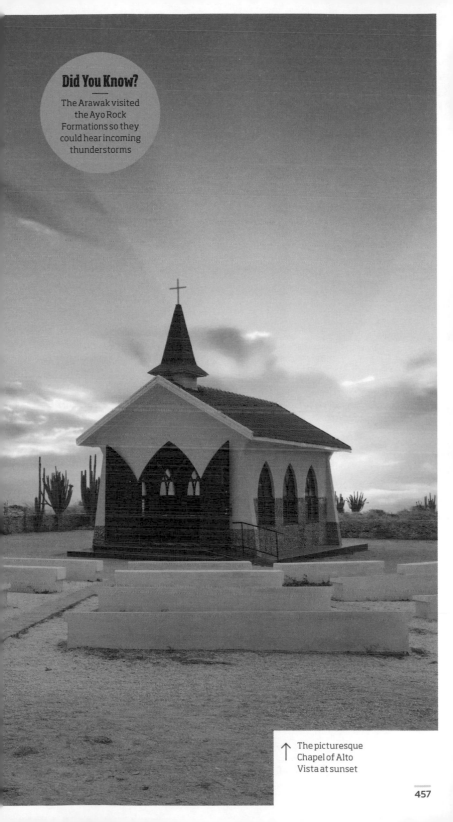

↑ The picturesque Chapel of Alto Vista at sunset

The vivid turqoise Caracas Bay, viewed from Fort Beekenburg ↑

A DRIVING TOUR
CURAÇAO

Length 22 miles (35 km) **Difficulty** The main roads are
paved but secondary roads may be rough and some pass
through rugged terrain

Locals call the eastern part of Curaçao "Banda Riba",
which means upwind. The countryside is dotted with
developments, yacht-filled harbors, and a few tourist
sites. About 70 *landhuizen* (old plantation homes),
with Dutch colonial architecture, sit on hilltops.

To the north of the capital lie the **Hato Caves**.
These were formed millions of years ago, when
Curaçao was underwater. There are underground
waterfalls, a lake, and chambers with stalagmites,
stalactites, and hundreds of bats.

**The Ostrich and Game
Farm** is the largest of its
type outside Africa. Jeep
tours get visitors close to
the world's largest birds.

In Salina Ariba is the
**Curaçao Liqueur
Distillery**. Housed
in the 17th-century
Landhuis Chobolobo,
it still uses 19th-
century equipment
to make the cordial
from dried orange
skins. Tours include
an overview of the
production process.

The trendy developments
of **Spanish Water and
Caracasbaai** are popular with
young locals and yachties.
Enjoy a meal at the Landhuis
Brakkeput Mei Mei and a tour
of Fort Beekenburg.

The scent of herbs lures
visitors to **Dinah's Botanic
and Historic Garden**
featuring local plants
that have been used for
centuries as folk medicines.
It has a model village and
lodge built by Amazon
Indians and the owner
Dinah tells visitors about it.

Curaçao
International Airport
Meiberg
Hato Caves
FINISH
Muizenberg
Playa Kanoa
Piscadera
Duena
Vista
Brievengat
Sint Michiel
Habaai
Ostrich and
Game Farm
Curaçao Liqueur
Distillery
Willemstad
Rooi Santu
Dinah's Botanic
and Historic Garden
START
Koraal
Specht
Seru Grandi
Spanish Water
Caracas-
baai

0 kilometers 5

0 miles 5

N

The incredible stalactites illuminated
inside the Hato Caves

PRACTICAL
INFORMATION

Here you will find all the essential advice and information you will need before and during your stay in Aruba, Curaçao, and Bonaire.

AT A GLANCE

CURRENCY
Aruban Florin (AF) Netherlands Antillean Florin (NAFl) and US dollar (US$)

TIME ZONE
Atlantic Standard Time, 4 hours behind GMT and 1 hour ahead of EST

LANGUAGE
Dutch is the official language, but locals speak a dialect called Papiamento, as well as English, and Spanish

ELECTRICITY SUPPLY
On Aruba, the voltage is 110 AC; 127/120 AC on Bonaire; and 110/130 AC on Curaçao. Most outlets accept US plugs

EMERGENCY NUMBERS

AMBULANCE

911 (Aruba, Bonaire)
912 (Curaçao)

TAP WATER
Tap water here is safe to drink

When To Go

Aruba, Curaçao, and Bonaire are well out of the hurricane belt and, though storms can occur, warm temperatures and cool breezes can be found all year round. Summer and fall are the best time to visit the three islands, when many cultural events are held.

Getting There

Aruba and Curaçao have a daily direct air service from North America and Amsterdam. Bonaire has direct flights with American Airlines from Miami, United Airlines from Houston and Newark, Delta Airlines from Atlanta, from Toronto with Sunwing and from Amsterdam with KLM and TUI Airways. Flights land at the international airports of Queen Beatrix on Aruba, Flamingo on Bonaire, and Hato on Curaçao. Delta flies non-stop to all islands from Atlanta. American Airlines flies to Aruba and Curaçao from the US, and to Bonaire from Puerto Rico. JetBlue and United Airlines have flights to Aruba from the US. Flights from Amsterdam to all three islands are on KLM. From the UK, TUI Airways has weekly direct flights (May–Nov) from London Gatwick and Manchester to Aruba. Regional airlines such as Divi Divi fly within the islands, and and Aruba Airlines connects Curaçao with Jamaica.

Personal Security

Crime is rare on the three islands, with crimes against tourists among the lowest in the Caribbean. Still, precautions should be taken, especially against theft from rental cars. Visitors should also avoid leaving valuables unattended. Drug-related crimes occur occasionally, so avoid secluded roads and alleys after dark. Any crime must be reported and receive a written report.

Health

Dr. Horacio Oduber Hospital in Aruba, San Francisco Hospital in Bonaire, and St. Elizabeth Hospital in Curaçao are the best hospitals.

Passports and Visas

Citizens of the EU nations as well as all other nationalities, including Canadians and Americans, must show a passport to enter the islands. Visits may extend to three months without a visa. In addition, immigration officials may ask for an onward or return ticket, proof of sufficient funds for the planned stay, and an address where travelers plan to reside on the islands. Visitors can also check with their concerned embassies.

LGBT+ Safety

The ABCs (and other former Dutch colonies) are LGBT+ friendly islands in a largely conservative, often hostile, Caribbean. Same-sex marriage is legal only in Bonaire, but recognised in Aruba and Curaçao. As these islands are generally socially tolerant, it's not essential to seek out specifically gay bars or resorts, though these are easy to find especially on Curaçao, which even has an annual gay pride parade in September.

Money

The official currency on Aruba is the Aruban Florin (AF or Afl), which is divided into 100 cents, and Curaçao uses the Netherlands Antillean Florin (NAFl or Fl). The NAFl is also known as the Netherlands Antillean Guilder (ANG). Bonaire uses the US dollar. US dollars and major credit cards are widely accepted on the islands. Banks and ATMs are located throughout the islands. Banking hours are Monday to Friday from 8am to 3:30pm.

Cell Phones and Wi-Fi

Visitors bringing cell phones should check with their service providers to determine if they will work on the islands and if they will be subject to roaming charges. The country codes for Aruba, Bonaire, and Curaçao are 297, 599, and 599 respectively followed by the seven-digit local number. To call from outside the Caribbean, dial the international code (011 from the US) plus the area code, and the local number. For example, dial 011, then area code 297, and the seven-digit number for Aruba. Internet access is provided at major resorts and airports, and there are many Wi-Fi hot spots. Local SIM cards are available at Digicel offices.

Getting Around

Ferries are not practical for travelling between the islands due to the long distance between them and unpredictable sea conditions. Aruba has a good bus service that connects the airport, Oranjestad, and resorts along the west coast. Bonaire has no public transportation, and Curaçao has limited bus and van service. Visitors must rely on tours or rental cars to explore the countryside. Taxis are easily found at the airports, cruise ship terminals, hotels, and major tourist attractions. The international airports have car rental agencies on-site. A valid driver's license and major credit card are needed to hire a car. Driving is on the right side, and all the islands have a network of paved roads connecting the main towns. Dirt roads run through the countryside, and a four-wheel-drive vehicle is practical for independent travelers touring out-side major tourist areas. AVIS, Hertz, AB Car rental, Amigo Rent-A-Car, and Michel Car Rental are popular car rental companies.

Visitor Information

Tourist information kiosks are located at the airports on Aruba and Curaçao. Government Tourist Boards including the **Aruba Tourism Authority**, **Tourism Corporation Bonaire**, and **Curaçao Tourist Board** have offices oneach island as well as public relations agents overseas.

Aruba Tourism Authority
🌐 aruba.com
Curaçao Tourist Board
🌐 curacao.com
Tourism Corporation Bonaire
🌐 tourismbonaire.com

NEED TO KNOW

Boats anchored at Grand Cayman beach

BEFORE YOU GO

Forward planning is essential for any successful trip. Prepare yourself for any eventuality by brushing up on the following points before you set off.

Passports and Visas

Entry requirements vary widely among the island nations, so always check before you travel. For most countries, visitors need to have a valid passport and a return ticket, as well as a tourist visa (typically good for 30- to 90-day stays). Refer to the Practical Information pages in each island chapter for more details.

Travel Safety Advice

Visitors can get up-to date travel safety information from the **Foreign and Commonwealth Office** in the UK, the **State Department** in the US and the **Department of Foreign Affairs and Trade** in Australia.
AUS
W smartraveller.gov.au
UK
W gov.uk/foreign-travel-advice
US
W travel.state.gov

Customs Information

Besides personal belongings, tourists are allowed to carry up to 2 liters (68 fl.oz) of alcohol and two cigarette cartons to most Caribbean islands. Certain drugs require a prescription. Local and Caribbean customs are on guard for drug trafficking. US Customs allows $800 of goods duty-free, including 2 liters (68 fl.oz) of alcohol, 200 cigarettes, and 100 non-Cuban cigars, plus an unlimited amount of original art. Visitors who travel to the US Virgin Islands plus another Caribbean island may bring back $1,600 of goods duty-free. No Customs declaration is required when traveling between Puerto Rico and the US. The UK permits £390 of goods, plus 200 cigarettes or 50 cigars, plus 2 liters (68 fl.oz) of wine, and 1 liter (34 fl.oz) of spirits.

Avoid buying items made from endangered species such as tortoise shell, black coral, or reptile skin. These are covered under the Convention on International Trade in Endangered Species (CITES) and anyone found in possession of such items can be fined.

Insurance

It is wise to take out an insurance policy before you go covering theft, loss of belongings, medical problems, cancellation and delays.

Vaccinations

Malaria is prevalent on some islands, and the region has experienced an epidemic of dengue fever in recent years; check **Fit for Travel** (UK) and **CDC Travelers' Health** (US) for for advice and guidance on recommended inoculations before traveling.
Fit for Travel
W fitfortravel.nhs.uk
CDC Travelers' Health
W nc.cdc.gov/travel

Money

A wide variety of currencies are in use throughout the Caribbean – refer to the Practical Information pages within each island chapter for specific details. However, the US dollar is accepted almost everywhere and many businesses also accept euros. Banks are ubiquitous, although ATMs often run out of cash. Most hotels are also happy to change foreign currency.

Travellers with Specific Needs

Facilities vary across the islands. Many historic buildings do not have wheelchair access or lifts, but most modern and renovated hotels provide toilets and other amenities for wheelchair-users, and many pavements now have wheelchair ramps. The following tour operator makes specialist arrangements:
Accessible Caribbean Vacations
W accessiblecaribbeanvacations.com

GETTING
AROUND

If you're thinking of moving between islands or planning a comprehensive tour of the Caribbean region, there are several ways you can island hop.

Cruises

The Caribbean is the world's most popular place for cruising, and with good reason. Whether it's aboard a large deluxe cruise ship or a small sailboat, no other place in the world offers such a diverse plethora of islands, stunning landscapes, and fabulous ports of call to tempt you to travel by sea.

Offering a perfect combination of multiple destinations and a roving resort-style hotel, it's not surprising that a large percentage of visitors to the Caribbean arrive by cruise ship. Most islands have at least one major port capable of docking large cruise ships (some have several), while on the smallest islands cruise ships often anchor in sheltered coves and shuttle passengers to shore via boats called tenders.

The main departure ports are Fort Lauderdale and Miami in Florida, and San Juan in Puerto Rico, while a few ships depart New York. Generally, the islands are spaced close enough together to allow passengers to arrive at a new destination each morning after sailing overnight, while cruises of a week or longer typically include at least one full day at sea. Options range from two-day cruises to The Bahamas to two- or three-week cruises that navigate most of the Caribbean and often include ports-of-call in Central and/or South America. A minimum of a week is recommended if you desire to sample a variety of islands.

Itineraries are generally divided by region, although many longer itineraries combine two regions, or even all three. Popular destinations in the Western Caribbean include Nassau, Turks and Caicos, Dominican Republic, Grand Cayman, plus Montego Bay, Ocho Rios and Kingston, in Jamaica, and often Mexican ports such as Cancun and Cozumel and stops in Belize and Honduras. Eastern Caribbean ports-of-call include San Juan in Puerto Rico; St. Thomas, St. Croix, and Tortola in the Virgin Islands; plus St-Martin/Sint Maarten, St. Barths, St Kitts and Nevis, Antigua, Guadeloupe, and Dominica. The Southern Caribbean's top destinations include Martinique, Saint Lucia, Barbados, Grenada, Trinidad and Tobago, plus the A.B.C. islands.

With over two dozen Caribbean cruise lines operating in winter (December through April), the choice of ship is as varied as the islands themselves. And it's not just a matter of size, which can range from 50-passenger vessels to Royal Caribbean International's four 5,500-passenger Oasis-class vessels – the world's largest cruise ships. Atmosphere also varies from ship to ship, depending on the cruise line. For example, budget-priced Carnival Cruise Line – the biggest company, with 24 large cruise ships plying the Caribbean in winter – appeals to party types who don't mind an excess of neon and noise. At the other end of the spectrum, the most expensive companies, such as Crystal Cruises, Seabourne, and Silversea, specialize in a more serene, deluxe experience that includes formal black-tie gourmet dinners and a strong educational component. You can even thrill to the snap of the wind in the sails on fully-rigged ships, such as the sumptuous, four-masted *Sea Cloud*. Then there are 'themed' cruises geared towards a particular topic or interest, from LBGT+ and singles to holistic wellness.

Almost all cruise ships offer a wealth of on-board activities and shore excursions. These can vary from Carnival's rock-climbing, mini-golf, and on-board waterparks to Seabourn's luminary speakers and wellness programs. Needless to say, the distinctions draw like-minded people to any particular ship or company. So, when choosing a cruise ask yourself what size ship do you want to be on, what type of experience you want to have, and what kind of shore excursions you would find most interesting. Before booking, don't forget to research the ports themselves to make informed decisions about shopping, beach time, historical tours or adventure activities like hiking, snorkeling or zip lining.

Cruising doesn't suit everyone, and ships and their passengers can completely overwhelm some Caribbean ports in peak season, when several enormous ships may be docked at the same time. But cruises require very little forward planning, no need for constant packing and unpacking, and no worry about how you're going to get from island to island.

Island-Hopping

Island-hopping is the best way to absorb as much of the Caribbean as possible in a short time. Flights and ferries link the main islands with their neighbors, and many are close enough that sailing between them by yacht or catamaran is a breeze. Rather than choosing three or four big islands spread far apart, more convenient island-hopping is to go to groups of islands close enough together to make traveling between them easy and less time-consuming. Be prepared to pack light for small planes, and if you're darting about on ferries, it's no fun being loaded down with heavy luggage. Alternatively consider using one island as a central jumping off point and do day trips or overnighters to other islands, leaving the bulk of luggage at a hotel or villa.

Flying

Many major airlines serve the Caribbean: From North America, these include American, Delta, JetBlue, Southwest, Spirit, United and Air Canada, plus such regional carriers as Air Jamaica, Bahamasair, Caribbean Airlines, and Cayman Airlines; from Europe, Air Jamaica, British Airways, Virgin Atlantic, Thomas Cook, Thompson Holidays, Air France and KLM have direct service. Some flights touchdown in more than one country, which can be useful when planning an island-hopping trip. For example, the British Airways flight from London stops in both Barbados and Grenada, and the KLM flight from Amsterdam, stops in Curaçao and St. Maarten. Also, it's quite possible to fly back home from a different island than the one on which you arrived.

Within the Caribbean, some two dozen airlines offer inter-island links or 'puddle-jumper' flights across the region. LIAT is the main carrier between the former British territories, and connects most of the islands between the Dominican Republic in the north and Trinidad in the south. Air Antilles serves the French islands, and the Dutch islands have Winair. Other airlines include Seaborne Airlines and SVG Air.

The very small island groups also tend to have local airlines that offer both scheduled and shared and private charter flights, usually using 19-passenger Twin Otter jet-props, 9-passenger Britten Norman Islanders, or small Cessna aircraft seating 4–12 passengers. For example, Mustique Airways links St. Vincent and Barbados with Mustique and the Grenadines; ABM flies between Antigua, Barbuda and Montserrat; St. Barth Commuter flies between St. Barths, St. Maarten and Antigua; Tradewind Aviation links Puerto Rico, St. Thomas, Anguilla, St. Barths, Nevis, and Antigua; and Vieques Air Link flies between Puerto and the Spanish and British Virgin Islands. As tickets are aimed for the local market, prices can be very reasonable.

Ferries

Ferries are a fun way to travel, and you'll enjoy beautiful views as you make your way between the islands. They range from hulking old mail ships to modern high-speed catamarans, and are usually plentiful between neighboring islands within the same countries. Routes include from Nassau to, and between, the Bahamian Out Islands such as Eleuthera and the Abacos; to Puerto Rico's offshore islands of Vieques and Culebra; the islands of the British Virgin Islands, like Jost Van Dyke and Virgin Gorda; between the islands of the Turks and Caicos; between Grenada and Carriacou and Petite Martinique; Antigua and Barbuda; St. Vincent and the Grenadines; Trinidad and Tobago; and between St. Kitts and Nevis.

There are few services linking the island nations themselves, especially the Greater Antilles, which means you may have to take occasional flights between them. But some international routes do exist. Ferries del Caribe operates between the Dominican Republic and Puerto Rico; GB Ferries links St. Maarten and Anguilla; L'Express des Iles links St. Lucia, Guadeloupe, Martinique, Marie Galante, Les Saintes and Dominica; Great Bay Express links St. Maarten, St. Barths, Saba and St Eustatius; and the Lady JJ links Union Island in the Grenadines to Carriacou in Grenada.

Sailing

The Caribbean is an exciting sailing destination, whether you want short island hops in calm, protected waters or longer blue-water passages. Many foreign visitors sail their own yachts through the Caribbean, while thousands of other annual visitors choose charter vessels from such companies as Sunsail, in Puerto Rico; Nicholson Yacht Charters, in the Grenadines; or The Moorings, which has bases on eight Caribbean islands. Experienced sailors can hire a bareboat charter in which they act as captain, while less experienced travelers can opt for a skippered charter with a qualified captain at the helm. Or you can join a flotilla vacation, where you'll sail will other yachts from one isle to the next.

The most popular destinations are the Abacos, in The Bahamas, plus the British and U.S. Virgin Islands, and – in the southern Caribbean – the Grenadines. All have relatively sheltered waters and plenty of coves. In general, the heaviest swells and strongest winds are on the windward (eastern), or Atlantic, side of most islands.

INDEX

ACKNOWLEDGMENTS

The publisher would like to thank the following for their kind permission to reproduce their photographs:

Key: a-above; b-below/bottom; c-centre; f-far; l-left; r-right; t-top

123RF.com: Maridav 38-9c; Altin Osmanaj 430-1b; Dmitry Travnikov 17t, 108-9; Dennis van de Water 216b.

4Corners: Werner Bertsch 456bl; Massimo Borchi 36cr; Pietro Canali 12t; Danielle Devaux 404-5c; Fyne Photos 285t; Giovanni Simeone 374-5t.

akg-images: 58cb; Album / Oronoz 58-9t.

Alamy Stock Photo: 24BY36 21t, 252-3; AGE Fotostock 31cla, 151b, 386br, / Alvaro Leiv 152-3t, / Katia Singletary 345tr; AGF Srl 26tr, 396-7; John Anderson 455cra; AndKa 32clb; Archisto Library 214t; Archivart 60tl; Arco Images GmbH 407bl; Avalon / Bruce Coleman Inc / Spence McConnel 191bc, / Photoshot License 113crb; Gary Bagshawe 56clb; Chris Bainbridge 193tl; Mark Bassett 145br; John de la Bastide 428-9t, 430t, 432-3t; Henry Beeker 448t; Buiten-Beeld 268-9t, 277tr; Debra Behr 261bl; Susanna Bennett 432b; Matt Bills 256b; Blickwinkel 12clb, 421tr; Bluegreen Pictures 57tr; BonkersAboutTravel 32t; Bryan Mullennix World View 212b; 213tr; Buzz Pictures / Neale Haynes 417cra; Kike Calvo 48-9b, 231br; Chris Cameron 177tr; Caribbean 401bl; Cavan Images / James + Courtney Forte 358b; Charles O. Cecil 344br; Chronicle 58br; Julia Claxton 378b; Roy Conchie 416t; Helmut Corneli 269cra; Cultura Creativ 130b; Jan Csernoch 405cr; Tim Cuff 34cla, 114b; Ian Dagnall 150tl, 156tl; Martin Dalton 49br; Danita Delimont 38-9t, 49tr, 227cra, 316tl, 379t, / Walter Bibikow 259tlr, 291tl, 320bl; Danita Delimont Creative 227cmu; DanitaDelimont.com / Jaynes Gallery / Wendy Kaveney 56cl; Simon Dannhauer 342-3t; David Davis Photoproductions RF 102bl; dbimages 171b, / Jeremy Graham 304-5b; Susan E. Degginger 361cla; Design Pics Inc 391; directphoto.b 180-1b; Reinhard Dirscherl 172cla,174cla, 357clb; Dleiva 8cl; DOD Photo 60br; Doug Houghton Carib 287bl; Sean Drakes 10-1b, 56ca; James Dugan 207cr; Michael Dunlea 414cr; Michael Dwyer / "Courtesy of the Arecibo Observatory; a facility of the NSF" 208t; Editorial, Alius Imago 291tr; EQRoy 284cra, 288-9bc; Everett Collection Historical 73tc; Eye Ubiquitous 407ca; Michele Falzone 206bl, 209br; Jakob Fischer 334-5t; Patrick Forget 346tr; Fotograferen.net 47ca, 269b, 271bl, 275bl; Kevin Foy 77tl; Roberto Fumagalli 28t; tim gartside 328bl; Víctor Gómez 174t; Granger Historical Picture Archive 58t, 133br; Hackenberg-Photo-Cologne, 170tr, 182b; Stanislav Halcin 178br; Nick Hanna 46bl; Rosemary Harris 81b; guy harrop 418bl; hemis. fr / Walter Bibikow 36clb, 273tl, / Aurélien Brusini 328tr, 330cr, 330-1b, 332b, 333bl, 356, 357bl, 357bc, 360b, 361tr, 363bl, / Bertrand Gardel 41cl, / Gil Giuglio 8clb, 28crb, 190bl, 191tr, 247tr, / Franck Guiziou 47clb, 332cra, 343bl, 346-7b, / Herve Hughes 452b, 454tl, / Camille Moirenc 376tl, / Richard Soberka 260-1t; Mike Hill 301cr; Keith Homan 419br; Horizons WWP / TRVL 42bl, 59cb; Clive Horton 80tl; Michelle Howell 61tr; Frances Howorth 275cra; George H.H. Huey 131tl; Ian Dagnall Commercial Collection 289r; Iconotec / Peter Alix 417tr; imageBROKER 28cr, 429bl, 455cr, / Martin Moxter 298-9t, 450tl, / Norbert Probst 438-9b; Imageplotter 73cr, 73br; INTERFOTO 59bc; International Photobank 301br; Kerrick James 233cl; Brian Jannsen 258-9b; Jon Arnold Images Ltd 30-1t, 233t, 373cra, 386-7t, / Michele Falzone 420-1b, / Gavin Hellier 303br, / Doug Pearson 142cra,152bl, 161tr, / Jane Sweeney 176b, David Jones 334cl; Philip Jones 217cla; Pawel Kazmierczak 54br; John Kellerman 392-3t; Keystone Press 60cr; Jim Kidd 226tl; Roland Knauer 403bc; Christian J Kober 61cb; Alexander Kondakov 305tr; Joe Kras 306-7t; Chris LaBasco 207br; LatitudeStock / David Forman 287tr; eric laudonien 102-3t; Lazyllama 88br; Frans Lemmens 257br, 272-3b, 273cla, 274t; Ian Littlewood 226-7b; Look 45clb; Elijah Lovkoff 229tr; Don Mammose 179t; Nino Marcutti 128-9b; MARKA 428bl; Martin Thomas Photography 234t, 235br; Mauritius Images Gmbh 70bl, 82-3b, / Walter Bibikow 230-1t, 276-7b, 277clb, 289cl, 290bl, 320-1t, / Michael Runkel 116-7b, 389br, 434tl; Matt May 51cl; Jon McLean 53cl; Michael DeFreitas Caribbean 39tr, 256crb, 458; Lucian Milasan 54t; Mostardi Photography 260bl; Graham Mulrooney 43crb, 158-9t, 286t, 419cl, 451tr; National Geographic Image Collection 147tl, 147cra, 273cra, 361tl, / Jad Davenport 362t, / Michael Melfor 156-7b, / Brian J. Skerry 235cbl; Nature Picture Library 113cla, 301t, 386crb, 429cl, / Alex Mustard 306br, / Doug Perrine 211br, / Onne van der Wal 403t; Newscom 57tl; Niday Picture Library 60-11t; john norman 419t; M. Timothy O'Keefe 27bl, 371bl, 442-3; Christian Ouellet 219br; George Oze 202t, 210-1t, 231c; Efrain Padro 19cb,198-9, 205b, 209tl, 216cra, 219tl; Sean Pavone 318-9b; Pbpvision 80bc; George Petrou 133cr; PhotoSpirit 140-1t, 145clb; Anthony Pidgeo 158bl; Anthony Pidgeon 31tr, 160br; Wolfi Poelzer 84b; Ingolf Pompe 8 333tl; Graham Prentice 307br; RayArt Graphics 316bl; Sergi Reboredo 34-5t, 127tr; Robert Harding World Imagery 195crb; Robertharding 21bl, 26cb, 112-3b, 264-5, 400t, 410-1, / Richard Cummins 319tr, / Roberto Moiola 302-3t, / Rolf Richardson 388br, / Michael Runkel 195b, 215bl, / Jane Sweeney 90-1t; Rolf Nussbaumer Photography 217cl; hannah russell 402b; Peter Schickert 173cl; James Schwabel 232b, 248-9t; Patrick Shyu 236-7t; Keith J Smith. 257tl; Kumar Sriskandan 379clb; Stock Connection Blue 41tr; Stockimo / Jay ernesto 180tl; Stocktrek Images; Inc. 101ca; Martin Strmiska 44bl; Sunshine Pics 459bl; Tom Hanslien Photography 434-5b; Torontonia 91bl; Torontonian 57crb; Rafael Vélez Torres 217clb; Travel India 405cra; travelstock44.de / Juergen Hel 175b; Peter Treanor 35tr; tropicalpix / JS Callahan 194t; Andrew Twort 392bl; USFWS Photo 217bl; Valentin Valkov 18cb, 164-5; Lucas Vallecillos 70tr, 75tc, 76bl; WaterFrame_jdo 12-3b; Westend61 GmbH 30cra, / Martin Moxte 148b; Nik Wheeler 38cl; White House Photo 143cra; Poelzer Wolfgang 84cl, 87tr, 239tr; Julian Worker 390bl; World History Archive 60cb; WorldFoto 126-7b; ZUMA Press Inc 202br.

AWL Images: Walter Bibikow 20tl, 222-3; Aurelien Brusini 23br, 324-5; Alan Copson 6-7b, 11cr, 25tl, 366-7, 406t; Christian Kober 19tl, 186-7; Nick Ledger 24br, 352-3; Richard T Nowitz 56cr; Doug Pearson 144-5t.

Main Contributers Christopher Baker,
Skye Hernandez, Sara Humphries, Fred Mawer,
Lizzie Williams, James Henderson, Lynda Lohr,
KC Nash, Don Philpott, Theresa Storm,
Lynne Morgan Sullivan, Polly Tomas

Senior Editor Alison McGill

Senior Designers Bess Daly, Laura O'Brien

Project Editors Sophie Adam, Alice Fewery

Project Art Editors Sarah Snelling,
Vinita Venugopal, Bharti Karakoti,
Ankita Sharma, Hansa Babra

Designer Kitty Glavin

Factcheckers Rukmini Tilara,
Lisa Voormeij, Skye Hernandez

Editors Rachel Thompson, Robin Moul,
Zoë Rutland, Lucy Sara-Kelly

Proofreader Laura Walker

Indexer Hilary Bird

Senior Picture Researcher Ellen Root

Picture Research Nimesh Agrawal,
Sumita Khatwani, Rituraj Singh, Mark Thomas

Illustrators Chapel Design & Marketing Ltd.,
Chinglemba Chingtham, Aurgho Jyoti,
Arun Pottirayil, Mark Arjun Warner

Senior Cartographic Editor Casper Morris

Cartography Uma Bhattacharya,
Zafar-ul-Islam Khan, Animesh Pathak

Jacket Designers Bess Daly, Maxine Pedliham

Jacket Picture Research Susie Peachey

Senior DTP Designer Jason Little

DTP Nand Kishor Acharya,
Jagtar Singh, Vikram Singh

Producer Rebecca Parton

Managing Editor Rachel Fox

Art Director Maxine Pedliham

Publishing Director Georgina Dee

**The information in this
DK Eyewitness Travel Guide is checked regularly.**
Every effort has been made to ensure that this book
is as up-to-date as possible at the time of going to
press. Some details, however, such as telephone
numbers, opening hours, prices, gallery hanging
arrangements and travel information, are liable to
change. The publishers cannot accept responsibility
for any consequences arising from the use of this
book, nor for any material on third party websites,
and cannot guarantee that any website address
in this book will be a suitable source of travel
information. We value the views and suggestions
of our readers very highly. Please write to: Publisher,
DK Eyewitness Travel Guides, Dorling Kindersley,
80 Strand, London, WC2R 0RL, UK, or email:
travelguides@dk.com

First edition 2009

Published in Great Britain by Dorling Kindersley Limited,
80 Strand, London, WC2R 0RL

Published in the United States by DK Publishing,
1450 Broadway, Suite 801, New York, NY 10018

Copyright © 2009, 2019 Dorling Kindersley Limited
A Penguin Random House Company
19 20 21 22 10 9 8 7 6 5 4 3 2 1

A CIP catalog record for this book
is available from the British Library.

A catalog record for this book is available
from the Library of Congress.

ISSN: 1542 1554
ISBN: 978-0-2413-6888-6

Printed and bound in China.

www.dk.com